An Introduction to School-Age Care in Canada

An Introduction to School-Age Care in Canada

Kevin Bisback
Pinecrest-Queensway Health and Community Services Centre
Leslie Kopf-Johnson
Algonquin College

Pearson Canada
Toronto

To all the families and their wonderful children whose laughter,
curiosity, creativity, and challenges inspired this book ....

Library and Archives Canada Cataloguing in Publication

Bisback, Kevin
  An introduction to school-age care in Canada / Kevin Bisback, Leslie Kopf-Johnson. — 2nd ed.

Includes bibliographical references and index.
ISBN 978-0-13-208201-3

  1. School-age child care—Canada—Textbooks. I. Kopf-Johnson, Leslie II. Title.

HQ778.7.C3B58 2010   362.71'20971   C2008-904594-7

ISBN-13: 978-0-13-208201-3
ISBN-10: 0-13-208201-2

Vice-President, Editorial Director: Gary Bennett
Editor-in-Chief: Ky Pruesse
Executive Acquisitions Editor: Christine Cozens
Marketing Manager: Loula March
Assistant Editor: Victoria Naik
Production Editor: Claire Horsnell
Copy Editor: Ann Borden
Proofreaders: John Firth, Allegra Robinson
Production Coordinator: Lynn O'Rourke
Compositor: Laserwords
Art Director: Julia Hall
Cover Designer: Brett Miller
Cover Image: Getty Images

9 10 11 CP 14 13 12

Printed and bound in Canada.

Contents

Preface

The field of school-age care has rapidly expanded as both families and society recognize the importance of providing high-quality experiences during out-of-school time. The approach in this text recognizes that children do not want to spend their out-of-school hours in an institutional setting engaging in activities similar to those found in school. At the same time, we recognize that learning experiences need to support all areas of development.

Designed for programs at the post-secondary level, this text provides the reader with general information on how school-age children develop and learn. It includes strategies for developing a sense of community and creating learning environments and experiences that children find fun and challenging. Educators will learn how to develop and facilitate learning experiences that complement and support the education that children receive in the school system by promoting social, emotional, physical, language, and cognitive learning in a variety of settings.

School-age children bring a variety of skills and knowledge to any program they attend, and are eager to become more independent and take on new responsibilities. With this in mind, the text emphasizes the involvement of the children in all aspects of the program, while at the same time recognizing that educators will have to help many children develop skills (e.g. leadership and conflict management) to become successful participants in the programming process.

Since theories of learning and child development are the foundation of curriculum development, there are references to both learning theories and child development throughout the text. As individuals become comfortable making the link between the theory and practice, they will be able to explain the approach taken as they help parents and schoolteachers understand the rationale behind their program and the learning that is occurring.

The approach to curriculum planning in the text is to identify the components that are common to effective curriculum development, regardless of the curriculum approach. We recognize, however, that there are at least two main approaches to curriculum planning and that each approach has an impact on what educators do when planning curriculum. As a result, we have included one chapter on the traditional curriculum approach and another on the emergent curriculum approach.

There is no separate chapter dealing specifically with issues such as special needs and diversity. For real inclusion to occur, one must not segregate this information from the rest of the text, and we have chosen to deal with such topics in each chapter as the need arises.

Individuals working in school-age care programs may be referred to by various titles, such as school-age care worker, caregiver, or day-care staff. The decision to substitute the term *educator* throughout the text was a deliberate one. Individuals who are creating high-quality out-of-school programs that support learning and development are educators, and should be recognized as such. The text looks at a variety of characteristics, skills, and roles required of the educator.

The second edition of this text also includes a number of new or expanded sections.

- Additional material on activities designed to promote and develop a sense of community
- Additional information on how to work with and complement the school
- Expanded bullying prevention section

- Added steps in the development and implementation of long-term projects
- Expanded theory section includes Kohlberg's and Gilligan's theories of moral development and self-regulation
- Expanded development section includes more on social and emotion development
- Added stories to help illustrate emergent curriculum
- Reorganized chapters to better support the reader's understanding of how all program components are interconnected

We hope you find the information relevant and the techniques useful. We have always believed that school-age children have the potential to work co-operatively with peers and educators when planning curriculum, and we have seen the enthusiasm shown and learning achieved by children when given the chance to participate in program development. We hope that you also experience enthusiasm and excitement as you develop programs *with* the children, rather than *for* the children.

The following section identifies pedagogical features included in the text:

1. A **Chapter Overview** provides a summary of the content of the chapter.

2. **Charts, tables, diagrams and photos** are used to highlight points, summarize information, and provide pictorial examples of what is being discussed.

3. **Anecdotes** are used to help bring the chapter contents to life.

4. A **Summary** is included at the end of each chapter to encapsulate the chapter content.

5. **Student learning experiences** are designed to stimulate discussion and thinking. They also help students acquire and/or apply knowledge in a practical way.

6. **Review questions** are used to help students reflect on the readings, recognize important points, and synthesize information.

7. A **Glossary** is located at the end of the text to help readers who may be unfamiliar with some of the terminology.

8. A **Bibliography** is provided to acknowledge sources and to provide the student with suggestions for further reading. It includes both text and web sources.

SUPPLEMENTS

This text is accompanied by an Instructor's Manual and PowerPoint Presentations. These supplements are available for downloading from a password-protected section of Pearson Education Canada's online catalogue (www.pearsoned.ca/highered). Navigate to your book's catalogue page to view a list of those supplements that are available. See your local sales representative for details and access.

COURSESMART

CourseSmart is a new way for instructors and students to access textbooks online anytime from anywhere. With thousands of titles across hundreds of courses, CourseSmart helps instructors choose the best textbook for their class and give their students a new option for buying the assigned textbook as a lower cost eTextbook. For more information, visit www.coursesmart.com.

Acknowledgments

We would like to acknowledge several individuals who were crucial to the writing of this book. We would like to thank Sarah Rea, program supervisor of Children's Village at Stoneway, as well as her staff and the children at her centre for allowing us to use photos of their program. We would like to thank our partners, Anthony and Hal, and our friend and colleague Joan McCullagh, who all told us to stop talking and start writing. We'd also like to thank the following reviewers who took the time to give us feedback on the text: Angela Foster, Georgian College; Diane Nyisztor, Vanier College; Gail Hunter, George Brown; Tricia Lirette, Grant MacEwan; and Heather Ross, Okanagan College.

Finally, we would like to thank the many children we've worked with over the years. These children, who came from various backgrounds and who had diverse abilities, proved to us that actively involving children in curriculum development and implementation is rewarding for educators and children alike.

Leslie Kopf-Johnson
Kevin Bisback

An Introduction to School-Age Care in Canada

PART 1

School-Age Care in Canada

CHAPTER 1

Children and School-Age Care

OVERVIEW

This chapter will provide an overview of the types of school-age care that exist and how the educator's **philosophy** will influence what the program offers. The chapter will introduce the reader to the children and families who use these programs. It will highlight some of the developmental needs that are common to most **school-age children** while also identifying some of the many ways in which children and families differ from one another.

WHY SCHOOL-AGE CARE?

What are school-age children doing from the time school is dismissed to the time their parents arrive home from work? Do they hang out at malls? Sit at home and watch television behind locked doors? Play a game of street hockey with friends? Join a game of basketball at a recreation centre? Attend a licensed school-age care program?

Do the arrangements meet the needs of school-age children? Are the various levels of government doing anything to address the needs of school-age children and their parents? Can all of these arrangements be referred to as school-age care?

Parents, **teachers**, social workers, and children themselves have all expressed concerns about what is happening when children are out of school and parents are still at work. Concerns range from the quality of the experiences children have to issues regarding their basic safety. These concerns have resulted in many institutions offering a variety of programs for school-age children: these range from licensed school-age care to the "Kids Help Phone"—a nationwide toll-free line that children can phone if they are worried or lonely. In a society where news reports of children being abducted, bullied, sexually and physically abused, or even murdered are given such prominence, it is natural for parents and children to worry about what will happen when a child is alone or in a program that is not regulated.

Some children may lock themselves into the house and panic if the doorbell rings while they are at home on their own. Some parents may spend their working hours after school wondering if their children are all right, or even phoning them on a regular basis to reassure themselves. Other parents may be concerned about with whom and where their children are hanging out. The saying "Do you know where your child is?" can become a nightmare for concerned working parents.

Since the 1960s there has been a gradual shift in family structures. While there have always been a variety of family structures in Canada, the dominant one tended to be the nuclear family, in which the wife stayed at home if there were young children. As late as the 1960s divorce was still difficult, unmarried mothers were strongly encouraged to give up their babies at birth, and alternative family structures were often frowned upon. Today, there is greater recognition that families come in a variety of constellations, each with its own set of needs. These changes in family structure have contributed to changes in attitudes toward child-care and school-age care programs. As society sees an increased number of dual-income families as well as single-parent families, one also finds more parents who are concerned about the care their children receive outside of school hours.

In today's society, although more and more families require school-age care, licensed child care cannot meet the demand. Most provinces and territories have spaces for fewer than 10 per cent

Children participate in a wide range of after-school activities.

of the school-age children who need spaces, and, as a result, the majority of parents have to find alternative types of care for their children.

A BRIEF HISTORY OF SCHOOL-AGE CARE

Although school-age care has been around in one form or another for decades, its history is sketchy because so much of it has been informal in nature, or the programs offered were an adjunct to preschool programs.

In the early 1900s out-of-school care was an urban phenomenon, since most children in rural settings went home after school to help on the family farm. In some larger Canadian cities (such as Toronto and Vancouver) crèches were established to provide care for both preschool and school-age children (Young, 1994). Around the same time, **recreational programs** in some cities were being introduced into parks in order to help keep children from playing in the streets (Young, 1994). As a result of these two developments, most provinces have two very different systems providing services for school-age children during out-of-school hours, with licensed programs falling under legislation for child care and unlicensed, recreational programs falling under legislation for recreation.

During the 1960s and 1970s, as more and more mothers entered the workforce, the demand for school-age care programs increased. Because the number of school-age programs in Canada was very limited, parents often used a variety of recreational and informal methods (such as grandparents or neighbours) to provide care for their children. By the

1980s, as a result of pressure from parents, school boards in a number of cities began to allow child-care agencies to provide school-age care space in schools that had empty class-rooms. In the late 1980s the Ontario government recognized the value of having school-age programs attached to schools, and legislated the inclusion of a child-care centre into every new school built. Although the Ontario legislation was later revoked, school boards in sev-eral jurisdictions in Canada (including some in Ontario) allow child-care centres to be built within schools (Jacobs *et al.*, 1998).

Today, despite the continued demand for high-quality school-age care programs, out-of-school programs continue to be provided under different mandates (such as daycare or recreation); are found in insufficient numbers to meet demand; and, where they do exist, are often unaffordable for many families.

WHAT IS SCHOOL-AGE CARE?

School-age care can be found in either licensed or unlicensed centres. It can be home based or centre based. It can be recognized by the provincial or territorial government as child care or it can be viewed as a recreational program for children.

The majority of provinces offer some licensed school-age care, and the legislation across Canada identifies licensed school-age care in very similar ways. Although the vari-ous provinces and territories may differ in terms of group composition and administrative structure, a key component of all school-age care definitions is that care is regulated out-side school hours for school-age children. Across the country the ages identified are usu-ally six to twelve, although there is some variation. Recognized, licensed care may be found in either centre- or home-based programs (CRRU, 2004).

Some programs may be offered only after school, while others provide both before- and after-school care. Some programs include **kindergarten-age children**, while others offer services only once children are in grade one. Some programs require children to leave after the age of ten, while others provide care for children through age twelve. Some programs offer separate summer camps, while others run throughout the year with the same children.

Although governments don't include recreation programs when defining school-age care, parents' definitions often include recreational programs (such as Boys and Girls Clubs or city-run recreation programs), lessons (e.g. music or swimming), and even the use of older children as part of their school-age care system.

Different types of school-age care operate under different regulations and provide dif-ferent experiences for children. When making a decision regarding out-of-school care, par-ents need to be aware of the differences.

TYPES OF SCHOOL-AGE CARE

Recreation Programs

Families frequently use **recreation programs** because they often offer several advantages. These programs allow for part-time participation and are usually cheaper than licensed child-care programs—a factor that can be appealing for parents who don't qualify for child-care subsidies. The programs are often located in the community and therefore allow children to be with their friends. The focus of recreation programs clearly complements rather than duplicates school activities; these programs frequently focus on skill development, often in the area of sports.

However, there are also some disadvantages to recreation programs. Their leaders usually have minimal levels of training—for instance, high-school students are frequently used. Because programs often focus on skill development, they may not meet the needs of a variety of children. The child who wants to engage in quiet activities like reading a book may find it difficult in some recreation programs where the focus is on group activities. The fact that the programs are unlicensed means that they may not meet health or safety standards, or provide the adult/child ratios that exist in licensed programs. As well, most recreation programs are not available before school, and some are not available during school holidays such as Christmas break.

Home Child Care

This is frequently used by school-age children, and there are several reasons why parents might choose it for their child. Because the care is in a home it provides children with a non-institutional environment. After being in school all day many children prefer a more homelike and relaxed environment. Like recreation programs, **home child care** is usually cheaper than licensed, centre-based care, and is more likely to take a child on a part-time basis; as well, it is more likely to accommodate extended hours of care. Frequently, home child care allows school-age children more independence than other types of programs. Children in these programs often have opportunities to go into the neighbourhood to play with friends and make decisions about the activities they will engage in.

Like all programs, the home setting has some disadvantages. Many programs lack a wide variety of materials and opportunities for children to develop diverse skills. For example, the program may not be able to provide opportunities for children to engage in activities such as working with clay, woodworking, tie-dying, or group games. As well, many home child-care programs are unlicensed and may not meet the health and safety standards required of licensed programs. In addition, home child-care providers are not required to have the same level of training as educators in licensed centres. Parents using these programs would have to ask each caregiver what training they have that will support a school-age child's learning and development.

Sibling Care or Self Care

Other children may go to their own home after school to be supervised by an older sibling or look after themselves. The type of care in these situations is often referred to as **sibling care** and **self care**. A frequent term for children in these situations is **latchkey kids**, since having their own front-door key is taken to indicate that no adult is waiting for them at home when they return from school. Parents turn to this type of arrangement for several reasons. They may not be able to access the other types of care, they may not be able to afford to pay for care, or they may feel that the children involved are mature enough to be trusted with this type of arrangement. However, self care often creates the most stress for parents, and it is in such situations that parents spend time at work phoning their children to make sure everything is all right.

Licensed School-Age Care

Besides recreational, home, sibling, and self-care arrangements, families may have the option of a **licensed school-age care** program. These programs have several advantages for parents. Children in these programs will have a variety of activities available that are designed for both individual and group participation. Because these programs are licensed, parents know that there are minimum standards for health, safety, adult/child ratios and educator training. Many licensed programs offer care both before and after school—which can be essential for parents—and in some areas centres have been opened that accommodate parents who work shift work.

As with any type of program, there are also disadvantages. Because of the various regulations governing the operation of the centre, children may not have the same amount of independence that they have in other programs. As well, some school-age programs, in order to provide a variety of activities, may become more structured than a child who has already been in school all day would like. Like recreation programs, licensed programs may come across as institutional rather than homelike. Unfortunately, licensed school-age programs are often more expensive than other types of care, and parents who do not qualify for a subsidy may find it difficult to afford licensed group care. A final disadvantage for many families is that often these programs cannot accommodate part-time care.

Although the above paragraphs provide some generalized descriptions of different types of programs, one must remember that great variations exist within each type. One organization may operate recreational programs that try to follow the regulations for licensed centres, while another may have very lax standards and hire mainly high-school students to run the programs. An individual operating an unlicensed home child-care program may have both an Early Childhood Education (**ECE**) certificate and a recreation diploma and provide a variety of appropriate and interesting **learning experiences** for school-age children, while another operator may have no training and provide few activities for the children. A young school-age child may go home to be looked after by his seventeen-year-old sibling, or an even younger child could go home to be looked after by her nine-year-old sibling (though this does occur, educators should be aware that in many provinces the minimum age at which children can legally be left at home alone is ten, and in some provinces, such as Quebec, it is twelve—check with the local Children's Aid Society for details in your province). Finally, a licensed centre may hire only people with ECE and recreation diplomas and make sure that there are a wide variety of learning experiences, while another licensed centre may hire very few people with training and have a shortage of materials and activities for the children.

Choosing a Program

When choosing a program for their child, parents need to look carefully at what is being offered and how it meets the needs of their child. Some of the questions they should be asking are: Do we need before- and after-school care? If my child needs a quiet time after school to be by himself, is there opportunity for this to occur? If my child is interested in a particular skill or sport, will the program foster this development? Will there be friends that my child can spend time with? Will my child have opportunities to help decide what activities she wants to take part in? Are there plenty of opportunities for my child to develop skills in, say, painting or music? What kind of opportunities are there to develop leadership skills? What are the qualifications of the staff? What are the adult/child ratios?

Educators working in school-age programs should also ask themselves similar questions. They need to know what the abilities and interests of the children they are working with are. If a child is interested in art, are they providing the types of experiences that will foster growth in this area? If the child simply wants to spend time with friends, is there a comfortable place where they can do this? If children are interested in developing their sports skills, are there opportunities and experiences that will support this? Educators need to ask themselves if they have incorporated opportunities for the children to make decisions regarding the learning experiences. Once educators have asked themselves these questions, they need to reflect on their answers and be willing to make any necessary changes to the program to ensure that the needs of the children are being addressed.

SETTINGS FOR SCHOOL-AGE PROGRAMS

School-age programs can be found in a variety of settings. Churches, school gyms, cafeterias and libraries, community centres and purpose-built centres are all used for school-age programs.

Spaces within schools have often been used for school-age programs. Sometimes this space is rented to outside organizations that provide the service, while in other locations the school board may operate the program itself.

Cities have often offered after-school programs through their recreation departments. These programs may be based in recreation or community centres. Programs located in recreation centres may have access to swimming pools and gyms, while those located in community centres may have very few sports amenities.

Churches are another location for many school-age programs. Some of these programs are run by the church, while others simply rent space in the church. These facilities may vary widely, since some churches will have a gym, a hall, meeting rooms, and a large outdoor space, while other churches may have only a large hall, perhaps in the basement.

Still other programs may take place in purpose-built environments. These may be attached to a school or a centre that also houses younger children. Some of these centres may be housed in buildings that were not originally designed for a child-care program but which were renovated to meet their new roles. The advantage of a purpose-built centre is that the environment is solely for the use of the program and therefore is designed with the needs of the children in mind and, unlike shared space, the educators and children will be able to leave the environment set up, or change it as needed.

Each setting for a school-age program results in unique challenges for educators and children, but within each setting creative educators can provide interesting and stimulating programs for children. Regardless of the setting, the goals of all educators should be to create a high-quality program for school-age children. Because our book will often refer to quality, it is important to identify what the research on high-quality school-age care indicates.

HIGH-QUALITY SCHOOL-AGE CARE

A variety of researchers and experts in the field of child care have identified quality indicators for child-care programs, and more specifically school-age quality indicators. In the

United States in the early 1980s, Baden and others looked at the matter of quality and concluded that there were common elements found in the best school-age programs. Some of the elements they identified were: sufficient and well-trained staff; an environment that fosters development; a range of activities that capitalize on the children's interests; usage of community resources; encouragement of interactions with parents; and places for children both to socialize with peers and to be alone (Baden *et al.*, 1982). Since then other research and literature reviews have been done in the area of high-quality school-age programs (Ontario Coalition for Better Child Care, 2000; Green, 2005; Jacobs *et al.*, 1998), and very similar results have been found.

In Canada, although there is no national statement devoted to school-age quality indicators, the Canadian Child Care Federation (CCCF) has developed a general statement on quality. The *National Statement on Quality Child Care* was published by the CCCF in 1991. It is based on developmentally and culturally appropriate practices relating to quality. The *Statement* identifies seven indicators, each of which contains at least three subsections—typically people, practice, and place. More recent publications by the CCCF continue to support the indicators identified in the statement (such as *Partners in Quality: Issues*, 1999).

Indicators of Quality (CCCF, 1991)

1. Suitability and training of care providers
2. Child development and the learning environment
3. Group size and ratios
4. Adult relationships
5. Health and nutrition
6. Safety
7. Partnership

In the United States the National School-Age Care Association (NSACA) has identified standards specific to school-age programs. Although the headings for the indicators of quality may differ from those developed by the CCCF, the content of each document is very similar. For example, one of the NSACA headings is "Human Relationships," which has no exact counterpart in the CCCF document. However, components of this standard (such as ratios of adults to youth, adults' interactions with children) are also important components of the CCCF standards.

The research on quality and the development of standards has led to the development of tools to determine how well programs are addressing quality issues. O'Connor *et al.* (1994) developed an instrument called ASQ (to assess quality in school-age programs). The system was designed as a self-assessment process to help programs determine quality and make improvements. Other tools have also been developed that are frequently used to evaluate quality. One of the common tools used in Canada is the School-Age Care Environmental Rating Scale (SACERS) (Harms, Jacobs and White, 1996). Like ASQ, it is a self-assessment guide. It is organized into six categories that address issues such as the appropriateness of the physical environment, safety, interactions, activities, health and nutrition, and administration.

WHO ARE THE CHILDREN?

Educators will find, particularly in large urban areas, that the children in their after-school program come from a wide variety of backgrounds—both ethnically and socio-economically—and have a wide range of abilities. Here are some examples of the types of children they might encounter.

Samantha is seven years old. Her two mothers are both professionals who work full time; one as a lawyer and the other as a social worker. Samantha is in French Immersion at a neighbourhood school, and attends this school-age program because her parents like the philosophy and **curriculum** being implemented here. Samantha has a four-year-old brother who attends a preschool child-care program. Samantha is also enrolled in swimming, skating, and dance classes. Some days her mothers pick her up early from the centre to get her to her various lessons. She lives with her family in a four-bedroom house with a pool in the backyard.

Muhammad is nine years old. Eight months ago he came to Canada from Somalia, where he saw several members of his family being killed and was himself subjected to a starvation diet and was uprooted from his village. Muhammad has had little formal education and is currently in English as a Second Language (ESL) classes at the school attached to the school-age centre. He is unsure of the whereabouts of his father, who is still in Somalia. His mother is also taking ESL classes while she tries to adjust to life in Canada and care for her five children, who range in age from two to twelve. Muhammad has a younger brother and sister attending the same centre. Muhammad and his siblings are picked up by their mother, who walks to the centre from her school and returns home with the children to their three-bedroom apartment located in a nearby high-rise.

Matt is nine years old. Both his parents work to support the family. His father works as the manager of a local clothing store and his mother works as a nurse in a local clinic. Matt attends the school attached to the centre. He has a thirteen-year-old brother who goes home after school, and Matt is trying to convince his parents that he too is old enough to be at home instead of at the centre. He enjoys hockey more than anything, and two nights a week his father picks him up early to take him to hockey practice. He lives with his family in a three-bedroom house, four blocks from his school and centre.

Gabriel is six. His mother has recently returned to school to complete her education since she dropped out at age sixteen to have him. Gabriel has been in child care since he was one year old and his mother went to work. Most of his experiences have been in home child-care programs because his mother worked shifts in a factory. Even with home child-care programs she often had to rely on her parents when working the late shift. Gabriel has seen his father twice in the past three years. For the past ten months his mother's boyfriend Joe has lived with them, and Gabriel has begun to call him *Dad*. Gabriel's mom drops him off as soon as the centre opens in the morning; however, she frequently picks him up within half an hour of the start of the afternoon program because her school day ends earlier than his. They live in a two-bedroom social housing townhouse within walking distance of the school-age centre.

Michelle is eight years old. She lives with her mother and stepfather. Her mother is currently on maternity leave after giving birth to Michelle's brother Alec. Michelle has cerebral palsy and uses a wheelchair to get around. She attends the school attached to the centre, and is in grade one. Michelle lives in a bungalow four blocks from the school and

School-age care programs often comprise a diverse set of students with varying interests and needs.

centre. She is bussed to school in the morning and one of her parents picks her up around 5:30 each afternoon. Once a month she spends the weekend with her dad and his new wife.

Samantha, Muhammad, and the others are typical children attending school-age care programs, to which they bring diverse interests and needs. They require programs that allow them to pursue their interests and provide them with new experiences. They need educators who demonstrate commitment, creativity, resourcefulness, and a good grasp of child development.

DIVERSITY

As the above scenarios indicate, children in school-age programs come from diverse backgrounds and have varying needs. In order to create a program that school-age children will want to attend, educators must respect this **diversity** and provide materials, resources, and a curriculum that addresses this diversity in a positive way.

Family Diversity

Religion The families of the children may have different faiths or no faith at all. Educators working with families that are religiously diverse may need to speak to parents about how religious celebrations can be recognized without offending others, or if all celebrations with a religious connection should be eliminated from the program. Through such discussions educators may also be able to help clarify which celebrations the families regard as religious in nature and which, if any, are predominantly secular.

Culture Although religion influences one's culture, educators must be aware that families of the same faith may still be culturally diverse and that this diversity will influence different family practices, the roles of the various family members, and the values that the family has. Some families may expect the father to deal with educators in the program, while in others it will be both parents, and in still others only the mother. Culture may also influence the expectations the families have for their sons and daughters. This may become apparent as the educator speaks to the parents about the learning experiences the children can engage in (such as sports) or the types of responsibilities the children are expected to take on (such as cleaning up after a snack).

Language More and more school-age children are coming to programs speaking more than one language. For many children English or French may be their second language, and until they started school they may not have spoken anything but their first language. Other children may have grown up in a household where more than one language was commonly used. Knowing that the language used in the program is the child's second or even third language can help the educator. A child who uses English as a second language will likely have a smaller English vocabulary than the child whose first language is English. This child may have to search for the word he wants, or may not know the meaning of a word the educator is using. At the same time, the child may be able to read words that he doesn't understand because the child has mastered the grammar and phonic rules common in English.

Family Structure The structure of the children's families will also differ. Some children may live in **single-parent families**. This family structure may result from divorce, death, or the mother and father never co-habiting. When working with these families educators must not make assumptions about the nature of single-parent families, since a variety of factors will influence how each one functions.

Other children may live in **extended families**, with several generations living under one roof. Educators working with these families need to recognize that adults other than the parents often play an active role in the decision-making process. For example, in a family that includes the child's grandparents, they may have the final say in some decisions because parents are expected to defer to family elders.

Some families may comprise **same-sex parents** and their children. Although research indicates that same-sex parents are equally capable and provide positive family environments for children (e.g., Gay and Lesbian Parents Coalition International Network, 1992; Flaks *et al.*, 1995), educators need to be aware of biases that these children and their families may face. Educators must be able to support these children if they encounter discrimination or are bullied because of their family composition. Family Services Ottawa, a family-counselling agency in Ottawa, created resources and curriculum about how to support same-sex parents in early learning and elementary school environments. This curriculum can be found at the following web site: www.rainbow-families.com.

Socio-Economic Background Family diversity is also affected by socio-economic backgrounds. Families from lower socio-economic classes often have slightly different values than those from middle- or upper-class backgrounds, and at times these differences may result in conflict. For example, families from lower socio-economic classes may support more authoritarian parenting styles than do middle-class parents (McLoyd, 1990; Steinberg, 1999), and this may result in parents disagreeing with some program policies.

Socio-economic background will also influence the children's ability to acquire many of the material objects that are becoming increasingly important to some school-age children (such as designer-label clothes and shoes, access to various lessons, and so on). This in turn can influence their interactions with peers, such as peer pressure and social isolation from the group, which may lead to social bullying (see Chapter 9). The educators will have to create different strategies and techniques to minimize the importance of material objects and the influence of media (television, music videos, and fashion magazines) in their program.

Disability Still other families may have a member with a **disability**. Regardless of whether the individual with **special needs** is the child in the program, the child's sibling, or the parent, the special need will influence family interactions. Educators recognize that adapting the environment or curriculum may be required if a child in the program has special needs; however, they may not have thought about how other family members with special needs might affect the program. If a child in the program has a sibling with special needs, he may at times resent his sibling because of the amount of time his parents spend with that child. This in turn can influence the child's behaviour in the program. At other times, the child may become very protective of his sibling, and this too may affect the child's behaviour.

It is also possible that a child in the program has a parent with a special need. In this situation the child may take on responsibilities that other children in the centre do not have to worry about. For example, a child with a quadriplegic parent may take on chores around the house that the parent has difficulty doing. As well, the child may at times resent that her parent is different from other parents, or may be sensitive to the reactions of other children toward her parent.

Regardless of which family member has special needs, the educator must learn how the special need is affecting the child in the school-age program, and how to best support that child's learning and development. At the same time the educator may need to look at how accessible the centre is to the family member with the special need.

Individual Diversity

School-age children also demonstrate individual diversity. Although family background contributes to it, individual diversity reflects the characteristics, interests, and abilities that make each child unique. Some children in a program would be happy spending the entire time chatting with friends; others may prefer more solitary activities such as reading or building with Lego, and still others may be interested in more physical activities such as sports or rollerblading.

Personality Diversity among the children will vary widely with respect to personality, abilities, interests and physical build. Some children in a program may be very shy while others are very outgoing, and educators will find that these differences will influence not only how the children respond to various situations, but also how the educators interact with the children.

Abilities Children will show great diversity in their abilities. Some children will excel in academic areas, while others will excel in the arts or in sports. Some children will be able to acquire new knowledge and develop new skills very easily, while others will struggle to learn new concepts or have difficulty mastering physical skills such as those required for writing or for playing soccer. Educators will need to be aware of these differences in order to provide appropriate support to each child.

Interests In a school-age program, children will also show diverse interests. Name a topic and there will probably be at least one child who is interested in it. Interests can range from playing with dolls to figuring out how a computer works.

Not only will there be a wide range of interests, but there will be differences in terms of how deeply the child wants to study or participate in a topic or activity. Some children may satisfy their curiosity by simply reading a book on insects, while another child will want to have a more hands-on approach that involves capturing and studying live insects.

Physical Build Finally, individual differences in physical build will affect children and the type of support they need from educators. Children who are obese are often bullied and may hesitate to engage in physical activities for fear of failure or for fear of the reactions they may get from their peers (such as teasing). Children who are very short may be babied by the other children, while those who are very tall may be expected to behave like older children. Children who are unattractive will have different needs than those who are very attractive, since appearance will affect how people respond to an individual. Physical diversity will affect different children in different ways, and educators need to observe the children to understand how it is affecting each one.

NEEDS OF SCHOOL-AGE CHILDREN

Despite the diversity found among children, school-age children have many things in common. When educators think about the needs of school-age children, physical, social, emotional, cognitive, and language needs automatically come to mind. It is also important to remember that children are usually coming to the program after a full day in school, and this will affect the focus of the school-age program (for instance, the need for a more relaxed atmosphere, with perhaps more physical activities).

Simply stating that the developmental needs of children should be met will not help the educator unless one breaks it down into more specific needs. The following sections will not only do this but will also indicate some of the learning and development theories that support these needs (the theories will be discussed in Chapter 3 and a more detailed overview of development in Chapter 4).

Social and Emotional Needs

Like all children, school-age children have a number of social and emotional needs (see Table 1.1). They are moving from the micro (smaller) **community** of the preschooler into the macro (larger) community where peers and interactions with the broader community play a more active role. Urie Bronfenbrenner's **ecological theory** (Chapter 3) helps to explain the influences the macro community has on the child, while other theories help one understand why peers are starting to exert such a strong influence on a child. Many of the school-age child's social and emotional needs revolve around developing his confidences, self-esteem, friendships, and peer relationships, and educators must look at how they can help children fulfill these needs. For example, the development of friendships is important

TABLE 1.1	Children's social and emotional needs
Social/Emotional Needs	**Theories That Address Each Need**
Emotional support to develop self esteem, self image, and self confidence, from warm and caring adults	Maslow and Erikson
A safe environment free from physical and psychological bullying	Maslow
Independence	Piaget and Gardner
Opportunity to take "safe" risks	Maslow, Erikson, and Vygotsky
Opportunity to make friends	Erikson and Vygotsky
Opportunity to be alone	Gardner
Affirmation of heritage, culture, and cultural practices	Bronfenbrenner and Vygotsky
Acceptance of peers	Vygotsky, Maslow, and Erikson
Individual and group responsibility	Maslow, Bandura, Kohlberg, and Gilligan
Opportunity to be involved in the local community	IPM, Bronfenbrenner, Kohlberg, Gilligan, and Bandura
Development of a sense of community and home-like environment	Bronfenbrenner, Gilligan, and Maslow
Positive adult role models with whom they can identify	Bandura, Kohlberg, and Vygotsky
Opportunities to develop self-regulation skills	Bandura, Kohlberg, and Gilligan

at this age, and educators must determine what they can do to help the child who may not be skilled at developing friendships to acquire this ability.

Cognitive and Language Needs

The school system addresses the academic needs of school-age children; however, the school-age care program can also provide children with opportunities to develop these very important academic skills. Programs do this in a variety of ways. Children can use their reading, writing, and math skills as they pursue a variety of interests and engage in projects related to these interests. For example, children interested in planting a garden may use reading skills by having access to science books or the Internet to determine plant growing requirements, writing skills to record their brainstorming ideas, and math skills to record plant data or plot out the garden.

After a day in school, which is usually teacher-directed, the school-age program can provide an environment where children develop cognitive and language skills through learning experiences that let them make choices, come up with their own solutions to problems and challenges, and be creative (see Table 1.2).

According to Erik Erikson's **psychosocial theory** of development, school-age children also want to engage in meaningful activities that are valued by society. By providing school-age children with real-world tools, educators address this need and help children develop a variety of skills that they can use both now and later on in life.

TABLE 1.2	Children's cognitive and language needs	
Cognitive and Language Needs	**Theories That Address Each Need**	
Opportunity to practise academic skills	IPM, Vygotsky, and Gardner	
Opportunity to achieve competence in some skill area	IPM, Erikson, and Gardner	
Time to explore and work at own pace and developmental level	Piaget and Vygotsky	
Opportunity to be creative and resourceful	Bandura, Piaget, and IPM	
Freedom of choice	Gardner and Vygotsky	
Opportunity to work with real tools	Erikson and Gardner	

Physical Needs

School-age children also have a variety of physical needs that can be supported in an out-of-school program (see Table 1.3). They need opportunities to engage in physical activities after having spent much of their day in school. They also need opportunities to improve on the fine and gross motor skills they have already acquired.

To help to promote the physical needs of school-age children it is important to provide the children with healthy snacks based on the Canadian Food Guide and the requirements of legislation. By providing a variety of snack food (proteins, carbohydrates, fruits) and drinks (water, juice, milk) at different times of the day, the children will be able to refuel and re-energize their bodies and will have the energy to engage in physical activities.

PHILOSOPHY AND SCHOOL-AGE CARE

The philosophy of a program is the framework and guide for how it will work. It is theory based, and usually reflects the values of the educators and the society at large. The roles of the educator, children, parents, and community in relationship to the program should be highlighted in the philosophy. It gives educators guidelines for how to implement and evaluate the program.

A philosophy, for these purposes, can be thought of as a written statement of the **5 Ws**: **Who, What, Where, When, and Why**? The 5 Ws should be used in combination with the educator's knowledge of child development (social, emotional, physical, cognitive, and

TABLE 1.3	Children's physical needs	
Physical Needs	**Theories That Address Each Need**	
Opportunity for outdoor and indoor play	Gardner, IPM, and Piaget	
Opportunity to use their whole body	Gardner, Piaget, and IPM	
Opportunity to have nutritional requirements met	Maslow and IPM	
Opportunity to develop meaningful, complex motor movements	Erikson, Bandura, and Gardner	

language) and theories of learning (such as Howard Gardner, Jean Piaget, Abraham Maslow, and Erik Erikson). It is a statement of who, where, when, what, and why the program is being implemented, and how children learn, interact, and behave in the physical and social environment.

In many jurisdictions it is a requirement for school-age programs to have a statement of their philosophy. For example, Ontario regulations require such a statement to be posted in the program.

The philosophy will guide educators in developing the indoor and outdoor environments, curriculum, links to the community at large, and **behaviour-guidance** strategies. The roles and responsibilities of educators with respect to children, parents, school, program, and the community should be prominent in the philosophy.

Typically, philosophies emphasize a child-centred approach to learning and programming. However, this might look different depending upon the developmental and learning theories the educators believe in and how they choose to apply them. For example, the philosophy for a program based on behaviourism might emphasize teacher-directed **learning activities** and de-emphasize group experiences, while a program based on Erikson's psychosocial theory of development might emphasize child-directed learning and group experiences. Regardless of the theories used to support the philosophy of the program, an observer should be able to see evidence that the staff is implementing the philosophy of the centre.

The Curriculum Approach and the Centre's Philosophy

In a traditional theme-based program (Chapter 10), the curriculum is developed by the educator for the children. The educator's role is to conceptualize, plan, and implement the layout of the physical environment and the curriculum delivery. The educator determines the desired learning outcomes for the children, the activities, and the behaviour-guidance strategies. A traditional program, therefore, should have a philosophy that lets parents recognize the centre's approach and the rationale behind it.

In an **emergent-curriculum**-based school-age program (Chapter 11), the curriculum arises from the interests of the children, and is developed with the children, who are actively involved in the process. They participate in the design of the environment and the development of activities. An emergent-curriculum program, therefore, should have a philosophy with a statement that lets parents recognize the rationale behind this type of programming.

Centres have a responsibility to families to make sure this link between the philosophy and the actual practices of the program exists. Parents looking for an after-school program know their child and what they want for their child. By reading the philosophy and the statement of principles they should be able to make an informed choice regarding their child's care.

Evaluating and Reviewing the Philosophy

The program philosophy should be reviewed and evaluated at least once a year to see if its goals are being met. If the program is not demonstrating the philosophy, it is important to ask questions like the following:

- What was successful?
- What practice was in conflict with the philosophy?

- What are the challenges?
- What does the program need to do to overcome the challenges?
- Is the program meeting the needs of the community it serves?
- Does the program need to identify steps that will allow it to meet its goals?
- How can the program make sure these steps occur?
- Does the program need to identify short-term and long-term goals?

Without regular review, it is easy for centres to drift slowly away from the philosophy statement and begin to offer a program that does not meet the expectations of the families or employees of the centre.

Summary

Although all school-age care is designed to provide care for children outside school hours, programs come in a variety of forms and offer diverse learning experiences. School-age children have some common needs, but children also come with diverse needs—for example, different cultural and family practices and interests. When choosing the type of program best suited to a particular child, parents and educators need to consider all the child's needs in order to make sure that the program will be appropriate. Educators also need to be aware of all the factors that could be affecting a child in order to ensure that their program meets the individual needs of each child and the group needs of the children. The philosophy of a program should help parents and educators determine the types of experiences children will encounter in a program. When looking at a philosophy one needs to make sure that it is based on a strong theoretical understanding of learning and development and that it is clearly reflected in the program's practices.

Student Learning Experiences

1. Interview a school-age child to discover what she wants to do in her school-age program.
2. Using the list of social and emotional needs identified in this chapter, observe a school-age program and give one example of how the program and educators can address each of the needs.
3. Interview two families with school-age children. Find out what is important to each family in the areas of culture, family, education, and recreation. Identify the similarities and differences in the answers of each family.
4. Review the needs identified in one of the developmental areas discussed in this chapter, and identify concrete ways in which educators can help children meet those needs.
5. Compare and contrast the school-age child care legislation from two provinces/territories. Reflect on why the differences and similarities may exist.

Review Questions

1. Explain how changing Canadian demographics have affected school-age care.

2. Using two examples, show how the theories identified in a program's philosophy might be reflected in the program's day-to-day practice.

3. List the common types of school-age care discussed in the chapter and identify the advantages and disadvantages of each.

4. Identify two types of family diversity that educators might encounter and explain how they might influence the program offered.

5. What type of environment has been found to be linked to quality in school-age programs?

CHAPTER 2

The Educators in School-Age Programs

OVERVIEW

This chapter will focus on the staff working in school-age programs. Throughout the text, individuals working in these programs will be referred to as *educators*. This term will be used instead of *teacher* to differentiate these individuals from teachers working within the school system. The terms *practitioner*, *worker*, or **child-care worker** will not be used here because the authors see the educational component (social, cognitive, and physical development) as key to any licensed school-age program, and they think that this professional skill should be recognized in the title given to the staff.

This chapter will include information on legislation across Canada that influences the training of individuals working in centres, their roles, and their responsibilities. It will identify characteristics that are important for educators to have if they want to work successfully with children in licensed school-age programs. The various roles that educators have when working with children and their families will be discussed, and the wide range of responsibilities an educator commits to when agreeing to work in high-quality school-age programs will be highlighted.

LEGISLATION AND THE EDUCATOR

All provinces and territories have some legislation regulating school-age child care (see Table 2.1). Among the provinces and territories there is some consistency regarding ratios and group sizes. Most provinces/territories require a ratio of one adult for every 15 children when the children range in age from six to twelve. This ratio influences the educators working in school-age programs, since they must be comfortable being responsible for larger groups of children than they would have in a preschool environment. At the same time most jurisdictions limit group sizes to 30 children, which influences the size of the team that will be working with the children.

Although there are some similarities among provinces and territories with respect to ratios and group sizes, the qualifications required to work with school-age children are another matter. According to legislation governing licensed school-age programs, the adults working in them may have a wide variety of training, or even no training at all. In some provinces and territories the only requirement is that the individual be able to administer first aid. In other provinces and territories some of the educators must have a diploma or certificate in early childhood education. If directors use this flexibility to hire individuals with complementary skill sets (for instance, some with ECE diplomas and others with recreation diplomas) it can help the quality of the program offered to the children. If directors use the regulations to hire as many untrained individuals as the regulations allow, it could lower the quality of the program offered. Research indicates that training is linked to quality (e.g., Cameron, 2004; Doherty-Derkowski, 1995).

TABLE 2.1	Legislation governing school-age child care

Alberta Child Care Licensing Regulation

British Columbia *Community Care Facilities Act*: Child Care Regulations Child Care

BC Act SBC 2001

Manitoba *Community Child Day Care Standards Act*: Manitoba Child Day Care Regulations

New Brunswick *Family Services Act 1980*: Family Services Act and Day Care Regulations as amended

Newfoundland *Child Care Services Act*: Child Care Services Regulation 37/99

North-West Territories *Child Day Care Act*: Child Day Care Standards and Regulations 1988

Nova Scotia *Day Care Act* and Regulations

Nunavut *Child Day Care Act*: Child Day Care Standards and Regulations

Ontario *Day Nurseries Act*. Revised Statutes of Ontario amended by the *Services Improvement Act: Ontario Regulations 262*

Prince Edward Island *Child Care Facilities Act*: Child Care Facilities Regulations

Quebec *Public Education Act*: Regulation on School-Age Child Care. *An Act Respecting the Ministère de la Famille et de l'Enfance* and amending the *Act Respecting Child Day Care Centres*

Saskatchewan *Child Care Act* (Bill 8): Child Care Regulations 2001

Yukon *Child Care Act 1990*: School-age Program Regulation 199

WHO ARE THE EDUCATORS?

Educators, like the children they care for, will be diverse in their backgrounds, education, and talents. Here are profiles of a variety of educators, to help give an impression of this diversity.

Courtney is 21 years old and is a recent graduate from a local community college. She received a two-year diploma in Early Childhood Education. She is energetic and enjoys being outdoors with the children. Reading action-adventure stories is one of her passions and she enjoys reading to the children in the program.

Malcolm is 36 and from Scotland. He has a three-year diploma in Early Childhood Education, with two certificates that qualify him to work with children with special needs. He is reflective in nature, enjoys the one-to-one relationships, and feels his strengths are in creating environments for children and developing a family-centred philosophy. Malcolm plays the guitar in a local band and brings his guitar to the program to teach a group of children how to play.

Fatima is 53 and emigrated from Ethiopia. She has a four-year degree in Psychology and a two-year diploma in Early Childhood Education from a local community college. She is very organized by nature and is family oriented. Cooking is one of her talents, and she feels it is important to celebrate the cultural diversity of the program by providing a variety of food and music activities.

Anu is 29, graduated from a two-year diploma program in Recreational Leadership, and has a one-year certificate in Conflict Resolution and Management. She is goal oriented and feels that having concrete goals will help to evaluate both the program and the children's learning. She brings her knowledge of sports skill development, leisure activities, and large-group experiences to the program. She also enjoys doing folk crafts with the children, such as sewing, knitting, crocheting, and quilting.

Darren is 41 and graduated from a three-year diploma program in Visual and Creative Arts. For many years, he taught drawing and painting to school-age children at a community arts school. He enjoys using the camera and camcorder for documentation, and taught the children how to use them. The children are using the camcorder to make a movie, and will be showing it to the parents at the program's next potluck meal.

Rosie is 25, a Native Canadian, and graduated from a three-year Child and Youth Worker diploma program. She has strong computer skills and a good sense of humour. She enjoys telling jokes, doing charades, and performing skits with the children. She feels the community meeting process is important because it gives the children the opportunity to voice their ideas and opinions, and helps to create a sense of community.

Sam is 20 and is a high school graduate. She has always enjoyed working with children and during high school she spent the summers working in day camps. She enjoys crafts and playing games with the children. She has no plans to further her education since she's happy with her position and doesn't want to become the director of a centre.

The above profiles show the variety of backgrounds educators have as well as the variety of skill sets that they bring to programs. The educators described have educational backgrounds that include Early Childhood Education, Child and Youth Worker, Recreation, Visual and Creative Art, and Psychology. There is a role in school-age programs for this diversity. The Early Childhood Educator bring to programs a strong knowledge of child development and curriculum development; the Child and Youth Worker brings a knowledge of older children and techniques for working with children with difficulties; the Recreation graduate has a knowledge of sports skill development; the Arts major brings an ability to help children develop art techniques and an appreciation of art; the Psychology major has an understanding of how children learn and how they are motivated to learn; the older woman brings her mothering skills and the young woman brings enthusiasm. By utilizing the skills of the individuals working with the children, programs will be better able to meet the various needs of children (learning sports skills, creating plays, teaching art skills) and broaden the types of learning experiences the children encounter.

CHARACTERISTICS OF EDUCATORS

Along with relevant training there are a number of other characteristics or qualities associated with competent school-age educators. Many texts on school-age child care list a number of these characteristics, but perhaps the place to begin the discussion is with the children.

During a group meeting with school-aged children in Ottawa the adult facilitator asked the following question: "What type of person do you have to be to work with children?" One child during the brainstorming session recorded all of the comments made by the others. Below is a list of some of their comments.

- Someone who knows how to have fun. They should be able to tell jokes and like to laugh a lot.

- They should be relaxed and not too stressed out; chilling out.
- Listens to our kind of music and who is up to date on "kids' stuff" like rap music, books, MuchMusic, etc.
- A good listener and supportive.
- There to help all of us when we are trying to figure something out.
- Someone who doesn't take sides but is there to help everyone.
- Who likes to play sports and is active. Not too active and pushy but the right amount of being active.
- Gives us space to be with our friends.
- A good snack maker. Someone who likes to cook and bake.
- They have to make sure we have things to do and materials to do things with.
- Someone who is respectful of our feelings.
- They should like having us help in planning the program: for example, planning snacks or having a special day.

The statements made by the children clearly describe the different qualities and roles that they feel an educator should exhibit. Children are very direct about what they want in an educator, and they see it as being a multifaceted role. What is also clear is that it is the qualities the educators bring to the program, not their gender or age, that are important to the children.

When describing the positive qualities educators need to facilitate children's learning, it is difficult to sum them up in one or two words. The educator will demonstrate a number of qualities and skills depending on the situation, their past experiences, and who is involved. Many researchers and writers have identified a number of educator qualities associated with good programs for children (Musson, 1999; Bender et al., 1984; Canadian Child Care Federation, 1999; Gestwicki and Bertrand, 1999). The following are some of the qualities and skills that it is commonly agreed educators should have.

- Patience
- Sense of humour
- Empathetic
- Organized
- Open to new ideas
- Curious
- Risk taker
- Respectful
- Responsive
- Flexible
- Creative
- Firm, fair, and consistent

At first glance one might be daunted by the list, but good educators will demonstrate all of these qualities and skills as well as their own unique qualities. Many of these characteristics may be an integral part of the educator's general personality (e.g., patience) while other

Educators are important for the success of the program.

educators may require training to increase the presence of the quality or skill. Training and practice can help educators develop any of these characteristics, just as skilled educators can help the children develop similar characteristics. In addition, programs that employ more than one educator can try to ensure that the strengths of the educators complement each other. One educator may be a very creative thinker while another may be very playful; combining these strengths in a program will lead to better learning experiences for the children.

Although each educator will tend to be stronger in some areas than in others, all of the qualities must be present if the children are going to have a quality program. Some educators might show more patience than others, but all the educators must be able to demonstrate this quality to some degree. An educator without patience will become frustrated when the children are unable to perform the way the educator expects them to. This lack of patience will, in turn, create stress and perhaps resentment in the children, who will know they are having trouble meeting the educator's expectations. Similarly, all educators must respect the children in the program. If an educator does not respect a child, this will often be demonstrated in his interaction with the child. It may come out in the tone of voice, in the words spoken, in the looks given, in the lack of responsiveness to the child, and so on. These inappropriate interactions create a poor environment, not only for that child, but for all the children, since the other children are also learning inappropriate interactions from the educator's example.

ROLES OF THE EDUCATOR

Facilitator

During the day the educator will have to take on many roles. One of the most important roles is that of a facilitator. As facilitators, educators help the children acquire new knowledge, concepts, and skills in all of the **developmental domains** (for instance, providing the loose parts, books, or other materials necessary to explore a new concept). As facilitators, educators help children develop problem-solving skills and self-regulation skills.

Educators also take on the facilitator role as they develop positive, effective, and professional relationships with children, parents, the school, and the community (for instance, by arranging to bring someone to the class who can help the camera club learn how to use different types of cameras).

Communicator

The school-age program is a social environment, and the educator's success as a communicator will have an impact on how effective the program is. Educators take on the communicator role as they help children understand why the program works the way it does and what the responsibilities of the children are in this environment. To be an effective communicator the educator must speak to school-age children with respect and at their level. Educators who speak to school-age children the same way they might speak to preschoolers (for instance, by using expressions like "indoor feet" and "listening ears") will quickly discover that the children resent this type of language and think the educator is talking down to them.

Educators need to be excellent communicators when interacting with the school and the community. They must be able to explain the program to these groups and convince them that supporting the centre supports children and their learning. Just as important as the above is the ability to communicate effectively with the parents of the children. Depending upon the background of the parents, this may provide the greatest challenge to effective communication. What do you do if the parents don't speak the language of the centre? How do you communicate in a way that is respectful of the parents' culture? Regardless of the challenges encountered, educators must find ways to communicate with the parents and to develop a rapport with them. Because communication skills are so important to the success of the program, educators would often benefit from training in effective communication skills.

Director

Although educators are often facilitators, at times educators must take on the director role. Especially in areas affecting **self-esteem**, self-concept, health, and safety, the educator will have to take a more directive approach. If an educator is aware of an occurrence of bullying or discriminatory behaviour that may affect the confidence and the self-esteem of the child, the educator needs to be directive. She must address the inappropriateness of such behaviour, outline its consequences, and then follow through on dealing with the behaviour. For the educator such discriminatory behaviour is not to be tolerated or negotiated.

In another situation the educator may become more directive if she sees that a child is wandering and not becoming engaged in any area of the room. In this situation the educator, after discussing the situation with the child, may need to be directive and move the child into a play area where the educator can then try to engage the child in learning experiences.

Model

In a variety of situations the educator may take on the role of model. He may need to model appropriate behaviours or attitudes. For example, in a conflict situation the educator should model conflict-resolution techniques for the children. As the children watch the educator use these skills and see the results, they will be more likely to try similar methods when they are involved in conflict.

Supporter

Frequently, educators take on the role of supporter as they acknowledge children who are engaged in meaningful learning experiences or practicing newly learned skills. Educators do this every time they stop to make a positive comment to a child who has successfully completed a challenging task (for instance, the educator says to the child who has finally made a paper airplane capable of flying across the room, "Wow, how far do you think your plane flew?"). They do it when they sit down beside the child completing a puzzle and comment on how quickly he put it together or on how carefully he looked at the colour of the piece so as to work out where to place it. They do it as they give children responsibilities in the program (e.g., caring for pets, making snacks), and they do it in a variety of other ways as well. They support a child's emotional development when the child comes from school upset because he felt a teacher was being hard on him, and the educator takes the time to listen to what the child has to say and acknowledges his feelings.

Planner

The role of planner is an important one for educators. Regardless of the amount of child participation in the planning process, the educators are ultimately responsible for the program. Educators are planners as they determine how to set up the environment for the children or how to get the children involved in setting up the environment. Educators are planners as they determine how to develop a system of ongoing communications with the parents using the program. They are planners as they determine how best to use the money in the budget to obtain the necessary materials for the program. Finally, educators are planners as they get involved in committee work both within the centre and in the larger ECE community.

Advocate

At times, educators must take on the role of advocate. They may need to advocate for the children and their families in a variety of ways. Educators may get involved on an individual basis as they advocate for support services for a child with special needs, or they may meet with teachers in the school system to advocate for a consistent approach to a challenging behaviour. At the community, provincial, or even federal level they may also engage in advocacy. This may take the form of lobbying for better funding for school-age programs, or it could take the form of providing information to the general public about the long-term effects of quality programs on children.

Peacemaker

The last role to be discussed is that of peacemaker. Educators will often be called upon to be peacemakers when working in school-age programs. An educator may have to be a

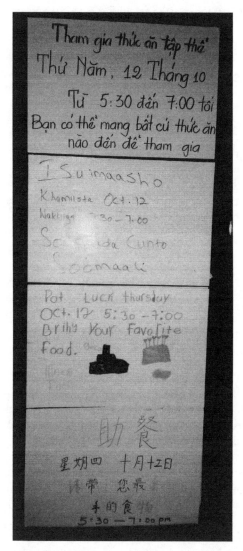

If families have difficulty reading English or French, important messages may be posted in other languages.

peacemaker between two groups of friends within the program, by helping the children to practice and implement various techniques, such as conflict resolution and self-regulated problem-solving strategies (see Chapter 9). An educator may at times have to be a peacemaker with members of the team who for one reason or another are unable to get along. Educators may also have to become peacemakers with parents who may be in conflict with staff or with other parents. An educator may have to be a peacemaker when another educator is caught up in a power struggle with children. Because this role is crucial for the well-being of the centre, educators may benefit from further training in conflict resolution skills.

RESPONSIBILITIES OF THE EDUCATOR

Educators have a variety of responsibilities in a program, ranging from implementation of government regulations to curriculum planning. The educators have a responsibility to follow the **occupational standards** set out in the various acts and regulations governing school-age programs. They also have responsibilities with respect to the children, program, schools, families, colleagues, and the profession.

All of the responsibilities that an educator has are in one way or another linked to responsibilities to the children. For example, educators are responsible for following the legislation governing school-age programs, which is directly linked to the needs of children. Similarly, the responsibilities to the program or to the families also come back to what the educator should be doing for the children involved. As a result, this section will not have a heading called "children" because responsibilities to children will be found under all of the headings.

Legislation

The various pieces of legislation that govern school-age programs in each of the provinces and territories are there to serve as a framework and reference when setting up a program. These regulations set minimum standards for programs, but it is the responsibility of educators within the program to ensure the quality of the learning experiences the children participate in.

Educators have a responsibility to know the regulations governing programs in their area. It is crucial that regulations influencing the daily operation of the program be known by heart. Educators are responsible for maintaining required staff/child ratios, implementing fire drills, developing the program, and dealing with children's health issues such as allergies; therefore, educators must know what the regulations are. The educator who does not know what the regulations are around fire drills and emergency evacuations will not have time to consult the manual if the alarm sounds.

Educators also need to know the legislation because parents may have questions they need answered. When a parent questions the behaviour-guidance approach used in the centre, the educator needs to be able to explain the approach in relationship to current research and to the legislation governing the techniques used. For example, parents may suggest that their child would benefit from corporal **punishment**. In this case it is the responsibility of the educator to explain how the theories governing their practice will not allow this, and that the legislation governing the program forbids corporal punishment. In another situation parents might ask permission for their ten-year-old child to walk home from the centre so that the parents don't have to come to pick her up. Although the educators might agree that this particular child is capable of walking the two blocks home, the educators must also know what the regulations state and be able to explain it to the parents so that they'll understand the limitations placed on the educators.

Educators have a responsibility to themselves with respect to the legislation. Regulations around health and safety issues are there to protect both children and educators. For example, legislation regarding **child abuse** identifies the reporting responsibilities of educators but also protects the educator from prosecution as long as the educator follows the regulations.

Legislation governing the reporting of child abuse varies among the provinces and territories. What constitutes abuse or neglect may also vary from province to province.

Despite these variations, all child-abuse legislation aims to encourage individuals working with children to report incidents of child abuse by providing legal protection for those who report suspected child abuse and sanctioning those who fail to report it. In order for educators to understand the local legislation and expectations regarding the reporting of child abuse, they need to refer to the relevant legislation (see Table 2.2) as well as to local policies that may have been implemented.

Although legislation attempts to protect the individual reporting the abuse, educators must realize that parents may be able to guess who it was who did the reporting. Recognizing that one's identity may not remain secret should not stop educators from reporting the offence, but it should help educators prepare for dealing with very upset parents.

The Program

Philosophy All educators have a responsibility to know the centre's philosophy and how it translates into action. Having a clear philosophy of how the program works is a responsibility of the educator. The educator should be able to articulate how development and learning theories influence their relationship with the children, the design of the environments, and the curriculum approach. The philosophy should be evaluated at least once a year.

Health and Safety The educator is responsible for making sure that all children are safe, both physically and emotionally, in the program.

The educator is responsible to make sure the environment is safe from hazards in the indoor and outdoor environment. It is important to inspect the play yard each day for hazards before children use it. Broken glass, damaged play structures, and uneven play surfaces (such as cracked asphalt) are some common hazards. In many urban environments educators may also need to check the play yard for used syringes and condoms. Making sure the physical environment is safe and free of hazardous materials allows children to play safely,

TABLE 2.2	Provincial acts dealing with child abuse
Alberta	*Child, Youth and Family Enhancement Act*
British Columbia	*Child, Family and Community Services Act*
Manitoba	*Child and Family Services Act*
New Brunswick	*Family Services Act*
Newfoundland	*Child Welfare Act*
Northwest Territories	*Child and Family Services Act*
Nova Scotia	*Children and Family Services Act*
Nunavut	*Child and Family Services Act*
Ontario	*Child and Family Services Act*
Prince Edward Island	*Child and Family Services Act*
Quebec	*Youth Protection Act*
Saskatchewan	*Child and Family Services Act*
Yukon	*Children's Act*

and to feel safe in the play environment. Educators must also make sure the materials in the classroom are not hazardous (for instance, that there are no poisonous plants).

Educators are responsible for maintaining an environment that promotes health in children. They do this by ensuring that sanitary practices are abided by (for example, by sanitizing tables both before and after serving food). It also means that educators have a responsibility to engage in a quick visual inspection of each child as they enter the room to ensure the child is well enough to participate and to discuss any concerns with the parents. Within the curriculum, educators support healthy development by ensuring that children engage in physical activities. These types of activities will be especially important for children who tend to favour sedentary pursuits, and those who are overweight.

Educators are responsible not only for the physical health of the children, but their emotional health as well. Educators need to maintain an awareness of the children's emotional health (self-esteem and self-concept) and respond when children appear to be depressed, traumatized, and so on.

Nutrition The educator is responsible for making sure children are receiving a nutritious snack and food supplement (such as milk) when attending an after-school program. Many programs will serve a daily snack to all children, and the educator may be responsible for planning and making snacks. They need to be aware of the Canadian Food Guide, cultural practices of the families in the centre, health policies (washing hands before serving the snack), and the food budget when planning and serving the snack. The educator is responsible for knowing if the children are affected by any food allergies or cultural restrictions, and to make sure they are following parental requests.

Environments The educator is responsible for creating and setting up both the indoor and outdoor environment of the program based on his observations and interests, and on input from the children. A home-like, community-based environment should be developed with the children. The physical environments should reflect the qualities of home and the community at large. Educators are responsible for providing materials, props, and equipment that reflect the culture of the classroom, the children's families, and the community. The educator is responsible for providing materials to expand play experiences.

Curriculum The educator is responsible for conceptualizing, planning, and implementing an age-appropriate curriculum with the children. Based on the educator's observations, knowledge of development, and the interests of the children, she is responsible for providing materials, resource books, guest speakers, and community trips to facilitate children's learning.

It is the responsibility of the educator to record the program delivery. The format for this may vary from centre to centre, and often reflects the curriculum approach of the program. In one centre the educators may use webbing (see Chapter 11) to develop a curriculum or planning chart, while in another a more traditional activity-based weekly planning sheet may be used (see Chapter 10). In some school-age programs, the program planning will be done and recorded collectively by the educators, while in other programs individuals will be responsible for planning and recording certain aspects of the curriculum. In still other programs, the children and educators plan the program together (emergent curriculum approach), but regardless of how planning occurs, it is the responsibility of the educator to make sure that the curriculum plans are completed. Once the planning has been put in place, a high-quality program will maintain such records, so that educators and parents can review them and ensure that the curriculum is meeting the needs of the children.

The educator has a responsibility to make sure all children develop the necessary social and communication skills to enter play, make friendships, and to challenge peer-group pressure when necessary. This is achieved when educators support the children and help them develop assertive communication and activism skills. When children develop these skills, they will have the necessary strategies and techniques to deal with aggression, bullying (both physical and social), and harassment.

The educator has a responsibility to facilitate the children's cognitive and language development. By providing appropriate materials, facilitating the play, encouraging the children to practice the skills they have, and facilitating the learning of new skills, the educator addresses this responsibility.

The educator has a responsibility to make sure children have a balance between indoor and outdoor play. At least once a day children should engage in active physical pursuits (for instance, a running game, tag, sport skills, or play rituals such as skipping rope, hopscotch, and clapping games). At times, the weather may limit these activities to ones that can be done indoors; however, this does not need to happen every time a light rain falls. Children who are dressed appropriately should have opportunities to experience activities in a variety of weather conditions, such as light rain, snow, or fog. Running on a sunny day may be fun, but running on a rainy day with all the puddles to jump into and the rain on one's face may be even better.

Behaviour Guidance The educators are responsible for guiding children's behaviour in a positive learning environment. They are responsible for creating an environment that encourages positive interactions and discourages inappropriate behaviour such as aggression and bullying.

It is important for educators to establish firm, fair, and consistent rules and consequences with the children. The educators will implement a variety of strategies and techniques which may vary because of the children's ages, the situation, the location, and the number of children involved. The educator's responsibility around behaviour guidance also includes involving the school-age children in the determination of rules and their consequences (see Chapter 9).

The School

When the school-age program is located in a school, developing an open relationship with the school is another responsibility of the educator. Creating opportunities for open communication is important (for example, sharing behaviour-guidance strategies, shared projects, fundraising, and use of the yard); however, educators must also be aware that confidentiality requirements mean that not all information can be shared without written consent from parents or guardians.

A collaborative approach will keep communication between families, school, and the school-age program consistent, and by demonstrating an open communication style the educator will have the opportunity to negotiate with the school about using resources and shared space. Table 2.3 lists a number of helpful tips the educator and school-age program can implement in developing a positive relationships with the school.

Educators should demonstrate new tools and materials so that children learn the appropriate way to use them.

TABLE 2.3	Developing relationships with the school

- Be friendly and approachable. Start a dialogue and connect with teachers in the hall, lunchroom, or outdoors. Make sure sharing-of-information consent forms are signed off by the parent before you share any information about the children with the school.
- Create an open-door policy for teachers to drop off and visit the children and the educators.
- Invite the teachers to specific open houses, family potlucks, or afternoon tea.
- Celebrate any special occasions, such as "day of the teacher."
- Drop off extra snacks to the staff room, such as muffins made by the children, with compliments of the school-age program.
- Have lunch in the school staff room.
- Invite the appropriate teachers to curriculum planning sessions. Plan together special activities, projects, or school-based curriculums.
- Share your resources and knowledge of child development.
- Submit information about the school-age program to the school newsletter.
- Add any school information to the school-age newsletter.
- Post the school-age curriculum in the halls of the school.
- BE VISIBLE!

Families

When families entrust their children into the care of educators, educators make a commitment not only to the children but to those families. Educators must respect the families and maintain effective communications with them.

The educator needs to be respectful of all parents and the diversity of the families. This respect is reflected in the body language, vocabulary, and verbal cues of the educator. It is demonstrated when educators listen to parents and follow up on parental requests (such as providing information on behaviour-guidance techniques). It is demonstrated when educators hang posters that illustrate the backgrounds and cultures of the families. Respect can even be shown in the way the educators dress (for instance, by following a dress code that avoids overly revealing clothes).

As well as respecting families, educators must develop and maintain effective communication with the parents. Open and meaningful communication with parents is essential and can occur in several ways. During the intake process the educator or director of the program will have an opportunity to meet with the parents, fill out registration forms, and discuss the philosophy and goals of the program. Parents will have the opportunity to share any goals they may have for the program and for their child, and provide other information, such as family or cultural practices and dislikes and interest of the child. The school-age program will have a written parent handbook, with policies, procedures (which may be set out by legislation), and information about the program.

Daily verbal communication with each parent is important to encourage open communication. At this time the educator may have the opportunity to discuss what the child is learning, who the child plays with, and any other issues or concerns, such as sharing any behaviour guidance techniques they are implementing in the program. When educators and parents touch base, parents have the opportunity to share information about their cultural and family practices and other interest in the program (volunteering their time and skills). Daily verbal communication may also be very mundane in nature (such as phoning the program to tell the educator who will be picking up the child), but even these simple exchanges help create a positive rapport with the parents.

Formal meetings provide the opportunity for the educator and the parent to spend an uninterrupted period of time connecting with each other discussing their impressions and observations of the child, and to work collaboratively in developing goals for the child. They might discuss the successes of the child, the development of social competency (new friends), new learning opportunities, and any issues or concerns the parents or educator might have.

At least once a year, programs should host a formal meeting with parents to discuss the development of the child, provide an overview of how and what the child is learning in the program, and suggest possible goals. In these meetings parents should have the opportunity to discuss the types of learning their children have been involved in, their goals for their children, and concrete ways both parents and educators can help the children achieve these goals. To facilitate these formal meetings, many programs use a portfolio and **checklist** system to keep track of each child's learning. During this time the parents have the opportunity to communicate and discuss how they can be involved in the program by helping to supply resources, volunteering during field trips, coming in as guest speakers, advocating for the program if needed, or helping with fundraising.

A formal meeting between the educator and the parent may be required at different times throughout the year if the educator or parent feels she need a longer period of time to discuss any positive and negative behaviours demonstrated by the child. This is an opportunity for the educator and parent to work together to share their observations of the child, and to develop goals and techniques to change the child's behaviour, in particular when dealing with atypical behaviour, such as moodiness, overt aggression, or bullying. By working together the parent and educator can be consistent in developing an action plan and in implementing the action plan to help the child to change her behaviour and to develop new skills and techniques.

Written and pictorial documentation, photographs, dictation, stories, and illustrations can be very effective ways to communicate to parents the kind of work and play that takes place in the program, and the values they reflect. A parent resource bulletin board and a monthly newsletter to all parents (perhaps produced in the languages of the program's families, if parents will volunteer to do the translation) are two other ways communication occurs. Regardless of the approaches used, educators must keep all parents informed.

Colleagues

In some school-age programs, a low number of children may require only one educator, but it is more common for several educators to work together to deliver a program. Whenever educators are working with others they have responsibilities toward their colleagues and, in turn, the other employees have responsibilities toward them.

Just as educators are required to respect families and maintain effective communications with them, educators have a responsibility to develop respectful relationships with, and communicate effectively with, their colleagues. When developing all aspects of the program, educators must respect the opinions of their colleagues and listen to their ideas. They must be willing to negotiate in order to create a learning environment that meets the needs of the children and accommodates the individual differences of the team members. When working in a team it is essential that a sense of trust be developed. This trust develops as colleagues make sure confidential information remains confidential, and when team members independently follow through tasks that have been assigned.

Educators have a responsibility to maintain effective communication with their colleagues. One method is through ongoing informal discussions that occur throughout the day. Information on the children's behaviour, play development, parental interactions, children's medications and allergies, set-up of the environment, and so on is recorded and shared with the team to ensure that all educators are kept informed.

When conflict arises within the team the educators have a responsibility to deal with the conflict in an effective and professional manner. They will need to use conflict resolution techniques, beginning by discussing the situation quietly with the individual rather than in the staff room with others present. If the issue is one that the educators can't handle on their own they have a responsibility to contact the supervisor and utilize the supervisor's skills to help solve the problem.

Although a good school-age program provides opportunities for educators to work collaboratively with the administration (such as the supervisor and the coordinator) the educator must recognize that often the final decision is the responsibility of administration, and once a decision has been made it will have to be adhered to by the educators.

When making any decision regarding the program and the children in it, educators and administrators in high-quality school-age programs have a responsibility to adhere to a professional code of ethics. The professional associations in some provinces (e.g., British Columbia and Ontario) have developed professional codes of ethics that they hope all practicing ECEs will follow. In jurisdictions without a written code of ethics, ECEs often use the code developed by the Canadian Child Care Federation (see Table 2.4) to guide their behaviour.

The Profession

Educators also have a responsibility to their profession. Educators should not expect to sit back and let others advocate for high-quality early learning and care programs. If educators think people aren't aware of the long-term implications of both good- and poor-quality programs for children, they must help find ways to make the public aware. Educators who feel that their profession is under-valued must speak up and let the general public know how their knowledge and skills support children's ongoing learning. If educators think they are underpaid, they must be willing to tell the general public how under-funded the profession is in relation to other educational and family support systems. For many educators, advocating for the profession may seem daunting, but there are a variety of ways one can advocate without having to stand up in front of a group of people! Educators can advocate within their centre as they discuss various issues with parents and colleagues. Educators who dislike public speaking may work on committees, research information, or develop letter-writing campaigns. Educators living in isolated communities may use the Internet, or financially support organizations that can advocate on their behalf. Regardless of whether the educator is advocating for better regulations to ensure quality, or fighting for more respect, advocating for the profession is something that all educators must do if changes are going to occur.

TABLE 2.4	The eight principles of ethical practice

- Child care practitioners promote the health and well-being of children.
- Child care practitioners demonstrate caring for all children in all aspects of their practice.
- Child care practitioners enable children to participate to their full potential in environments carefully planned to serve individual needs and to facilitate the child's progress in social, emotional, physical, and cognitive areas of development.
- Child care practitioners work in partnership with parents, recognizing that parents have primary responsibility for the care of their children, valuing their commitment to the children, and supporting them in meeting their responsibility to their children.
- Child care practitioners work in partnership with colleagues and other service providers in the community to support the well-being of children and their families.
- Child care practitioners work in ways that enhance human dignity in trusting, caring, and co-operative relationships that respect the worth and uniqueness of the individual.
- Child care practitioners pursue, on an ongoing basis, the knowledge, skills, and self-awareness needed to be professionally competent.
- Child care practitioners demonstrate integrity in all of their professional relationships.

Source: **Doherty (2003). Reproduced with the permission of the Canadian Child Care Federation.**

Summary

Legislation regarding the training of educators working in school-age environments means that programs may hire individuals with complementary skill sets; however, directors must recognize that all staff, regardless of their training, need a solid knowledge of child development and an understanding of how children learn.

Although educators may come from diverse backgrounds, there are qualities and skills that all educators should have. Imagination, an ability to nurture, respect for children, empathy, and openness to new ideas are just a few of the traits identified as important for early childhood educators.

There are also specific roles that educators will have to take on as they interact with children and develop the curriculum. At times the educator will be a facilitator, while on other occasions he will be a director, a supporter, a planner, a communicator, a model, an advocate, or a peacemaker. The children, the situation, the location, the families, and the colleagues will influence the role the educator takes on.

Closely linked to the roles are the responsibilities educators acquire when agreeing to work in a school-age program. Educators working in school-age programs have a responsibility to know and follow the various regulations governing programs in their local and provincial jurisdictions. They also have responsibilities with respect to the program, the schools, the families, the colleagues, and the profession, along with their over-riding responsibilities to the children they care for.

Student Learning Experiences

1. Interview a group of school-age children to find out what type of educator they would like at their centre and why they think these skills and qualities are important. In class, share the information and draw some conclusions regarding characteristics educators should have.

2. Interview an educator who has just begun working with school-age children and another who has worked in the field for at least three years. Compare and contrast their answers regarding the skills one should have to work with school-age children.

3. Locate the provincial or territorial legislation governing staff training and curriculum in school-age programs. Cite one legislated requirement and explain how it might influence the learning experiences found in the program.

Review Questions

1. The director has been told that the budget is being cut by 10 per cent and she in turn has decided that no new material purchases will be made for a year. Does the classroom educator have a responsibility to speak to the director and discuss how this will affect the quality of the program? Justify your answer using references from the section above on Responsibilities of the Educator.

2. Explain what is meant by the term "educator as advocate."

3. Do the roles of an educator in a school-age program differ from those of one in a pre-school program? Justify your answer.

4. Identify three roles of the educator and explain when each would be appropriate.

5. Identify two responsibilities that educators have with respect to families.

6. Describe three ways an educator could work with elementary school teachers to improve the quality of the after-school program. Justify your answer.

PART 2

Development: Theories, Ages, and Stages

CHAPTER 3

Theories of Development and Learning

OVERVIEW

Educators in school-age programs face a variety of challenges that are different from those faced by educators working with younger children. Being bullied or bullying other children, wanting independence from adults, working on academics, increasing competitiveness among peers, emerging sexuality, and needing a change of pace from the school environment are just some of the challenges facing children—and therefore educators—in school-age programs. On top of all these challenges, educators may have in their program children of a wide range of ages, perhaps all the way from five to twelve. However, educators who have a thorough understanding of a variety of developmental and learning theories can effectively use this knowledge to help develop school-age programs that address the needs and challenges of such diverse groups of children.

This chapter will briefly review a number of theories that can provide insight into the challenges facing school-age children and show how to program effectively for them. Piaget's cognitive developmental theory or Erikson's psychosocial theory of development provide insight into how children at different ages might behave, while theories such as information processing models (IPM) and Vygotsky's sociocultural theory focus on how children learn regardless of their age. Still other theories address intelligence and look at how this influences a child's approach to problems and the types of activities they prefer.

School-age children are not learning in isolation. Many of the learning theories indicate that the people most immediately involved with the children, as well as the broader society in which they live, will influence the learning that occurs.

Since school-age children are actively reaching out toward the larger community around them, it is useful to review Bronfenbrenner's ecological theory to help one better understand how the children's immediate environment and the larger culture will influence both the children and their behaviour.

GARDNER'S THEORY OF MULTIPLE INTELLIGENCES

The theory of **multiple intelligences** developed by Howard Gardner states that there are at least eight types of intelligence (see Table 3.1). His theory attempts to show how people differ in the content areas of intelligence—in other words, in their abilities. He sees each of the intelligences as unique and indicates that a child can excel in one type of intelligence while having challenges in another area. Gardner also indicates that the intelligences within which a child is strong as well as those that are challenging will influence how he approaches learning and the types of activities that the child he will prefer.

For the educator, this provides a challenge when programming, because it means he should present a concept to the children in more than one way. For example, in a school-age program he may decide that the children need to deal with the issue of ostracizing others. The educator decides to call a group meeting to discuss the issue and hopes the children will come away with a better understanding of how ostracism can affect all of them. Depending on how he conducts the group meeting, it could work very well for the children who have strong linguistic, interpersonal, or intrapersonal intelligences, but it may not work nearly as

TABLE 3.1	Gardner's intelligences	
Intelligence	**Characteristics of the Intelligence**	**Some Activities that Support the Intelligence**
Linguistic	Strengths in areas requiring oral and written language. Uses language effectively to express concepts and emotions.	• Storytelling, chanting • Role-playing • Documentation • Reading books, etc. • Writing • Word search activities, etc.
Logical-mathematical	Strengths in areas that require logical thinking and problem-solving, seeing patterns and math skills	• Construction play • Puzzles • Organizing air bands • Sudoku and logic games • Weaving folk art, origami, etc. • Cooking, baking, gardening
Interpersonal	Strengths in areas that require working with others and understanding others' emotions, thinking, and body language	• Group meetings • Dramatic play • Construction • Leadership activities • Peer mentoring
Intrapersonal	Strength in areas requiring self-reflection: understanding your own skills, abilities, and emotions	• Music • Art • Reading • Writing • Unstructured activities with loose parts available • Construction play
Spatial	Strengths in areas that require the ability to see and understand dimensional relationships between objects	• Art • Construction • Dance • Sports and active games • Cooking • Charting
Bodily kinesthetic	Strengths in areas that require the understanding of what is needed to effectively control your body in a variety of activities	• Sports • Dance • Art • Obstacle courses • Musical concerts
Musical	Strengths in areas that require one to recognize, understand, and appreciate various aspect and component of music	• Air bands • Singing and chants • Playing instruments • Writing and creating music • Listening to a variety of music
Naturalistic	Strengths in areas requiring an appreciation and understanding of the interplay of the various elements of nature, including people	• Gardening • Taking care of pets • Outdoor activities (e.g. digging, field trips) • Caring for indoor plants • Science activities using natural elements and natural loose parts • Cooking

well for some of the other children. Children with strong musical intelligence but challenges in interpersonal intelligence may learn more effectively if the educator invites them to create a song or has them listen to various types of music and identify music that would reflect how one feels when ostracized. By dealing with the concept through more than one type of intelligence, the educator will help all children have a better understanding of it.

Gardner's Theory of Multiple Intelligences does not aim to determine which children are "more" intelligent; instead, it aims to help educators understand the nature of these multiple intelligences and determine the ways in which children of differing intelligences learn best. In an after-school program there may be one child who has a strong musical intelligence but is weak in the area of logical-mathematical intelligence. There may also be a child in the program who is very strong in the area of logical-mathematical intelligence but weak in the area of language intelligence. Because of the different intellectual strengths of these two children, they will be interested in different activities and will learn differently. The child with the logical-mathematical intelligence may love to engage in construction play or enjoy doing puzzles, while the other child might prefer to put on an air band performance. When approaching the learning of math facts, the child with strong musical skills may learn better if the facts are incorporated into a song, while the other child might ignore this learning strategy altogether. If the two children are given an activity requiring them to use measuring skills, the child stronger in logical-mathematical intelligence might appear to be more intelligent, but if placed in a situation requiring musical skills, the other child might appear to be more intelligent.

According to Gardner's theory, a child may be strong or weak overall in all intelligences; however, she will still demonstrate different ability levels among the intelligences and have some preferred types of intelligence. By observing to learn the child's strengths, needs, and preferences, educators obtain knowledge that will help them develop curriculum the child finds both interesting and challenging.

Along with being aware of children's intelligences, educators need to be aware of their own intelligences, and how their abilities and preferences might affect what they do. If an educator has very strong linguistic and interpersonal abilities but very few abilities in musical and intrapersonal intelligences, for instance, this will probably influence what she offers the children in the program. The strong linguistic abilities may make the educator a great storyteller in the program, while the interpersonal skills may mean that she quickly responds to a child in distress. On the other hand, her weakness in the area of musical intelligence may result in a failure to provide many musical experiences, while the weaknesses

TABLE 3.2	Insights the educator can obtain from Gardner's theory

- Each child will have his or her own preferred ways of learning.
- Each child will have strengths in some ability areas (intelligences) and find other areas more challenging.
- Educators should provide opportunities for children to learn through all types of intelligences.
- Educators should ensure that their own challenges and preferences aren't interfering with learning opportunities for the children.
- Educators should periodically evaluate their program to make sure that the development of all types of intelligences is occurring.

in intrapersonal intelligence may result in few opportunities for children to be on their own or engage in daydreaming.

Gardner indicates that everyone will have some intelligences that they prefer to use; however, children have the potential to develop in all of them. Educators, therefore, should assess their programs to determine what types of intelligences are encouraged and what types appear to be ignored or even discouraged. Educators need to identify the intelligences they avoid using themselves and understand how their avoidance may be influencing the program. Educators also need to brainstorm ways to ensure that all types of intelligences are promoted (see Table 3.2).

PIAGET'S THEORY OF COGNITIVE DEVELOPMENT

Jean Piaget's theory of **cognitive development** (see Table 3.3) has had a major influence on early childhood educators and how they interact with children. According to Piaget, typical children in a school-age program could be at the preoperational, concrete operational, or formal operational stages of development. For the educator, this can provide some real challenges.

Preoperational Stage

The preoperational child in the program has difficulty seeing another person's point of view (egocentrism) and can think operations through in only one direction (he lacks reversibility in his thinking). This child will have some difficulty following the rules of a game and will try to change them to meet his needs since he has trouble taking into account the perspectives of the other children.

TABLE 3.3	Piaget's theory	
Developmental Stage	**Approximate Ages**	**Description**
Sensorimotor	Birth to 2 years	Children construct an understanding of their world through sensory experiences and physical actions.
Preoperational	2 years to 7 years	Children use their understanding of language and symbols to help construct their knowledge of the world.
Concrete Operational	7 years to 11 years	Children are able to reason logically in real-life situations and use their understanding of logical reasoning to help construct their knowledge of the world.
Formal Operational	11 years and older	Children and adults are able to reason logically when dealing with abstract concepts and use abstract thinking to help them construct their knowledge of the world (both ideal and real).

Concrete Operational Stage

At the same time, the educator will have other children who are in the concrete operational stage of development. These children will be better able to take another's perspective and logically solve concrete problems or challenges. These children have developed a number of concepts that allow them to think logically. These concepts include reversibility (being able to work backwards through something to arrive at the starting point), classification (being able to group things into classes), and seriation (being able to order objects). When these children play a game, they recognize that everyone must follow the rules for it to be fair and may become frustrated or upset with the preoperational child who isn't following the rules (especially if the child is the same age). The concrete operational child will, when playing a team sport, use classification skills to understand how different players have different positions and her logical thinking skills will result in her expecting team members to play those positions. This understanding can create conflict when preoperational children are involved in the game, since the preoperational child's concept of a position would be much more fluid; he would see no problem in changing from defence to offence, for instance, because he wants to follow the ball and be involved.

Formal Operational Stage

In the school-age program, some older children may have already moved into the formal operational stage of development. These children are able to solve abstract problems and are more systematic in how they approach them. These children are also developing concerns about social issues and identity. With their increased skills at solving problems and taking perspectives, these children may actually become the peacemakers in the above situation. Their ability to understand *why* the preoperational child behaves as he does means that the older children are more likely to accept the seemingly inappropriate behaviours of the younger children and help guide them through the game. At the same time, they can understand the concrete operational child's desire for organization and adherence to rules. With their ability to understand both ways of thinking they may be able to help the younger children reach a compromise, such as making some changes to the rules of the game that will accommodate the preoperational children's needs.

Assimilation and Accommodation

Piaget's theory indicates that regardless of childrens stage of development, they learn to adapt to their environment and learn new concepts through the processes of **assimilation** and **accommodation**. Assimilation refers to the process by which the child takes in new information and simply incorporates it into an existing schema or concept. A school-age child might consistently mix up the rules of a game of tag if she uses only assimilation when learning the new game. As she simply incorporates the information about the new game into information she already has about tag, she may incorporate it into rules for another game of tag, which results in the child now trying to play both types of tag with the same rules. Instead of having two distinct games of tag, the child now has trouble playing either game effectively.

In contrast, the child who uses accommodation when learning the new information is making changes in the way he thinks. In the situation above, such a child wouldn't mix up

TABLE 3.4	Insights the educator can obtain from Piaget's theory

- Educators cannot expect children of different ages to behave or think in the same way.
- Although all children go through all of the stages, they will go through them at their own pace, so educators must observe each child to determine what type of learning experience is most appropriate for her.
- Knowing how each stage influences a child's thinking can help educators provide more appropriate learning experiences for him.
- Knowing how each stage influences a child's thinking can help educators engage in more appropriate interactions with her.
- Different children may learn different concepts from the same experience.
- The environment that a child has lived in (and has therefore adapted to) will influence what she learns and how she adapts to new experiences (assimilation/accommodation).

the rules of the old game with those of the new one because he would have reorganized his mental schemas to accommodate a completely new type of tag game. Instead of having a simple category for tag that incorporates more than one game, the child may have created a subcategory for each game. If this child is asked to play freeze tag, he will know that the rules for it are different than those used for ordinary tag.

Accommodation and assimilation determine what is learned and how it is learned. As seen above, two children exposed to the same learning experience may come away from the experience having learned different things.

Although Piaget seldom refers to the social environment of the child, one can see how the individual's construction of knowledge will be influenced by the child's social environment and culture. A child's past experiences will be determined by the social environment in which she lives, and this will in turn influence what is assimilated or accommodated, and how.

INFORMATION PROCESSING MODEL (IPM)

The **information processing model** (IPM) focuses on the processes individuals use when learning new information (see Figure 3.1). This model gives educators a better understanding of what children might be learning in various situations. This approach to understanding learning helps educators realize that what's going on around the child as well as his child's past experiences can influence what he actually learns.

Sensory Register

The first component of IPM is the sensory register. This part of the cognitive process merely registers all of the sensory input to which the child is exposed. In order for children to attach meaning to, and learn from, the input they're receiving, they must first pay attention to the input. It is up to the children to determine what they will attend to; however, educators can make it easier for them to focus on a particular input by reducing the number of other inputs that could distract them. The educator who is trying to have a group

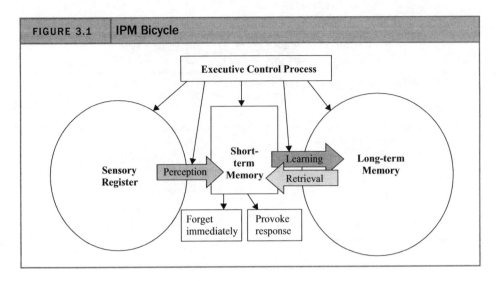

FIGURE 3.1   IPM Bicycle

discussion with the children about programming for the March break, for instance, might help by avoiding having:

- the meeting right next to a window (especially if it's a beautiful day outside).
- the children's favourite music playing in the background.
- other activities going on at the same time (e.g., other educators setting up an activity).

According to IPM, if the meeting occurs where the above stimuli are also occurring, the educator should not be surprised if a child learns the lyrics to the songs or asks questions about today's activities rather than thinking and asking questions about the March break. If the children are able to focus and pay attention to the question "What do you want to do during March break?" they can then attach some meaning to the words that they are hearing (perception) and move the information into their short-term memory, where they can then think about it.

Short-Term Memory

While the information is in short-term memory, children can use a variety of strategies to help them understand the information they have heard and respond to it. The strategies can range from simple rote memorization to creating rhymes or linking the new information to similar past experiences. Children frequently use rehearsal strategies such as chunking or mnemonic devices (like acronyms) to help them remember new information. In fact, a child who uses several different strategies to help her learn new information is more likely to remember it than a child who uses only one strategy.

Long-Term Memory

When children use information from past experiences to understand or remember new information, they are relying on memories that have been stored in their long-term memory (in the March break example, *episodic memory*) to help them understand and respond to the question of what they want to do (for example, by recalling that "last year we went bowling"). Other children may not have past experiences to use, but they may be able to use their understanding of the English language (stored as *semantic memory*) to help them respond to the information. This type of memory is how specific concepts (such as concepts of water or animals) are stored. In other situations, children will store new information in their *procedural memory*. This memory is how action memories are stored (for instance, riding a bike, skating, or swimming).

Executive Control

The relationships among the various IPM components are dynamic. The child continually takes in new information (moving some of it into the short-term memory); manipulates it in the short-term memory (which operates over a period of no more than a few seconds); and pulls information out of long-term memory to help her understand the new information being processed while moving the freshly processed information from short-term into long-term memory, where it can be stored for later use (whether seconds, or years, later). This movement does not occur randomly. The executive control process encompasses the cognitive processes that determine the decisions being made. When the child in this example hears the educator along with all the distracting sounds in the room, her executive control process determines which sounds to filter out immediately and which ones to pay attention to. Without this cognitive function the child would be overwhelmed with all of the stimuli that are going on in the room. At each step of the learning process this function determines the decisions that will be made.

Remembering What Has Been Learned

IPM theory indicates that the more frequently an individual uses information, the better it will be remembered. Each time the information is brought out of long-term memory and used in short-term memory, new connections are being made. IPM indicates that information

TABLE 3.5	Insights the educator can obtain from the information processing model

- A child may learn something completely different from what the teacher expected because the task he was attending to was different from the one the teacher expected him to be attending to.

- The more connections children can make between new information and information they already have, the easier it will be for them to remember the new information.

- New information that has connections to a variety of sensory inputs, as well as a number of different types of long-term memory, will be easier to recall than information that has only one type of link for each component. For instance, reading this passage may only involve input through the visual sense and may be moved only into your semantic memory. If this is the case you will have more trouble remembering this information than someone who read the passage out loud and thought of a past experience that illustrated the point being made.

- The more you revisit information (use it) the easier it will be to remember. If you don't use information, the memory will decay and eventually be forgotten.

- The connection made between previous memories and new information can influence what is learned.

that is not used will often begin to decay, and over time it will become harder and harder to remember.

VYGOTSKY'S SOCIOCULTURAL THEORY

Lev Vygotsky's **sociocultural theory** provides information about how children learn and helps educators understand how to support children's learning (see Figure 3.2). A major concept of this theory is that learning is not done in isolation but is dependent, to a large extent, on interactions with others. These interactions take place within the context of the family and societal culture into which the child is born; therefore the child's family and culture will influence what is learned. An educator should not expect all of the children in the program to have the same knowledge base, or to react the same way when encountering similar situations. Educators in after-school programs see these influences all of the time. A child from a visible minority may interpret a comment differently from a Caucasian child. Children who come from families that emphasize manners and politeness may behave very differently from children who are growing up in an environment where acting "tough" is important.

Another key component to this theory is the need for individuals to be in the **zone of proximal development** (ZPD) for learning to occur. This means that the child should be engaged in learning experiences that are neither too easy nor too difficult. If the educator does not provide activities or materials that offer the children a challenge, they will not be learning. They may have fun at times engaging in activities that require no real thinking on their part, but since there isn't any learning occurring they may quickly become bored with these activities and find other ways of providing themselves with some challenges. On the other hand, activities or materials that are too difficult for a child will also create problems. Children who can't do an activity, even with the support of an adult or a more knowledgeable child, will become frustrated and probably stop trying. An example of this in an after-school program would be if the educator decided that all the children were going to make

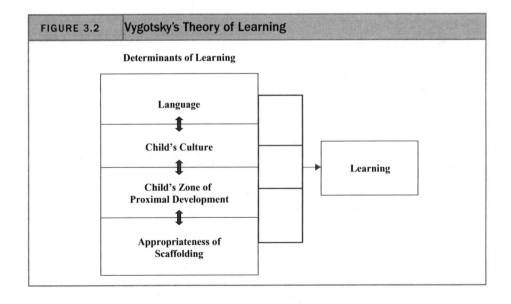

| FIGURE 3.2 | Vygotsky's Theory of Learning |

Determinants of Learning

Language ⇕ Child's Culture ⇕ Child's Zone of Proximal Development ⇕ Appropriateness of Scaffolding → Learning

friendship bracelets, and one of the children couldn't follow the directions even when others tried to demonstrate the process and provide step-by-step instructions. In this case, the child would probably become very frustrated and give up.

When a child needs support—think of it as **scaffolding**—this can take a variety of forms. The educator may encourage children to work together so that a child with particular skills may help other children. This type of peer teaching often occurs around craft activities. A child who knows how to sew is often eager to help his friends learn the skills. In a school-age program an educator can offer support by providing materials and equipment that engage children in problem-solving activities that are challenging yet possible. When the educator provides the children with tubes, buckets, water pumps, pulleys, and books on aqueducts, for instance, she is supporting the children's exploration of and experimentation with plumbing systems and the properties of water. The educator can also provide additional support by asking children questions or giving them a challenge that's connected to the materials. In some activities the educator may even need to provide hand-over-hand support to help the child learn the task. An obvious example of this is when parents or educators help a child learn to tie her own shoes by guiding her hands through the process.

Many parents and educators use some "scaffolding" techniques naturally, but it is important for individuals to recognize what type of scaffolding might be most useful to the child at a particular time, and recognize when a different type is called for. As an example, educators recognize that children will need support in order to develop successful conflict-resolution skills. Initially, educators will often take on the role of mediator because they know that children cannot be expected to develop those skills without support from others. What many educators have difficulty doing is recognizing when to change the level of their support. When should they encourage the children to take a more active role in the solution of the problem, and how should they do it? As adults we may find it very difficult to allow children to come up with a solution that we know won't work. Instead of letting them think through the solution or try it out, we jump in and tell them that it won't work or tell them that another solution is the right one. If the children are ready to solve problems, perhaps a better support would be to ask them to brainstorm all the possible benefits and challenges that could occur with the chosen solution. Another support might be to say, "If you try the solution and it doesn't work, we need to meet again to discuss the problem before anyone gets upset." Children will learn the necessary skill only if educators are able to change the types of supports to meet the children's increased level of competence.

TABLE 3.6	Insights the educator can obtain from Vygotsky's theory
• Recognize and respect how the children's cultures will influence what is learned
• Recognize that learning is influenced by the children's understanding of language
• Recognize when the experiences available to the children may not be effective learning experiences for them (either because they are too difficult—even with scaffolding—or too easy)
• Recognize that scaffolding by adults or peers can help a child learn new skills and learn them more quickly
• Recognize that you need to change the type of scaffolding you provide as the child's skill and knowledge changes

This theory also looks at the important role that language plays in what is learned. Most of the information a child receives is filtered through language, and the child's language will influence how information is interpreted. The child who has grown up surrounded by adults with large vocabularies will come away from a group discussion with a different understanding of what was said than a child who has spent most of his time in groups of children and whose parents use a more limited vocabulary when speaking with the child. As well, the child who is surrounded by language that includes swearing will learn that this is an appropriate way to express one's feelings, so he may have difficulty understanding why it bothers some people.

ERIKSON'S PSYCHOSOCIAL THEORY OF DEVELOPMENT

The focus of Erik Erikson's **psychosocial theory** is on social and emotional development (see Table 3.7). Erikson's theory differs from many other developmental theories in that he looks not only at changes that occur in childhood but also at those that occur in adulthood.

TABLE 3.7	Erikson's theory	
Erikson's Stage of Development	**Approximate Ages**	**Description**
Trust v. mistrust	Birth to 1 year (infant)	Through interactions with parent/caregiver, child develops a sense of trust or mistrust of the world. How well the child's needs are met will influence the outcome of this crisis.
Autonomy v. shame	1 to 3 years (toddler)	Child begins to seek autonomy, self-control, and doubt and control of her interactions with her world. Responses of others can foster this or lead to a sense of shame and doubt.
Initiative v. guilt	4 to 6 years (preschool)	Child wants to make choices, meet challenges, and solve a variety of problems. At the same time he is learning that not all explorations and approaches are acceptable. Adults who are supportive of a variety of explorations can help a child's initiative. However, if adults respond negatively to many of the child's initiatives, the child may develop a sense of guilt.
Industry v. inferiority	6 to 12 years (school age)	Child wants to become accomplished at many of the tasks that society values. If she is successful at accomplishing these skills and if she is recognized for her accomplishments, she will have a sense of industry, but if she has difficulty achieving success or receiving recognition for her success, she may develop a sense of inferiority.

Although early childhood educators tend to focus on the development of children, Erikson's theory indicates that educators should also focus on adult development. Educators interact not only with children but also with the children's parents. Different parents may be at different stages of development, and this could affect the types of interactions educators have with them. If one of a child's parents is in the "intimacy v. isolation" stage while the other is in the "generativity v. stagnation" stage, the educator should not expect both parents to view the world in the same way or to express the same type of concerns.

Initiative v. Guilt

In a school-age program there may be younger children who are at the initiative v. guilt stage of development, while many of the children will be in the industry v. inferiority stage. The children in the initiative stage are often those in kindergarten or the primary grades. They are still learning how to take initiative in appropriate ways. They may be working out how to enter group play situations successfully (for instance, by asking if they can play rather than barging in and trying to take over) or how to understand more about their world by initiating exploration of the materials available to them. Using their curiosity as a springboard, these children may explore the uses of a plumbing pipe by using it as a wand one day, a dumbbell another day and as a marble run on still another day. The educator's role is to support these active explorations while also letting children know, when necessary, the boundaries of the exploration (for example, that the pipe can't be used as a weapon to hurt another child).

In a school-age program there may be children whose past experiences make them hesitate to take the initiative, and they may experience a sense of guilt about their desire to explore the world actively. When working with these children, educators will actively encourage them to try new experiences and to explore their world. For example, there might be a child who is interested in art but is afraid to participate because he has always been discouraged from getting dirty. Knowing this, the educator would include materials such as crayons and play dough (make sure it's not sticky!) along with messier materials such as pastels, clay and paints. Initially, she may locate the non-messy materials slightly away from the messy materials in order to encourage the child who hates getting dirty to get involved in art. As the child explores what can be done with non-messy materials and sees the different things that the other children are doing with the messier materials, the educator can show support and enthusiasm for what the child is already doing, thereby encouraging further exploration. Once the child is willing to take more initiative, the educator can encourage him to try messier materials, and help minimize a sense of guilt by showing him how to keep relatively clean while using messier materials.

Industry v. Inferiority

The majority of the children in a school-age program will be in the stage of development that Erikson characterized as industry v. inferiority. These children want to become accomplished at tasks that society values. Unlike younger children, their exploration is not just about discovering how the world works (although that's still important); they are also becoming much more goal oriented. They're no longer content to just kick a ball around. They want to know how to use the ball to play soccer or basketball. They want to learn to read, and to be recognized as readers. They want to engage in and be successful at crafts and art projects that have a product, because they want to be able to do things that are valued in the culture and society in which they live. An educator in a school-age program supports this by having a variety of materials available to the children, and helps them learn the techniques required to be successful. This doesn't mean that every educator needs to know all the rules of soccer, or to understand how to create perspective in drawings. It does mean that educators working with school-age children have to be willing to learn some of these skills or to find individuals in the community who would be willing to come and share them with the children.

The children's desire to develop skills that are valued within their culture and society also means that children in the program will show preferences for different experiences. A child growing up in a family that values sports will probably want to spend a lot of time in the program working on sports skills, be it through pick-up games of soccer or shooting hoops in the gym. Another child, growing up in a family that values more academic pursuits, may want to spend time reading or even doing homework projects. Other children may be interested in pursuing activities that are closely related to their ethnic or religious background. A child with family ties to Chinese culture may wish to spend time learning or becoming better at writing Chinese script. If there is no educator in the program who has this skill, there may be a member of the community who could come in and support this learning.

Educators in school-age programs must also be aware that children who struggle to develop the skills that society values may develop a sense of inferiority. Educators with children in their program who are struggling with basic skills such as reading and math see firsthand how it affects the children's self-image. Many of these children will openly describe themselves as stupid, and may tend to give up quickly when presented with a challenge. Educators can help children overcome this by providing them with opportunities to engage in activities that they are capable of completing successfully and, at the same time, are valued by society. Educators may help them become good at a sport, learn a craft, or even provide them with opportunities to develop some academic skills while in the school-age program. A child who is struggling to read but who loves to cook may be motivated to read simple recipes or to get involved in putting together a recipe book that will be sold to help raise money for a field trip. A child who is having problems with math may be encouraged to develop these skills if he is asked to help decide what materials should be bought with the $100 the program has to spend, or if he is involved in shopping for the program's food.

TABLE 3.8	Insights the educator can obtain from Erikson's theory

- Educators must know what developmental stage the child is at in order to anticipate her needs.
- Educators need to observe children to try to determine what stage they are at and what crises have been positively resolved.
- If the child has not positively resolved previous crises, the educator will have to address those crises as well.
- Educators need to provide positive support for children's explorations when they are in the initiative v. guilt stage.
- Educators need to help children successfully develop skills that are valued by the child's culture and society when children are in the industry v. inferiority stage

Although the children will likely be in one of the two stages discussed above, Erikson's theory recognizes that not all of the children will have positively resolved the crises from the previous developmental stages. Erikson indicates that if children have developed mistrust or a sense of shame and doubt, there will be additional challenges for the educator. A child who has developed a sense of mistrust will also have difficulty working through industry v. inferiority, and is more likely to come to an unsatisfactory resolution of this crisis. Educators will therefore have to help the child develop a sense of trust while continuing to help him work on the current crisis. If the educator doesn't help the child to develop a sense of trust, it will be very difficult to help him successfully develop a sense of industry.

MASLOW'S HIERARCHY OF NEEDS

Abraham Maslow, the leader of the humanistic psychology movement of the 1950s and 1960s (Hunt, 1993: p. 502), was interested in what motivated individuals and the link between this motivation and their social, emotional, and cognitive development. He hypothesized that individuals are motivated by a **hierarchy of needs** and that the lower needs (deficiency needs) must be met before the individual can move on to higher-level needs (being/growth needs). According to the hierarchy of needs theory, everyone will go through the stages at his own pace. The types of experiences a person has had will help determine what stage she is in. Therefore, through observations and conversations with a child and his family, an educator can learn what stage a child attending the program might be in.

Physiological Needs (Deficiency)

The first level of Maslow's hierarchy consists of physiological needs. At this very basic level a person is motivated to obtain food, water, and shelter. Unless these basic needs are met, the person will not be motivated to engage in other types of interactions. Educators should not expect children who are very hungry and tired to be interested in art activities or even social interactions. These children want something to eat and a place to sleep before they engage in other learning experiences.

Safety Needs (Deficiency)

The hierarchy of needs indicates that once physiological needs have been met the child is now at the second level, motivated by safety needs. A child who is subject to abuse at home or bullying at school would be one whose safety needs are not being met, and she will not be motivated to participate in many of the learning experiences available in the program. This child will be dealing with her feelings related to the lack of safety, or she will be engaged in activities to increase her safety. The fear and stress the child is feeling may show itself in the child lashing out at peers or teachers. On the other hand, the child may be very withdrawn as she attempts to eliminate any behaviour that might result in someone abusing or bullying her. In either of these cases the child is not focusing on the learning experiences being offered by the program.

Belongingness and Love Needs (Deficiency)

The third level of the hierarchy is belongingness and love needs. Everyone needs to feel that they belong. It may be simply with one or two friends, or with a larger group, but regardless of the type or size of the group, the sense of belonging is necessary if a person is to continue to grow. This stage of development is often actively supported by educators in school-age programs, who create a sense of community by encouraging friendships and helping children who may have difficulty with social skills to develop relationships with other children. By expressing interest and concern for the children in the program, educators also help meet the belonging needs of the children in their care.

Esteem Needs (Deficiency)

The fourth and last deficiency level is esteem needs. As the name indicates, individuals at this level are motivated by a need for self-esteem. They need to feel confident and competent. Children at this level will certainly engage in many of the learning experiences offered by the program; however, they may hesitate to truly challenge themselves for fear of making a mistake. Educators must also be aware, however, that children may attain self-esteem by engaging in activities of which the adult might not approve, since for the school-age child peer expectations are just as important as adult expectations.

Need to Know and Understand (Being/Growth)

Once self-esteem needs have been met, the individual has successfully fulfilled all of the deficiency needs and moves on to the being/growth needs. Although the needs in this part of the hierarchy are shown as three different levels, none of these needs is ever completely filled. An individual at the level of needing to know and understand will be motivated to find information on a particular topic, but even as he learns, he realizes that there is more information to be discovered and digested. Instead of losing interest, he is motivated to find out more about the topic, or a related one. Individuals at this level begin to see that learning is a life-long process rather than simply a means to an end.

Aesthetic Needs (Being/Growth)

As individuals continue to work on knowing and understanding, they will also have a need for order, truth, and beauty. Individuals who are at the level of understanding and appreciating truth, beauty, and order will, rather than having this need satisfied, find themselves continually motivated to learn more.

Self-Actualization Needs (Being/Growth)

Self-actualization needs are an individual's need to become the most that they can become—in other words, to try to attain one's full potential as a human being. This ongoing motivation results in individuals continuing to work on all three types of being/growth needs. According to Maslow, one can never attain full self-actualization because an individual at this level will always find new experiences to enhance her knowledge and growth as a human being.

Maslow's scheme of deficiency and being/growth needs has been criticized because it suggests that movement, especially in the deficiency needs, is in one direction, when in real life people appear to move back and forth between levels. Many educators have worked with children who appear to have all their deficiency needs fulfilled, but who, if

TABLE 3.9	Insights the educator can obtain from Maslow's theory

- Educators must observe children and know what is happening to them both within and outside of the centre in order to determine what their needs are.
- Life experiences will influence what a child is interested in and willing to learn (motivation).
- If basic needs aren't being fulfilled, educators shouldn't expect children to be motivated to learn academic subjects or concepts.
- Educators need to create a sense of community if they want to meet the belonging needs of all the children.
- Life experiences, not just age, will determine where the child is on the hierarchy of needs.

their parents divorce, appear to be dealing with belongingness or even safety needs. Another criticism is that some individuals seem to consciously deny themselves an aspect of a deficiency need in order to obtain greater understanding or knowledge. An example that is often used is the spiritual leader who appears to deny himself food or physical comforts in order to attain greater understanding. A response to this criticism might be that the individual's most basic needs are simply satisfied at a lower level than those of the average individual.

If one accepts that life's situations can result in a person returning to a previous level on the hierarchy, and that individuals can have needs fulfilled in different ways, this theory can help educators understand what might be motivating a child's behaviour, and how physical, emotional, social, and intellectual needs are all interrelated.

BANDURA'S SOCIAL-COGNITIVE THEORY OF LEARNING

Albert Bandura's **social-cognitive theory** helps explain how children learn not only as others respond to their actions with rewards or punishment, but how they can learn simply by observing what is happening to those around them (see Figure 3.3). This theory also looks

FIGURE 3.3	Bandura's theory

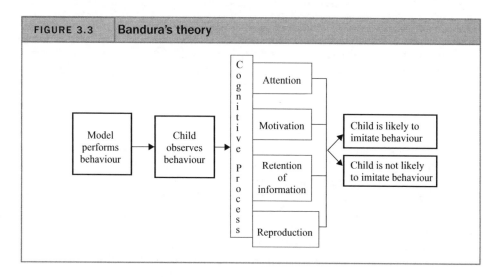

at internal mechanisms that may influence the choices people make or how much effort they put into a task (self-regulation and self-efficacy).

Observational Learning

Bandura's theory refers to observational or **vicarious learning**. For this to occur, Bandura suggests that there needs to be someone who is modelling the behaviour as well as someone observing what is happening. As one child (model) performs a cartwheel, another child (observer) is watching him. Because the observer has a desire to learn how to cartwheel, she carefully pays attention to the model and will then imitate his behaviour. In the above example, four processes are involved. First, the observer has to pay attention to the model. Second, the child has to be motivated to learn the behaviour. In this example, the motivation was internal (desire to do cartwheels) while in other examples the motivation might be external (the observer might want the reward that a model receives, for instance). The third process is retention; the child must be able to transfer the information to his memory. Finally, the child has to be able to reproduce the behaviour. In this example the child has to be able to try the cartwheel, while in another situation a child may need only to recall information (for example, remembering to say thank you when handed a package).

Attention

The above processes indicate that the child has some control over what is being learned. The child can think about what is occurring and make some decisions that will affect the learning. The first process requires attention: the child decides what he will attend to. In order to make a decision, the child will consider several factors:

1. The popularity of the person performing the task (children are more likely to imitate behaviours of someone who is popular).

2. The attractiveness of the person performing the task (children are more likely to imitate someone who is considered attractive).

3. The competence of the person performing the task (children are more likely to imitate someone who is skilled).

4. The degree to which the child wants to learn the task (children will imitate those things they want to learn). The reason they want to learn a task may vary. Sometimes they may want the knowledge, while other times it is an external reward that is motivating them, such as a good grade.

Motivation

A second process required for learning is motivation. Every child determines for herself what is or is not motivating. Educators often assume they know what will motivate a child because past experience has indicated that a particular reward (for instance, praise) is effective; however, educators should never assume that a particular reward will work. Every child is an individual, and only by observing the child and interacting with him can the educator get a fairly clear idea of what will motivate him.

According to Bandura, past experience plays an important role in determining what is motivating for a child. If a child has been previously successful at a task, she will probably be motivated to engage in the task again. If she has previously been unsuccessful at a task, however, she will probably not be motivated to try again, because she will anticipate failure. A child who is having trouble with reading in school is probably not going to want to get involved in reading activities in the school-age program. She is going to want to participate in those activities in which she knows she's going to do well. If the child is good at sports this means that she will seek out sports activities and avoid the reading corner. Bandura refers to "self-efficacy" as the idea that people will use past successes and failures to determine how successful they will be in the future.

Retention

A third process is retention. In order for a child to learn the new information or skill, memory is required. In order for the learning to succeed, the memory must be accurate. A child who is trying to learn to ride a mountain bike must be able to remember how to change gears and not confuse the gear shift with the brake. If he confuses the two parts of the bike, he won't be successful at learning to ride. Children's ability to use the retention process effectively will influence how easily they learn new skills and information. One child may need to be shown several times how to kick a soccer ball with control, while another may need only one demonstration before he is successful.

Reproduction

The fourth process is reproduction. This requires the following abilities: cognitive organization, initiation, monitoring, and refinement. Cognitive organization is the ability to organize the information in a way that makes sense and helps one use the knowledge or skill later. Initiation is the ability to actually use the knowledge or skill in order to determine if one has learned it. Monitoring is the ability to think about the way one just used the knowledge or skill, to determine if there are changes one might make to improve performance. Refinement is the ability to take the information obtained from monitoring one's previous performance and use this information to make actual changes in future performance.

All four cognitive processes working together determine what and how the child learns. A child who is able to attend to the task, is motivated to complete it, has a good memory for it, and is able to use a number of cognitive abilities to complete it effectively will be successful at the task. A child who has the attention, the memory, and the cognitive abilities—but is not motivated—is less likely to learn and successfully complete the task. Another child may have all of the skills necessary, but was paying attention to something else instead and so is not able to replicate it. This child may successfully complete a task; unfortunately, it may not be the right one. Because all four stages are important to the learning process, educators need to observe children to determine what kind of support might be needed in each area.

Rewards and Punishments

The social-cognitive theory recognizes that rewards and punishment can also determine what is learned. According to this theory, learning will occur when a person is directly rewarded or punished, though a person can also learn vicariously (indirectly) as he observes someone else being rewarded or punished. An educator who wants a child to participate more may reward the child by praising him when he participates (as long as he likes praise), but the educator will also recognize the importance of praising the other children who are participating. She will recognize that a child who needs to participate more and who likes praise might watch the other children receive praise and decide to participate so he too could receive praise.

Self-Efficacy and Self-Regulation

Social-cognitive theory also looks at several additional internal mechanisms that affect a child's self-image and decision-making process. Self-efficacy is the individual's assumption regarding the likelihood of success or failure on a particular task. These assumptions result from the child's understanding of past experiences. If the child has had repeated success in math, she will assume that future math activities will be successful. If a child has had difficulty in math in the past, he is likely to assume that he won't be successful when confronted with a new math problem even if he has the skills necessary to solve it. In addition, the child is more likely to have negative opinions about math in general. In other words, self-efficacy refers to the child's prediction of success or failure based on past experiences with the activity.

Whereas self-efficacy refers to a child's prediction of success or failure, self-regulation refers to the child's determination of the appropriateness of a particular behaviour in a particular situation. It also refers to the child's ability to control behaviours she has determined to be inappropriate and to use behaviours she deems appropriate. A child who has mastered self-regulation will refrain from hitting another child if he has determined that this is an inappropriate behaviour. The child will refrain from the behaviour despite being aware that hitting the other child is what he really wants to do. According to social cognitive theory, self-regulation is successful because the child finds a way to reward himself for the appropriate behaviour. Therefore, the child who uses words over hitting because he's determined that words are the appropriate response may reward himself by thinking of how he can get on with his play as soon as he's told the other child what he thinks.

TABLE 3.10	Insights the educator can obtain from Bandura's theory

- Children can learn by watching others (vicarious learning).
- Whether or not a child (observer) will imitate another person's (model's) behaviour is influenced by the model's social status, appearance, and ability to perform the task, as well as by whether or not the observer is actually interested in the task he is observing.
- Rewards and punishments will influence what is learned.
- Past experiences will influence what one chooses to learn.
- Children have to pay attention in order to learn.
- Children have to be motivated to learn.
- Children have to be able to remember the task or concept in order to learn it.
- Children have to be able to reproduce the behaviour in order to learn it.
- Children who have acquired self-regulation will be better able to display emotions and behaviours in a socially acceptable way.
- Children who have acquired self-regulation will be able to work more effectively in group situations.

BRONFENBRENNER'S ECOLOGICAL THEORY

Urie Bronfenbrenner's **ecological theory** looks at how the social context in which an individual lives influences the person's development. His theory looks at the individual in relation to his immediate social contexts and to the larger social contexts or systems in which he lives. Bronfenbrenner focuses on the interactions between the individual and the various social contexts or systems in order to determine how these interactions affect the growth and development of the individual. He points out, however, that the observer cannot simply look at the interactions that are occurring and determine how they will affect the individual's learning and development. It is the individual's perceptions of those interactions that will determine the learning that occurs. This concept is clearly illustrated in the following example.

In a school-age program, the educator might ask the children to help plan the activities for the March break. Although the request of all children is the same, there might be one child in the room who thinks that the educator is just being lazy and resents having to take time out of his play to get involved in a planning meeting. This child will probably contribute little to the meeting and learn very little from the experience. Another child who is eager to help might ask questions about how the meeting is to be run, decisions made, and so on, and as a result acquire some new knowledge and skills that will be remembered and used later. Because each child perceived the request differently, their responses were also different, and they left the meeting having learned different things.

Bronfenbrenner's theory is not limited to childhood. His theory looks at development across the human lifespan and includes time as one of the systems influencing development. According to Bronfenbrenner, five environmental systems influence our development.

Microsystem

The system most closely connected to the child is the microsystem. This consists of the various social contexts of the child's life. This encompasses the environments where the child is engaged in face-to-face interactions with peers, family, educators, and so on. The school-age child's microsystem would include the after-school program, the neighbourhood in which she lives and plays, her family, and the school. In all of these environments the child is interacting directly with other individuals, and these interactions have an impact on her development. In the microsystem, the influences flow in both directions; for while others will influence the child's development, her personality and interests will also influence the others and their actions. Bronfenbrenner makes it clear that interpersonal interactions are not the only factors influencing the child's development. He indicates that the physical environment and the activities available to the child will also have an impact.

Mesosystem

Surrounding the microsystem is the mesosystem. The mesosystem encompasses the linkages between the various social contexts and settings that make up the microsystem. Two settings or contexts that the school-age child has in the microsystem would be the after-school program and the school environment. The mesosystem, therefore, would include links between the school and the after-school program. One of these links would be how experiences in the school affect the learning and development that is happening in the after-school program. If the child is having difficulty in the school (especially with behaviour), it is possible that this will affect what is happening in the after-school program. The school teacher and the educator may meet to discuss how to co-ordinate efforts to support the child and together may implement a specialized program for him. The mesosystem for this child could also include, for instance, various links amongst the family, recreational programs in which he is involved, his neighbourhood, and the health care services he uses.

Exosystem

Moving away from the child's immediate world, one finds the exosystem. Although the child is not directly involved with the experiences that occur within the exosystem, these can influence her development. The child who is having difficulty in school won't have direct contact with the school board, but decisions made by the board can have an impact on her development. If the school board reduces funding to special education, the child may not receive the support she needs to succeed academically. Other social and economic structures that could affect the child might include the employer of the child's parents, hospital boards, the larger community in which the child lives, and the administration of parks and recreation.

Macrosystem

The macrosystem involves the broader culture in which the individual lives. This system incorporates the values and customs of the society as well as the more global influences that occur between cultures around the world. The general structure of the individual's society and its ideologies will influence the other system levels (exosystem, mesosystem, microsystem) and ultimately the child's development. A child growing up in Canadian society will, as a result of Canadian societal values, have different types of interactions with adults than a child growing up in a society that emphasizes very traditional gender-specific roles.

These societal views of gender roles will influence not only the child's microsystem but also all of the other systems. The societal values are reflected in the microsystem when the parent encourages the child to engage in non-traditional activities. It is reflected in the mesosystem when the family expectations influence what happens in the after-school program. In this situation the family expectations may result in parents expecting the centre to actively engage both boys and girls in team sports and to use certain behaviour-guidance techniques. The exosystem is clearly influenced by societal values. Society's view that roles are not restricted to one gender may mean that the employer of the child's mother promotes her to a very senior position in her company, which in turn will influence the amount of time the mother has to spend with the child. In all of these examples, the macrosystem has either directly or indirectly had an influence on the child's development.

Chronological System

Besides looking at the child in the context of the society and world in which he lives, the ecological theory addresses the issue of time, both past and present, and how it can influence an individual's development. The chronological system emphasizes that the era in

TABLE 3.11	Insights the educator can obtain from Bronfenbrenner's theory

- Educators should try to understand how other aspects of a child's life might be influencing her behaviour in the centre.

- Educators need to be aware of how their own microsystems (such as relationships, family culture, and personal values) are affecting what they are doing in the program.

- Educators need to recognize how societal values affect families, children, and the program being implemented.

- Educators should try to develop links with other components of the child's microsystem.

- Educators need to recognize that the child's personality, appearance, and so on may be having an influence on the educator's own behaviour.

- Educators need to recognize that how the child interprets the educator's behaviour is as important as what the educator is doing.

which an individual grows up will influence development. For instance, one should not expect children growing up in today's technological age to be the same as children who grew up during the Great Depression of the 1930s. One should also recognize that the age of an individual as they live through different eras will affect learning and development. A child living in this technology era will respond differently to the environment than an adult living in the same era. Therefore, the time system encompasses not only the whole period during which the individual is living, but also the individual's age during different eras throughout his life.

Bronfenbrenner's ecological theory emphasizes that learning occurs within a social context, and that the social context is different for each individual because everyone perceives things differently. Bronfenbrenner views learning and development as something that is life-long, for new experiences are always occurring and social contexts are always changing. Although the theory indicates that the study of children is very complex, it clearly shows that one cannot study children in isolation.

KOHLBERG'S STAGES OF MORAL DEVELOPMENT

Kohlberg's theory of moral development consists of three levels of moral reasoning, with each level consisting of two sub-stages for a total of six developmental stages (Table 3.12). These stages are sequential in nature and are influenced by four factors.

The first factor influencing one's moral reasoning is the person's level of cognitive development. Kohlberg agreed with Piaget's theory of cognitive development and thought that one needed to be at the stage of cognitive development where logical thinking occurs in order to develop moral reasoning. A child at the preoperational stage of development would not be able to truly engage in moral reasoning because the child is egocentric and doesn't think logically when trying to solve a dilemma. A child at this level of cognitive development would be unable to move past the first stage of Preconventional Morality.

The second factor is the motivation behind the person's moral reasoning. A person may be able to reason at one level but for practical purposes may chose to reason at a lower level. A school-age child may be able to understand that it is wrong to bully another child and ostracize her; however this child may worry that by standing up for the excluded child

TABLE 3.12	Levels and stages of moral development

Level 1: Preconventional Morality

Stage 1: Punishment: Avoidance and Obedience	Make moral decisions strictly on the basis of self-interest; determine if an action is good or bad by whether it results in a reward or a punishment.
Stage 2: Exchange of Favours	Recognize that others have needs, but make satisfaction of own needs a higher priority; the idea is "you scratch my back and I'll scratch yours."

Level 2: Conventional Morality

Stage 3: Good Boy/Good Girl	Make decisions on the basis of what will please others; be concerned about maintaining interpersonal relationships.
Stage 4: Law and Order	Look to society as a whole for guidelines about behaviour; think of rules as inflexible, unchangeable.

Level 3: Postconventional Morality

Stage 5: Social Contract	Recognize that rules are social agreements that can be changed when necessary.
Stage 6: Universal Ethical Principle	Adhere to a small number of abstract principles based on human rights that transcend specific, concrete rules/laws; answer to an inner conscience.

he risks his own exclusion. In this situation, the child may choose to ignore what is happening (even though he knows it's wrong) for fear of what may happen to him.

The third factor relates to the opportunities a person has had to see situations from another's perspective. As one interacts with others, one begins to see situations from another's perspective. This ability to see a situation from more than one perspective is necessary to develop higher levels of moral reasoning. A child's social environment plays a large role in the development of this ability. A child who is exposed to individuals from a variety of backgrounds and with a variety of viewpoints will, all things being equal, more rapidly learn to see issues from more than one perspective than a child who is raised in a very homogeneous environment where everyone tends to view issues from similar perspectives.

The final factor identified by Kohlberg is the justice structure of the society in which the child lives. When Kohlberg refers to society, he is referring to all levels of social structure ranging from the child's family, to the child's school, to the local community and on up to society at large. He claims that children raised in a society with a justice system that promotes a high level of equality and reciprocity among all members will more easily move to higher levels of moral reasoning than a child who lives in a society with lower-level justice structures. In other words, one should not expect to see the same level of moral reasoning in people raised in an autocratic dictatorial society as in those raised in a more egalitarian society. Kohlberg would predict that in the autocratic and dictatorial society one would see fewer individuals at the higher levels of moral reasoning because the society doesn't support this type of reasoning and the individual will have had fewer opportunities to see issues from various perspectives.

Educators working in school-age programs know that there is a wide range of moral reasoning within this age group. There may be younger children or children with cognitive delays who are at the first stage of the Preconventional Level of Morality while other children may be entering the Postconventional Level of Morality. All of the children will bring with them experiences that will influence how they respond to situations requiring moral reasoning. Children who have experienced only very authoritarian justice structures at home and in the school environment may find it difficult to take another's perspective, since this ability hasn't been encouraged. Educators need to be aware of this as they try to develop a sense of community in the group and as the children identify and implement the group's rules. These differences can lead to conflicts. A school-age child who has experienced an egalitarian justice structure at home may be functioning at stage 5 and will understand that the rules need to be bent at times. A school-age child who has experienced only an authoritarian structure is more likely to be at stage 4 (or less) and will insist that the rules must remain the same (or, if functioning at a lower stage, change the rules only if it benefits him).

Educators also need to ensure that they practise what they preach. Educators who want children to demonstrate more egalitarian behaviours and reciprocity will have to create a classroom/community environment that supports these behaviours. If they want children to respect others and listen to other points of view, they must also respect the children and listen to what they have to say. If they hope to have the children using higher-level moral reasoning, they can't take an autocratic approach to behaviour guidance. Educators need to help children see others' viewpoints when dealing with conflict situations. They should not

TABLE 3.13	Insights the educator can obtain from Kohlberg's theory

- Life experiences, not just age, will determine where the child is at in his moral reasoning.
- A child needs to be a logical thinker to develop moral reasoning.
- Educators need to understand the stage of moral thinking the child is at in order to effectively deal with her
- An autocratic social structure will not encourage a child to move to the higher stages of moral development.
- An egalitarian social structure will encourage a child to move to the higher stages of moral development.
- Opportunities to take on another's role/perspective will encourage moral development in a child.

TABLE 3.14	Insights the educator can obtain from Gilligan's theory

- Gender can influence how a child responds to situations requiring moral reasoning.
- The gender of the teacher can influence how a child responds to situations requiring moral reasoning.
- Educators should help children learn to take into account both group and individual justice perspectives.

quickly impose solutions on the children since this will not encourage them to take different perspectives or help resolve conflicts in a way that respects the rights of others. In many school-age programs, conflict-resolution skills are taught. These skills help children develop higher levels of moral reasoning.

GILLIGAN'S CARE PERSPECTIVE OF MORAL DEVELOPMENT

Carol Gilligan criticized Kohlberg's theory of moral development as being too focused on the rights of the individual as opposed to the interrelatedness of individuals within a society. Much of Kohlberg's work was done on males, and Gilligan felt that this biased his results. When females are tested using Kohlberg's dilemmas, fewer tend to attain stage 6 reasoning. Gilligan argued that this reflected the greater emphasis women place on relationships. Rather than indicating that women function at a lower level of moral reasoning, the differences in men's and women's responses merely indicate that females are socialized differently. A woman will view issues from the perspective of the group as well as from her individual justice perspective, whereas a man will tend to focus solely on the individual justice perspective. Gilligan, in her studies on girls and women, found that moral dilemmas were viewed with respect to human relationships rather than only from an individual justice perspective. She emphasizes "connectivity" between group members and discusses how this influences moral decisions. Gilligan does not recommend that Kohlberg's theory be discarded; however, she would like to have the care perspective included, and argues that the highest level of moral reasoning includes both the care and justice perspectives.

Educators working with school-age children need to be aware of possible differences between how the boys and the girls respond to different situations and issues. The different emphasis boys and girls place on relationships will influence their responses to situations. Gilligan's research indicates that the differences between men and women emerge at the Postconventional Level of Morality, and some children in a school-age program may be entering those stages.

Summary

Each theory provides educators with different insights on learning and motivation. Educators may find that certain theories relate more to behavioural issues, curriculum development, or creating environments, while others provide more insight into how to present new concepts to the children. Many of the theories complement each other or address aspects of learning that are not discussed in other theories. Most educators find that one theory is not comprehensive enough to explain all aspects of children's learning, and choose to use aspects of several to help guide their teaching strategies.

Student Learning Experiences

1. Observe an educator interacting with school-age children. Record the teacher–child interactions. Analyze the information to identify what the educator is doing to support the children's learning and development. After identifying the educator's behaviour, determine what theory supports the techniques you have observed. Explain how you came to your conclusion.

2. Teach a group of children or adults a new game. Review what happened as you taught the game (what you did, what they did, and so on) that helped them learn it. Identify a theory you think supports the techniques you or the participants used, and explain how it supports the techniques.

3. Observe a group of school-age children. Record an example of a child in the zone of proximal development (ZPD). How do you know the child is in the zone? Record an example of a child who seems to be outside his ZPD. How do you know the child is outside the zone?

Review Questions

1. Compare and contrast Piaget's theory of cognitive development with Vygotsky's socio-cultural theory.

2. What are three insights into children that educators can gain from Maslow's theory? Provide an example for each insight.

3. Describe Bronfenbrenner's theory and explain how it can help educators plan more appropriate programs for school-age children.

4. According to information processing models (IPM), how does perception influence learning?

5. In Bandura's theory, there are four processes required for learning to occur. Identify these processes and explain why each is important.

6. Indicate if you think Kohlberg's theory or Gilligan's theory provides a more accurate description of the moral development encouraged in Canadian society. Justify your answer.

CHAPTER 4

Growth and Development

OVERVIEW

This chapter will review the developmental changes that occur during both the kindergarten years and the school-age years (six to twelve). When discussing the younger children (kindergarten) we will be referring to children in Piaget's preoperational stage of development, and when discussing school-age children we will be referring to children entering into, and at, the concrete operational stage. We recognize that throughout the country there are differences in the age at which children begin grade one and this, along with individual differences in development, will result in some of the younger school-age children having characteristics that are better described by the kindergarten section, and vice versa. As always, children are individuals and never fit the neat labels we assign them. An older school-age child with learning disabilities may, in some of the cognitive skill areas, have the skills of a young school-age child, while at the same time having relatively sophisticated social skills. The gender of the child may also influence development. For example, boys tend to spend more time in throwing and catching activities, and therefore those skills are often better developed in school-age boys than girls even though there are few physical differences between the genders at this age.

The domains used to discuss development will be physical, cognitive, language, and social/emotional. The authors recognize that other domains are sometimes used (such as creative and spiritual) but this text will use only the four identified.

PHYSICAL DEVELOPMENT

Walk into a kindergarten/school-age program (K/SAP) and one will see children who are confident in their movements and who can easily manipulate a variety of materials. Many kindergarten children demonstrate that they have mastered the basic skills associated with preschoolers, and the school-age children are becoming adept at complex movements. School-age children are actively participating in sports activities that require the ability to combine a variety of physical movements. The older children among them make these complex movements look easy, and it is difficult to imagine that a few short years ago they were having difficulty accomplishing them.

Kindergarten Physical Development: Gross Motor Skills

Out in the playground, kindergarten children demonstrate that they are becoming increasingly competent in a variety of gross motor skills (that is, large movements involving the limbs or the whole body). Some children are involved in chasing games, while other children are busy climbing, jumping, or playing with balls. Both boys and girls are very similar in their physical development at this age, although boys tend to be a bit more muscular. Boys tend to be more active than girls, and girls tend to do better with activities that require co-ordination. Because there are so few physical differences between the genders at this age, it is speculated that socialization, rather than physical build, may account for these differences. Parents may spend more time in rough-and-tumble play with boys while providing girls with more activities that

School-age children have learned to combine a number of skills in order to engage in complex activities.

promote the fine motor skills of eye–hand co-ordination (dress-up activities, dolls) rather than large muscle development.

The young kindergarten child can still have body proportions that are top-heavy compared to the older kindergarten child, who is noticeably taller and has a lower centre of gravity. A higher centre of gravity will play a role in all skill areas requiring balance, and many of the changes in gross motor abilities that occur during the kindergarten period are due to changes in the child's centre of gravity as well as his opportunities to practice the skills. By the end of the kindergarten years children are confident runners and will be able to maintain their speed when running and trying to avoid others in "chasing" games.

The children in this age group are trying to master increasingly difficult gross motor skills. They enjoy the challenges provided in trying to co-ordinate the movements and balance required to gallop and skip. Children often practice galloping while engaged in pretend and co-operative play. Given the space and opportunity to try galloping, most four-year-olds will have developed the skill. Skipping is a more difficult skill than galloping, since it incorporates a hop and also requires the child to alternate the feet. Because of the complex movements involved, most children do not skip before they are six.

Jamie (five-and-a-half years old) confidently jumps off the climber and races over to where a group of friends are digging in the sand. Meanwhile, Lei (three-and-a-half) who'd been following him, is still on the climber looking at the ground, not sure if he can safely make the leap. Only two years separate these two boys, but these years are important in the development of jumping skills. The older child has learned (probably at around age four-and-a-half) to move his arms forward and up when taking off and to lean forward at the same time. Children who can do this are likely to end their jumps in a more controlled manner and quickly move on to the next activity.

Ball skills are being developed during the kindergarten years but many will not be mastered until the school-age years. Younger kindergarten children can throw a ball, but many will throw using only their arm and a slight twist of the shoulder to follow through with the arm movement. Children at this stage of throwing keep both feet in the same position. Because the child is not using the rotation of her body and her body weight to help with the throwing, her throwing will not be as accurate as an older child's, nor will she be able to throw the ball as far. Educators working with kindergarten children see changes emerging in how they throw. During this period children begin to use the entire body to help throw a ball. As the child has more opportunities to engage in throwing activities, she begins to step forward when throwing. At first, she will step forward with the foot that's on the same side as the throwing arm and, although the body will be used to help with the throw, the movement will be a forward one with very little body rotation involved. Only after repeated opportunities to engage in ball activities does one see mature throwing skills emerge, and for many children this skill will not be mastered until some point during the school years.

For children, one of the biggest physical accomplishments that often occurs during the kindergarten years is the ability to ride a bike. Younger preschoolers can pedal tricycles, but by the end of the kindergarten years many children have the balance and co-ordination to use a bicycle, a skill that they see as important, and a sign that they have made it to the school-age years.

Kindergarten Physical Development: Fine Motor Skills

An observer in an after-school program will notice that kindergarten and school-age children are also refining their fine motor skills. This refinement shows considerable progress between entering junior kindergarten and beginning grade one. As children improve their control of finger, wrist, and arm movements, finger dexterity, and eye–hand co-ordination, educators notice qualitative differences in the activities that children can successfully accomplish. The young kindergarten child may attempt to cut by holding the scissors in both hands, hoping the paper won't slip away or bend when he closes them. By the time he is almost ready to move on to grade one, however, he can usually hold the paper in one hand and manipulate the scissors in the other. This change in ability did not happen overnight, but came about as the child gained more control over his fine motor skills through repeated opportunities to practice them. In order to use the scissors effectively, the child had to learn to hold them in one hand and the paper in the other. He also had to learn to hold both scissors and paper in the correct relative position. On top of this, he had to recognize the need to line the scissors up with the picture he wanted to cut out and to turn both scissors and paper as needed, so as to cut around the object rather than through it. Clearly, children need opportunities to use scissors in order to develop cutting skills, but increased control of finger and wrist movements, as well as eye–hand co-ordination, are also essential in the development of this skill.

The ability to manipulate writing instruments is another fine motor skill that kindergarten children are developing. Younger children often hold a marker, crayon, or pencil in their fist (using a palmar grasp) rather than resting it on their middle finger while holding it in place with the thumb and index finger. A palmar grasp requires the child to use the wrist and arm to move the marker, and as a result control is limited. As the child shifts from using the fist to the fingers, she gains more control over the marker. As the child practices using the marker this way, the educator will notice that she is able to create more precise and detailed drawings.

Educators need to ensure that children have opportunities to use drawing materials that will allow them to develop this precise control. As well as ordinary markers, children need access to fine-tipped markers and ordinary pencils. When using paint brushes, children need to have access to fine-tipped brushes as well as the fatter type typically seen in kindergarten programs. As a child gains more finger dexterity, strength and control, he is able to move from the fatter crayons and pencils to the narrower ones. By the end of kindergarten, many children no longer benefit from having thicker pencils, but other children will still require them because they are still developing this fine motor skill. The overall trend of progress is clear, however. Compare children of ages four, five, and eight writing their names, and witness how the ability to use a pencil grows by leaps and bounds (albeit still using block letters rather than joined-up writing).

As children play, they engage in a variety of activities that help them improve fine motor skills. Activities like beading and lacing help them work on finger dexterity and eye–hand co-ordination. Younger children may need bigger beads with holes that accommodate larger lacings, but as practice results in improved skills the beads used become increasingly smaller and the lacing becomes smaller and more complex. Other activities, such as using Lego bricks, also help with fine motor skills. Eye–hand co-ordination, finger dexterity, and an ability to control finger pressure are all necessary when carefully placing that final piece on the top of the model spaceship. Press too hard, or lose control of the pieces, and part of the ship will be destroyed. The task may be challenging, but once completed the feeling of success is well worth the effort. Although the older children may enjoy the challenge of Lego or Kapla blocks, younger kindergarten children may prefer to use larger blocks (such as Duplo) because they have yet to develop the finger dexterity needed to use the Lego or Kapla blocks successfully. As they manipulate the larger blocks, they gain these skills and with enough practice are able to use smaller blocks successfully or develop very complex structures with the larger ones.

Finally, fine motor skills are developed as the child becomes increasingly independent. The younger child in a kindergarten program may have difficulty closing a zipper by putting the two parts together, or she may have problems doing up small buttons or snaps. All of these tasks require a combination of finger dexterity and eye–hand co-ordination; she also needs a certain level of finger strength to effectively apply pressure to the snap as well as the ability to line up the two pieces so they can snap together. Given opportunities to practise these skills, most children will have mastered them by the end of kindergarten. In fact, by the time they leave the kindergarten program, many have even mastered tying shoelaces—as long as they have had the opportunity to wear shoes with laces.

School-Age Physical Development: Gross Motor Skills

A number of physical changes are occurring in children during the school-age years. Children are steadily growing taller during this time, although there may be intermittent growth spurts and their accompanying "growing pains." Changes in body proportions occur so that the school-age child's head is smaller in proportion to the rest of the body, and the legs and arms are longer than those of the preschooler. These physical changes result in improved balance, and the ability to move faster and with more control.

For younger school-age children, losing baby teeth is a major milestone. Throughout this developmental period boys and girls are fairly similar in their skill development, although boys tend to have greater upper arm strength and girls tend to be more flexible. Toward the end of this period you may see the beginning of sexual maturation, especially in girls.

School-age children are mastering the ability to combine a variety of different gross motor skills (such as skipping rope or dribbling a ball while running). As their ability to combine skills improves, children become increasingly competent at a variety of sports. Many children engage in organized sports throughout the school years and their skills develop rapidly. A group of children in grade one will eagerly play soccer, but their ability to dribble the ball or kick it while running is limited. By grade four, these same children will have no difficulty controlling the soccer ball as team members pass it back and forth between them and try to score a goal.

Skipping is another skill that is mastered during the school years. Most kindergarten children find jumping over a rope that is being swung back and forth challenging, but during the school-age years children learn the ability to co-ordinate many actions, meaning they can now flip the rope over their heads while skipping. Many become proficient at more difficult skipping games such as "double-dutch" or "pepper."

Children continue to develop throwing and catching skills. If children who are eager to learn these skills have opportunities to practice them and are given appropriate support when learning various techniques, they may become very competent by the time they reach the teenage years. At the end of this period the educator will be able to observe a child who rotates the body as she brings her arm back and then rotates again as she moves the arm forward to complete the throw, while also leading with the foot on the opposite side from the throwing arm. Mastery of throwing is difficult because it requires the co-ordination of a wide number of movements, and many children continue to lead with the wrong foot until they have been shown how to make the shift.

School-age children can jump further, climb more difficult objects, and control a ball better than kindergarten-age children. The improvements in these abilities are partly a result of increased strength and endurance; though improvements in reaction time, co-ordination, and spatial awareness also play important roles in the mastery of these and other abilities.

As children near the end of the school-age years, many girls will begin to enter puberty, but it will be later before most boys begin this stage of physical development. As girls enter puberty they will begin to experience a major growth spurt, and the typical girl at this age will be several inches taller than the boys. The average age for the onset of puberty in girls is eleven, but this is merely the average and many girls experience emerging body changes much earlier. Educators could easily have eight- or nine-year-old girls in their program who are beginning to develop breasts and other signs of physical maturity. Unfortunately, this early onset can have a negative impact on the child's social and emotional development. Children who are beginning to show physical changes in their bodies may be teased or taunted by their peers. Educators can help prevent this type of reaction by developing a climate that encourages respect for all individuals and accepts diversity.

School-Age Physical Development: Fine Motor Skills

Like gross motor skills, a refinement of fine motor skills occurs in school-age children. As children master fine motor control over finger and wrist movements, and as eye–hand co-ordination continues to improve, they are able to engage in complex activities such as writing, knitting, or building models.

Although many young school-age children have learned how to hold a pencil correctly, they continue to develop writing skills as they discover additional control techniques. As the children continue to practice they discover that by resting the side of their hand on the table they gain more control of the pencil. This control allows the child to write increasingly smaller letters, and to place those letters between or on the lines on a paper. The educational system has recognized this skill progression, and therefore the paper children use in grade three has less space between the lines than that used in grade one.

Increased finger dexterity, as well as hand and wrist control, results in a wide range of new activities opening up for the school-age child. School-age children enjoy a variety of hobbies involving fine motor skills, ranging from woodworking to knitting, and as they

engage in the activities they gradually become more competent. The young school-age child may build simple objects (such as a rough-made box) while an older child will want to create more complex objects (such as a working birdhouse).

The child's increased precision control and co-ordinated movements allow her to manipulate materials in very complex ways. Using precision finger control, she can create tiny but complex origami objects, intricate friendship bracelets, or extremely detailed pictures.

Increased muscle strength also affects fine motor skills. Those snaps kindergarten children may have had trouble with are now easy to manage.

At any age, most children show an interest in music and a desire to use musical instruments, but it is during the school-age years that children usually learn to play an instrument. At this age children have acquired a level of finger dexterity, eye–hand co-ordination, and other fine motor skills that will allow them to be successful.

Improved fine motor control is not limited to the child's hands. Children become more adept at manipulating numerous muscle groups, and this ability results in children becoming able to whistle or wriggle their ears.

Fine and gross motor skills help the school-age child succeed at a variety of activities beyond the reach of younger children, yet their success is due not only to physical changes but to changes in social, emotional, language, and cognitive development as well.

COGNITIVE DEVELOPMENT

Observe children in an after-school program and you will see numerous signs of the rapid cognitive development that occurs during the kindergarten and school-age years. The young kindergarten child might be showing only the beginnings of mathematical skills as he uses one-to-one correspondence to set enough places for his friends at the table, while the older school-age child may be able to divide 164 by 2 without any difficulty. These changes in cognitive skills are seen in many other areas as well. Just look at the differences between kindergarten children and ten-year-olds in their ability to play games with rules, or to play a musical instrument.

Kindergarten Cognitive Development

According to Piaget, the majority of kindergarten-aged children—as well as some of the younger school-age children—will be in the preoperational stage of cognitive development. Children in this stage will view the world differently from older children. They will approach problems and learning experiences in a less logical way, and will require more guidance and support from the educator or from older children in the program. For instance, imagine a four-year-old and an eight-year-old in a program, each choosing to do a puzzle. At first glance one may initially think that the main difference is in the complexity of the puzzles, but the more striking difference may be in the children's approach to solving the puzzle. The four-year-old randomly selects a piece to put into place. Sometimes he looks at the colour or the design on the piece and attempts to match it with those already in place, while at other times the process appears to be more trial and error. Conversely, the eight-year-old begins by sorting the pieces into edge pieces and other pieces. He may even proceed to sort the remaining pieces into piles according to colour or design, and all of this occurs before he even begins to put the puzzle together. Although the four-year-old uses some simple logic, he does not tackle problems with the same systematic approach of the eight-year-old. As well, the four-year-old still has difficulty classifying the puzzle pieces according to the fragments of the design found on each piece.

Preoperational children's cognitive development is also influenced by the fact that appearances will influence their thinking. They are still great believers in magic and magic tricks. A magician in a room of kindergarten children will have a rapt audience full of believers. When the children see the magician pull the rabbit from an apparently empty hat, they accept that this is what has happened. Preoperational children are often firm believers in myths such as Santa Claus and the Tooth Fairy because they've seen the evidence with their own eyes. Didn't the Tooth Fairy leave money in place of their tooth? Unfortunately, this same type of thinking can lead children to be convinced there are monsters in their closet because they heard them make the floor creak.

Kindergarten children are learning many concepts. While painting at school or in the kindergarten program, they continue to learn more about colour and texture. As educators provide opportunities to build with blocks, and as they talk about them with the children, the children are learning a variety of science and math concepts (such as symmetry, balance, size comparisons, quantity, and measurement). As the children converse with their friends they also develop a better understanding of humour (see Language Development on page 74).

In the area of math skills the youngest kindergarten children may have limited counting abilities. They may be able to count to ten, but make sequencing, positioning, or co-ordination errors. By the time they are ready to enter the school-age program most will be able to count accurately to 20 or higher. They will recognize that they need to make sure that only one number corresponds with one object, and using everyday concrete objects many children begin to understand simple addition and subtraction. The child setting the table for a pretend meal will recognize when she needs to add some more plates so all her friends can eat, and is able to indicate how many more are necessary.

School-Age Cognitive Development

In many children, cognitive changes occur around the time they start grade one that make it possible for them to engage successfully in games with rules, along with a variety of other new and exciting activities. Piaget would say that these children are entering the concrete operational stage of development, while recent neurological research would indicate that structural changes are occurring in the brain at this time that may result in children becoming more logical in their thinking and therefore better able to follow games and activities that have a number of rules. Of course these abilities do not suddenly appear overnight. Younger school-age children are still developing these skills and, being somewhat egocentric, will often become upset when the game doesn't go their way. You can expect older school-age children to more easily handle games with rules and to understand that they will not always win, but never take this for granted.

Changes in cognitive abilities result in the emergence of new interests and skills. School-age children are known for their collections, be they rocks, stickers, or action figures. This interest results from the child's emerging ability to simultaneously categorize objects in a number of different ways. The ability to see the relationship between two or more items is also reflected in the child's greater understanding of a variety of math concepts. It is during these years that children learn to understand the concept of time properly, as well as the very important concept of money. Opportunities to be involved in real-life situations that require these skills will help the child be successful both in and out of school. When children in the school-age program are given a budget for games or art supplies, they have opportunities to practice math skills (such as addition, subtraction, and percentages) and problem-solving skills, and begin to understand that the money from the ATM is not an endless supply.

These logical-thinking skills result in children needing environments that contain more complex challenges. The children are becoming more product-oriented and want to learn the skills necessary to complete adult-like projects and products. Look at the drawing of a young school-age child and compare it to that of an older school-age child. The older child's picture will contain more techniques (like shading or perspective), resulting in a more adult-like product. Unfortunately not all children will develop these complex skills without support from more knowledgeable peers or adults and, unlike younger children, many will become frustrated and end up claiming that they don't like the activity.

Apart from the creative arts, school-age children are also interested in developing craft skills such as sewing, model making, and woodworking. Their logical thinking skills, along with their increased attention spans, improved memory skills, and a desire to create a product rather than simply exploring materials, make crafts a natural choice for many school-age children. Their improved task completion skills also mean that they can stick with a project even if it takes days or weeks to complete. The desire to participate in these types of activities is so strong that many teachers in after-school programs take classes to learn how to knit or work with wood so that they can, in turn, help the children develop these skills.

However, this is also the age at which many children discover they have a learning disability. Problems such as dyslexia, lack of short-term memory, and attention deficit disorder begin to have a big impact on children as they enter the academic world of school and discover how these disabilities influence their success. Although help is available, most children with learning disabilities experience repeated failures before the problem is diagnosed and help can be given. These failures can influence their perceptions of their abilities and, as a result, many such children will assume that they can't do well in school. By working co-operatively with teachers and with parents, educators in the after-school program may help these children develop more confidence in their academic potential.

LANGUAGE DEVELOPMENT

Cognitive development in both kindergarten and school-age children is inseparable from language development, since almost all the concepts children learn are influenced by language and their understanding of it. As Vygotsky's theory indicates, most of the information a child receives is filtered through language, and the child's language will influence how information is interpreted.

Kindergarten Language Development

The vocabulary of kindergarten-age children may appear to be relatively sophisticated, but educators will find that children sometimes use words without having a clear idea of their meaning. Children this age have already acquired a sizeable vocabulary, but most of it has been learned by listening to adults and older children using the words in a sentence. As the children listen and try to understand what the person is saying they will quickly place the word in a cognitive schema that already exists (for example, the child hears the word "orangutan" as another child talks about a visit to the zoo, and therefore places the word within the schema of "zoo animals"). Since most vocabulary is learned this way rather than by being taught definitions of words, it is important that educators use words in more than one context to help children develop accurate meanings.

Kindergarten children can be very creative in their use of language. Educators will encounter children who make up words because they don't have a suitable word in their vocabulary. Other children, because they are still learning the grammar of the language, may overgeneralize grammatical rules they have learned.

Many kindergarten children still have some problems with their pronunciation of words. Because children may not master some of the more difficult consonants sounds (such as *r* and *l*) until the early elementary-school years, educators can monitor and document their progress in this area. If the child is making enough pronunciation errors that it interferes with his ability to communicate thoughts and ideas effectively, he will benefit from further assessment. Such a child is less likely to "grow out of the problem" and is likely to become frustrated by his inability to get others to understand him.

Conversational language skills are important for kindergarten children because they are engaging in co-operative play with their peers. The pragmatics of language are seldom formally taught to children, but by kindergarten age most children have discovered that you need to take turns in a conversation and make eye contact to help keep the other person interested (though this can be dependent upon culture), and that you can get a response from someone by asking questions.

Although it is evident that kindergarten children have successfully developed a variety of conversational skills, they often have difficulty describing situations or telling someone else a story. This is because they will often leave out important pieces of information or change the order of events. For example, a child might blurt out to her mom on being picked up from the program, "I want shoes with bows, too!" The statement only makes sense to the mother when, by asking additional questions, she discovers that her daughter's friend was wearing shoes with bows that day. Mixing up the order of events often occurs as a child tries to retell a story that she heard, or when trying to describe an event that she was involved in.

Kindergarten children often combine language with physical actions to express humour. A giggling child will shout, "I'm dying!" and then collapse in a heap while his friends laugh hysterically. At other times children will deliberately say "taboo" words and then break out into laughter. Kindergarten children are becoming aware of more structured forms of humour such as jokes and riddles, though the knowledge of language that is required for these types of humour is often beyond them. The young child trying to tell a knock-knock joke may break out laughing even though the joke makes no sense to older children or adults.

The kindergarten child is also developing literacy skills. Children this age are increasingly interested in the sounds as well as the meanings of words. Children enjoy rhyming games and songs, especially if they can make use of a word that sounds funny to them or that adults might not want to hear. If a child is beginning to read or to show interest in playing with word sounds, the educator needs to provide activities to support this learning.

Kindergarten-aged children are becoming interested in the printed word. Of course, one of the most important words that children want to learn to read is their name. Some children at the beginning of kindergarten may be able to recognize only the first letter of their name, but the majority will know all of the letters by the end of the year. Because each child is unique, some will just be starting to show an interest in letters while others are already beginning to read books.

Writing skills are also developing along with reading skills. Kindergarten children are often very interested in writing letters and using writing to record important information and messages. However, the development of writing skills is again very variable between children. Some of the younger kindergarten children may scribble when writing, while others may write some of the letters only, or write the words with their own (either guessed-at or invented) spelling. They may also write randomly anywhere on the page, or put large spaces between letters.

Educators support writing skills by giving kindergarten children opportunities to use their writing skills in meaningful ways. In an after-school program the educator might, for instance, have all the children record the ideas that come out of a brainstorming meeting around what to do on an upcoming teachers' Professional Development (PD) day, when the children will be off school and consequently the program will be active for the whole day. Some of the children will scribble while others will try to write actual words, but all of their writings can be posted along with the list that the educator has recorded. If the meeting also includes the school-age children, the examples of writing can range from scribbling to very skilled and conventionally formatted writing.

Kindergarten children will show wide variations in all aspects of language development, and many factors will have influenced the development of the child's English- or French-language skills. A child who is learning English as a second language (ESL) should not be expected to have the same level of fluency as a child who has grown up using the language. Educators need to recognize this and find ways to support the ESL child's language development. Educators also need to remember that a child's comprehension skills (receptive language) are usually much better than his oral skills (expressive language).

School-Age Language Development

Cognitive development is inseparable from language skills. During this period of childhood, vocabulary is rapidly expanding and children are developing reading and writing skills. Given opportunities and encouragement, children eagerly embrace these skills as they see the usefulness of them. Children who want to cook see the value of reading a recipe, just as children who want to know more about cars will read to locate the desired information. Many school-age children read to gain information about topics they are investigating, or to learn how to do something (such as directions for a game), but they also read simply for enjoyment. As they become more proficient readers, they begin to read chapter books rather than storybooks. Many school-age children prefer books that have children their age as the protagonist, and particularly enjoy stories in which the children outsmart the adults. Other children are drawn to comic books, which may seem to be their exclusive reading material. In school-age programs there will be a wide range of reading abilities, and the educators need to make sure that the children have resources that accommodate their reading levels and interests. These resources should include materials the program owns as well as those borrowed from libraries. In one school-age program there may be some children who are struggling to master the simplest reading skills while others are reading at a high-school level. Some children may read only fiction, while others read only non-fiction or comic books.

Just as educators take into account reading abilities when providing books, they should also take them into account when posting information for the children. Is the language simple enough for all the children to understand it? Is the print large enough for children with a visual disability to read it?

Writing skills usually develop simultaneously with reading skills. As children's writing skills develop they will likely write notes to their friends, create secret codes, and record important information (such as the food they've decided on for the afternoon snack). Story, poetry, and songwriting are enjoyed by many school-age children. They have discovered that these creative media are effective ways to express their ideas, feelings, and humour. Unfortunately, other children will have learned that writing is a process that they do not enjoy. Educators can support these children's writing skills by involving them in planning the program. When they are involved in group meetings to plan what is going to happen, the children will begin to see the importance of using their writing skills to record ideas (perhaps using planning webs), strategies (such as directions), and documentation (for instance, meeting minutes, project panels). When educators encourage these types of activities they must model respect for every child's efforts. Since the skills will vary greatly, it is important that children not be allowed to use the activity as an opportunity to belittle each other's writing skills. If one child can't read another child's work, simply tell her that she needs to ask the other child to read it for her.

The child's increasingly sophisticated language skills have an impact on the type and length of the conversations you are going to hear in an after-school program. Getting together and talking to one's friends is important for school-age children. This type of social ability is facilitated by their language skills as well as their improved memory skills

School-age children's ability to read allows them to follow recipes to make snacks for the group.

and attention spans. School-age children can discuss a wide variety of topics, although they will continue to have difficulty discussing abstract concepts (such as the "meaning" of life). The children not only know even more words, but they understand that the same word can have more than one meaning. As with the other changes, this is a gradual one; the younger children in the program may be stumbling over "knock-knock" jokes while many of the older children will be quick in using puns or sarcasm. As their understanding of the format of various jokes and riddles improves, the children begin to create their own jokes—jokes that even adults understand.

As already discussed, fluency in English or French will be affected by the child's first language. Children with limited English- or French-language skills will continue to need support from educators and peers to successfully participate, as they did in the kindergarten-age programs.

Because school-age children are interacting more with the larger community and are increasingly influenced by their peers, slang becomes more common at this age. Some of the slang will be common terms used by society at large, while other words will be created by the peer group and will be common only to that group.

As anyone who has worked with school-age children knows, changes in language and thinking skills also result in children who can and will present logical arguments for or against any particular situation. Arguments among the children are bound to happen and, especially with younger school-age children, the cry of "That's not fair!" is frequently heard. Successful educators realize that they have to be able to justify what they do with the children, and the limits that are set (hopefully these have been developed in collaboration with the children). Simply using one's role as an educator to enforce seemingly arbitrary limits will result in arguments. Sound reasoning will appeal to school-age children much more than the simple authoritarianism of a statement such as "You must do it because I tell you to do it." Educators also need to help the children develop conflict-resolution skills to settle arguments. Children at this age have the language skills, the logical-thinking skills, and the ability to take someone else's perspective—skills necessary for successful resolutions to occur.

SOCIAL AND EMOTIONAL DEVELOPMENT

As children move into and through the school-age years, a major change in the area of social development is the increasing importance of peers in their lives and a desire for more independence. In the area of emotional development, children are displaying ever-increasing self-control/self-regulation.

Kindergarten Social and Emotional Development

Although parents and adults continue to play a major role in the social and emotional development of the kindergarten child, the influence of peers is becoming more evident. The children do not seek out the educator as much as they used to. Although children this age will still show educators their work, they are just as likely to turn to the child beside them to show their work or to ask for advice.

Friendships, although still fairly superficial in nature, are becoming more important. Friendships may frequently change, but it is still important to have a friend. It is the rare kindergarten child who would not identify at least one child as being his friend. As the

Most school-age children want to participate in activities with their peers.

child becomes increasingly aware of the importance of friends, threats regarding friendship often become the method for striking back at another child. "You're not my friend!" or "You can't come to my birthday party!" are a couple of the worst insults or threats that children can use at this age.

Kindergarten children have developed, and are beginning to master, a variety of prosocial behaviours. Most children have learned how to share, although depending upon the situation they might choose not to. By the time children have reached kindergarten they have often had many opportunities to practice turn-taking skills and to help others (signs of empathy and compassion). If adults have responded positively to those children who have waited patiently or offered to help others, it is likely that children will usually comply with these types of requests.

Co-operative play frequently occurs in kindergarten programs, and is successful because the children know how to share the materials, take turns, and negotiate with each other. This does not mean that everything will always run smoothly. Even though the children have been developing these skills, many of them are still somewhat egocentric and will want others to do things their way. Educators frequently find differences among the children in how successful they are at convincing others to co-operate or go along with their ideas. Even at this age, educators observe children who manage to control social situations through aggressive behaviour, as well as those who use reason or flattery when taking on a leadership role. Educators will also see that there are children who seldom seem to get to make decisions, even when their decisions would benefit the group. These children will need to have the educator's help to develop the social and communication skills that will allow them, in turn, to develop leadership skills.

As the children develop their negotiation skills, educators can help them use these in conflict situations. Children can tell their peers why they're upset and what they think should be done to resolve the conflict. Educators, however, need to recognize that the children still have egocentric tendencies and will need some guidance in conflict situations, since a child may have difficulty seeing another child's perspective.

Kindergarten children have developed concepts of gender roles. At this age, children can be very rigid in their concepts of what is appropriate for each gender. What they consider appropriate roles will be influenced by the culture into which the child has been socialized. Williams and Best (1990) conducted a study of gender stereotypes in 30 countries and found wide variations in what was considered appropriate for one or the other gender. Along with concepts of gender roles, kindergarten children have developed a sense of gender identity, and tend to show a preference for play with peers of the same gender.

Kindergarten children tend to have positive views of themselves (Harter and Pike, 1984). They have mastered most of the skills associated with the early years, but they have not yet had to face the academic challenges of the school-age years.

School-Age Social and Emotional Development

During the school-age years, educators will see dramatic changes in the children's social and emotional development. A desire for increased independence and responsibility emerges in children during this period. According to Erikson's theory, children at this age are in the "industry v. inferiority" stage of psychosocial development. Children need to see themselves as successful. School-age children frequently use their success or failure in school as a way of measuring their self-worth. If they are struggling in school they often fail to see themselves as successful unless they're able to excel in another area that is also valued by peers and adults (such as sports). In a school-age program, educators can help children feel successful by giving children responsibilities in the program, by helping them become more successful in academics, and by offering them activities that they can do well. In addition, programs that allow the children more independence help them realize that adults trust their abilities.

School-age children pay more attention to what their peers think than younger children. They often compare themselves to their peers in order to determine how well they are doing. You will often hear children this age say something like, "See Mike's drawing. I'm no good at this!" As educators we try to support children who see themselves as less successful than others, though we must also be aware that what we say may have less impact than it did when the children were younger.

School-age children are also better at reading the social cues of individuals. They will more accurately read facial expressions and body language than younger children. School-age children who have difficulty reading these cues are often responded to negatively by other children and are frequent victims of bullying behaviour.

Peer opinion is becoming important, as is being part of a group or clique. Children will tend to form groups with others whom they see as similar to themselves; therefore, groups will often have members of only one gender, and with similar interests. You may also see children wanting to dress similarly (for instance, as skaters or with a preppy look) in order to show belongingness. The perceived need to belong to a group is so strong that some children will do almost anything to be a member of one, including demeaning other children. Educators need to be aware of the development of cliques or clubs and monitor whether discrimination against or segregation of some children is occurring as a result.

It is important that during the school-age years every child develop at least one significant friendship. Unlike the somewhat superficial friendships that occur during the preschool years, school-age friendships tend to be longer term and deeper. The younger school-age child is more likely to have only a couple of close friends who like to engage in similar activities. As the children grow older, their circle of friends widens. At this age they expect more of their friends than they do from other peers; loyalty and support are important in a friend. Their rapidly improving conversational abilities mean children find it easier to share ideas, interests, and skills with each other. School-age children will want to spend time with their friends and discuss topics that interest them, be it the latest computer game or their favourite singing group. Many of these conversations are meant to be private. At this age, the children don't want an educator hovering over them listening in on their conversations.

As mentioned earlier, new cognitive skills make it possible for school-age children to engage in a variety of group activities, such as sports and games. Success in these activities also results from the children's improved social and emotional skills. During this period children are increasingly able to compromise and "play by the rules," an ability that is necessary to participate in games with rules. Their ability to see another's point of view and to empathize with others is also essential for the development of conflict-resolution skills. These skills are important not only when involved in sports or games, but when involved in any type of conflict.

At the same time, children are developing their ability to self-regulate their behaviours, a development which will allow them to deal with a variety of social and emotional situations. Self-regulation provides children with the ability to inhibit impulsive responses which, in turn, allows them to focus attention on the task at hand and to control their actions even when they're emotionally upset.

Working together, the social, emotional, and cognitive skills developed during the school-age years result in children who can actively participate in group decision-making. School-age children are capable of enjoying the responsibility involved in the process of developing class rules and curriculum. As long as educators help children develop group meeting skills (such as chairing a meeting, turn-taking, debating, brainstorming) children can successfully conduct meetings for curriculum planning, budgeting, and club development.

DIVERSITY

In any school-age program there will be a wide range of abilities and interests. These differences will reflect not only the varying ages of the children, but also their family backgrounds and individual needs. In Canada, the word "diversity" is most often associated with cultural diversity, but this is only one type of diversity. In this text, diversity encompasses special needs and family diversity—which includes cultural, economic, and individual family differences.

Special Needs

In one sense, every child has special needs because each child has unique skill sets and interests. For the purpose of this text, however, the term will be used to refer to those needs that are usually identified by provinces as entitling a child to additional services and funding.

A school-age program may include children who have cognitive disabilities and others who are gifted. Educators have the challenge of providing learning experiences for all of the children, so they must carefully observe them all to learn what their abilities and interests are, and to make sure that the materials and activities in the program take these into account. The educator may need to provide materials that vary greatly in complexity. For example, the educator may have musical instruments that range from rhythm sticks to keyboards, since one child may be learning to keep a simple beat while another child needs the challenge of learning to play a complex instrument. Other materials may meet the needs of all children, since they lend themselves to a variety of uses. For example, hollow blocks can be used by a child who is in the preoperational stage of development as well as by a child in the concrete operational stage. The preoperational child may make simple structures while the child at the concrete stage will make more complex structures.

Educators will also have to consider the variation in physical abilities of the children when planning both the environment and the curriculum. Some children may be very agile and well coordinated, while others may require a wheelchair or walker and have very limited fine motor skills. Some of the adaptations that educators may need to make are identified in other chapters. However, rather than making adaptations based on assumptions about a child's particular disability, the adaptations should be based on a knowledge of the individual child's abilities that has been acquired through observation along with input from the parents or guardians and other professionals.

Some children in the program may have difficulty with social skills. In a school-age program, this type of developmental difference will have a greater impact than in a program for younger children. During the school-age years, peers are becoming increasingly important to the children, and being able to read social cues and respond appropriately is crucial for successful interaction. Children who tend to be aggressive, egocentric, or demonstrate Pervasive Developmental Disorders (PDD) are often ostracized by other children because of their poor social skills. Because each child is unique, and the reasons for poor social skills vary, educators may need to work with the family and other professionals in order to develop successful strategies. In one case, the educator may coach the child through social interactions, while in another, the educator may use a behaviour-modification type of program.

Some physical differences may not receive the label "special need," yet still have an impact on the child. Obesity is a condition that affects many school-age children. It can have a direct impact on social, emotional, and physical abilities. Children who are obese are more likely to suffer from poor self-esteem and have more difficulty with a variety of motor skills. They are also more likely to have health problems than children of normal weight, and are more likely to be bullied by other children.

Language Diversity

In Canada, an increasingly common form of diversity among children is English or French as a second, third, or fourth language. If the child has only recently arrived in the country, her limited language skills may be very obvious, while for other children it may be seen in more subtle ways (such as not understanding some slang words). Even when the child's understanding of English or French is good, his accent may create some difficulties when communicating with peers or adults. In order to support his language development, educators therefore need to observe the child to determine his skills and, when necessary, consult with professionals in the area of language development. It is also important that educators remember that all children have receptive language that is more advanced than their expressive language—that is, they can understand more than they can speak.

Family Diversity

Children in school-age programs come from a variety of diverse backgrounds, and as Bronfenbrenner's ecological theory indicates, these backgrounds will have an impact on the children's participation in the program.

A child's culture has an impact on her development. Cultural diversity can mean that some families don't encourage boys and girls to engage in the same activities, and this can result in differing abilities. If girls are not given the opportunity to play catch at home, they won't have the same skill level as children who do. Culture can also affect the child's social and emotional development. If educators aren't willing to accommodate children who are fasting for Ramadan (for instance, if there is a set snack time and children who can't eat have to wait for the other children to finish), it could affect those children's self-esteem. Instead, educators should schedule an open snack time where children can choose to get involved in another activity if they don't want to have a snack.

Although diversity is often associated with differences in religious and ethnic backgrounds, educators need to recognize that socio-economic backgrounds or sexual orientation of parents are also types of diversity. Socio-economic backgrounds may influence the vocabulary and grammar used by a child. It can influence the strategies used in conflict situations, a child's self-image, and the type of physical skills he spends time developing. Children growing up with same-sex parents may have a different understanding of what it means to be a family than a child growing up in the stereotypical nuclear family. In addition, children growing up with same-sex parents may experience negative attitudes from some children and adults, which may require educators to look at how they approach situations like Mother's Day or Father's Day.

Educators must also remember to avoid stereotyping families within a similar group. Even within a particular culture or socio-economic group, families are unique. One family may emphasize academics and music, while another may emphasize social interactions and sports. If academics are emphasized, the children within that family may have advanced cognitive and language skills, while an emphasis on sports may result in precocious physical skills. In order to plan successful school-age programs, educators need to recognize that special needs, religious, ethnic, and socio-economic backgrounds, and family differences all influence the child's development.

Summary

Educators working with school-age children recognize that they are, in many ways, very different from children in preschool programs. Some school-age programs include children ranging in age from younger than four to twelve years of age, while other programs are limited to children of six to ten or six to twelve years of age. The focus of this text is on programming for children of six to twelve years of age, though within that age range children will demonstrate a wide range of skills. Younger school-age children may still function at the preoperational stage of development, while some of the older children may be entering formal operations. If educators want to develop after-school programs that will both challenge and excite children, they must embrace their developmental diversity and accommodate their needs.

Educators must develop programs that provide children with opportunities for independence and responsibility, while giving them the skills to handle both. Educators need to recognize the importance of friendship, and provide space and opportunities for children to develop. They need to recognize that children want to be successful in a variety of situations, and help them see that they can succeed in physical activities, social situations, and academics.

We must provide after-school environments that challenge children in ways that are different from those found during the school day, and we must provide learning experiences that recognize the children's unique needs, interests, and abilities.

The subsequent chapters are designed to help educators working with school-age children to create programs that will meet their diverse needs. By recognizing and embracing the abilities that school-age children bring with them, educators, with the help of the children, can create challenging and exciting places for children to spend time both after school and on non-school days.

Student Learning Experiences

1. Design a board game for six- to nine-year-old children. Use your knowledge of development to justify the following: type of game, language used in game and in directions and subject matter of game.

2. Observe eight- to ten-year-olds and four- to five-year-olds, and record observations for each developmental domain. Compare the two age groups and indicate how this data would affect your programming.

3. Go to an after-school program and look at five books that are available to the children. Review the books and determine the age range for which each would be most appropriate. Use child-development concepts to back up your answer.

4. Create a chart identifying the developmental differences, in each domain, between a kindergarten child and an older school-age child.

Review Questions

1. Identify two fine motor activities that educators might offer older school-age children (nine to ten years of age) that younger school-age children (six to seven years of age) would have difficulty doing. Use child-development concepts to back up your answer.

2. Use child-development concepts to explain how school-age children can successfully help plan the curriculum in a school-age program.

3. Use child-development concepts to explain why conflict resolution is a behaviour-guidance technique that should be used in school-age programs.

4. Identify three ways in which kindergarten language skills differ from school-age language skills.

5. Identify three social skills that school-age children typically have, and explain how these will influence the type of program that is offered.

PART 3

Planning the Environment and Creating a Sense of Community

CHAPTER 5

Creating Indoor and Outdoor Environments

OVERVIEW

When coming home from a hard day's work, do adults want to drop onto the couch or sit on a hard dining room chair? Do they want to continue working on the same tasks they had at work, or would they rather take a break from work and engage in other activities?

During the school year children spend much of their day in a school classroom environment. This environment can be compared to the adult's work environment, and like the work environment it often lacks home-like touches. Rows of desks or tables, glaring artificial lighting, lots of hard surfaces, and no private or small-group space describes many of these rooms. When school is out, children need an environment where they can relax with friends or be by themselves. They need spaces where they can engage in a variety of non-academic or academic pursuits of their choice.

Children who attend school spend up to six hours participating in learning activities that do not require many large motor movements. When school is finished they need to release their physical energy and engage in learning experiences that promote physical development. They need large amounts of outdoor time for active play. School-age children require an outdoor environment with enough space to play games, spend time with friends, be by themselves, create and invent, explore the natural world, and experience the weather and the seasons.

Educators need to create a home-like environment regardless of the location. Educators need to look at both indoor and outdoor spaces when trying to create a comfortable environment. This chapter will discuss not only what an appropriate

school-age environment might look like, but how educators might overcome some of the challenges they encounter when creating these environments.

THE INDOOR ENVIRONMENT

When parents and community visitors first encounter a program set up with a home-like environment, you might hear them make comments like the following: "It looks relaxing, comfortable, and peaceful." "It feels and looks like home." "It reminds me of a kid's room or a loft." "You can tell that children play and spend time here."

If educators want to create environments that evoke these kinds of positive responses, they will have to look at what is being provided and encouraged in all aspects of the physical environment. Does the layout of the school-age space evoke a sense of home, or does it look more like a modified classroom? Do the materials and equipment provided reflect and enhance what is available to children at home? Does the environment reflect the diversity of the children and their families?

Although the creation of a home-like environment is important, educators must also keep in mind that the environment must be interesting and challenging for school-age children. The school-age environment is not simply a preschool environment with more complex puzzles and games.

Dramatic play demonstrates how educators need to recognize the differences between preschool and school-age children in order to create an environment that will challenge children while providing them with an enjoyable experience. Although dramatic play will occur in both preschool and school-age programs, the type of play the children engage in and the way that play is made available to both groups can be very different. Educators in preschool environments recognize that children enjoy imitating the roles of individuals with whom they interact in their daily life. The dramatic-play/dress-up area reflects this not only in the clothes available (such as doctors' jackets) but in the equipment provided (like a toy fridge or stove).

Although some children continue to engage in this type of dramatic play in school-age programs, their approach to it is changing, and they often prefer to create air bands or put on a play that they've made up. This change means that the educators must provide the children with more flexible materials (like fabrics and accessories) to allow the children to create the variety of costumes required. The change in the needs of the children means that they are less likely to want fridges and stoves for their backdrops, and are more likely to require fabrics and loose parts, such as wood, to create their own forts, stages, instruments, and so on.

Layout of the Environment

School-age children do not want a room that looks like a preschoolers' room or a school classroom. When children leave school at the end of the day they want to come to a home-like environment. Whereas a preschool environment is usually designed around activity centres, the school-age environment should be designed around multi-use areas that are similar to areas found in the home, such as a kitchen or a living room area. When designing the layout of the environment the following points may influence how the space is used or designed.

- Location of doors and windows
- Access to water
- Type of lighting (natural or artificial)
- Flooring or carpeted space
- Storage space
- Air space (high or low ceilings)
- Traffic flow into and through the room

For example, if you have access to water and a sink this may dictate where the kitchen or dining area should be located. A door going into the room or a door leading to another room will dictate the traffic flow of the room. Furniture or equipment should not be kept in front of or too near the doors for safety reasons (fire drills) and also to give children easy access into and out of the room.

Entry Area   Like in a home, the first area one sees in the school-age program is the entry. This area should create a sense of welcome to the program for both children and their families and invite them to come into the space and to stay. Like an entry at home, this area provides the children with a place to store their coats and bags when they come in. It also provides space in which to put messages, display pictures, and document learning experiences, projects, or clubs. Ideally this space will have a comfortable place for children or other family members to sit and relax and to spend time observing the program or connecting with other families. To make the entrance area inviting for parents and children, include home-like furnishings such as couches. Magazines, photo albums of children, finished projects or scrapbooks, and snack food such as a bowl of fruit can be added to help to create a home-like environment. In one program they turned the couch and the coffee table toward

Flexible materials can be used to create children's forts.

the entrance door and by doing this created a welcoming and inviting environment. By making this simple change parents and family members felt they had a place to sit down and observe their children in the environment, have discussions with an educator, or connect with other parents.

The entry area is also used as a transition/flexible area for children to enter and leave the program. In this area children may wait to go outside, get dressed for winter, or have an impromptu group meeting. Projects and physical activities (such as dancing) can also be expanded into the entry area on a short-term basis if the space is needed.

Living-Room Area Upon entering a home a child may decide to go to the kitchen, dining room, living room, rec room, the child's room, or even the study. In a school-age program children should find areas that serve similar purposes. One area may be set up as a living room, with couches, chairs, rugs, and a coffee table. In this area children may sit down on the couch to talk with their friends. They may bring out a game and play it on the coffee table, or they may use the table as a surface for making a Lego construction. They may curl up in chairs to read a book while eating a snack, or they may decide to do homework or individual projects (such as crafts) in this area. This is also an area where children may listen to music, play board games, research ideas, or plan activities with their friends. Because this space often promotes quiet, reflective activities, educators may choose to hold group meetings there.

Rec-Room Area Instead of going into the living-room area a child may decide to spend time in the area equivalent to a rec room. More active play usually occurs in this area than in the living-room area. Large constructions such as fort-building tend to occur here, as does messy play like art activities or science experiments. Because this area tends to be

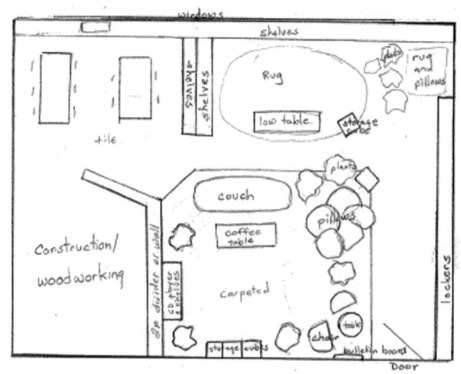

With creative thinking, a school classroom can be turned into a home-like environment.

larger and more open than the living room, this is where children often engage in dramatic play. This is where skits, air bands, and slapstick, impromptu plays occur. Woodworking often occurs in this area, as do many art activities. Because the space is often larger than other areas, it is likely to be popular for socializing in larger groups and engaging in activities that require room, such as dancing. At the same time, activities such as games and crafts that often happen in the living room will also take place in this area.

Kitchen Area Another child in the program may choose to go to the kitchen area. In some centres this might be an actual kitchen, while in others it may simply be a food preparation area within the room. Aside from using this area for cooking, children are likely to spend time here talking about food and planning activities that involve food, such as discussing snacks. In the kitchen area, different types of utensils, equipment (for example, pots and pans) and simple and complex machines such as blenders and juicers may be found. Some science experiments and messy activities that require water may be done in this area. A variety of loose parts may be located in this area for children to access when exploring, experimenting, or concocting their next science experiment. If the kitchen is a separate space, an educator may need to supervise the children in this area to ensure safety and safe handling of food.

Dining-Room Area The area corresponding to the dining room in a home is where one will find some tables for the children to work at and eat on. If space is set aside for this purpose, the educator has the opportunity to use actual dining room or kitchen tables, rather than the institutional tables found in school settings. These tables are an ideal area for children to do homework, games, art activities, and crafts. Children and educators may also meet around a table to discuss issues and engage in program planning. Finally, the large flat surfaces are great for working on individual or group projects, or for documenting previous learning experiences. Because the space is ideal for so many diverse activities a variety of loose parts, materials, and equipment should be located in this area.

Child's-Room Area   A child coming home might choose to go to his own room, because this is a space that is truly the child's own and where he can be alone and away from adults. Every school-age program should include this type of space for children. Because the functions of a child's room (privacy, individual space, a space where a child has a sense of ownership) are not easily met in just one area of a school-age program, the centre might look at creating different spaces to address the different functions of the room. Educators and the children can create small, private spaces where children can be alone to read or daydream, or where they can spend time with a couple of friends. This area needs to provide children with a feeling of privacy, even though most centres will not have a truly private area. Educators should expect to see private spaces change over time as children move materials to expand or contract the space in order to achieve the sense of privacy they desire, and to create a space that reflects them.

In order to address the function of individual space, another area in the centre might be used. Although most program space is communal, many programs ensure that some individual space is provided by assigning boxes or shelves to individual children. In this space children can store personal items or projects that they are working on, and know that these items will be left alone. Depending upon the program this space may be in a storage area, in the rec-room area, or in the entry.

Another function of the child's room is the creation of a space where the child has control. This function can be incorporated into all areas of the school-age program. If children are given responsibility for helping to create and maintain the indoor environment, the educators have created an entire program where the children have a sense of ownership.

Study Area   The last area that will be discussed is the study. This area is not found in all homes, and unfortunately it is also missing in some school-age programs. In the home, the study is usually an area used for more quiet pursuits by both adults and children. In school-age programs, this type of space is also required for both children and staff. The staff room or director's office often best serve this quiet type of activity, but many programs that share space may not have these facilities. As with the study in the home, educators will use this space for research, discussion, planning and administrative duties. This is also an area where educators can spend time documenting what has occurred in the program. Although children may not spend as much time in this space, it does not mean that children can never access the area. A child may use this space to work on the computer, research projects, or work without distractions.

Successful school-age programs provide living spaces similar to those found in homes, and as in homes, the layout of these spaces varies from program to program. It is the components that are important, and result in the home-like feel. The actual layout will be influenced by the children, staff, families, and the activities that take place there. Table 5.1 shows each of the living spaces, indicates the purpose of each, and highlights the types of learning experiences that can occur in these spaces.

TABLE 5.1	School-age indoor environment areas	
Area	**Purpose**	**Types of Experiences**
Entry	• Welcome children and families • Provide information	• Informal interactions between families, children, and educators • Documentation
Living room	• Socialization • Group skills • Variety of cognitive pursuits • Some gross motor activities (e.g., dancing)	• Informal interactions with peers • Music • Group meetings • Club meetings and activities • Reading • Board games, crafts, etc. • Creating documentation • Computer activities • Snacks
Dining room	• Socialization • Group skills • Variety of cognitive pursuits • Some fine motor activities	• Informal interactions with peers • Snacks/lunch • Board games, crafts, etc. • Small group meetings • Club meetings and activities • Art • Science
Rec room	• Socialization • Group skills • Active play • Variety of cognitive pursuits • Variety of gross and fine motor skills	• Informal interactions with peers • Dramatic play • Construction activities • Music • Science • Art • Group meetings • Club meetings and activities • Creating documentation
Kitchen	• Variety of cognitive pursuits • Variety of fine motor skills • Small group skills	• Cooking • Snack preparation • Science and art activities requiring water, etc. • Club activities
Child's room	• Quiet retreat • Small group interactions • Individual spaces • Variety of cognitive pursuits	• Reading • Homework • Writing • Computer activities • Board games, crafts, etc. • Storage of unfinished projects
Study	• Staff space • Research area	• Computer activities • Researching information • Small group planning • Creating documentation • Staff time to be alone or with peers • Staff meetings

Home-like environments can be created using plants and soft furniture.

Creating a Home-Like Environment

In order to create a home-like environment that meets the needs of the children and their families, there are several factors to keep in mind.

1. Use materials that reflect the children's home environments
Materials in the physical environment should evoke the qualities and physical characteristics of home. Living rooms are not full of hard tables and wooden chairs, but incorporate softer furnishings like couches, rugs, and overstuffed chairs. Educators can develop the feeling of a living room by creating a space that contains a couch, overstuffed chairs, a coffee table, lots of large pillows, an area rug, baskets of toys and magazines, art posters on the wall, and window treatments (see Table 5.2). The style of the furnishings will vary from one centre to another, and will incorporate items that reflect the cultures of the children, families, and the surrounding community. Fortunately, unlike preschoolers, school-age children do not need scaled-down furniture, and educators can buy inexpensive used furniture that will help create a home-like atmosphere.

2. Use actual tools and machines that children might have at home
School-age children have developed the necessary fine and gross motor skills to use a variety of tools, and they have the logical thinking skills to understand the safety issues around the use of the tools and machines. With proper instruction from the educator, even young school-age children can competently use a variety of tools.

TABLE 5.2	A home-like environment

Furniture and Equipment

Couches; overstuffed chairs; wooden chairs and wooden tables rather than institutional ones; drafting tables; coffee/end tables; modular wooden cubes; bookcases; bamboo floor screens; picture frame screens; area rugs; pillows of a variety of shapes, textures, and sizes; plants in a variety of shapes and sizes.

In Shared Space: Couches and chairs (if in a storage space, or if opportunity to negotiate leaving furniture in place for other parties to use arises), large pillows, various rugs, floor screens on castors, wooden storage cubes (on castors) that also serve as dividers, large storage bins that can be draped with cloth and used as coffee or end tables, some large plastic plants on wheels if real plants aren't viable (softens space, creates barriers).

Lighting

Natural lighting, floor lamps, table lamps, hanging lights, theatre spotlights, pot lights, flashlights, candles, twinkle lights.

In Shared Space: Try and get at least a couple of lamps for the living-room area.

Air Space

Lanterns, kites, beaded/bamboo curtains, cloth canopy, branches, trees, plants, crystals, stained glass, wire sculptures, mylar strips, banners, macramé hangers, mirrors, mobiles made with CDs; laminated documentation hanging from the ceiling can do double duty as dividers.

Wall Space

Wall hangings, children's art work, children's documentation, a variety of posters (art posters, skyscrapers, songs, families, etc.), vines, mirrors.

In Shared Space: Use of air space and wall space will have to be negotiated since this isn't something you'll want to take down each day. Consider the benefits your additions will create to the other uses of the space (e.g., in a gym you could put a couple of large laminated children's murals on a wall near the stage, which would also brighten the space when you're not there and wouldn't interfere with games that use the walls of the gym).

Storage Materials

Baskets, copper/ceramic pots, metal bowls, tin containers, and wooden storage cubes, as well as the more traditional plastic containers. Make sure larger storage units (e.g.,wooden storage cubes) can be safely moved by children.

In Shared Space: Store the baskets, bowls, and tins of supplies in the large bins. Once the items have been removed from the bins, the bins can be draped to be used as coffee tables, etc. Make use of wooden storage cubes on castors that have shelves for the materials and home-like containers but that can be quickly moved and rearranged as necessary. Take advantage of local carpenters who can custom build storage units to suit your space. Make sure storage units can be safely moved by school-age children.

Diverse Materials

Baskets, fabrics, art materials, books, posters and pictures, music, etc. should reflect the diverse backgrounds of the children.

Art and Building Materials

Old pieces of tile, drywall compound, mylar, proper clay tools, all types of fabrics for creative uses, a variety of woods in various states of refinement, real tools for creating with wood, plumbing parts, Sono tubes, computer programs such as Adobe Photoshop, MS Paint (see attached list of materials and loose parts).

Tools and machines should appear in the environment naturally and should be available on an everyday basis. When creating a home-like environment, educators locate cooking and baking tools and machines in the kitchen, or in an area designated for food preparation. Although providing these types of materials may, at times, be opposed by the local health department, the learning opportunities they provide mean that educators should work with the department to overcome any objections they have.

Everyday tools and machines are not limited to kitchen appliances. Woodworking is a very popular activity for school-age children, so woodworking tools should be part of a school-age program. Like the equipment involved in cooking, woodworking requires educators to teach the children the correct usage of the materials and all of the safety measures that must be taken (e.g. using safety goggles). Given appropriate training and proper supervision, children can very successfully create a variety of objects in the woodworking area. One child may simply want to hammer nails into wood, while another child will design a cradle and follow it through to completion. In one program a child spent most of the afternoon using wood, old wheels, a hammer, nails, and duct tape to create a set of dumbbells which he then used in his play.

Tools and machines included in the program may be complex, like drills or sewing machines, or they may be very simple, like pulleys, levers, and screwdrivers. The key to inclusion is to provide clear and reasonable guidelines for their use, and to teach the children the correct way to use them. Many educators worry about including electrical tools or tools with sharp edges in their programs, but school-age children have the skills and abilities required to use them effectively, enjoy the challenge these tools provide, and appreciate the opportunity to take on greater responsibilities and learn skills that are valued in our society. Educators must of course remember that they are legally responsible for the children's safety, so use of such equipment should be under their supervision to ensure safe handling.

3.   Incorporate the natural world into the classroom

By using natural materials in the room, educators can create warmer, softer spaces, divide large spaces, create a sense of privacy without sacrificing the educators' ability to supervise the room, and expose children to natural elements in our world.

Along with shelves and panel dividers, plants can be used to break up large expanses into several different spaces. Large plants can be grouped together to create a screen between areas. Plant screens give the effect of a wall and create private spaces without blocking the view of the children or the light. Smaller plants can be placed on top of shelves to soften their hard lines and to add texture and colour to the room. Grouping plants on top of storage units helps to extend the upward space. Plants grouped on the floor help to soften and screen out any hard surfaces. By placing small plants around the pots of larger plants, you can create a "plane" of plant life. Children can also add small plants to their dramatic play experiences.

Small plants can be used to create miniature ecosystems if placed in terrariums. These can then be placed on top of a storage unit to create a high visual screen between areas, or on the floor to create visual interest at another level. The children may create a variety of terrarium environments (such as woodland, savannah, desert, semi-aquatic, and green-house). When children and educators work together to create these miniature ecosystems, the physical environment of the program becomes more dynamic and the children learn a lot about the ecosystems in which we live.

Educators can use plants to change patterns of movement through the space. Educators know that a straight path down the centre of the room will encourage running, but a number of large plants jutting out into a running path will break up the straight line that the child sees and thus reduce the likelihood of running. If you place the plants in small,

Using everyday materials can change the dynamics of a room.

zigzagging groups, you can create a wandering pathway that not only slows the children down but that can create the feel of being in the woods. If the plants are large enough—say 1.5 to 2 metres in height—you can create pathways, entrances and exits to certain areas of the room. Breaking up or changing the shape or direction of pathways is not, of course, the same as blocking the path. Whatever their shape or pattern, paths must be kept clear of extraneous objects that might become a tripping hazard (particularly for someone with a visual impairment) or create problems for someone in a wheelchair.

Plants are not the only natural materials that can be used to help create a warm, home-like environment. Educators can use logs to define a low space. By placing a log length-ways in front of a window, educators can create an inviting sitting space for groups of children to socialize or simply view the world outside. Logs can be moved around the room by the children, and used when they wish to create their own space.

Many children find stumps even better than logs because they are so versatile. Stumps can be used for individual children to sit on, or as surfaces to play on (for instance, as a landing pad for their Lego spaceships). Stumps are often used by the children in their own constructions. When building forts they will use stumps for roof supports and for tables, beds, and chairs.

Small animals and their habitats can help create the home-like atmosphere educators want, while also defining space. Having small animals in the environment has the added benefit of providing children with the opportunity to be responsible for the care of other living things. Although children's allergies may limit the types of animals brought into the environment, these small animals and their habitats can draw children into various spaces, bring colour and movement to spaces, and even act as dividers between spaces. Fish in aquariums, birds in cages, small mammals in cages, and reptiles in terrariums are common pets that help create interest in a room.

Storage space for unfinished projects should be included in the environment.

The fact that many programs are in a shared space will, however, make it challenging to incorporate natural materials, and educators may need to come up with creative solutions to this challenge.

4.   Make the materials accessible to the children

In the school-age program children should be able to access most materials easily. Their increased desire for independence means children do not want to always have to ask an educator to get materials for them, and educators should be happy that the children are capable of obtaining materials for themselves. Because many children are tall, the shelves in a school-age program can be taller than those found in programs for younger children. When placing storage containers on the shelves, educators need to remember that higher shelves should not be used to store large containers if they want children to be able to remove them. The containers used should be aesthetically pleasing, but they don't always need to easily display what's inside, since the children can read a label if necessary.

The storage room should also be well organized, with shelves that the children can reach. They should know where to go to get equipment that isn't used every day. A child who wants to use the sewing machine to make a pillow should know where the machine is kept. After checking with the educator to make sure that it's okay, the child can get it out of the storage room and set it up himself. The educator's role is to ensure that the child is setting it up and using it correctly, with due regard for safety.

Because school-age children often engage in activities that can't be completed in a short time, the environment needs to include places for each child to store materials they are using. This can be achieved by providing children with individual boxes or shelves that they can easily reach. A child making a costume will need several days to complete it. If she has a storage box, she can return it to the storage cart or shelf when she's done as much as she wants to on any given day.

5. Use flexible materials and loose parts

Few adults arrange a room once and then never change the design again. In fact, everyone knows someone whose hobby seems to be rearranging the furniture. Just like adults, children in school-age programs will want to change the layout and look of the room as their interests and needs change.

For several months in one school-age program we observed, most of the children had converted large areas of the room into forts where they could read, play games, or simply spend time with their close friends. Just when the educators thought that this was going to be "the look" for the room, the children's interests shifted to drama, woodworking, and science experiments. Now, instead of a third of the room being covered by forts, there is only a small area devoted to forts. The workbench has come out of storage, there is a large table containing a number of science "experiments," and an open area is being used as a stage. These changes occurred easily, and most could be made by the children themselves because many of the materials and equipment were designed to be flexible. Rather than using large shelving units, many of the shelves and dividers were composed of storage cubes that were stackable and that could easily be lifted and carried by the children. These cubes could store art supplies, drama supplies, or games as the need arose. As the children and educators worked together to change some of the spaces in the room, the children were even able to move all the plants, because the educators had put the large plants on wheels, and the smaller plants were in pots that the children could carry.

Besides having equipment that was easy to rearrange, the new spaces were possible because other flexible materials had been incorporated into the room. Plumbing pipes that had been used as a communication system between forts were transferred to the science area to be used in experiments involving marbles and to the dramatic play area to become part of a prop for a play. The program also had a variety of fabric that was easily transformed from a roof for a fort to a costume for an air band. The educators took care, when purchasing materials like fabric, to incorporate materials that reflected diversity. The fabrics reflected various cultures and, instead of having only traditional cotton fabric products, the program incorporated fabrics made from bamboo and other more diverse materials.

Flexible materials and loose parts are usually familiar to children. These materials are found in children's homes and are often the materials most appealing to them, even though parents may think of them as junk. Fabric, wood, pipes, rocks, string, old machines, and so on are all flexible materials that children can use in a wide variety of ways. These loose parts (see Table 5.3) challenge children's thinking because they are open-ended in nature. Unlike toy cars or board games, there is not one correct way to use the material, so children have to use their creativity and logical-thinking skills to incorporate them into their activities.

6. Use soft lighting when possible

Depending upon where the school-age program is located, creating soft lighting may be very easy or next to impossible. A program located in purpose-built space may be fortunate enough to find it designed with natural lighting taken into account, but programs located in school gyms may have no option but to make do with the fluorescent lights already present.

Natural light should be used as much as possible. It is warmer and softer, and helps to create atmosphere in the environment. In areas of the room that don't receive much natural light, or during the winter, educators may need to provide additional lighting. Many spaces come with overhead fluorescent bulbs, but the light from these is harsh and can't be focused into specific areas. Floor lamps, table lamps, hanging lamps, twinkle lights, and spotlights can provide softer lighting as well as direct light to specific areas and so help define the area.

As long as there are sufficient electrical outlets available, using lamps in a school-age program can be done without fearing for the children's safety. School-age children have good spatial awareness and motor control, so educators don't have to worry that they'll accidentally knock over the lamps. The children also know that they need to be careful with electrical equipment, so the educator doesn't have to worry that they'll play with the cords or the outlets.

7. Make sure that the materials will be interesting and challenging to school-age children

School-age programs address the varied needs and interests of children from six to twelve. As the previous chapter indicated, the children in this age range have a wide variety of skills that differ from those of preschoolers. Although educators may continue to provide some picture books for younger school-age children who are still struggling with reading, the majority of books found in the program will be designed for readers. Reading materials should include magazines, comics, and non-fiction both to entice children to read and to provide resource materials for children engaged in projects. Puzzles and games are important materials to include, and like the books, these should provide various levels of difficulty in order to challenge the children.

When purchasing art supplies, educators need to remember that most school-age children have had opportunities to experiment with tempera paints and play dough as preschoolers, and many will be interested in trying other art media. Learning how to paint with acrylics or watercolours; creating paintings on a variety of art papers; using clay and perhaps even firing it; tie-dyeing fabrics; or using tiles to create mosaics are just some of the new art experiences children will enjoy trying.

Engaging in craft activities that are valued by society—such as knitting, building with wood, and sewing—are only a few of the activities that school-age children enjoy. Although many of the raw materials needed for the activities are the same as those found in preschool programs, the way the children use them will differ, as will the equipment they need to do their activities. The school-age child will use yarn to knit—and therefore requires knitting needles—while the preschool child will be more interested in gluing the yarn to the paper. Unlike the preschooler pounding nails into a piece of wood, the school-age child building a bird house will require a drill, a saw, screwdrivers, and a square, among other tools.

Sharing Space with Others

One of the biggest challenges for educators in school-age programs is sharing space with other users. Many programs are located in school gyms, libraries, or classrooms. Other programs may be in spaces that are also used by recreational or religious groups. Shared space often means that educators must set up and take down all the furniture and other equipment each day. How does this influence the storage space required and the types of containers used to store the equipment? How does one create a sense of ownership or a

TABLE 5.3	School-age materials and equipment

This table contains lists of various loose parts and materials that provide opportunities for school-age children to engage in a variety of developmentally appropriate learning experiences.

Machines	Fabric and Fibres	Drawing and Painting
Loose Parts/Material List	**Loose Parts/Material List**	**Loose Parts/Material List**
Watches	Needles: a variety of sizes,	Pencils
Computers	shapes, tips	Pencil crayons
Printers	Embroidery frames and hoops	Watercolour pencils
Small appliances	Pins	Pencil sharpeners
Telephones	Thimbles	Charcoal: pencils and stubs
Motorized cars	Crochet hooks	Pastels
Cameras	Knitting needles	Conté sticks
Clocks	Scissors: a variety of types and	Chalk
Overhead projectors	sizes	Markers: fine and wide
Hair dryers	Spindles	Calligraphy pens
Fans	Lattice	Ink: a variety of colours,
Lamps	Weaving looms: table, floor, etc.	watercolour inks and
Old electric tools	Thread: a variety of colours	drawing inks
Any other old machines	and types	Erasers
you can find	Embroidery floss	Ballpoint pens
	Yarns: a variety of colours,	Brushes: a variety of sizes
	textures, materials	and types
	Natural materials: wools, sticks,	Rollers
	shell, feathers, wood, rocks,	Natural materials: sticks,
	cane, reeds	feathers, reeds, etc.
	Wire	Paint: tempera, acrylic,
	Fabric: a variety of materials,	gouache, watercolour
	textures, patterns, weights	Paper: a variety, including
	Netting, meshing, mylar, etc.	watercolour paper, finger
	Beads: a variety of shapes,	paint, shelf, foil, newsprint,
	colours, sizes, materials	butcher paper, carbon,
	Sequins and other decorative	tissue, tracing, graph,
	materials	origami, canvas
	Ribbons	Plexiglas
	Elastics: a variety of widths,	Wood
	types, tensions	Masonite
	String, cord, twine, rope, jute	Acetate/transparencies
	Gimp	
	Buttons, snaps	
	Dyeing materials: natural	
	(vegetables, flowers, etc.)	
	and packaged	
	Nylons/pantyhose	
	Wax, crayons, etc.	
	Cotton batten	
	Cardboard	
Exploration Equipment	**Exploration Equipment**	**Exploration Equipment**
Screwdrivers: a variety of	Sewing machines	Containers for storing paints
types and sizes	Measuring tapes	and other materials
Tweezers	Catalogues and pattern books	Rulers

(Continued)

TABLE 5.3	School-age materials and equipment, continued		

Machines	Fabric and Fibres	Drawing and Painting
Loose Parts/Material List	**Loose Parts/Material List**	**Loose Parts/Material List**
Clamps	Paper: regular and graph	Geometry sets
Hammers	Pencils	Easels
Pliers and wrenches	Glue	Light table
Tape	Large tubs and access	Overhead projectors
Graph paper	to sink	Books on techniques
Storage containers	Books on techniques	Art books
Pencils		
Clipboards		
Books and manuals	**Woodworking and Construction**	**Sculpturing**
Cloth	Wood: a variety of types and	Clay
Paper: a variety of papers	sizes	Polymer clay
that will absorb ink/paint	Cardboard and boxes	Plasticene
Light-sensitive paper	Rope, twine, etc.	Clay sculpting tools (several
Drafting paper	Plumbing pipes	sets)
Transfer papers: both	Bamboo	Air-tight containers for
iron-on and computer	Plastic tubing: both rigid and	storing the clay
Wood: soft (e.g., pine)	flexible	Containers for slip mixture
Old cloths that will absorb	Wheels (ones for wheelbarrows,	Wire: variety of types and
ink/paint	etc.)	thicknesses (must be
Cardboard	Nails	bendable)
Collage materials: papers,	Screws	Wood
magazines, cards	Glue	Thread (for cutting clay)
Sandpaper	Tape: especially duct tape	Kitchen utensils that can be
String, twine, etc.	Nuts and bolts	used to help sculpt clay
Natural materials: sticks,	Wires	(e.g., garlic press)
grasses, rocks, leaves,	Pulleys	Pliers: a variety for bending
flowers, etc.	Hammers	the wire
Wax	Saws: handsaw, mitre saw,	Natural materials: sticks,
Water-based ink	hacksaw	feathers, rocks, grasses, etc.
Paint: tempera, acrylic	Clamps, vises	Paints
Silkscreen	Drills	Beads, sequins, etc.
Soft lino	Wrenches	Glue
Foam	Gears	Podge
Brayers	Sandpaper	Tape
Acetate (stencilling)	Screwdrivers	Scissors
Stencils	Hooks and eyes	
Stencil brushes	Natural materials: logs,	
Cutting tools	branches	
Glue	Fabrics: variety of sizes, textures,	
Pencils and markers	materials	
Pencil sharpener	**Protective gear:**	
Erasers	Goggles, work aprons, particle	
Wood	masks	
Ceramic tiles (get		
broken scraps from a		
tile centre)		
Adhesive		
Grout		

TABLE 5.3	School-age materials and equipment, continued		
Exploration Equipment	**Exploration Equipment**	**Exploration Equipment**	
Computer and copier	Workbench	Books on sculpting	
Drawing software	Saw horses	techniques	
Picture software	Mitre box	Art books, posters, etc.	
Large flat surface area	Graph paper	Oven for polymer clay	
Trays for paint	Pencils	Kiln (if available)	
Drying rack	Rulers		
Books on mosaics,	Drafting plans		
printmaking, etc.	Books on buildings, pulley		
	systems, etc.		
	Art books		
	Marbles, small balls, baskets		

home-like atmosphere when the space isn't permanent? How does one provide for all of the different types of spaces without spending large amounts of time every day simply setting up and dismantling the environment? Shared space certainly provides challenge, but it does not mean that creating a home-like environment that meets the needs of school-age children is impossible.

Gym or Large Hall (Large Open Spaces) Educators working in a gym or hall require a large storage area in or near the gym for all of their materials and equipment. Although the school board, YM/YWCA, or religious groups may not think that a lot of storage is required, this is something that educators must negotiate. Limited storage means limited materials, and will result in an environment with little variety for children and one that might encourage inappropriate behaviour (running and jumping in a gym is fine, but without other options the play will get out of hand).

Once educators have obtained adequate storage space, they need to determine how to get the most out of the space. Storage space found in large buildings often has a high ceiling, and therefore one needs to utilize the vertical space as well as the floor space. Spare materials may be located on very high shelves since they don't need to be accessed every day. Wall hooks can also be used to store materials like hoops and hockey sticks that children could access once the movable storage units have been removed from the closet.

Movable (wheeled) storage cabinets should be included when discussing storage units. These cabinets can hold a variety of materials and, when wheeled into the gym, can help define spaces. Because these units are high, safety precautions have to be used to ensure that health and safety inspectors are not concerned. Along with locking wheels, the cabinets need to be constructed so that the lower portion is heavier than the upper. As well, the dimensions of the lower half of the cabinet should be larger than those of the top half to ensure stability. A high cabinet could also include a hinged table attached to the lower section. When this table is flipped up to the working position it can extend the dimensions of the lower part of the cabinet, further increasing stability and creating a more home-like work space for children. All storage containers need to be designed so that once in the gym they become attractive elements of the room, functioning as a divider, a table, and so on. Hiring a carpenter may be less expensive than purchasing storage units from specialized catalogues. Carpenters can create customized units that fit your specific storage space, are movable but safe, and create a home-like rather than an institutional feel. Along with cabinets and shelving units, one can use small storage cubes that children themselves can lift up and move around. These cubes may be stuffed with blankets, rugs or small beanbag chairs when in the storage room, but can be adapted for other purposes once emptied of their contents. For example, a couple of cubes could be converted to a low table or end tables when the room is set up.

Whether or not the program is in dedicated or shared space, it still needs to be welcoming for families to enter, and divisible into specialized areas for children to use in different ways.

1. Entry area

Creating an entry to a gym or hall may not seem feasible, but educators can try a variety of strategies to make it brighter and more home-like. A portable appliquéd wall hanging could be placed by the door each day to greet families even before they enter the space. Educators could also include in this area a hinged screen with attached messages and documentation for the families. The documents could include photos, curriculum webs, children's brainstorming ideas, and so on. If the institution renting the space to the program doesn't object, the educators might even put out a couch or chair that could remain there at all times.

2. Living-room area

Even in a gym or hall the educator should be able to create a space where children feel comfortable and want to spend time. A living-room space might be located on the stage (if one exists) or in a quiet corner away from high-traffic areas and near an electrical outlet so music can be played there. The space can be made to feel cozier by using soft furniture such as beanbag chairs (which are easy to store), folding camp chairs, pillows, rugs, a storage bin serving as a coffee table, and even artificial plants to soften the space and create a greater sense of seclusion. If the storage space is large enough, or if some equipment can remain on the stage, one might include an overstuffed chair or loveseat as long as it is on castors for easy movement.

3. Kitchen area

Educators should also negotiate for use of kitchen space if a kitchen is located close to the gym or hall. As indicated earlier in the chapter, this space is important because it encourages children to take on responsibilities for snacks, and is a casual environment for spending time with friends. When the program is located in a gym or hall this area becomes even more important, because it provides a space where children can easily access water, be it for experimentation purposes or for clean-up.

Areas for art and science exploration are often messy, and will need to be thoroughly cleaned each day. If a messy activity is taking place, large drop-cloths simplify the cleaning up. If a water source isn't close at hand, a bucket of water should be made available to contain the mess to a limited area. If the space being used has direct access to the outdoors, the educators could move many art and science activities outside during good weather, further simplifying clean-up.

Both art and science activities will require table space, resource materials space, and storage space. Although it would be ideal for the tables to reflect those found in a home, the tables in shared space will have to be collapsible so they can be moved in and out of storage. For these areas a less institutional touch can come from the furniture used to store resources or unfinished projects. If a cabinet is used in this area, it might include the foldout table, be decorated with children's artwork, and have shelves with wicker baskets to store supplies. Like the cabinet, the containers used to store uncompleted projects could be personalized to each child, and the storage unit itself could be decorated like the cabinet. For activities that aren't as messy (i.e., those that don't involve water) a rug with no pile can help define and brighten up the area, while still being easy to clean up (it just needs to be shaken out).

4. Child's-room area

Getting private space can be a daunting challenge in a gym setting; however, corners of the room can become more private by using dividers, large artificial plants, and, if possible, wall hangings or banners to help deaden some noise and divide the space. Within the space, rugs and pillows can be used to create a softer, more relaxed feel and to reduce noise levels. Small pop-up tents with pillows are another way to create a private space where one can be alone to read quietly or spend time with one's best friend. If a stage is available, it is often used to create a more private area. As indicated earlier, the living-room space may be located there, and smaller private spaces are also suitable for this area.

5. Rec-room area

At first glance the rec-room area would appear to be the easiest area to create in a large shared environment like a gym. A gym or hall usually has lots of room for children to engage in more active play. It is easy to find the space to shoot hoops or have a game of dodgeball in a gym. However, it is also easy for these activities to interfere with the other things going on in the room. Children throwing a ball could easily hit the art area if the recreation area has not been designed appropriately. The ball could also destroy some of the activities which were identified as being associated with a rec room in a purpose-built environment. Activities such as block play, fort-building, or a board game could easily be damaged by a stray ball. In order to prevent this, the space being used for gym activities must be clearly divided from other areas of the room.

In some larger gyms or halls there may be a folding door that can be partially closed to prevent stray balls causing such accidents. In other large spaces the program may want to invest in some dividers or other visible barriers. In programs where dividers are needed, it is important that the children recognize that active play is not allowed to come too close to the dividers or the other play areas. It is also important that educators leave a clearly defined gap between the active play area and the other areas of the room to ensure safety.

In a space like a gym, fear of potential accidents may lead some educators to eliminate most gross motor activities. This should be avoided, however—children in out-of-school programs need to participate in these activities. If they are not provided with an area and materials to engage in active play they may discover less appropriate outlets for their energy.

Another typical type of play in the rec-room area is construction play. Unfortunately, although the space in a gym is an advantage, gyms have a couple of drawbacks for construction play. One is that the constructions have to be taken down each day; another is that the acoustics of the space can result in a lot of noise as the children use the materials, constructing and destructing. This area will require a rug that will deaden the sound without destroying the stability of the constructions. It also needs some dividers or storage units to help disrupt sound travel and identify the space. When deciding on the type of unit, the educator must consider that the children need to be able to put the blocks away quickly before moving the storage units into the storage room.

The rec-room space contains still another area. Children not engaged in the large motor activities and construction play may want an area to work on a puzzle, play games, or use smaller blocks such as Lego or Kapla. This area may be defined with tables, rugs, pillows, dividers, and cubes. A divider might hold the games or puzzles, and children might sit on a rug in front of the shelves while playing. Other children might prefer to lounge on pillows while using the top of a storage cube or bin as a playing surface, and still others might prefer to sit at the table to play or build. By providing the children with options for their play, the educator is giving them choices, allowing them to play in environments similar to those in the home and accommodating different learning styles.

6. Study area

The last area that needs to be addressed in shared space is the study area. This space is often non-existent in this type of environment. Educators may simply keep their files in a locked cabinet with the rest of the supplies, or there may be a small office in another area of the building that is not likely to be accessible while the program is in operation. Staff seldom have a designated space to relax while on break, although some programs are able to access a general staff room found in the building. Staff working in this environment will probably discover that they do most of their planning and documentation at home, where they can be comfortable and have the work space to complete the job.

Libraries Although educators might find the gym environment challenging, gyms do allow the educators the opportunity to add to the environment and transform it into the areas the children require. This task is much more difficult when sharing an environment where there are already well-defined areas, that are not what the educators require for their program.

Some programs may be located in the library of the school. This room is seldom set up to accommodate the messier types of play such as art and science, or the more active types of play such as construction and gross motor activities. This space is designed for one use, and educators may be told not to make many changes or bring much into the environment. Despite the inherent problems, educators should not assume that nothing can be done. Educators can negotiate some changes that might benefit both the out-of-school program and the library.

1. Living-room area

If the library has only tables and hard chairs for reading, the educators may negotiate the creation of a reading area for the library that could also double as a living room in the out-of-school program. Working with the librarian, the educators could determine a good reading area and look at supplying a couch, chairs, plants, and so on to soften the space. If the out-of-school program agrees to buy and care for the plants, both the library and the program benefit. The library becomes a more inviting place and the program has materials to help create an appropriate environment.

2. Kitchen area

Because a library is not suitable for messy activities, educators will have to look for other areas where they might take place. In a worst-case scenario the educators may have to negotiate use of the hallway outside the library. Although far from ideal, a hallway—with its tiled floors and lack of furniture—is relatively easy to clean up.

3. Child's-room and rec-room areas

Private space in a library may be created by using lots of pillows in a corner of the room, perhaps with some large plants surrounding the space. On the other hand, construction space may be difficult to provide in a library setting, since it requires open space for the children to build forts, for instance. If a more suitable space such as a gym is not available, the educators may have to limit the materials used in fort-building to items like blankets, which can be used with the tables already in the library. Because hollow blocks require large spaces, educators may have to limit block building to unit blocks, Kapla, and Lego, since these lend themselves to smaller spaces. The limited opportunities for construction indoors also means that the program will have to ensure that there are lots of opportunities for construction outdoors. Wood, Sonotubes, blankets, tape, and twine are great building materials for outdoor play, and will help compensate for the restricted construction and fortbuilding inside.

Shared Classroom Like libraries, shared space in a classroom will create challenges for the educator and will restrict the areas available to the children. In many schools where a kindergarten classroom may be in use for only half a day, this is the space educators are given. Although the advantage of this space is that the educator may have plenty of time to set up the room before school gets out and children arrive, it can also pose challenges. The first challenge the educator may face is that some of the children are embarrassed to have to come to this "baby" space while their friends go straight home. Because this attitude regarding the space is often held by many children in the school and can result in teasing, the educator needs to support the children in the program by using appropriate terms for the space. For example, the educator should never say to a child of this age, "Come down to the kindergarten room" or "See you in the child-care room." Something like, "See you in the after-school program" would be more appropriate, since it focuses on the activity rather than the space.

When sharing kindergarten space, other challenges are an environment where the furniture is too small for many of the children, and areas that are designed to appeal to pre-school, not school-age, children. Educators in these programs will have to work with the teacher to try to create space that can be used by both kindergarten and older children. This may be done by bringing couches and chairs into the room, and by adding a table and some chairs that are adult height. These additions will make the space more appealing to older children but also to many kindergarten children. The educator will also have to make sure that the materials brought into the room offer challenges for school-age children. In the art area, instead of using tempera paints on newsprint, educators can help children learn to use acrylics on canvas or watercolour pencils on proper art paper. In the dramatic play area, the educator might move items like the play stove against the wall, and instead of dress-up clothes provide fabrics and sewing equipment so the children can create their own costumes for plays.

Despite the identified disadvantages of a kindergarten classroom for school-age programs, there are also advantages. Although most kindergartens have an area for construction play, the blocks have been purchased by the school, and after-school educators won't automatically have access to them. Through negotiations, access might occur if the program agreed to split the cost of the blocks with the school, or to buy another set of blocks so that children in both the kindergarten and the out-of-school program have access to a larger supply of blocks.

Ideally, any out-of-school program should have some sole-use space, but educators working in the field know that this is not always possible. Educators using shared space have to find creative ways to develop a home-like environment and to store the materials needed for a successful program. Along with this creativity and the ability to design equipment to meet the needs of the program and the environment, educators using shared space must also have excellent negotiation skills in order to work successfully with other individuals using the space.

Making Sure All Children Can Access the Indoor Environment and Materials

The children in an out-of-school program come in all shapes and sizes, and with varying physical abilities. Just as educators take into account the size of children when buying shelves, they need to take into account children's muscle strength, co-ordination, mobility, vision, and so on when designing the physical environment. Educators should think of the equipment and materials they're providing in relation to the needs of the individual children in their program, and ask themselves questions like the following:

Can the tables accommodate wheelchairs and children of different sizes?

The program may have children ranging in age from six to twelve.

What types of containers are holding the materials?

Children with physical disabilities may have difficulty picking up containers if they are too large, too heavy, or do not have easy-to-grasp handles. More space on the shelves between the containers may be required for children to successfully maneuvre the containers.

Are the pathways open enough and clear of materials?

Children who use wheelchairs, crutches, or have difficulty walking will require pathways that are wide enough that they don't bump into dividers or other objects. Pathways also need to be clear of materials so the movement of a wheelchair won't be impaired, and children won't stumble. Children with visual impairments will also need to know that the pathways are clear in order to feel comfortable moving around the environment.

Are there materials to challenge children who vary greatly in their cognitive abilities?

Besides having children from a wide age range in out-of-school programs, educators might have children with a wide range of cognitive abilities. By providing a variety of loose parts and other open-ended play materials, educators can support all the children. For example, a six-year-old with cognitive delays may enjoy stacking blocks to create towers, while another child might use the blocks to build an elaborate fort system. In both cases the children are using the blocks successfully and are learning from the play. Less open-ended materials such as books and puzzles will suit a wide range of abilities. For example, books may range from picture books to novels, and puzzles from 12 to 500 pieces.

Can the available equipment and materials be adapted to make the environment user-friendly, or is additional equipment needed?

Children with visual impairments may require Braille on the outside of a container or textural cues to help them locate specific materials or areas of the room. Children who are deaf or have hearing impairments may need visual cues to let them know when **transitions** are occurring. Children with physical disabilities may need to use larger handles, and so on. Children with less visible disabilities, such as attention deficit disorder, may also require some adaptations. Some children may need to have areas that are less open in order to help them remain focused. If this is necessary, educators will have to find ways to create higher dividers or screens and, in shared space, will probably require more time to set them up.

The above are only some of the questions educators may need to consider in order to create a successful environment for all children in the program. Observations of the children, discussions with the children and their parents, and creative thinking are the key components for making sure educators meet the needs of all the children.

Creating a Safe Environment

In any out-of-school program educators must consider safety when creating the physical environment. As previously mentioned, educators should always make sure that the furniture used is sturdy (for instance, that cabinets have a low centre of gravity) and that if the equipment is movable it has castors.

Fortunately, school-age children don't require the same protection as younger children. Their cognitive abilities result in a better understanding of potential hazards and a better memory of what should be done to make something safe. If educators talk with school-age children about the damage water can do to wood, they can easily transfer that knowledge to how water spilled in the gym or brought in on snowy boots might damage a wooden floor. This is not to say that the children will always be conscientious about water, but it does mean that, when reminded, they know why they have to follow through. Often the educator won't have to finish the sentence before the child responds with, "Yeah, I know, it'll damage the floor!" and reaches for the mop located near the science area. Their cognitive skills also mean that children understand that they need to lock the castors on the shelves when they help set up the environment, or that climbing on the cabinet is not a wise thing to do.

School-age children can successfully engage in a variety of activities that require excellent eye–hand co-ordination and finger dexterity. This means that equipment like sewing machines, woodworking tools, cooking utensils, and so on can be used by children. If educators provide sufficient supervision and clear instructions on how to use the machines safely, they shouldn't have to worry that the children are going to get hurt.

The major safety issues in an out-of-school program probably arise not from a lack of skill or understanding of how to do tasks safely but from the social pressures being placed on children by their peers. Whereas toddlers may climb a shelf/divider because they have an urge to climb and don't think about potential hazards, school-age children may climb something unsafe because they want to prove to friends that they have the nerve to do it. To promote safety in the program, educators need to focus on the social factors influencing the risk-taking behaviours; the chapters on Community and on Behaviour Guidance will cover this topic.

THE OUTDOOR ENVIRONMENT

Imagine being in a yard with an asphalt surface, a grass playing field, one or two basketball hoops, and a climbing structure with sand beneath it. The yard is filled with children running about, yelling, screaming, bumping into each other, and throwing balls—in general, there is a feeling of chaos. Is this the kind of environment that you would like to spend time in by yourself or with your friends? Is this a space that readily provides areas for all the outdoor activities that school-age children enjoy? Do children using this space feel like they're playing in a neighbourhood, or like they're still in school?

Neighbourhood Play Spaces

In many neighbourhood play spaces children will find hidden lanes to run up and down or play skipping games. Children enjoy playing tag between fences, buildings, and houses; exploring hiding spaces; searching for insects; observing people; and planting vegetables and flowers. They enjoy eating popsicles and ice cream on the front porch, and riding bikes and scooters down dirt trails, on the sidewalk, and over grassy hills. School-age children will build incredible mazes, space ships, or forts from refrigerator boxes and large pieces of cloth in the backyard. In the winter children will skate on a backyard ice rink, while in the summer there's nothing better than running through waters sprinklers or playing in a pool.

Educators designing outdoor environments should try to reflect the ethos of the neighbourhood and offer similar play spaces, materials, and activities. When observing an outdoor environment for school-age children, the following questions may help evaluate the space. Does it evoke the neighbourhood play spaces? Does it reflect the diversity found among the children, their families, and the community? Does it reflect a rural and urban environment? Can the yard be used during all seasons and in all kinds of weather? In addition, when planning the outdoor space, educators need to keep in mind that school-age children are larger and faster than preschool children and therefore require much larger areas for active play. If space connected to the centre is not large enough for some of the more active play of school-age children, educators must locate and use nearby community space that will accommodate the needs of the children. This may require negotiations with community agencies but is necessary to provide the children with the physical movement they need.

Play Zones

The work by Steen Esbensen, who taught at the University of Quebec and spent years researching playgrounds, indicates that the outdoor play yard should be based on play zones, or neighbourhood play spaces. Play zones are broad (macro) play spaces that

Children combine different types of loose parts to create their own private fort.

consist of specific (micro) types of play, equipment, and materials. Educators should think about children's "neighbourhood play spaces" as consisting of the same elements as "play zones." When developing play spaces, educators need to determine how the children might use each one. Will they have the opportunity to combine different types of play? Does the space allow for the manipulation of different types of loose parts? Do children have the opportunity to explore and to use materials and equipment in different ways? For example, logs and stumps might be draped with cloth to be used as a campsite for a "Survivor" game.

Play zones should be scattered throughout the outdoor environment. Clearly defined pathways going in and out of each play space should be created to lead children to and from each play area. Pathways will also help to make sure that the play in one space does not interfere with play in an adjacent area. Spaces should be grouped in such a way that active play will not interfere with quiet play. Materials, loose parts, and props should be available, and children should be able to move them from one area to another, since combining materials will expand their learning, help them to make new connections, and develop their creative thinking. Children who are involved in a game of tag in the yard should have sufficient space so that they don't interfere with other children who might, say, be making rivers and building dams in another space.

Various playground surfaces can define the boundaries of play spaces, providing messages about what should happen in that area. An asphalt space with a hopscotch pattern painted on it is meant for small groups of children to be involved in social games with rules. A large open field is meant for large groups of children to play active games with rules.

Natural elements such as low cedar hedges or flowers can be used as edging along pathways.

Transition Spaces

Transitional areas lead the children into and out of different play spaces and from the building to the community. These areas should be open enough for large groups of children to move about, or for smaller groups to move into play spaces. The openness of transitional areas visually creates space to direct children through the yard and play spaces, and will help to reduce the likelihood of overcrowded areas or accidents. Transitional areas can be used to gather children for discussions, for parents to greet their children, or to serve snacks. A variety of tables, benches, and natural loose parts, such as stump stools, can be placed in these transitional areas so that children can sit around, participate in art activities or science experiments, or eat snacks. Also, administrative information, backpacks, and personal belongings can be kept in this area. Wooden tubs of flowers, or wooden planters, can be used as natural directional guides when children are leaving play spaces.

Pathways

Wandering, zigzag pathways throughout the yard can also help children make the transition from one area to another. Pathways also provide children with opportunities to ride bikes, run, or skip with friends. In addition, pathways can separate active and quiet play areas. For example, a cobblestone pathway between a sand area and basketball area will help to keep the diggers and ball players separated. Pathways can consist of paving stone, cobblestone, logs, asphalt, gravel, or sand.

Although outdoor environments should incorporate the various play zones and transitional areas, educators may find it challenging to ensure they do so when they share the outdoor space with a school or a community organization. Making changes may require negotiation and compromise to respect the needs of the different parties.

Materials in the Outdoor Environment

Outdoor Loose Parts Natural loose parts (such as rocks, boards, bamboo, sand, or snow) and man-made loose parts (like plastic foam core, plastic tubing, rope, or tape) should be available throughout the different play zones. Children need access to a quantity of loose parts in order to be creative and successful in their play experience. Because of the quantity needed, loose parts should be kept in large storage containers or stored in a specific area of the yard. Additional supplies can be kept indoors. When loose parts are in use, children need to be made aware of the safety issues. For example, if a plastic pipe were to be left out on the playing field it might be a danger to children playing an active game.

1. Logs, stumps, and poles
Logs, stumps, and poles are natural loose parts that should be available throughout the outdoor environment. Logs and stumps can be used as benches to sit on, as materials to build with (as when making forts), or as a decorative feature. Decorative stumps and logs can be painted, carved, glued, nailed, or decoupaged with photographs or found objects like shells, rocks, or tiles.

2. Boulders and rocks
Large boulders or rocks can also be used as dividers, and as places to sit and relax. Include a rock pile in your yard, but make sure it is kept away from the active play area and located near a manipulative play zone such as a sand area.

3. Water
Children should have access to water to drink and for their play. An outdoor faucet with a garden hose should be made available. If access to water—or volume of use—are issues, large plastic water containers with faucets can also be used. They can be kept beside the sand and garden area for messy play or for watering the garden.

4. Sand and Digging Pits
Every space should contain sand and a variety of tools to work with the sand. A variety of digging instruments, containers, vehicles, building materials, and loose parts should be made available.

Materials to Support Environmental Awareness and Appreciation of Nature

Natural materials, especially plants, can support the children's understanding of their environment and the role they play not only in their lives but in the larger ecosystem.

1. Vegetation
Trees, bushes, hedges, and vines can be used successfully in your layout. They can be utilized as barriers, visual aids for safety, and protection from the weather. Trees will help

A large section of a tree can be used as a bench, a roadway for cars, or a prop in a dramatic play.

A rock garden can help separate an active play area from adjoining areas.

to provide shade during the summer and protection from rain. Trees give the space a sense of height and connect children to the seasons and to the weather. The area under the tree can be turned into a play space by adding a blanket and play materials. Tents can be created by suspending cloth from branches or by using the trunk as a support. Fallen leaves in the fall can be used to create a leaf house or necklaces, and can be raked up and put on the garden for the winter.

During the winter months, bushes will add interest to the yard and berries for the birds to eat. Vines grown over gazebos or arched trellises will create another play space for children to use and another area for protection from the sun and rain.

2. Gardens

Gardens provide children with opportunities to connect with their natural environment. If the children plant sunflowers, for instance, they are creating their own play space. When the flowers grow, wildlife will begin to visit the sunflowers and children will be able to observe butterflies, finches, and squirrels. To promote this type of activity, educators need to find spaces where children can plant a garden and obtain the tools needed to work it. As with all materials, there need to be sufficient quantities so that several children can work together in the garden area.

Materials to Foster Social Interactions and to Allow for Privacy

Outdoor environments should have areas for children to socialize with their friends and peers. A small gazebo, a playhouse, or hammocks can encourage children to meet and spend time with friends, or curl up with a blanket and a book.

It is important to group tables, benches, and natural materials throughout the yard so children can create a number of areas to be with friends or to be by themselves. Try to develop at least one or two social or private spaces in each play zone.

Materials to Encourage Active Play

The outdoor environment should have space and materials to encourage active play. Educators need to remember when providing these spaces and materials that school-age children are larger than preschoolers, and have refined many of their physical skills. Baseballs that wouldn't be used with younger children are now appropriate to include with the outdoor materials, as long as the educators also make sure that mitts are available. The climbers will also need to be higher and more complex (with ropes, pulleys, or swinging bridges) than those available to younger children.

Loose parts such as boards, barrels, crates, Sonotubes, and sawhorses can promote a variety of large-muscle development and eye–hand skills. Given sufficient space for the children to work, and some method of storing their unfinished projects, these materials are very successful in the outdoor environment.

Materials to Encourage Fantasy and Dramatic Play

Fantasy and dramatic-play materials should be available in the outdoor environment so that children can perform plays, skits, and air bands. Having access to an electrical outlet will give children the option of listening to music, dancing, or singing their favourite songs.

The ideal yard should have an area for children to put on their performances. A variety of loose parts, construction materials, and building materials should be kept in various play zones for children to create props, costumes, and structures when involved in fantasy play experiences.

Art Materials

Just as they have indoors, children should have access to art materials when they're outside. In fact, many art activities can be done much more easily outdoors. Working with clay, tie-dyeing fabric, or painting are all activities that may be easier to clean up when done outside.

Storage

Every program needs to have secure storage for outdoor materials. The educators may need to negotiate with the school or community centre to get a storage space built outdoors, but it will be well worth the effort. When determining the storage space needed, educators must consider the sizes and quantities of the materials that need to be left outside. Besides a variety of balls, there will be numerous loose parts, sand, play materials, gardening supplies, scooters, and so on. If the storage unit is too small, the educators and children will end up having to drag most of their equipment outside each day, and as a result the variety and quantity of materials will naturally be limited.

Shared Space

When sharing the outdoor play environment with schools and the community, the educator will face several challenges. Most school play yards are designed to hold large groups of children at one time. Because of this, most outdoor school environments tend to be very open, large spaces, although many inner-city outdoor school environments are open, small spaces. Many of these environments are designed with a large asphalt area and a large grassy playing field. The focal point of many outdoor environments is the metal or plastic brightly-coloured play structure. Typically, sand is found under the play structure. Most of these yards have very few natural green elements and protected areas.

When negotiating with schools or communities for changes to play yards, educators must be aware of the different needs of the various programs and provide officials with concrete evidence that changes can benefit both groups. M.S. Rivkin's book *The Great Outdoors: Restoring Children's Rights to Play Outside* provides excellent information on how to transform schoolyards into environments that are more natural and provide a greater variety of spaces, while also helping to eliminate the conflicts and bullying that can occur when children have limited play opportunities.

Although creating an appropriate yard is more difficult when the space is shared, it is important that educators take the time to do this. After having spent most of the day in the school environment, children need opportunities to be outside, to move about actively, and to connect with their natural environment. There are many movements to create greener schools, and educators need to discover what is happening in their community and access these resources to create an outdoor environment that truly meets the needs of school-age children.

Making Sure All Children Can Access the Outdoor Environment

Just as educators have to think about individual children's needs and abilities when setting up the indoor environment, they will have to ask themselves similar questions when planning the outdoor environment, and work with parents and other professionals to create an environment all children can access. Some of the questions to ask are:

- Can the tables and climbers accommodate wheelchairs? (Specialized climbers are available that allow wheelchair access.)
- Can all children access all outdoor play areas?
- Can all children access the storage area where the outdoor equipment and materials are kept?
- Are the storage containers easy to manipulate?
- Are the pathways open enough and clear of materials?
- Are there materials to challenge children who vary greatly in their cognitive abilities?
- Are additional or adapted equipment and materials required to make the environment more user-friendly?

INVOLVING CHILDREN AND FAMILIES

Indoor and outdoor environments should be inviting to children and their families. In order to achieve this, educators need to include the children and their families in the development of the environment.

Smooth surfaces that lead to various play spaces help children with physical disabilities access the yard.

Educators can use a couple of methods for involving children and families. An indirect method is talking to them to find out what they like, and then incorporating these ideas into the environment. A more direct method involves asking children and families specifically what materials or equipment they would like to see in the environment, and how they think this could be accomplished. Many parents may not want to be very involved in the planning, but many children will be very interested in helping to create physical spaces that they will enjoy and for which they will have a sense of ownership.

Involving the children may occur informally, on a daily basis, when educators allow children to rearrange the room by moving dividers and plants to create new or larger play spaces as needed. In one school-age program we observed, a group of children were sitting on the rug playing a game on the coffee table. Because this was the living-room area, there were a couch and two chairs right behind the children. Lea and Fatima were building a fort/house behind the couch and decided they needed the couch to anchor the blanket they were using as a roof. The two girls leaned over the couch and asked Mark, who was sitting against the couch, if they could move it. When Mark said he didn't care, the girls shifted the couch about half a metre, draped one end of the blanket over the back of the couch and the other end over some boxes they had stacked up. Once this was done they disappeared into the house where they could be heard discussing what they needed for their home.

More formal planning can occur during group meeting times. During these meetings educators and children discuss problems they are encountering with the physical environment. For example, some children may indicate that they cannot talk to their friends because the children making forts are too noisy. Once a problem has been identified, the educators and children can brainstorm ways to solve it and agree to change the environment accordingly.

Group meetings are also good places to find out what new materials and equipment need to be purchased. After spending some time discussing what the children are interested in and what they want to do in the program, the educator and children can determine what materials they would like to purchase, the feasibility of the purchases, and how to go about doing it.

When educators involve children in the planning of the physical environment, children have opportunities to develop numerous skills, such as negotiating and problem-solving. It also provides opportunities for increased independence and responsibility. By giving the children a sense of ownership (which includes responsibility) for the environment, the educators will find that many children will demonstrate a greater willingness to set up and care for it. This is especially desirable in a shared space, where the environment has to be set up and taken down each day.

THE HOME-LIKE ENVIRONMENT AND THE THEORIES THAT SUPPORT IT

Creating a home-like environment that reflects aspects of the children's backgrounds and involving children in the development of it finds support in various learning and development theories. IPM theory, for example, indicates that children learn more easily when they can make connections to things they already know, and by using materials they are

TABLE 5.4	Theories and the environment
Environmental Component Theories	**Theories**
Home-like atmosphere	Vygotsky, IPM, and Gardner
Child access to materials	Piaget, Vygotsky, Maslow, Erikson, and Gardner
Child involvement in creating the environment	IPM, Vygotsky, and Bandura
Flexible materials, equipment, and space	Piaget, Gardner, Erikson, and Vygotsky
Involving families	Bronfenbrenner, Vygotsky, Maslow, and Bandura
Using diverse materials	Vygotsky, Gardner, IPM, and Piaget

familiar with and involving them in the process, these connections can more easily be made. As well, Vygotsky's theory identifies the importance of language and culture in the learning process. By providing opportunities for children to work together to plan the environment and solve problems, and by incorporating materials that reflect diversity, educators are creating richer learning opportunities.

Table 5.4 highlights some of the components of the school-age environment and identifies some of the theories that will support each component.

Summary

School-age children spend a large part of their day in the institutional environment of the school, so they will generally not want the same institutional feel when they come to the out-of-school program. By creating a home-like environment, educators can help create a space that children will enjoy coming to. In order to create this type of environment, educators need to think about the various spaces children have available to them in their homes and how these spaces are used—that is, the materials and experiences that are located in each room. Keeping these home-like spaces in mind, educators and children determine how to create similar spaces in the program, regardless of the setting.

Student Learning Experiences

1. In groups of three, design a layout for a school-age program located in a gym. Identify materials that you would include in the space, and show how you would store all the materials and equipment.

2. Explain how developmental theories support the idea that school-age children should be involved in designing the indoor space.

3. Imagine that you are working in a school-age program where the educators have never allowed the children to help design the environment. You want to start involving the children. Discuss how you will begin doing so.

4. Your school-age program is located in a school and shares a play space with it. Design an outdoor play space that will meet the needs of the children. Explain how you will involve the school in the design process.

Review Questions

1. Describe what a living-room area in a school-age program would include, and back up your choices in terms of child-development concepts.

2. Explain why it is easier to design a home-like environment in a gym than in a library.

3. Identify four outdoor loose parts and explain how they can support the cognitive development of the child.

4. Identify three adaptations an educator might need to make to ensure that a child who is paraplegic and uses a wheelchair can participate in outdoor activities.

5. Identify three challenges you might encounter when sharing outdoor space with a school. Describe how you might overcome these obstacles.

CHAPTER 6

Introduction to Curriculum and Program Planning

OVERVIEW

Where do educators start when they want to create a school-age curriculum that children will find challenging and enjoyable? Although the program philosophy will influence an educator's curriculum approach, there are aspects of planning that will occur regardless of one's approach to curriculum.

When developing a curriculum educators must keep in mind the legislation governing school-age programs, the places children spend their time outside the program (the school, the family, the local community), and the children's developmental levels. This background knowledge will influence what educators do regardless of their curriculum approach.

Since the 1970s many researchers and educators have identified *time, space, materials*, and *people* as essential components of child-care programming (Nash, 1979). In school-age programs each of these four components is influenced by each type of background knowledge outlined above (*legislation, school, family, community,* and *development*) and this in turn will affect the development of the curriculum.

In order to create a program that will meet the needs of the children, the educators will have to observe the children to determine how individual backgrounds and curriculum components will influence the program. Once the educator is aware of the skills and interests of the children and families attending the program, she will be able to combine this with her knowledge of the four curriculum components (time, space, materials, and people) to set goals and create learning experiences that will excite the children and support their development and learning.

INFLUENCES OF BACKGROUND KNOWLEDGE AND THE "FOUR CURRICULUM COMPONENTS"

When planning, curriculum educators always need to be aware of the time required to complete the learning experience, the space required, the materials needed to make it a success, and the people required to support the learning. If, for example, the educators want to plan a cooking activity, they will need to consider how long it will take to complete, the equipment needed (for instance, will each child need individual baking utensils, or can it be done as a group?), the space required and available, the number of children that can be involved at any one time, and the role of the educator in the process.

If children come to the program without any previous cooking experience, the educator will also need to introduce them to the various utensils, and show them how to use a recipe, before jumping into the cooking activity. Or there may be a child with severe food allergies, and the educator will have to adapt recipes to maintain a safe environment and learning experience for the children.

The following sections will identify some of the ways that background knowledge (legislation, school, family, community, and development) can influence the four curriculum components (time, space, materials, and people) and the educators' curriculum planning.

Legislation

Educators must have a thorough knowledge of provincial legislation on school-age programming,

119

since it will affect the curriculum and its delivery in school-age programs. In Ontario, for example, the *Day Nurseries Act* requires school-age programs to provide children with opportunities to help plan curriculum.

Educators and programs are legally responsible for following provincial regulations. In provinces and territories with little legislation on school-age programs, educators will be guided mainly by their knowledge of development and understanding of how children learn. When educators know the legislation, they will be able to plan their curriculum within the framework of their legal obligations.

Time If legislation requires some involvement of the children in curriculum development, educators will require time to meet with the children to determine what they want in the curriculum. Educators may also need to be flexible with the time allotted to this type of experience, since this will be a new skill that the children are developing.

Sufficient time will also be necessary to allow children increased opportunities for independence. For instance, a group of children may decide to put on an air band show. In this situation it would be easy and much less time-consuming for the educator to take the lead role and direct the development of the show, but to support the children's increased independence and responsibility around planning the educator will have to take more of a facilitator role. The children will need to make the decisions and this of course will take time as they share their ideas, negotiate with each other, change their minds as to what should happen, and so on.

Space Legislation in many provinces requires that the premises in which after-school programs are held have a minimum area of space per child. Because space can be very expensive, many programs may provide only the minimum required by law. In order to provide the types of learning experiences the children need, many educators will have to find creative ways to use the space, or find ways that they can share additional space with other institutions.

Materials Legislation is usually very vague in this area, which allows educators leeway to purchase the types of materials their group needs and to involve the children in the decision-making process, thus increasing their independence, sense of responsibility, and commitment to the program.

People Legislation will provide regulations concerning adult/child ratios and qualifications of staff. It may also identify some types of interactions that are required (such as behaviour-guidance approaches). Such legislation will affect the curriculum. Because the ratios are higher (1:15) for school-age than for younger children, educators will need to make sure that many activities can be done without a lot of adult supervision. This may be done by making sure there are clear instructions, and by making sure more knowledgeable peers can help children who are just developing the skills.

Regulations around behaviour-guidance practices and increased independence may also affect curriculum, since educators may need to help children learn conflict-resolution skills in order to successfully solve conflict.

Issues Regarding Legislation One issue that arises is that regulations governing licensed school-age programs differ from those regulating the educational system. Many families and children have difficulty understanding why licensed centres won't let children do what they can do in school.

In provinces where there is little legislation for school-age child care, there is a concern regarding the lack of standards for programs, and little control over issues such as curriculum or the qualifications of the individuals working with the children.

School

In the afternoon, children arrive in the program after having spent five to six hours in a school environment. During the school day the majority of the children's time has been spent in teacher-directed cognitively oriented activities. Most of these activities require few gross motor movements and the peer interactions encouraged are directed to the goal the teacher has identified (such as working in pairs to solve a science problem).

When children arrive from school they are coming from a competitive environment. Marks are used to determine how well children are meeting the curriculum goals, and school-age children are quick to compare marks and identify who is or is not skilled in each subject area. Unfortunately these comparisons often lead to ridicule and teasing of certain children. Competition is not found only in the academic aspects of the school but is frequently present in physical activities. Many sports activities emphasize winners and losers rather than simply focusing on skill development. In an after-school program it is important to present a variety of experiences that foster both skill development and co-operative activities.

Finally, schools often have strict policies around behaviour, such as a "zero-tolerance" approach to bullying. Although children may have initially been involved in identifying class rules, once these rules are in place many children feel that adults in the school seldom listen carefully to what all the participants have to say when a conflict occurs, and that they often enforce rules without thinking about the uniqueness of a particular situation. Children will also indicate that bullying is a common occurrence in the playground and in the school, and some of the children coming to the after-school program may be bullies or victims of bullies.

Educators need to be aware of what the children in their program are encountering during the school day; know how the school day is affecting the children; know how the after-school program can work with the school to complement their academic learning, and know how to support children who are struggling in the school environment. When educators use this knowledge in conjunction with the four components of programs, they can plan an after-school curriculum that both complements and supports the school.

Time Since the school day does not allow children many opportunities to simply spend time with their peers, educators in after-school programs will incorporate time for this into the curriculum. This can help children develop a sense of belonging, which, according to Maslow, is an important need of all individuals. Because children learn from each other (Bandura, Vygotsky) such opportunities will help them develop social skills (like understanding how tone of voice influences how one interprets a statement). Spending time this way will also support cognitive and language skills. As the children share jokes, they obtain a better understanding of subtleties in language, and increase their vocabulary. As they discuss what they were doing in school, they end up reviewing some of the content and may even help a friend understand a difficult concept. Simply by sharing their interests and personal discoveries, they are expanding each other's knowledge base (although parents and educators may not want to learn what some of this knowledge is about!).

The after-school curriculum also provides children with sufficient free time for them to make their own decisions. In school, most decisions have been made for them, but the ability to make meaningful decisions and then act on those decisions is an important skill.

Children need opportunities to work together in a non-competitive environment.

Along with helping children learn some decision-making techniques, educators need to provide them with time to develop this skill. An example of this is children creating their own game. Watch them try to come up with a plan for the game. By the time decisions have actually been made there may not be enough time to start the project. Many educators can anticipate this outcome, and want to jump in and help them quickly come to a conclusion. However, for children to learn how to process all the information needed to come to a decision, they often require time rather than assistance.

During the school year children will attend the school-age program in the morning before school, and in the afternoon after school. There are many variations to the time that children are in school and in school-age programs. In some school-age programs children will go to the program for lunch, while in other programs they will have lunch at school.

An example of the school and school-age program schedule might look like the following:

7:00 to 8:30 – School-age before-school care

8:30 to 3:00 – School

3:00 to 6:00 – School-age after-school care

The time children are in school will affect the amount of time for participating in community activities, playing outdoors, practising behaviour-guidance strategies (Chapter 9), and planning activities. The time and schedule guides the planning for snacks, participating in community meetings, opportunities for indoor and outdoor play, implementing long-term projects, and visiting the community. With limited time it is more difficult to plan and implement field trips, and long-term projects may require an extended period of time. Projects that may take two months to complete during summer programs might take up to six months or more to complete during the school year.

During summer holidays and during Professional Development (PD) days, children could potentially be in the school-age program from 7:00 a.m. to 6:00 p.m. With more time to schedule, educators have larger blocks of time to plan activities and play experiences, and more flexibility during the day to implement activities, clubs, and field trips. Children will have more time, flexibility, and freedom, as well as the opportunity to relax and read books, build forts, participate in leisure activities, exercise, be by themselves, develop new friends, and be with friends. Because there is more time in the program, parents may have more opportunities to participate, such as being part of a field trip or activities.

Space During the school day, the space children have to move around in is often limited. The classroom is full of desks or tables, and much of the work requires fine motor, not gross motor, movements. Keeping this in mind, educators in after-school programs need to make sure that children have sufficient space to use their entire bodies as they engage in a variety of activities. They need space to run, jump, twirl, and so on. They need space to participate in an activity lying down rather than having to sit on a chair as they have been doing for most of the day.

After spending most of their day in a classroom of 20 or 30 children with no opportunity to be alone, they also need space to get away from others. The school-age curriculum needs to include activities that children can do on their own if they wish.

Additional space may be required for Professional Development days and during summer holidays. Educators will need to develop positive relationships and open communication with the schoolteachers, custodial staff, and administrators in order to negotiate additional space. During these time periods programs will have more opportunities to use other spaces in the school, such as the library, gymnasium, or science lab. Use of space other than that designated for the program can also occur throughout the school year. The authors have observed some programs expanding from the school-age space to the halls of

Not all activities should require children to work at tables.

the school when children are working on specific projects, such as creating a mural or practicing a play.

It is important to note the need to communicate to the school administration your intent of using other school space. In some situations, a contract and financial remuneration will be required for other space. If other programs, such as recreational programs, are using the school space, it is important to negotiate with the program how the space will be used and the needs of each program.

Materials During the school day the children spend most of their time with paper, pencils, and books. In the after-school program the educators will ensure that a wide variety of outdoor and indoor materials are available, because the curriculum should support children's learning in a variety of ways (Gardner, Bandura, IPM). Many of these materials will be open-ended in nature so that children, alone or with peers, can explore them and use them in a variety of ways (Piaget, Vygotsky). Loose parts (such as plumbing pipes or machine parts), construction materials (like wood or plastic blocks), and art supplies (for instance, clay and fabric) will complement and expand the learning that occurs during the school day.

During the summer holidays and PD days school-age children may have the opportunity to use school gym material, such as gym mats, basketballs, or floor hockey equipment. It is important to negotiate with school administrators for the use of their materials and work with them to develop a plan for dealing with lost or damaged ones. One school-age program used a portion of its equipment budget to purchase badminton rackets, floor hockey nets, and small balls to be used by the school and school-age children.

Some children may find most of the learning experiences in school either too challenging or not challenging enough. To support learning for these children, educators must create experiences where the children can be challenged and successful. In order to do this, educators must make sure there are appropriate materials available for all the children (such as easy games for some children and more complex ones for others).

People   During the school day more learning occurs alone than in groups. Educators in the after-school program ensure that most learning experiences offer children the option of working either with peers or on their own, and recognize that often children need the support of others to learn (Vygotsky). Educators will also plan a variety of learning experiences so that all children have opportunities to share their unique skills. During the school day it is usually the academically oriented children who are seen as skilled. By providing a variety of learning experiences in the after-school program, a child who may not be seen as skilled in the school environment may have a chance to become the more knowledgeable peer who facilitates the learning of others.

Finally, during the school day the children are in classes, where the teacher's role is often that of director. In the after-school program the educator's role is usually that of facilitator, so that children might have more decision-making opportunities and freedom of choice.

With the expanded hours and schedule during the summer holidays and PD days, your budget may allow you to hire more program staff. The program may have the opportunity to hire staff with various cultural and educational backgrounds, based on the needs of the program, such as music expertise, recreational and health care education, or youth work. If programs feel the need for a recreational component in their program, hiring a staff with a recreational background may be desired.

Issues: School Experiences and the After-School Curriculum   One of the most common issues is whether or not after-school programs should deal with the academic curriculum the children are receiving during the day. Some programs and parents think that it is important to use the time to allow children to complete homework, while other programs and parents insist that children need a break from school, and that homework can wait until the child gets home. The approach taken may well be determined through discussions with families. In many centres a quiet area is provided where children can complete homework if their parents have requested this, and the educators provide some support for the children but do not spend a lot of time helping them complete the homework.

Because many centres want the curriculum to complement the school day rather than duplicate it, they focus on recreational types of activities and avoid the more academic ones, such as science. Other centres, while focusing on non-academic activities, encourage children to use their academic skills. For example, when woodworking, the educator will encourage the children to design what they want to make (using their graph skills), list the materials they need (writing, spelling), and take measurements (a number of math skills) before cutting the wood. Whether a program chooses to avoid academic-related activities or to support academics, the learning the children receive in school is influencing what happens in the after-school program.

Family and Culture

A high-quality school-age curriculum must be sensitive to families and cultures. In order for this, educators must be aware of how family and cultural differences might affect the curriculum provided. The educators also need to be aware of, and be prepared to deal with, conflict that might arise between the centre's philosophy and values and a family's values.

Time When planning the curriculum and scheduling necessary routines, educators recognize that a child's family background can influence the amount of time needed to complete some activities. For example, for some families eating is a very social event and one that should not be rushed. A child with this background may spend more time at the snack table than some of the other children. In this case the educator may want to ensure that an open snack time is provided, instead of scheduling the snack just before all the children go outside.

Space Space may be influenced by the family background of the children. Some families and cultures require fairly large personal spaces. If some children in the program require more personal space, educators may need to look at how many children are using the locker/cubbie area at one time, and plan routines and transitions accordingly. It may also influence the number of children expected to share a table when doing an activity.

Materials The backgrounds of the children in the program should be reflected in materials found in the centre. Not only do these materials support the development of positive self-esteem by acknowledging the importance of the child's background, but they also facilitate learning, since children learn new information better when it is linked to things they already know (IPM theories). When program materials incorporate items from various cultures (for instance, fabrics, games, or drums) children share their knowledge with their peers, comparisons are made, and all children learn more than if only the materials from one culture were present.

People Family diversity means some children will be more comfortable learning through observation and will expect the educator to determine what they should learn and when they should learn it, while other children will be more comfortable with a very active decision-making role and may see themselves as peers with adults. When planning group meetings educators will have to make sure that the procedure helps both groups of children learn to participate effectively. The educator may need to support the quiet children's efforts to speak out and encourage the listening skills of the more vocal children.

Educators may also find that some families will have different expectations for daughters and sons. Daughters may not be expected to participate in sports activities with boys. This should not mean that the girls simply sit out. What it does mean is that the educators may have to plan a variety of activity options for the children including, at times, options that allow for gender segregation.

Family diversity may also influence the choice of community members brought in to support the curriculum. For example, if some of the children celebrate a festival that educators are unfamiliar with (Chinese New Year, say), and families have indicated that they would like it included in the curriculum, educators may invite family members or someone from the community to share their expertise.

Issues Around Family and Culture One of the most common issues around curriculum and family sensitivity is whether or not holidays that have religious connections should be celebrated. Many educators worry that such celebrations will offend some families and thus avoid celebration of any holidays, while others make sure that only the secular aspects of the holidays are celebrated, and still others make sure that celebrations occur equally around holidays from a variety of religions and cultures. Which of these approaches is best? It may depend upon the families in the program. Programs that are sensitive to families should discuss the celebration of holidays with the families. Such a discussion could be part of the intake process, but it should also be periodically discussed, since a parent may change his or her mind on this issue. When the educator takes the time to discuss issues like this she may be surprised at the answers. In one school-age program the non-Christian parents did not object to the children participating in Christmas celebrations because all the celebrations were secular in nature. This same group of parents did, however, object to Halloween celebrations because of the apparent disrespect for the dead involved. The educators had not expected this response, since from their perspective Halloween seemed a more secular, light-hearted festival than Christmas.

Family diversity may also influence the curriculum with respect to competition. Many families think that competition is good for school-age children and expect it to be present in the curriculum, especially in sports. In a high-quality school-age program educators must take into account not only the family expectations but also the research on competition. By knowing the children in the program as individuals, educators become aware of which children can deal with competition and which cannot, and will provide options for the latter to reduce their exposure to competitive situations. In the area of sports, educators can help the children work on skill development rather than simply focusing on competitive games. Indoors, board games are usually competitive in nature; however, the educators can emphasize the fun of playing rather than the winning. They can also provide comments that indicate how much luck is involved in winning a game. Focusing on the aspect of luck helps the children realize that something other than ability on their part can determine the outcome of a game. Besides de-emphasizing winning, educators should also provide school-age children with co-operative board games (such as "Mountaineering," by Family Pastime), so they can experience working together to win rather than always competing with each other.

In the area of family diversity, a school-age program can sometimes accommodate families' expectations and requests, but at other times the educators may need to discuss with the parents why the staff's expectations may result in conflict with parental expectations. For example, some families may not expect their sons to prepare food or clean up. Because the staff are encouraging children to take responsibility for their actions and to become more independent, they expect all children to clean up when they have finished an activity and to help prepare and serve snacks. In this case the educator may need to explain to the family why the expectations are in place, the learning that occurs, and what could happen with the group if some children did not have to take on these responsibilities. Although the program cannot always change parents' expectations, discussion can help both educators and parents to better understand one another's perspective, and help the child realize that what is appropriate behaviour in the program may differ from what is appropriate behaviour at home.

Community

The average school-age child's world is much larger than that of most preschoolers and, according to theorists such as Bronfenbrenner, this will have an impact on what occurs in all areas of a child's life, including the school-age program.

When discussing community, educators need to remember that just as families are very diverse, the communities the children and the program are involved in will also be very diverse, and this diversity will affect the curriculum developed.

Time When developing curriculum, educators will need to consider the time required to take children out into the community or to bring the community into the program. Educators frequently think about trips to the library or swimming pool, but when working with school-age children they will also need to think about trips to the hardware store to price out what they need to buy for the woodworking club, or trips to the fabric store to find out what they can afford to buy to create their costumes for the play. They also need time to plan these trips with the children so that they are all prepared for the experience.

Space When educators bring the community into the centre they will have to plan for this, and part of the plan will involve space. If a musician is coming in to demonstrate how to play a keyboard, the educator needs to create a space that will allow the musician to interact with the interested children while not interfering with other learning experiences that may be occurring.

Materials The community will also influence the types and quantity of materials available for programming. A program in a rural community may have access to a wide variety of natural materials, while an urban program may have more access to recycled materials (such as broken tiles or cardboard boxes). The ethnicity of the surrounding community will also have an impact on the materials in the centre. If it is located in a community with few recent immigrants, the materials donated to the centre or bought in the community may be very traditional in nature. On the other hand, a centre in a community with lots of recent immigrants may find it easier to obtain materials that reflect a wide range of ethnic backgrounds. When developing curriculum, educators may find that the more diverse materials often provide greater curriculum options (for instance, discovering how things are made, where they come from, and comparing and contrasting different types of materials).

People Educators also need to consider bringing people from the community into the program. When educators get to know the community they will find that there are many skilled and interesting individuals who might be willing to share their skills with the children. Perhaps there is a musician who is willing to donate some time to the music club. Perhaps there is a grandparent who can come in and teach some of the children to knit. Bringing in experts will enhance the curriculum offered the children. When doing this, however, educators need to check if there are any local and provincial regulations regarding volunteers (such as police record checks).

Development

In all of the developmental domains, school-age children demonstrate skills and abilities that are uncommon in younger children (see Chapter 4); they also engage in different kinds of play (see Chapter 10). Educators working in school-age programs must make sure that the curriculum they develop acknowledges the skills, abilities, and interests that the children possess. When school-age children are bored and complain of having nothing to do, they are more likely to display apathy or exhibit challenging behaviour. To prevent this from happening, educators need to examine the program to determine if they are creating a learning environment and experiences that motivate and challenge the children. They need to see if they are providing the time, space, materials, and people that school-age children need.

In addition, educators need to plan curriculum for children with diverse developmental needs. Some of the children in the program may have physical disabilities, while others may have developmental disabilities, or may be gifted.

Time   School-age children do not develop skills overnight. They need time to practise the skills they are working on, and educators need to provide them with this time. Whether learning to knit, building a fort, or developing soccer skills, time is required. All children learn at different rates, and children with physical or developmental disabilities may require extra time to complete activities or learn specific skills. Educators should not assume that by the end of a given period, all children should have had sufficient exposure to a topic, materials, and so on. Educators need to use their observation skills and conversations with the children to determine when they have had enough time to explore a topic or develop a skill.

School-age children are more goal-oriented than younger children, and therefore require time to complete projects that they start. When painting, a child is not satisfied with simple experimentation but will want to complete a picture, and will need the time to do so to her satisfaction. This also applies to more complex activities. Be it sports or science "experiments," the activity will be composed of many elements, and each element will take time. When developing the curriculum, educators must provide sufficient time for children to complete these more time-consuming and goal-oriented activities.

Space   When planning learning experiences, educators need to ensure that the space is easily accessible to all the children. For example, the educator arranging a small group meeting with children to plan the snack menu must ensure that the child in a wheelchair can actually get the chair up to the small table where the meeting is being held.

When planning curriculum, educators need to remember that, physically, many older school-age children may be as large as some adults, and will require sufficient space to engage in the activities.

Because peers are increasingly important to school-age children, the curriculum must include space for children to work together in both large and small groups as well as space to simply spend time together.

School-age children need activities in which they can use their whole bodies, and understand their bodies in relationship to the space around them, thus developing spatial awareness. Programs help children develop these skills and abilities when they include the activities and the space for children to take risks in a safe environment. This can be seen in programs that provide the space and opportunities for children to climb a variety of materials and engage in activities like tumbling. When providing experiences to encourage the use of the whole body, one must remember not only the size of the children but also the great variations in terms of physical co-ordination and balance, and make sure that the space is appropriate for all the children. For example, a child who easily loses her balance and has very poor co-ordination may require more space for some of the activities, and perhaps more safety measures than those provided to the other children.

Children need opportunities to develop their interests.

Materials Because educators will be developing curriculum for a wide range of ages and skill levels, they need a variety of materials that range from simple to complex, open ended to structured. If there are children with physical disabilities in the program educators may also need to make some adaptations to materials, such as making a larger-than-normal mitre box so the child can saw successfully.

People   School-age children are logical thinkers and can demonstrate logical decision-making abilities. Educators must therefore be able to develop curriculum that supports the cognitive skills the children are demonstrating. In the art area, educators must be able to support the children's desire to learn specific art techniques (such as shading). A skilled educator will take the time to show the interested child how it is done and then encourage the child to practice it himself. Although educators recognize that the children still need time to experiment with materials, they also recognize that children want to be taught specific skills to help them with their more goal-oriented projects.

Educators in these programs will also take the time to help children with limited social skills develop abilities, such as socially acceptable ways to enter a group, so that they become more accepted by their peers. In addition, if there are children with special needs in the program, the educators may need to call on the expertise of psychologists, speech and language specialists, and other professionals who provide support for children with special needs.

Educators should take advantage of the fact that many children enjoy learning from more competent peers. Encouraging peers to support each other's learning is an important aspect of school-age programs.

Issues Regarding Development   Many issues arise around development and the school-age curriculum. Some have to do with the amount of direction given to children, while others are about the content of the curriculum. The following are some of the more common issues.

Some argue that educators should not be teaching children specific art techniques, and that children should instead simply be given the materials to explore and use the way they want. Advocates of skill training do not disagree with providing materials for children to explore, but argue that the majority of school-age children want to learn specific skills, and some skills will not necessarily be learned without the support of a more knowledgeable individual. Few would argue that children should not be expected to learn to read on their own, so why should children be expected to learn to draw without the help of others? Educators must remember, however, that teaching children how to draw is not the same as drawing for the child. Many children who lack confidence in their drawing abilities will try to get the educator to draw an object for them. The skilled educator will use this opportunity to help the children learn how to draw the object and offer encouragement as they develop the skill.

Another issue is the amount of time the curriculum devotes to developing the physical skills of children. The Canadian Fitness and Lifestyle Research Institute (CFLRI) and the Canadian Paediatric Society have done research on childhood fitness that indicates that Canadian children spend too little time in physical activities. "Two-thirds of Canadian children are not sufficiently physically active for optimal growth and development" (CFLRI, 1999), and recent reports indicate that the fitness level of children has continued to decline. In many schools the amount of time spent in physical activities is very limited (perhaps three gym periods a week), so it is crucial that the after-school curriculum complement schools in this respect by providing enough time for children to engage in a variety of physical activities and to develop physical skills. A well-designed curriculum offers opportunities to develop the co-ordination of large motor skills (such as dribbling and passing a soccer ball, or running games) and more generalized skills (such as providing heavy materials to build arm strength when erecting play forts, and structures on which to develop climbing skills). Educators in after-school programs need to be models for physical activity; as they engage in and demonstrate enjoyment of more active pursuits they will encourage many of the children to become more physically active.

PLANNING THE CURRICULUM

In a school-age program, children will spend most of their day exploring, manipulating, experimenting, and investigating materials and loose parts in their play environment. Children learn many things through play, such as how to develop friendships, negotiate conflicts, expand their thinking and language skills, develop their physical attributes, process moral dilemmas, and understand the values of society.

By observing children playing, the educator will be able to gather information about what they are interested in, how they are learning, and what they are learning. When the educator uses this knowledge to ask thought-provoking questions, to provide additional materials, loose parts, or resource books, to plan new learning experiences, and to link the children with community resources, she is developing, planning, and implementing a curriculum. As the educator asks the appropriate questions, provides the appropriate materials, assists in supplying resource books, and supports or expands the learning experiences, she is helping the children achieve a variety of learning and developmental goals.

A few years ago in a school-age program where we were observing children, we were able to see how the Pokemon cartoon show motivated the children to re-enact many of their favourite characters. They used their imaginative abilities to assume the voices, the different powers, and the physical movements, to transform from one Pokemon to another. During a Pokemon play episode the children were having conversations about making costumes. Having observed this play and discussion, the educator gathered a variety of materials (cloth, paper, cellophane, crepe paper, tin foil, tape, string, and scissors) and placed them in the play environment. The children gravitated to the materials and proceeded to make Pokemon costumes. In this example the educator was able to use *knowledge* she gained through observations to develop a piece of the curriculum that supported goals such as eye–hand co-ordination, the development of problem-solving skills, and co-operation with peers. Using the four curriculum components, she provided the children with uninterrupted *time* to play, *space* to play, appropriate *materials*, and opportunities for the children to *interact with others*.

Steps in the Planning Process

Regardless of the curriculum approach used by the educators in a centre, there are steps that should be taken during the planning and implementation of the curriculum (see Figure 6.1).

Step 1 *Observations* that have been made in the past are used to help the educators determine the children's interests and learning goals, and the types of experiences and activities that would support the their ongoing learning.

Step 2 Educators, with or without input from children, will *brainstorm* possible learning experiences for the program. At this point, educators may indicate in which areas of the program certain experiences or activities might be located. If they are using a theme-based approach to curriculum this would play a role in identifying the appropriate learning

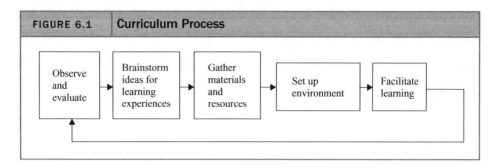

FIGURE 6.1   **Curriculum Process**

Observe and evaluate → Brainstorm ideas for learning experiences → Gather materials and resources → Set up environment → Facilitate learning

experiences. Educators analyze suggested learning experiences to determine how they might support the children's learning.

Step 3 Educators and children *determine the materials, equipment,and resources* needed to support the learning experiences. Once these have been identified, they need to be *gathered*.

Step 4 Educators *facilitate the setting up* of the environment to accommodate the learning experiences.

Step 5 Educators *facilitate the children's learning* as they engage in the experiences. This may be done by asking appropriate questions (both convergent and divergent), providing additional materials when needed, listening to children's comments, and answering questions, or simply by giving them the space to engage in the experience and trusting their ability to complete the activity without the direct intervention of the educator.

Step 6 Educators *observe and evaluate* what is happening as the children participate in the learning experiences and use this knowledge to try to determine what additional materials, resources, and learning experiences might be needed to help children further their learning. In a **theme-based curriculum**, this knowledge may be used to help determine activities that can be incorporated into the new theme.

Using Observations to Help Focus Curriculum Planning

In order for educators to obtain background knowledge, observations are crucial. It is through observation that educators learn what the children are really interested in, what their health is like, what their past experiences have been, what knowledge and skills they have, what their values are, and how their community, school, and family backgrounds influence them. Only after observing the children are educators in a position to set meaningful goals for them, and to create a curriculum that supports all children's learning.

When many educators think of observations, they envision jotting down notes on a piece of paper to be written up later and placed in the child's file or log book. Other educators think of the dreaded "**running record**" that they may have been asked to keep as a student or when trying to obtain detailed information on a child with special needs. Although observations include both of the above, they are much broader than that, and may include some techniques that are not automatically identified as observations.

Informal Observations Jotting down quick, **informal observations** about the children (always carry paper and pen) can help educators identify some of the interests and skills that the children have. An educator outdoors with the children may make a quick note that Hana kicks the soccer ball but never dribbles it, and that James has spent the entire time digging roadways in the sand with Trevin. Making notes like these and recording them so they can be reviewed when planning will help the educators create a curriculum designed for their group of children. After reviewing the notes, the educators may decide—with or without input from the children—to practise dribbling with them, and they might decide to put additional loose parts in the sandbox to encourage James to experiment with different ways of creating roads.

Anecdotes Anecdotes can be used to obtain similar information to that found in informal observations. Although **anecdotes** briefly describe what is happening in a particular situation, they contain more information than jotted notes, and educators often find this useful when trying to analyze the information later. For example, the educator may write in the anecdote that Hana kicks the ball when it comes to her and then comes to a stop and looks at children in other parts of the play yard before redirecting her gaze to the soccer game. With this information recorded, the educators may come to different conclusions regarding Hana and her soccer skills. They may conclude that the observation doesn't tell them what her skill level is, and instead that the issue is whether she is interested in soccer.

Checklists **Checklists** can be a quick way for educators to obtain information on the knowledge and skills the children have. There are a variety of checklists one can use, or educators can create their own lists of behaviours they want to observe. When using checklists educators need to be careful about connecting ages to different skills. Parents who see ages attached to skills may become very concerned if their child does not have the "age-appropriate" skill, forgetting that experiences affect how long it takes a child to develop a particular ability. If a child has never been encouraged to skip, one should not expect him to be able to do so straight away, even if he is eight.

Checklists are useful because they can help the educator determine what type of learning to support. An educator using a checklist might notice that the child appears to have difficulty with a variety of fine motor skills, but does well with gross motor activities. By noting the commonalities popping up in the checklist, the educator can now look at the situation more closely and take action. It may be discovered that the child seldom participates in activities such as painting, drawing, Lego, and crafts, which would help develop the fine motor skills. Instead, the child is usually found building large structures with the hollow blocks or playing sports in the gym or outside. If this is the case, the educators may want to plan activities for him to participate in that require the use of fine motor skills (such as taking minutes at team meetings, or documenting a project he is engaged in).

Event Samples Educators in school-age programs need to know and use a variety of **event-sampling** tools. As will be discussed in the behaviour-guidance chapter, many educators use the ABC (Antecedent, Behaviour, Consequence) observational method when dealing with behavioural problems. Sometimes educators might want to use the technique referred to as "charting" to determine how the various areas of the room are being utilized, while other times they may want to know the number of times that an event occurs per hour (**time sampling**). Or they may need to develop a more detailed event sample to look at a particular area or routine to determine if it is not working the way they expected it to. To analyze children's dressing routines, for example, the educators might devise a chart that records how long the quickest children wait for the slowest children; what activities are available to the children while they wait; what the educators do with and say to the children during the routine; the location of the routine; and how close children are to each other as they get dressed. By identifying what might affect the success of a routine and then observing what is happening during it, the educators develop a better understanding of how they can change it to produce a better learning experience.

Discussions/Meetings Through discussions and meetings with parents and children, educators can obtain a variety of information on the children. Discussions can help educators determine what the interests of the children are, since parents and children will often talk enthusiastically about topics that appeal to them, and what children find challenging. Along with informal discussions, educators should regularly have formal meetings with parents to discuss the child's skills and development, and to identify goals that the family might have. Such a meeting should occur during the registration process, and then regularly throughout the time the child participates in the program. The registration meeting ensures that the program is able to provide appropriate activities from the moment the child enters it, while the further meetings ensure that educators and families stay updated, and that the centre continues to provide interesting and challenging experiences for the child.

Technology Many educators find that photos and video cameras are enjoyable ways to observe and document what children are doing. If educators keep a small camera (preferably digital) in the room, they can quickly take photos of the children engaged in a variety of activities. Besides the obvious benefit of being able to share the pictures with families, educators can use these photos to identify what children are capable of and interested in. If children are given the camera and taught how to use it, educators will get added insights into the interests of the children, and may motivate the children to develop some additional skills, like creating a picture collage on the computer.

Video cameras, although useful, may be more difficult for educators to incorporate into the program. When videotaping, the educator must focus for a fairly long period on what is being taped, and so will not be as aware of what is happening in the rest of the room. In the school-age program the educator may be able to involve the children in this process. Children interested in using the camcorder could be part of a film club, and they could be taught how to use the camcorder effectively. Once they have this skill, the educator could enlist their help in taping various activities that could be viewed by the group and later analyzed by the educators.

The observational tool used will vary depending upon the equipment available, the information desired, the activity occurring, and the preference of the educator. All of the above tools will be used at one time or another in a school-age program, but just as important as taking the observation is what the educator does with the information obtained.

If the information is intended to help create a meaningful curriculum, it should not simply be put in the child's file. Educators might want to have a curriculum log book in which they can keep their daily observations, and to which they can refer when working on curriculum development. The organization of a log book would vary according to the needs of the educators involved. One book might have sections for development and interests, while another might be broken down into program areas. In some programs educators might use sticky notes to record informal and anecdotal observations so that they could simply be stuck into the log book. Other programs might prefer having the observations transcribed into the log book each day. How the book is organized is not nearly as important as the fact that the observations are available, and are used by the educators when planning the curriculum.

SETTING GOALS AND LEARNING OUTCOMES TO HELP FOCUS CURRICULUM

After observing the children and speaking to them and their parents about what they want out of the program, the educators are able to identify goals and learning outcomes that they are seeking. These may be general (for instance, "demonstrate leadership skills") or more specific (such as "demonstrate ball control skills for soccer"). Many goals or learning outcomes will apply to the entire group, with expectations being modified for individual children within the group. Other goals and learning outcomes may be very child specific, certainly so if the child has a special need.

The development of curriculum goals and learning outcomes should not be a make-work activity where they are identified, placed in the children's files, and never looked at again. The purpose of identifying goals and learning outcomes is to help educators plan programs that support children's learning.

For example, the educator who has identified "leadership skills" as a goal should keep it in mind while planning the curriculum and whenever she is interacting with the children. During community time, this educator will make sure that the children have opportunities to take on the role of the chair, the secretary, and so on. In contrast, an educator who fails to keep in mind the goal to develop leadership skills may always chair the group meetings and record the minutes herself. Although in both cases the children have opportunities to participate by sharing ideas or answering questions, only the children in the first situation are having real opportunities to develop their leadership skills.

USING RESOURCES AND MATERIALS TO FACILITATE CURRICULUM IMPLEMENTATION

Educators need to think creatively when trying to determine the appropriate materials and resources that will support their curriculum goals, such as developing *math skills*. As educators, we recognize that math skills are not limited to teacher-directed, paper-based activities. Many great curriculum goals can be supported through daily routines and hands-on learning experiences. When children are developing, implementing, and documenting a schedule for watering plants, they have the opportunity to practice *math skills* in a real-world context. When educators ask children questions about how different watering schedules can affect the plants and ask them to test out their hypotheses, additional math skills can be addressed.

USING QUESTIONS TO FACILITATE CURRICULUM IMPLEMENTATION

Along with having a willingness to learn with the children, educators need to know what kinds of questions to ask that will extend the learning experience and get the children to think. At times, educators will want to use convergent questions to help children recall specific information (for instance, "What colours did you mix together?"), while at other times, divergent questions (often referred to as "open-ended questions") will be needed to help generate creative thinking and solutions to problems (for example, "What else could you use to … ?"). Although convergent questions will not stimulate discovery and exploration like divergent questions, they can be useful in certain situations. Table 6.1 highlights the purpose of questions, types of questions, and examples of both convergent and divergent ones.

TABLE 6.1	Questions	
Purpose of Question	**Type of Question**	**Example**
Directing attention	Convergent	The educator can ask a question that directs the child's attention or allows the child to review what has happened. For example, when children are planting bean seeds and a child forgets to put the bean in the soil, the educator might ask the child where he planted his seed. By asking the question, the educator can help the child successfully complete the task without embarrassing him.
Recalling temporal order	Convergent	When the children are trying to build a fort and the roof keeps falling in, the educator might ask what they did first, next, *etc.* By walking through the steps, the children may discover a mistake that was made and be able to correct it.
Recalling prior conditions	Convergent	When children are keeping a garden and the tomatoes are ripening, the educator might ask if the tomato looks the same today as it did at the beginning of the week.
Eliciting predictions	Divergent	When children are experimenting with water and loose parts, the educator might ask how they think they can make the water move faster, or what would happen if … ?
Instigating discovery	Divergent	When children have taken apart the old machines but are now ignoring the various pieces, the educator might ask what else they think they could do with the materials or what would happen if … ?
Serving as a catalyst	Divergent	If the children are trying to develop a pulley system between two forts and it isn't working, the educator might ask: What else could you use, or what could you change to keep the rope from getting caught?
Probing for understanding and reasoning	Divergent	When the children are trying to make black paint, the educator might ask: Why do you think the colour looks more brown than black? What do you think would happen if you added white paint?
Reflecting feelings	Divergent	When children have been working on or have completed their fort, the educator might ask: What was the best part of the fort-building? How did you feel when the roof kept caving in? How did you feel when it finally worked?

EVALUATING CURRICULUM

In the curriculum process it is important that educators remember to record observations of the children and their responses during the implementation of learning experiences. These observations then need to be reviewed and analyzed. As educators engage in this review they are actually beginning a new cycle of curriculum planning, because they are using the information from these observations to determine the next learning experiences. This continuous cycle allows the educators to develop future curriculum experiences, to determine if goals have been met, and to plan for future goal development.

PLANNING CURRICULUM THAT LINKS TO THE SCHOOL

The experiences the children have in their school-age program will be and should be influenced by the experiences that are occurring in the school environment. These influences may be either indirect (when information from the school influences what a child does) or direct (when the educators and teachers actually work together).

Story: Mapping Exercise

During a community meeting, the children and the educator in a school-age program were having discussions about planning the garden for the upcoming season. As a group they brainstormed the location and size of the garden and the amount of sun required for certain types of vegetables. Once they decided on the location and size of the garden, the educator asked the children the following questions: "How are you going to know if there is enough room for all the vegetables?" and "How do know if you left enough room between each type of vegetable?" A number of children in grade three mentioned they had been learning about mapping in school and suggested using a mapping exercise for the garden. It was agreed by the children to use mapping as a way to pre-plan their garden and to see if they have enough space for all the vegetables. They taped large sheets of paper together to create a map the size of the garden. Information from garden/plant resource books helped the children to understand the required space needed for each vegetable. The above resources and questions enabled the children to pre-plan the size of the garden and space requirements for the vegetables.

The above story illustrates the interfacing between the school curriculum and the garden project in the school-age program. The children at school were learning about the math concept of mapping, and in class they had the opportunity to use a pre-planned worksheet to practice the concept. The children were able to integrate their knowledge of mapping from school to the school-age garden project by applying the mapping concept to a direct experience: creating a full-scaled map of the garden.

Another way for the educator to find out about what the children are learning at school is by developing clear and direct lines of communication between himself and the teacher. By developing a positive relationship with the teacher, discussions about what the children are learning in the classroom will happen naturally and a connection between the school and the school-age program will develop. The educator may have the opportunity to visit the classroom to see the application of what children are learning and the teacher will have the opportunity to visit the school-age program to observe learning in the school-age environment. In the above example, if the educator already had discussions about mapping with the teacher, she could ask the group the following questions: "Does anyone know what mapping is?" or "Does anyone know how to map the garden?" She could ask the grade three children what they were learning in school and this could trigger discussions about the mapping. These questions might be enough to stimulate a discussion about mapping and help the children to see the relationships between what they are learning at school and the mapping exercise for the school-age garden project.

Research and Presentation Skills

In the school-age program, with the facilitation of the educator, children should have the opportunity to use resource books or the Internet to help them to complete school projects. Children have the opportunity to practice public speaking skills by presenting their research or project to the rest of the children during community time. For example, a grade five student was researching gorillas and needed to create a panel board based on his research. He researched gorillas by using specific science habitat books located in the school-age program. Once he gathered all the information, he word-processed his information and posted the information and photos of gorillas on the panel board. He asked the educator if he could practice his gorilla presentation at the next community meeting, because he is expected to present the gorilla project to his class. At the next community meeting he presented his gorilla research to the group; in fact, he presented it a number of times. The children gave him feedback about his presentation and about what they learned.

After the student presented his research at school he commented to the educator that he felt very comfortable with speaking in front of the class, and the teacher said he was quite knowledgeable about gorillas. At a later time the educator connected with the teacher and asked about the presentation. The teacher had been very impressed with his public speaking skills and with the information. The educator shared with the teacher how the child had worked on the project in the school-age program and practiced the presentation in front of the other children. By continuing to develop a connection and a dialogue between the teachers and educators of the school-age program, children will have the opportunity to practice their new knowledge of concepts and skills in both settings, transfer what they are learning at school to activities and play experiences in the school-age program, and have opportunities and access to research material (books and Internet) for school projects.

CURRICULUM MODELS FOR SCHOOL-AGE CHILD CARE

Although background knowledge and curriculum components result in educators taking the same general steps to develop a curriculum, the curriculum model used by a program will influence what occurs in each of the planning steps.

In many school-age programs educators use a **traditional curriculum** model (Chapter 10). In others, they use an **emergent curriculum model** (Chapter 11). Both approaches have their proponents, and educators who choose one approach over the other should be able to justify their choice by referring to the centre's philosophy statement and to theories of learning and development. Table 6.2 identifies some of the characteristics of each model.

TABLE 6.2	Curriculum approaches	

Traditional Curriculum	Emergent Curriculum
Developed by the educator:	Driven by the child:
• preplanned experiences are based on goals for the group	• educators meet regularly with children to plan the program
• goals are based on observations and knowledge of development	• goals are developed through observations, and children and family input, as well as the educators' knowledge of development
• planning usually done for a week or a month in advance	• planning meetings occur regularly to plan for both short- and long-term experiences
• spontaneous learning experiences arise from ongoing play and serendipitous events	• spontaneous learning experiences arise from ongoing play and serendipitous events
Usually based on a theme	Program is not theme-based although there will be a number of short- and long-term projects occurring that may have the appearance of a theme.
Environments are often arranged around specific activity centres that remain constant throughout the year. They include private, small-group, and large-group spaces.	Environments are often arranged around a variety of loose parts and resources that might change throughout the year as interests and skills vary.
	• materials can move from one area to another
	• the play areas are flexible in nature and include private, small-group, and large-group spaces
Learning activities are identified as appropriate for one activity centre or another.	Learning experiences can arise in one play area and move into other areas.
Planning tends to occur around the activity centres.	Planning tends to occur around the children's interests and play.

Curriculum Approaches

Both the traditional and emergent curriculum approaches will begin curriculum planning by looking at the observations to determine what the children are interested in, the skills and learning the children are demonstrating, and how this knowledge can help when planning the curriculum. As the educators move to step two, they begin to see differences in the implementation of the step.

Step two involves brainstorming ideas, but how this is done will be different in traditional and emergent curricula. In the traditional curriculum approach the educators will use their knowledge to brainstorm appropriate ideas (ones that support the learning and skills the children are developing) within the context of the theme for that week. All of the planning for the week will be done prior to the start of the week, and is unlikely to change once the week has begun.

In the emergent curriculum approach, the educators will brainstorm ideas for long-term projects, clubs, and various learning opportunities over a period of weeks and even months, with the input of the children. The educators will use knowledge based on their observations and discussions with the children to help determine how the ideas raised can support the learning the children are involved in and the skills they are developing. Although planning will occur in advance, it will be more fluid in nature, and the educators will add and change materials and resources throughout the period they are planning for as the need arises.

Summary

The starting point for planning any curriculum effectively is knowing and using observational techniques to discover where the children are in their development and learning, what their interests are, and what is important to their families. Without the background knowledge obtained from observations, any curriculum will fall short of meeting the needs of the children. The knowledge that educators gain from observations is the foundation for all planning.

As educators plan learning experiences for school-age children, they need to remember that there are three major factors working together to determine the curriculum: background knowledge (such as legislation), curriculum components (such as time), and a curriculum model (whether traditional or emergent). The first two factors—background knowledge and curriculum components—are composed of several distinct elements, all of which must be considered when developing the curriculum. Educators cannot pick and choose the elements they want to use and ignore the others.

The last factor, curriculum model, is unique in that educators can choose the model they wish to use, and by doing so they are selecting a particular planning strategy (for example, child driven) and ignoring other strategies (for example, theme based). The model chosen will reflect the philosophy of the centre, and therefore will be based on the theories supporting that philosophy. Once a model has been chosen, educators will use it, along with background knowledge and curriculum components, to create an environment that is full of learning experiences that excite the children and support their learning and development.

Student Learning Experiences

1. Observe a learning experience in a school-age program. Describe how the space used in the experience is influenced by the children's development, legislation, family sensitivities, and the fact that the children have been in school all day.

2. Locate an article that describes holiday-based curriculum planning. Using examples from the article, determine if it is sensitive to families from various cultures. Identify what else could be done to make the curriculum more inclusive.

3. Using the chart on traditional curriculum and emergent curriculum, discuss how the two approaches might influence the school-age program's use of materials, space, time, and people.

Review Questions

1. Describe four ways educators use observations to determine curriculum.

2. List the four curriculum components and explain how they influence the school-age curriculum.

3. Identify three questions the educator might use while supporting the development of the children's soccer skills. Determine which ones are convergent and which are divergent. What influenced the use of each type of question? How could you change the convergent questions into divergent questions? Why might you want to do this? When would you avoid doing this?

4. How does the traditional curriculum model differ from the emergent curriculum model?

5. Identify and describe the six steps in the planning process.

CHAPTER 7

Play and Play Activities

OVERVIEW

During the school day children do not have many opportunities to engage in play activities, therefore when they arrive at the after-school program they need to be able to play. Fortunately, educators recognize the importance of play and the learning that occurs during play experiences.

Educators working with school-age children recognize that their play will often differ from that of preschoolers. According to Piaget's theory of cognitive development, most school-age children will be in the concrete operational stage of development. Social interactions with peers also change from the preschool to the school-age years, as do friendships and play behaviour. These changes in thinking and social interactions result in types of play that differ from those of preschool children.

This chapter will look at different types of play, such as games with rules, and some of the changes that occur in play as children move through the school-age years. It will also look at developing appropriate play activities for this age group, and provide the reader with resources to

Outdoor play can lead to new friendships.

help develop activities that school-age children will find interesting and challenging. Included in this chapter will be information on developing activity plans and information about field trips.

ROLE OF PLAY IN LEARNING

Many people associate school-age learning with the activities that take place within the elementary school system. Although educators recognize the importance of the learning that occurs at school, they know that play still has a crucial role in a child's learning. Play provides children with opportunities to practise skills being taught in school. Educators have often seen children pretending to play school, and in doing so practising spelling or math skills. Play also allows children to practise their skills in a less structured environment than a school, and to learn skills and concepts that are not being taught in school (see the section on skill development in Chapter 12).

Simple to Complex Play

As children initially explore concepts or materials, they engage in simple exploration and play activities. For example, a child who has never seen children playing jacks, when given a set of jacks may simply play with the ball and the jacks separately. If the child knows that the aim is to bounce the ball and pick up the jacks, that may also occur. But only after the child has had time to explore the materials and learn more about the game will he begin to experiment with more complex play (such as incorporating different movements when picking up the jacks, trying to pick the jacks up in a certain order, creating a jacks competition, and so on).

School-age children have developed a variety of physical, social, language, and cognitive skills that result in an interest in and an ability to engage in complex play. Unless the materials are new to the children, they will not be content simply to use them the same way they did during their preschool years. Their Lego structures will become more complex and detailed; their water play will require siphons, irrigation systems, and so on. Often children require more time in order to experiment with materials and develop more complex play. As educators plan activities, they need to review the materials being provided in order to ensure that the play can move from simple to complex, and that enough time is provided for this movement to take place.

TYPES OF PLAY

Just as the play of school-age children becomes more complex than that of younger children, the types of play that children engage in also changes. As indicated in previous chapters, school-age children will continue to participate in many activities that were introduced during preschool years, but will want to expand on the skills that they have already developed. In addition, school-age children develop an interest in types of play that preschool children seldom participate in (such as putting on a play) or are only able to participate in under the direct guidance of an adult (such as simple games). Play rituals, collections, games with rules, and dramatic productions are some types of play that build on the skills learned during the preschool years but do not tend to appear until children enter school-age years.

Play Rituals

Play rituals are games or activities that have been handed down by one generation of school-age children to the next. Older children naturally teach the younger children the rules involved in these play rituals (such as tag, hide and seek, marbles) and support them as they learn the games. Many of these games are centuries old, but there is concern that this type of play is being lost in our modern age. As children spend less time in unstructured play and more time in organized activities, some play rituals are disappearing. Some school boards have even hired consultants to help children learn games that have traditionally been part of recess play but which are no longer known by some children.

Play rituals include games like hopscotch, jacks, clapping games, and four square. They support eye–hand coordination, dexterity, problem-solving, balance, and strategic planning. There are also more specialized types of play rituals. These are counting rituals and storytelling rituals. Counting rituals are used during games when selecting teams or deciding who starts the game. They usually consist of rhymes with a counting component included. Examples of counting rituals are Su-sum-see, One potato two potato three potato four, and Rock–paper–scissors.

Story rituals include ghost stories, poetry, riddles, chants, cheers, and chapter books, which get handed down from one generation to the next. Children may pass some story rituals down through activities like skipping. There are many chants associated with this type of play. Like chants, some stories are part of the children's oral traditions, and both chants and oral stories may change over time to accommodate local conditions, current trends, new technology, and so on. Regardless of where they grow up, children will tell each other stories with common elements, such as mysterious disappearances, the supernatural, and old houses.

On the other hand, books can become a type of play ritual, but they are not as changeable as the oral rituals. Books like the Narnia series, or more recently Harry Potter, capture the imagination of children, and as younger children listen to the older ones they become interested in the books and read them when their abilities allow. Many of the books included in storytelling rituals are widely recognized as classics of children's literature. Table 7.1 illustrates

TABLE 7.1	Play rituals	
Type of Play	**Play Experiences**	**Learning**
Play rituals	Jacks, kick the can, statues, hide and seek, marbles, hopscotch, cat's cradle string games, skipping, tag, clapping games, four square, ball games, rhymes, red rover, Pogs, etc.	• eye-hand coordination • dexterity • spatial skills • balance • strength development
Counting rituals	Black shoe, black and white, Su-sum-see, one potato, two potato, three potato, four..., rock-paper-scissors, etc.	• large motor coordination • problem solving • strategic planning • group dynamics
Storytelling rituals	Skipping chants, riddles, oral stories (usually scary), books (e.g., Harry Potter series, Narnia series, *Black Beauty, Holes*), poetry	• co-operation • memory skills • rhythm • math skills • reading • classification • concept development sequencing of events, etc.

the type of play (play rituals), play experiences (hopscotch, skipping, clapping games), and learning (dexterity, balance, eye–hand co-ordination) that occurs during play.

Collections

School-age children are avid collectors. Their collections can consist of many items based on one characteristic, or many items based on a variety of characteristics (colour, size, shape). Unlike adult collectors, children may use the objects in their collections during play or incorporate them into a game. Collections are often used for social trading and borrowing. The collections of school-age children may be composed of everyday found objects like rocks, or of bought items such as hockey cards or stuffed animals. Collections can consist of almost anything the child finds interesting and of value (bearing in mind that a child's view of value often differs from an adult's).

Collections allow school-age children opportunities to develop their classification skills. It helps to refine their ability to make comparisons, develop negotiating skills (trading), and practise conversational skills (discussions around collections). Some children may require support from adults as they develop the above skills. Trading can be an awkward issue for a program, because the wide range of negotiating skills among the children means those with weaker skills often end up feeling cheated, and their parents may become very upset when they realize that the trade was very one-sided. To avoid these consequences, educators may ban trading or may severely restrict what can be traded. At the same time, educators may decide to incorporate activities into the curriculum that will help children develop negotiating skills in an environment where they have less to lose (such as negotiating what snacks will be served or what field trips will be taken).

Collections also help children learn how to engage in more in-depth studies of a concept. Children who are into rock collecting may initially pick up any rock they find interesting. As they begin to show the rocks to others, talk about them, and classify them, their knowledge begins to expand. As they have opportunities to look more closely into the rocks that they have, and as they expand their collections, they begin to discover the various ways rocks are created and the different types of materials in rocks. Because a collection tends to be a topic that sustains a child's interest over time, it has a great deal in common with long-term projects. In fact, if the collection motivates a child to really study the objects being collected, it is one of the most child-directed types of long-term project that can occur in a program. Table 7.2 illustrates

TABLE 7.2	Collections	
Type of Play	**Play Experiences**	**Learning**
Collection	Collections may consist of: rocks, stamps, comics, dolls, horse figurines, Beanie Babies, postcards, marbles, shells, songs, crystals, rock band posters, CDs, bugs, sand, cards (hockey, basketball, Magic, Pokemon, Digemon), etc.	A wide variety of classification skills (often very complex), concept/knowledge development, organizational skills, negotiation skills, math, memory, peer relationships, etc.

the type of play (collection), play experiences (collecting rocks, cards, toys) and learning (classification, peer relationships, negotiation skills) that occurs during play.

Games with Rules

School-age children have the cognitive skills to successfully play games with rules. They are able to follow the logic of the game, and recognize the importance of following the rules. Although most school-age children recognize that many games result in only one child winning, some will have difficulty accepting losing. This is especially true of younger school-age children.

Games with rules are bound by the set of rules specific to that game or play. Changes to some of the rules can be negotiated and agreed upon by the players before the game, but the main concepts of the game are fixed. For example, a group of children playing Crazy Eights may decide to make Threes wild as well as Twos, but everyone will still be expected to play the cards according to suits, and one can win only by getting rid of all one's cards.

Although changes to rules can be discussed before the game starts, children playing the game expect everyone to play by the same rules once it is under way. If children are changing the rules during the game it is the educator's role to remind them of the rules, or to see if all the players are willing to agree on the new rules.

Traditionally, games with rules have been considered competitive in nature, with either individual children competing against one another, or children in teams competing against other teams. A more non-traditional approach is to have children work together toward a common goal. These games are considered co-operative in nature, and all the children playing work together in order to "win." The rules in co-operative games may be fixed as in competitive games; however, there is often more flexibility regarding changes to rules once the game has begun, since all the children are working together to achieve the same goal.

Because of the difficulty many school-age children have with losing, educators should be sure to include co-operative games as well as competitive games in the program. When educators do this, children have opportunities to develop the skills involved in playing a game without having to always deal with the concept of losing. Table 7.3 illustrates the type of play (games with rules), play experiences (baseball, chasing games, co-operative games), and learning (classification, peer relationships, negotiation skills) that occurs during play.

Rough-and-Tumble Play

Rough-and-tumble play is what children do naturally with each other and with co-operative adults. It is viewed by many as play wrestling, and is often referred to as horsing around. Boys are much more likely than girls to engage in this type of play, and men are much more likely to engage children in rough-and-tumble play than women are. Men are also more likely to view it as appropriate play than women are.

Rough-and-tumble play is non-competitive, builds self-esteem, and helps children learn to control their bodies and set limits. Educators tend to confuse aggression with rough-and-tumble play in children. Rough and tumble is not fighting or bullying. It is a win–win approach, while aggressive play is a win–lose approach.

In rough-and-tumble play children alternate roles, and the power is shared. Children involved in this play need to demonstrate good social problem-solving skills, since they

TABLE 7.3	Games with rules	

Type of Play	Play Experiences	Learning
Competitive games	Organized sports: soccer, basketball, football, baseball, badminton Organized games: tag, chasing games, board games, marbles, hop scotch, dominoes, card games	• co-ordination of several movements • controlled movements refined for accuracy, distance control, etc. • eye-hand and eye-foot control • problem-solving • reaction times • strategic planning • social acceptance • concept development
Co-operative games	Dramatic play: assuming different roles during play Parachute and blanket games, board games, group challenge games, group chants and rhyming games. Creating plays and skits. Creating and performing group dancing with choreographic moves.	• appropriate expression of emotions • socially acceptable ways to enter group situations • co-operation • group dynamics • self-esteem

need the skills to stop the play before it becomes aggressive. In rough-and-tumble play emotions do not escalate; the children will finish playing as friends.

Aggressive play is very different. In aggressive play one child has the power and the other child is the victim. Children demonstrate poor social skills during an aggressive play episode. They fail to read or ignore the signs that the other child is in distress. Emotions will escalate and the children will finish playing as enemies.

Children with poor social skills will have difficulty engaging in rough-and-tumble play because they will be less able to discern the boundaries between it and aggressive play. This means that educators must be willing to support such children as they develop the social skills and abilities necessary to engage in this type of play.

When a program decides to develop opportunities for rough-and-tumble play, the educators and children will have to establish clear limits and rules. An important safety measure is to agree on a code word that children can use to signal that they want to get out of the play. As well, educators will have to supervise such play to ensure that the rules are being abided by and that the children are accurately reading the body language and listening to the other child. In addition, programs should create a suitable space for this type of play. Mats, carpets, sand, or soft grass are necessary to ensure that children don't get hurt.

Although there is research to indicate the value of this type of play (Pellegrini and Perlmutter, 1988; Hughes, 1999) many educators discourage children from engaging in it, and many programs do not allow it for fear that it might escalate into fights or that someone might get hurt. If a centre is fearful of allowing this type of play it should then consider a more structured type of rough-and-tumble play, such as Greco-Roman wrestling, in order to provide children with the opportunity to develop some of the abilities

TABLE 7.4	Rough-and-tumble play	
Type of Play	**Play Experiences**	**Learning**
Rough-and-tumble play	Play fighting, horsing around, testing of strength, king of the castle	• socially acceptable limits of behaviour • ability to read the body language • ability to read voice tone of individuals • spatial awareness • co-ordination • muscle strength • strategic planning • co-operation • problem-solving • flexibility

found in such play. Table 7.4 illustrates the type of play (rough and tumble), play experiences (testing strength), and learning (spatial awareness, strategic planning) that occurs during play.

Dramatic Productions

The dramatic play of the young school-age child may differ considerably from that of older children in the program. The younger children will still engage in a lot of the traditional fantasy play used by older preschoolers. This tends to be very spontaneous, and the direction of the dramatic play emerges as the children actually engage in it. Two six-year-olds pretending to be superheroes will make up the plot as they go along, and when it is over they will move on to a new plot. On the other hand, older school-age children are more likely to pre-plan their dramatic productions. A group of ten- and eleven-year-olds will likely decide ahead of time that they want to create an air band. After making the decision, they will decide on the content and the dance moves, and finally, they will rehearse the words and actions until they have got them right.

School-age children's dramatic play experiences are complex. The type of dramatic play the children engage in will be influenced by their peers, their community, and pop culture (such as music videos, books, magazines, slang, comics). Children will imitate their favourite characters or personalities from movies, books, comics, or musical groups. They will often assume the speech patterns of the characters they are imitating, recite dialogue from videos word for word, and build props for their dramatizations. During the school-age years, a dramatic play can easily turn into a long-term project that may or may not be directed by the educator.

School-age children are capable of organizing pre-planned dramatizations and music productions. Children engaged in these activities will assign roles to various members of the group, create props and costumes, plot out the content of the production, and spend a great deal of time and energy rehearsing their performance. Because such performances require negotiations, compromise, and co-operation, educators involved with children putting together a play or air band need to be tuned into the discussion, and be ready to act as facilitators if necessary.

Even though school-age children show interest in pre-planned, long-term dramatic play, they continue to engage in spontaneous dramatic play as well, though it is usually more extensive than in preschool programs. Educators can accommodate longer-term dramatic play by allowing children, whenever possible, to maintain some of their dramatic-play props over a period of time. For example, a program that has space designated for the sole use of dramatic play can support the children's fort-building by allowing children to keep the forts up overnight. When educators do this, children have the opportunity to expand on the play that occurred the previous day. Instead of trying to rebuild a fort, children can try to develop communication systems between forts or create storage spaces within the structure. Table 7.5 illustrates the type of play (dramatic), play experiences (charades, dramatic games, creating plays), and learning (social interaction, conversational skills, problem-solving) that occurs during this activity.

CHANGES TO PLAY IN SOCIETY

Dramatic changes are occurring in the play of school-age children in Canada. Children are engaging in less spontaneous play organized by and for themselves, and many children have less time to play than previous generations. Not only is there a concern about the amount of homework compared to previous generations, but children are participating in more organized activities, which take up much of the time they have outside the school and child-care environments. Children are registered in art classes, language classes, Cubs or Brownies, choirs, and organized sports, to name just some of the activities.

TABLE 7.5	Dramatic productions	
Type of Play	**Play Experiences**	**Learning**
Dramatic productions	Dramatic play activities: performing plays and skits, air bands, charades, miming, character tag games and dramatic games (creating machines) Creating and wearing costumes and props Writing songs, dialogue, poems, stories. Recreating choreographic dance movies.	• social interaction skills (e.g., turn-taking, leadership and follower roles) • refined conversational skills (e.g., timing) • problem-solving • strategic planning • vocabulary (e.g., similarities in words, new words) • imagination • math skills (e.g., measurement, counting, graphing) • numerous cognitive concepts • reading • drawing techniques • writing • public speaking • rhythm • co-ordination • balance • memory • sequencing

Our society is seeing increased participation in computer and video games by children, with boys having a higher participation rate than girls. Although these types of games do provide some skill development, there are concerns about the amount of time being spent on them, since they tend to be both more sedentary and more solitary than traditional play.

SCHOOL-AGE ACTIVITIES

As the types of play change from preschool to the school-age years, the types of materials and activities provided and supported by educators will change as well. Knowing that children are interested in collections, educators in school-age programs will make sure that they provide activities that support this interest. Knowing that children are interested in crafts as well as in experimenting with art materials, educators will provide craft activities as well as introducing more complex art materials for them to experiment with.

In order for educators to create activities that will work in their program, they need to know which activities are appropriate for children of school age and might also interest their particular group of children. As educators determine how to implement these activities, they need to be aware of any adaptations required for all children to participate, and they need to provide alternative activities if some children are unable to participate successfully, perhaps because of a disability. Activity plans can not only help educators determine if an activity is appropriate, but also help them ensure that they have included the necessary materials for the activity to succeed.

ACTIVITY PLANS

What Are Activity Plans?

Activity plans are the written records of learning experiences. They contain information regarding the learning one expects children will gain from the experience, the materials required, and how the experience should be set up. Activity plans are one more tool to help educators ensure the curriculum is addressing goals the children need to attain.

Activity plans may be kept on file or in theme kits, and either reused unchanged or modified to support the learning the children are involved in. For example, the educator may have an activity plan for an obstacle course that involves children dribbling a soccer ball, and has kept this activity on file with other soccer activities. Having observed that the children are really interested in playing soccer but are having difficulty controlling the ball, the educator may decide that this would be a good activity to incorporate into the curriculum. In a traditional program, the educator would then review the activity to make sure it supported the type of learning and skill development the children were working on. While reviewing the activity she would also determine if modifications needed to be made for this group of children, or even for one child in the group.

An educator working in an emergent-curriculum program might use the same activity plan slightly differently. After reviewing the activity plan she might decide to take it to the group of children interested in soccer for discussion. The children would then help determine if the activity should be implemented, and if there should be any changes made to it. In both of the above situations the activity plan helped the educator plan the curriculum and provided information that would assist the educator when setting up the environment, namely the materials needed for the activity.

Where Does One Get Activity Plans?

Educators will be able to find activity plans in resource books, but many plans originate from the program educators themselves. In order to facilitate planning, educators should develop an activity plan whenever the group is undertaking a particular learning experience for the first time. As educators add new plans to those already on file, they are increasing the number of potential learning experiences that children have access to in the future.

What Does an Activity Plan Look Like?

Activity plans vary from centre to centre both in their form and in the amount of detail included. Regardless of the type of plan being used, an activity plan should contain information on the learning one expects children will gain from the experience, the materials required, and how the experience should be set up. Table 7.6 is just one example of an activity plan.

Things to Remember When Using an Activity Plan

Activity plans, whether from a book, from a file, or brand new, have the potential to help educators and children plan a challenging and interesting curriculum. They also have the potential to create a rigid curriculum that fails to address the interests and goals of the children in the group.

Activity plans are effective when they are used as a starting point for learning experiences. As indicated earlier, educators should review existing activity plans before putting them into effect again, in order to make sure that they meet the needs of the current group

TABLE 7.6	Soccer activity plan
Name of Activity:	**Soccer Obstacle Course***
Objectives	Eye-foot coordination Coordination of several movements Kicking with control
Materials/equipment	Pylons Wood to make ramp Wood U-shaped tunnel Soccer balls Additional materials children decide to include
Set up	In large area, set up obstacle course or have children set it up
Educator's role	Provide materials Help set up or let children take on this task Facilitate discussion around rules for use Let children use it on their own
Suggestions for future	Use different types of balls. For example, beach, tennis, and Nerf balls Use a variety of sizes of balls in the activity Create an obstacle course without using a soccer ball
* Evaluation	Evaluation questions will help to guide the educator's thinking when observing and reflecting on the play.

of children. If the educator discovers that the activity is too simple, and therefore makes modifications (with or without input from the children), the modified activity plan will likely support the children's learning more effectively than the unmodified activity. If, on the other hand, the educator simply pulls out the activity plan and implements it unchanged, the plan is less likely to support the children's learning effectively.

If educators view the activity plan as a learning experience that can lead into other, more complex or in-depth learning experiences, or provide additional practice for skills children are developing, then the implementation of the plan will support the children's learning. If the educators view the plan simply as providing one more learning experience for the program, however, it is less likely that the activity will support children's learning as effectively.

Evaluations and Activity Plans

Activity plans may contain a section for evaluation, or educators may simply use their ongoing observations for evaluating activity plans. As the educators observe the children engaging in the various learning experiences, they should note whether or not the objectives of the experience are being met. If they are, then the plan is appropriate. If the observations consistently show the children using the materials in unanticipated ways, the educators should incorporate this information in the activity plan, so they can recall it the next time they use the plan.

FIELD TRIPS

Besides the day-to-day activities provided in school-age programs, many special events and activities are planned throughout the year. One important type of event is the field trip, and successful field trips are carefully planned with input from the children and families. During field trips children will have the opportunity to connect with the people and places in the macro community. For example, a field trip to a local radio station will give the children the opportunity to see how a radio station works, observe adults in their work environment, and ask questions.

Planning Field Trips

Whenever educators decide to take children on a field trip, a number of steps are required for the trip to be successful, both in terms of the learning provided and the organization of the trip. This section will identify steps that must be taken to ensure a successful trip. Some steps are important for all field trips, even if it is only walking to the local bowling alley or library, while others will be relevant to trips involving transportation.

Regardless of what the field trip is, it is important that the educator understand the objectives of the trip before undertaking it. Is the purpose to give children an opportunity to obtain information or expand the learning component of a long-term project or a club? Is it to provide them with a different type of physical activity (such as swimming) or opportunities to explore and connect with their community? Is the purpose to purchase materials and loose parts for an activity or project? By determining what the objective of the field trip is, the educators can critically discuss the trip to brainstorm how good the idea is. Once they have discussed it they should also visit the location in advance (if unfamiliar with it) to determine if it will really interest the children and address the learning outcomes.

The length of an outdoor field trip will depend not only on the objective and activities, but the weather, the facilities, and the ages of the children. Flexibility is also important. Children who are uncomfortably hot, cold, or wet are not going to learn well. If this happens because of a turn in the weather, cut the trip short or transfer some activities to a more comfortable inside venue if possible. It is important to note if children are appropriately dressed, (for example with raincoats and rubber boots if it is raining); then, being out in light rain could be a wonderful play and learning experience.

Educators also need to anticipate what could happen on the trip that might result in different outcomes from those expected or create organizational problems. For example, before going to the beach to swim the educators should first find out whether all the children in the program can swim. If they can, the next thing to consider is what they will do if the children decide the water is too cold or too dirty and do not want to go swimming. If the trip is going to a studio where pottery is made, the educators need to think about what might happen if not all the children can fit into the studio at the same time, or if some children will have trouble seeing what is happening. Will there be something else to see if the group has to be divided into two, or will one group simply have to sit around and wait? Background research into the field trip is not the only thing needed for the trip to be successful. There are a number of important details that may or may not be involved in the outdoor visit you are planning. What is the cost of the field trip? Has the director approved the trip? Will you need a bus or other transportation? Will you be going on the field trip with another school-age program, which may help to reduce costs? Arrangements should include the date, time, and place of pickup, destination, and route, as well as plans for the return journey.

Preparing for a Field Trip: What Do You Need to Take?

Emergency Materials and Information

- Bring a first aid kit (carried by an educator) and any medications that need to be administered to specific children at specific times.
- Know in advance if any children have allergies that may require special attention.
- Bring attendance sheets and emergency information for each child (carried by an educator). Check attendance before, during, and after the trip to make sure no one is left behind.
- Carry an emergency cell phone at all times.
- Have parents sign a consent/permission form before leaving. Make sure all parents have signed the forms before you leave.

Food, Materials, and Clothing

- Will a meal or snack be required on the trip? If children are bringing their own lunches, they need to pack them in their backpacks. Remind the parents ahead of time not to send food that needs to be microwaved and to add ice packs to keep food fresh.
- If you are going to bring any other materials/equipment, such as science equipment, with you, it is important to think about how you will carry them. Individual educators' knapsacks may be useful to carry a number of items such as guidebooks, plastic bags, containers for collecting, writing materials, binoculars, and hand lenses. Take as few

materials and equipment as you can carrying extra items may not only be tiring, but may limit the activity as well.

- Wear appropriate shoes and clothing suitable for the outdoor environment and weather, such as running shoes, sun hats, and layered clothing that can be removed or added depending on whether it is too hot or cold.
- Have sun screen available even if children have already applied it before the trip, because later application may be necessary.

Documentation Materials

- Bring digital cameras to document the trip. If possible, bring disposable cameras for children to use. This will be a great opportunity to document what they are seeing during the trip.
- Supply clipboards, pens, or markers so children can document their own experiences and illustrate or write about what they are seeing and thinking. Small hand-held clipboards can be purchased from any office supply store and can be stored in each child's knapsack so they can access them easily.

Enlisting Volunteers Naturally, the larger the group, the less individual attention can be given to each child. If possible, keep the groups small. Generally speaking, the younger the children, the smaller the group should be. If you can enlist some parents to volunteer to come along, this may help to reduce the number of children each adult must supervise. When enlisting volunteers make sure the expectations and boundaries regarding their roles are identified at the time you ask for help.

Preparing Children for a Field Trip Before going on a field trip make sure the children are prepared. Without a doubt, the three most important preparations are that making the children are safe, dressed for the weather, and know what to say.

Before the trip, discuss and brainstorm with the children where they are going, what they may see, what types of transportation they will be using, and the expectations for the group. It is important to discuss safety rules before and during the trip, such as staying with the group or identifying what is expected when travelling on a bus.

If collecting items is a part of a trip, help the children follow a conservation ethic. For example, do not pick flowers or remove plants from the pathways; leave them for others to enjoy also. Explain that if each visitor took just one sample of a plant, it would quickly disappear. Such attitudes will help children to develop a feeling of responsibility for the environment.

After the Trip: Discussions, Reflections, and Documentation After the trip, during a community meeting, discuss what the children saw, their favourite parts, what they learned, and what they were surprised by. Encourage the children to draw pictures and write stories or poems about their field trip experiences.

When the photographs from the field trip are available, the children and educator can work together using the photos, drawings, or stories to create documentation panels or a bulletin board to be displayed in the environment. The children will be able to tell their parents about what they saw, how they felt, and what they learned during the trip. The educators should also include their reflections, dictations, and stories about the trip and add this information to the display as well as, if needed, the goals of the field trip and the learning opportunities.

The main goal of any outside field trip is to develop a sense of wonder and joy in the children.

Summary

When children move from the preschool years into the school-age years, their play begins to change. It becomes more complex and results in types of play typically associated with school-age children. These types of play include play rituals, collections, games with rules, rough-and-tumble play, and dramatic productions.

Educators working in school-age programs take these changes into account when planning play activities and make sure that the activities provide the children with challenges that they will enjoy.

When planning an activity or field trip, the educator looks at the objectives to make sure they are appropriate for the children. Educators also use their previous observations of the children to examine the activity and determine if changes will be needed to create challenges or increase interest in the activity among their own particular group. As educators look at possible activities (in resource books, on file, and so on) it is important to remember that these activities should always be considered a starting point. Changes and extensions may be required to make an activity truly appropriate for a particular group of children. In addition, when planning field trips educators must ensure all the preparatory work is completed before leaving on the trip.

Student Learning Experiences

1. Resource Book Activity

Examine an activity from a resource book or other source to determine the following:

1. What ages and/or gender would this appeal to the most? Use child development concepts to back up your answer.

2. Describe how you might modify the activity to accommodate younger or older children.

3. Determine whether or not you might have to modify the activity to accommodate a child with the following:

- Disability affecting fine motor movements
- Disability affecting social interactions
- English or French as a second language

Identify two other activities that might arise from this activity, and explain why you think so.

2. Internet Search

Search the Internet for an article on school-age children and collections. Bring it to class and, with a partner, discuss it. Determine how the information in the article could help an educator provide appropriate collection-based activities for children in a school-age program.

3. Interview

Interview school-age children and find out what skipping chants or tag games they know. Ask how they learned the games. Interview adults and find out if they remember skipping chants or tag games they did as children. Do adults and children remember the same chants and games? What do you think accounts for similarities or differences between the two age groups?

4. Activity Plan

In groups of four, use the format of an activity plan (See Table 7.6). Complete the plan around the following play activities:

- Monopoly (board game)
- Skipping and skipping chants
- "Survivor" (dramatic re-enactment)

5. Planning a Field Trip

Plan a field trip to a local museum, recreational centre (swimming or skating), and restaurant. Create a file system to organize your information by using the following headings:

- Where are you going? (Location, address, etc.)
- Who is the contact?
- What is the cost? (Admission charges, transportation)
- What do you need for the trip?
- How are you going to document the experience?
- How will the children document the experience?
- What kinds of things can you do before and after the trip?

Review Questions

1. In your own words, describe why field trips are important for school-age children. Explain why an educator should have visited the location of a field trip before taking the children there.

2. List and describe the different types of play. Describe one activity that would support each type of play. What is the educator's role when implementing play activities?

3. Describe what an activity plan looks like and explain the importance of each component.

4. Create a diagram to illustrate the relationship between play rituals and games with rules. Justify your diagram.

CHAPTER 8

Developing and Building Community

OVERVIEW

This chapter will review our perception of what community is—what it looks like, what it feels like, and why it is important for school-age programs. We will look at the process of building community under the headings of a set of five foundation skills and a set of nine building blocks for making a community. Community meetings will be reviewed, and practical examples and steps will be illustrated. The importance of teachers' roles, children's roles, and a set of three power structures through which they can be viewed will be highlighted throughout the chapter. Stories and activities from a community-oriented program will be woven throughout the chapter to demonstrate how the idea of community might be consciously created and built up over time. Finally, a series of steps will guide the educator over time when building community.

In a community-based program, children should have opportunities to connect with each other and develop friends.

COMMUNITY BUILDERS

The following observation is from a school-age program with thirty children in attendance and two educators. The program is located in a purpose-built school-age environment in an elementary school in Ontario. All the children in the program go to the school, and the core group of children has been attending the program for at least five years.

The Initial Observation

When visitors arrive at the Bungee School-Age Program (not its real name), they first notice photographs of children engaging in play and projects and participating in group meetings. Around the photographs are stories, drawings, and paintings representing what they are learning in the program (such as creating natural dyes from fruits and vegetables). Many of the stories are written in different languages to accommodate the diverse cultures of the program. A bulletin board on one wall contains information for parents about creative packed-lunch ideas, fact sheets about how to promote self-esteem, an invitation to the community fall festival, and websites for bullying-prevention resources. Photographs of all the families in the program taken during the last potluck supper are included.

Observing Children and the Educators

Entering the playroom, you first notice a large red sign saying "DARE TO TAKE RISKS"; under it are a number of lists and posters containing information about different strategies and techniques to use when dealing with conflict (for instance, steps in the mediation process, using respectful language, and the "think-twice" process). The environment feels like a home, with couches, overstuffed chairs, lamps, and plants. It feels safe, secure, and stimulating. There is a hum of activity, and it looks like children play and live in the space. A number of children are sitting around a table eating snacks and discussing their favourite music groups. Some children are taking old machines apart (toasters, telephones, old computers, hair dryers, and so on) using screwdrivers, wire cutters, and wrenches. The more skilful children are showing the less-skilled children how to use the tools.

A group of children are building a "Shark Laboratory" in the "rec room" area. All the children are participating in a discussion about what materials they need. They are taking turns and sharing their ideas by using "I" statements (for example, "I think we should have lots of film canisters and plastic bottles to collect shark blood"). One child is making a list of all the materials they need. An educator is close by, listening to the discussion, jotting down notes, and acting as a facilitator when needed. One child is moving plants to different locations in the room. Another child is reading a book with a friend on a small red couch. A small group of children are sitting on pillows with an educator, making friendship bracelets. The children are teaching each other different techniques and one child is helping the educator with his bracelet. A number of children are starting a card game and are discussing the rules of the game. Two parents have entered the room and announced to the educators and their children that they are here, but that there is no rush to leave. They sit down on the couch and have a discussion with each other while observing their children.

What Does Community Look Like?

The previous observation describes how communities can look and feel in a school-age program. Community reflects a particular philosophy of how people work and live together. It is an approach and attitude based on mutual respect, trust, inclusion, support, equality, sharing of power, developing partnerships, and ownership of the program. A sense of community can be felt in the social environment as children and educators socialize with each other and participate in co-operative learning experiences. It can be seen in the environment as children play and interact with each other, and it can be heard as children and educators communicate, tell stories, sing songs, and discuss various issues. The community environment that made the scene described above possible was not built up over a few days or weeks, but took many months to develop.

A Story: What Is Community?

At the beginning of the school year, a new group of school-age children was gathered together in a comfortable area of the room to discuss community. The educator asked the children to find their personal space, get comfortable, and relax their bodies. Then he asked them to close their eyes, think about community, and conjure up mental pictures that would encapsulate it. The following questions were used to help the children focus their minds when thinking about community and to guide them through the process: What is community? What does your community sound like? What does your community feel like? What happens in your community? Is community the same in school and in the school-age program? How would you develop community in the classroom and the play yard? Who is in your community? What happens in your school community? What happens in your home community?

After the visualization, the children illustrated and wrote stories about their ideas and concepts of what community is. They used their illustrations and stories to discuss the above questions. Here are some of their comments:

"Community is where we play and live. My parents, brothers, grandparents, and my dog are part of my community. It is a safe place."

"Community feels safe and it is a trusting space. People listen to us and respect us for who we are and for our ideas."

"My friends are part of my community. A friend is someone who helps you do things. When you need something, they get it. You do the same for them."

"We are allowed to give input into the program. Like what we want for snacks and we even can help to make snacks."

"Community is helping people when they need help. If we have conflict because of racism we can talk about what we can do about racism in our community."

The children's community consists of buildings (where they live and go to school), relationships (friends, parents, siblings, pets, educators), feelings (being safe, being respected and trusted), working together (helping each other, giving input into the program), and activism in the broader community (dealing with conflict, racism).

Different Types of Community

There are different types of communities where children will connect with other children, families, and other community members. Community can be both macro (large) and micro (small) by nature. The following are examples of different types of community:

- Larger communities. In the larger community you will find places where families live, different types of neighbourhoods, meeting spaces (community centres, multicultural centres, and parks), places to learn, places to keep you safe and healthy (recreational centres, hospitals, police stations), and places for religious beliefs (churches, mosques, temples).

- Smaller communities. In smaller communities children help in the neighbourhood by raking leaves for the senior residents, or help to keep the school-age program clean, or develop rules for the program.

- Some communities are planned ahead of time. During community meetings children will have the opportunity to plan different community experiences—for example, fundraising for a food bank.

- Some communities happen by chance when children solve problems and negotiate during play experiences (such as where to build a fort) or volunteer to pick up litter from the play yard.

- Communities can last for a short time or a long time.

In this chapter, the type of community discussed is based on all aspects of the above examples, such as helping in the macro and micro community, participating in community-based activities, being part of planning curriculum and the environment and social action activities (adopting a whale). In a school-age program community occurs in the social environment (interactions and developing friendships) of a well-designed physical environment based on a home-like approach. Children will have the opportunity to play, socialize, and participate in community activities and community meeting in this type of social community. Community builds trust in a safe and secure environment, where all children are respected and have the opportunity to work as a group in building their own sense of community. Whether communities are planned or unplanned, long-lasting or brief, they can be a powerful means to connect children to a specific goal.

The Goals of Community

The goals of community are for children and families alike to feel safe, respected, secure, and involved in group decisions, and to have opportunities to develop friends and to interact with people in a supportive environment. Community gives children the opportunity to feel connected to the group. For instance, when children and educators are working together to plan and implement curriculum, such as deciding what to make for a snack, they are connecting with each other through brainstorming, planning, making, and eating. They learn different skills—to collaborate, negotiate, compromise, and work in partnership toward specific goals. Children will learn to become effective and productive community members by participating in:

- Community meetings, to be part of making decisions and to develop rules, routines, transitions, and the curriculum

- Character-building activities such as showing respect, developing trust, and being responsible for your own actions

- Social-justice and activism activities, to help others in the community, reject peer pressure, and stand up for what you believe in

- Co-operative and group experiences, to develop leadership skills and group skills
- Making connections with each other, to have the opportunity to be friends and play with groups of children
- Connecting with the broader community by participating in field trips and helping (volunteering) in the community
- Making connections with parents, family members, guest speakers, and experts in the community who visit the program to share their skills and talents
- Helping to plan what should be in the physical environment, and being involved in the designing of the space

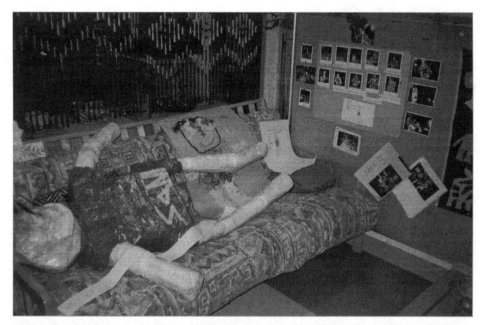

In a community-based program children should be encouraged to use the environment and furnishings in different ways.

POWER OF COMMUNITY

Educators working in a community-oriented program need to be aware of the different types of power structures that can occur when working with children and parents. The goal of the community is to focus on being safe, foster respect, develop relationships, and connect with each other. It can be easy to misuse our own sense of power. This power can be thought of as belonging to one of the following three types.

Directed Power

In this scenario, the educator has all the power and controls all aspects of the program, including the children's behaviour, the rules, the consequences of breaking them, and programming decisions. This type of power can be the kernel of developing a sense of community when used appropriately, since it can help all children feel physically and emotionally safe, with the educator taking full responsibility for making sure the environment is safe. There are times when it will be appropriate for the educator to use this type of power, such as making sure all children are safe from bullying behaviour and other safety issues (such as how to walk as a group on a busy street).

Although directed power can be found in any community, when it is the main type of power it will also result in children feeling controlled, with no real choices in the program. This type of environment tends to lead to high levels of competition, and it can leave children with poor communication skills. Conflict-resolution skills are not implemented, and it can even lead to an atmosphere of intolerance.

Guided Power

Guided power is the main building block for developing a sense of community in a school-age program. Children are provided with experiences that contribute to the development of self-esteem, co-operation, and group membership. The educator helps the children acquire new knowledge and skills by encouraging them to have some input into developing rules and consequences, setting up the environment, and developing planned experiences such as field trips, clubs, and projects.

Facilitated Power

Facilitated power is a model of how a community can work by motivating both educators and children to be productive members of the broader community. The educator, children, and parents are partners in learning together. There is an atmosphere of co-operation, team building, inclusion, and assertive communication skills. Group membership and leadership skills and advocacy and activism skills are all developing, and the child acquires new power from the experience.

Children and educators work together to discuss safety issues to make sure all children feel safe. Community meetings are an essential part of the program. Children actively participate in community meetings by brainstorming, developing, and implementing rules, consequences, and strategies in dealing with, for instance, bullying situations. During community meetings children and the educator brainstorm, develop and implement community learning experiences (such as fundraising), co-operative activities (like building a fort), and collaboration (for example, planning for the summer).

The goal of a community-oriented program is to move away from the directed-power approach toward guided power and eventually to facilitated power. Moving from directed power does not mean that educators abdicate their role in the program. Part of the role of educator is to understand when to use the different types of power, and there are times when she will use directed power to make sure children are safe and secure in the program. The question is how the educator can work with children to share power, and to understand how power works. As children gain experience with power and understand the responsibility it entails, the community will become stronger.

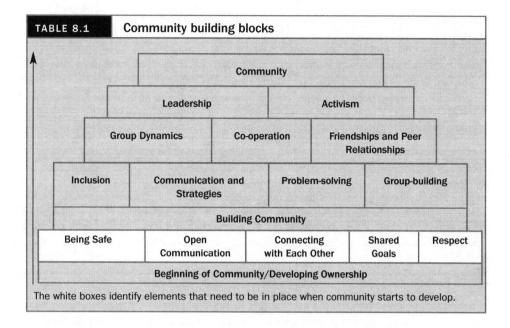

TABLE 8.1	Community building blocks

The white boxes identify elements that need to be in place when community starts to develop.

COMMUNITY BUILDING

The previous section discussed what a community is and why it is important in a school-age program, and identified goals of community. The next question is how to make community happen, since it takes time to develop and does not happen overnight.

Table 8.1 illustrates the elements that are necessary to create community. It is a pyramid form because educators need to facilitate the development of foundation skills before the children can develop more complex ones. The pyramid illustrates the necessary foundation skills practised at the beginning of community, such as being safe and having respect. As the children practise the foundation skills, they will progress up the pyramid to building community such as group-building, co-operation, and leadership. All of the identified elements are within the grasp of most school-age children (even the aggressive ones), but children who have not had past opportunities to practise foundation skills cannot be expected to master more complex skills before they do. For example, a child who has not had exposure to open communication cannot be expected to successfully practise conflict-resolution or leadership skills. Children need to practise and demonstrate skills, but do not have to master everything for a community to be successful.

Beginning of Community: Developing Ownership

Community begins in a school-age program by giving children responsibilities and starting to encourage them in a sense of ownership. Children can be responsible for watering plants, taking care of the program pets, cleaning the environment, preparing activities (such as setting out clay and tools for sculpting), or serving snacks. Developing a system of taking turns—for example, a monthly chart to keep track of whose turn is next for a specific job—will enhance the sense of ownership. The chart will eliminate any disagreement between the children about whose turn it is, and can be used as a self-checking system. Children love to help in the program, and the above activities will help them start to develop a sense of responsibility for its smooth functioning.

To develop responsibility and a sense of ownership, children need to be able to experience and practise to develop the necessary skills. The five foundation skills are: being safe, open and direct communication, connecting with each other, shared goals, and respect.

Being Safe

When developing community, children need to feel safe. They need to know that their feelings, body, materials, ideas, and families are safe in the environment. The educator should make sure that everyone feels safe, and that all children are respectful of each other. If children do not feel safe or feel threatened in their environment, then community is more difficult to establish.

1.   Safe Feelings

Children feel safe to express themselves and to share ideas and challenge opinions in a community-based program. Children are safe from any emotional abuse or social exclusion— for example, teasing about appearance, size, sex, or race, or name-calling, threats, gossiping, and being excluded from a group. Children are encouraged to include others in their play and projects, communicate in an assertive and respectful manner, and respect the feeling of others.

2.   Safe Body

Children are safe from physical harm due to any violent acts such as being hit, kicked, punched, or tripped. Children are safe from any physical harm, from being targeted by an individual or group, and from repeated negative action. Children are encouraged to communicate in a non-defensive manner and to solve problems that arise.

3.   Safe Materials, Loose Parts, and Equipment

Children feel safe to explore a variety of loose parts and materials in the environment. All loose parts and materials should be in working order and safe for children to use. Children are encouraged to experiment and to use the materials in different ways in a safe environment. Children in one program used a large piece of satin as a table-cloth, kite, cape, turban, sari, canopy, and hammock, to transport materials around the room, and as a backdrop for a play. They need to have implicit confidence in the safety of the materials to use them in this inventive way.

4.   Safe Ideas and Words

Children feel they can express their ideas in a safe environment. They are encouraged to take risks, to think in different ways, and to be critical thinkers. They are encouraged to express their individuality and personality by sharing ideas and feelings with the group. They develop collective ownership of ideas and products by working collaboratively during play or on projects. Opinions, ideas, and concerns are expressed in a positive way, and children are helpful and supportive of each other. For example, they may have different opinions about what type of music they would like to listen to in the program.

5. Safe Families

The environment in a community-based program should be a place where all families feel safe and secure no matter what their sex, race, orientation, religion, learning style, socio-economic status, cultural practice, type of disability, or skill level. A non-sexist, non-racist, and multicultural setting should be developed by promoting each child's own culture and the cultures of others not represented in the group, and by demonstrating the same expectations for boys and girls. All children and families should have the opportunity to participate in celebrations. In one program, four families would organize an annual potluck meal, inviting all the other families. During this event some 250 participants showed up with dishes representing 15 different countries.

The celebration of children and families should be visibly on display in the environment, using photographs of the program's children and their families and success stories in different languages, and by creating family-based workshops and social gatherings. This will help to create a sense of belonging, making children and families alike feel secure and trusted.

Open and Direct Communication

In open communication, all members of the community (children, educators, parents, family members, etc.) are empowered by knowing it is all right to talk about ideas, issues, and opinions openly. They should be able to share freely what they enjoy, who they enjoy playing with, what they need, and what concerns them. Everyone involved will have the opportunity to communicate and to practise communication in an open, safe, and trusting environment. For example, if any particular child's behaviour causes others to feel unsafe (perhaps through bullying), children are encouraged to communicate and address the issue during individual discussions, small group meetings, or community meetings.

Children who learn to use respectful, caring, and inclusive language when communicating in an open environment (for instance, see the "I" message in the following chapter) will be empowered to gain ownership of the problem and communicate effectively. A variety of communication strategies will help children to observe carefully, communicate accurately, and listen attentively. When children learn how to use "I" statements by having opportunities to role-play different situations, they will gain the necessary experience and practice. With practice, children will be able to use these strategies during their play experiences and when interacting with other children.

In a safe community, issues are not ignored or swept under the carpet, and all points of view are heard. Children should have a forum to raise issues in a safe and trusting environment. In one program where it was the educator's responsibility to plan and prepare the snacks, the children said during a community meeting that they were tired of the same type of snack and wanted to try something new. Because open communication had been an essential part of this program and the children felt safe to express their feelings, the educator listened to their views. The educator asked questions to clarify what the children wanted so that together they could solve the problem. The resolution was that the children, with the help of the educator, were going to plan a five-week rotation snack menu based on the Canadian Food Guide, which was one of the requirements of the program.

Connecting with Each Other: Children, Families, and Broader Community

Connecting with each other—the educator, parents, other family members, and the broader community—is what community is all about. Building relationships gives children the opportunity to communicate, express themselves, develop group dynamic skills and leadership skills, and explore and connect with new people and environments. Without having the opportunity or experience to connect with each other, children will not have the skills to develop friendships, leadership, co-operative learning experiences, and opportunities to experience and explore their community and become citizens in their community.

In a trusting environment, children feel they are part of the group and have the opportunity to connect with each other. When designing the physical environment it is important to create natural gathering areas where children can come together and have discussions. Areas with pillows, a snack table, a reading area, or a couch can be used successfully to do this. Children will also have the opportunity to connect during planned activities such as building a box, learning a new co-operative game, planning a club, and gardening. Children learn to connect with each other by participating in community meetings where they have input into making decisions in the program and the planning process. They become aware that they are part of a group, and are needed and valued members of it. They have the opportunity to express their ideas, to get to know each other, to practise saying positive things about each other, and to practice group dynamic skills.

Children need to have opportunities to connect with the broader community by participating in field trips, perhaps visiting a seniors' residence, or by volunteering to help others by raking leaves or cleaning a park. Also, it is important to bring the community into the program. If the children are working on a project about music, bring in musicians.

Parents and family members are a vital part of community and it is important to involve them in your school-age community, curriculum, social activities, and celebrations. Children will develop a sense of pride when they see their parents or a family member (grandparent or sister) visiting the program to share a specific skill or talent. Table 8.2 illustrates different activities or ways to create the connections through participation with each other, the broader community, and families.

Shared Goals

In a community environment, it is important for the educator, parent, and child to have shared goals about the program. They may share goals such as achieving open communication or giving children the chance to design the environment and the curriculum. By having shared goals, the power structure will start to shift from guided power to facilitated power.

In an environment where children and adults have created shared goals, you will hear the children refer passionately to "our rules," "our projects," "our community meetings," and "our planning." When children and educators work together to create these things, the children are given a stake in upholding them. They develop a "we" framework of thought

TABLE 8.2	Creating connections through participation

Children Connections:

- Develop a mentoring/peer-support program where children teach each other and younger children different skills or techniques, such as making play dough, knitting, science experiments, origami, or reading.
- Involve children in planning and teaching each other co-operative and team spirit games.
- Get groups of children to take turns making snacks or baking food for snacks. They can also serve snacks to the group or to other groups of children (kindergarten program).
- Involve children in rearranging or redesigning the indoor environment.

Broader Community Connections:

- Participate in field trips into the broader (macro) community. For example, museums, swimming pools, ice rinks, provincial parks, movies, and various art groups.
- Participate in local (micro) field trips such as libraries, seniors' residences, restaurants, grocery stores, parks, community walks, farmers' markets, or hardware stores.
- Invite experts from the community to visit the program to enhance any projects or clubs. For example, musicians, artists, scientists, health care professionals, architects, landscapers, mechanics, etc.

Families Connections:

- Create a "We Are Family" bulletin board and invite families/parents to post information such as favourite stories, interesting lunches and snacks for children, articles, photographs, etc.
- Develop a family culture in the program by planning and facilitating family pot lucks, after-hours discussion groups, workshops, and cleaning days, or invite families for different celebrations.
- Create a community garden where parents can be actively involved with the school-age program by planting, taking care of, and harvesting the garden.
- Invite parents and family members to volunteer their time, skills, and talents to the program. For example, carpenters, musicians, landscapers, firefighters, chefs, etc.
- Encourage families to bring in resources to be used in the program, such as loose parts, music, posters, or artifacts to represent their family culture.

instead of a "me" framework. When parents are involved in helping to develop goals for their child or the program, they will feel the same about the program as the children do and will experience the same "we" philosophy.

Children and educators work together to develop shared goals or objectives during community time, play experiences, and participation in projects and clubs. For example, shared goals are developed when children are brainstorming rules and consequences for the program, creating a group mural for the hallway, cleaning the room, or brainstorming different strategies when dealing with a bully.

Respect

One of the essential elements in developing community is encouraging and developing respect for self and for others. Children are encouraged to be respectful of each other's talents, skills, personality, and passions. The child's sex, size, race, culture, learning style, disability, or socio-economic status should not influence the children's opinions of each other. Rather, their feelings should be based on developing equal relationships by fostering a sense of self and a celebration of the strengths of the group. This does not mean that everyone is the same, but that we all have the responsibility to be respectful of each other, learn to encourage each other, and understand that we all have special talents and skills.

The following points illustrate the role of the educator in this process, and the areas the educator should emphasize:

- *Be a good role model*. The educator should think about how he communicates and how his actions and words affect others. The attitude and tone of voice is also important to consider.

- *Build self-esteem*. The educator should focus on giving children the appropriate praise and encouragement, always focusing on the positives, which will help to develop and enhance their confidence, self-image, and self-concept. Children will start to understand who they are as a person, and their relationship with others and with the community. It is important to recognize and acknowledge the contributions of all the children in the group and to make sure credit is given equally to both girls and boys.

- *Encourage co-operation and collaboration*. The educator should provide opportunities for children to work together when playing games and developing projects and clubs. Children should have opportunities to be active members of the group and to be involved in co-operative activities. They should have the opportunity to contribute to classroom meetings and develop classroom values. The focus during this process is on developing confidence, realistic expectations, and appropriate choices.

- *Teach acceptance*. The educator should support positive attitudes and inclusive practices in relation to differences in personality and cultural practice between individuals and groups of children. Children should be encouraged to have discussions about sexist and racist attitudes, and all prejudiced behaviour should be challenged.

Respecting and appreciating other children's points of view and understanding the value of differences is an essential learning experience in community. Children learn to respect other children's likes and dislikes (such as favourite music, food, or movies). Children have the right to agree or disagree with opinions expressed in a positive manner by other children. However, they need to be respectful of each other, and this can be demonstrated by the tone of voice and the choice of words. For example, saying "That band you like really sucks," is not respectful either in tone or wording. The child could instead choose to say, "I'm not really into that band," and "I prefer to listen to. . . " or "because I like . . . "

The authors have been asked many times, "Does equality mean the children or the educator can do whatever they want in the program?" The following story will help to answer this question and will also illustrate the role of the educator during the process.

In one school-age program, the children felt it was all right to gossip about each other and decided as a group that it should be allowed. The educator respectfully listened to the children's comments and various points of view without passing any judgment. When the children were finished, the educator made it clear he heard what they were saying and understood what they wanted. He read the written philosophy of the program, about being safe, to the children. When he got to the part about everyone being emotionally safe in the program, he stopped and asked

TABLE 8.3	Building community

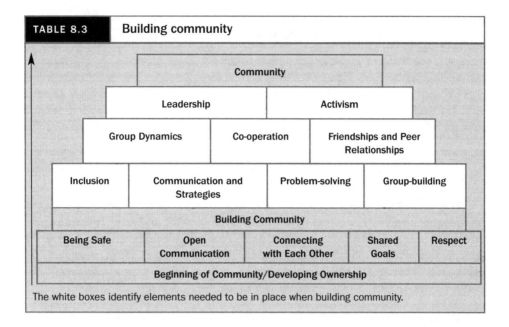

The white boxes identify elements needed to be in place when building community.

the children if everyone would feel safe if children were allowed to gossip. A discussion followed, and the children decided that they would not feel safe or secure if other children were gossiping about them.

In the above story, the children felt they could do what they wanted, because they all seemed to be in agreement that it was all right to gossip. The educator demonstrated respectful communication but also demonstrated the ability not to give in to the children's sense of equality, and related the information to the safety of children and the development of the community. His role in the story is to guide the children's moral development and the development of respect for self and the group.

Next Step: Building Community

When building a sense of community, the lower foundation skills (being safe, open communication, and so on) combine to support the more complex skills, as illustrated in Table 8.3. It is important to note that during certain times of the year the educator may need to revisit some of the lower foundation skills. For example, if a group of younger children have joined the group, it might be important for everyone to revisit the issue of respect. This need not be a root-and-branch review, but a reminder of selected points that might be in danger of being forgotten.

Nine Building Blocks for Making a Community

When children have had practice communicating in a respectful way, sharing goals, and connecting with each other in a safe environment, they should have the necessary skill to start to build community, as the following scenario shows.

A group of children in a school-age program wanted to create archways to highlight each area in the room. They used large sheets of paper, pencils, and rulers to design their archways. Everyone helped each other to measure the height and width of the arches in the room. The educator kept the process going by asking questions about what kind of materials would be used, how they would attach the arches to the ceiling and walls, and how big the arches would be. They designed arches made from a variety of materials, such as wood, Plexiglas, papier mâché, beads, and cloth. During the process, children supported each other by sharing information about what they were learning about arches, critiquing each other's designs and suggesting changes, and helping with the drafting of the designs. Each group presented its design to the larger group and described the materials needed, the location of the arch, and how it would be made. The group decided there were enough designs to construct all the arches in the room. Everyone agreed to take turns helping to construct all the arches.

This story illustrates how a group of children worked together to create archways in the playroom. It demonstrates how children can create their own community by having opportunities to practise and demonstrate some of the community's characteristics. All the children were included in the experience, communicated their ideas, solved problems, and worked together toward a common goal. The children's different personalities and learning styles emerged as they worked together in a supportive environment. The group dynamic was positive and developed naturally as children learned about arches, analyzed each other's designs, and helped each other in creating them. Finally, the children were involved in creating and designing their own environment, and you get a sense they are creating their own community in the environment.

The nine elements of building community are: inclusion, group-building, group dynamics, co-operation, friendship and peer relationships, communication and strategies, leadership, problem-solving, and activism.

1. Inclusion

Inclusion is important when building community because children, educators, and families become more inter-connected to each other and to the values and culture of the group. In an inclusive community, diverse cultures, socio-economic backgrounds, family practices, skills, and needs are respected and included in all areas of the program. By implementing a safe, trusting, and respectful community, all children, families, and educators are included, and not excluded because of gender, personality, learning styles, race, language, sexual orientation, special needs, age, skill level, past experience, or cultural, religious, and family practices.

Inclusive Environments

When developing the environment, different cultures and family structures should be reflected in both the indoor and outdoor spaces. The following are examples of what could be used to develop inclusive practices in the indoor environment: chapter and picture books, visual materials (such as posters), fabric, loose parts, props (such as artifacts and baskets), and photographs of families. Children and families should be encouraged to donate materials and props from their culture. A family in one program donated a number of African baskets from Ethiopia, which they brought back from a family trip, to be used for displaying and storing materials in the room. In the same program, one child brought in a music cassette with Arabic singing to share with the group. Both of these examples demonstrate how families and children in the program feel that they are part of the community of the program.

Inclusive Practices

Inclusive practice is an active/proactive approach to challenging prejudices, stereotypes and personal bias. The focus is on the inequality and the source of discrimination, and children are taught strategies to challenge prejudices, stereotypes, and their bias. In a community environment, children are encouraged to ask questions about how to deal with racist, sexist, homophobic, and classist comments and behaviour. They are encouraged to talk about differences and stereotypes, and to confront prejudice by developing activism skills, such as the ability to stand up for themselves and for others. For example, if a group of children exclude another child from their play because of the child's skin colour, their behaviour would be considered racist. The educator's role is to challenge comments, behaviours, and attitudes, and by asking questions to get at the root of the problem. Children should be taught different strategies to deal with conflict, violence, and bullying behaviour (see Chapter 9). By example, children can learn to observe each other, listen carefully, and communicate with caring language. The educator needs to support this effort by introducing discussions, stories, songs, or group-building activities that address stereotypes and prejudices.

2. Communication and Strategies

Communication in a community-oriented environment should be positive and non-defensive, and is crucial to developing community. Children will have the opportunity to develop, practice, and demonstrate their communication skills by brainstorming ideas, discussing issues, and developing the rules and values of the program. The educator teaches and models the appropriate communication skills and strategies when she interacts with the children, with other educators, and with parents. Children should have the opportunity to practise and demonstrate communication strategies (such as listening skills or picking up on non-verbal clues) by role-playing, being involved in planning, and play. Once practised, these skills will later emerge naturally during play and in planned experiences. Children will have the opportunity to express their feelings and to share their ideas, concerns, and personal history in a safe environment. Also, children should have the opportunity to develop their conversational skills by talking with each other during snack time, during play, and in community meetings.

3. Problem-solving

Problem-solving involves open communication and co-operation skills, which are important to have when working in a group and building community. Problem-solving allows everyone the opportunity to express themselves and to contribute their own ideas, needs, and concerns in order to come up with a decision that is acceptable to everyone. Children need to be able to negotiate and compromise during the problem-solving process, and it is important to teach these skills through various play experiences. The educator's role is to help the children to develop and practice problem-solving skills by implementing a step-by-step process or framework to develop problem-solving strategies. The following five steps illustrate the process or framework that can be used when building community, conflict-resolution skills, and curriculum development.

Five Steps in Developing Problem-solving Strategies

Step 1: Define and identify the problem. What is the problem and why is it a problem?

Step 2: Think about the problem and solutions. Explore and think about different solutions and ask questions about which solution is the most appropriate.

Step 3: Make a decision and create a plan. Gather all the information and materials needed to carry out the plan and allow for the appropriate time, space, and people to follow through.

Step 4: Follow through with the plan and continue to ask questions and seek feedback from others in the physical and social environment.

Step 5: Look back and think about (reflect) what the challenge was and how you solved it. What worked and what didn't? What did you learn about yourself and the problem? How will you deal with the problem next time?

4. Group-building
Group-building is the first step in developing basic skills of working with a group. These experiences will help children to develop open communication by sharing ideas, solving problems, and working toward a collective goal, as the following scenario illustrates.

> In a school-age program, a group of 20 children were given a group-building challenge. A large blanket was placed at one end of the gym. The children were asked to each find a space to lie down on the blanket. They were then challenged to move the blanket, as a group, from one end of the gym to the other, with their arms and legs remaining in contact with the blanket at all times. The children negotiated and shared space, making room for everyone on the blanket. They talked and listened to each other about different ways to work together and how to move the blanket from one end to the other. They supported, encouraged, laughed, and giggled as they worked the blanket across the gym. When they finally made it to the other side, they cheered and congratulated each other.

The educator gathered the group to talk about what they learned from the experience, how they were feeling during the challenge, how they felt about each other, and how they felt as a group. The children said they learned the following group-building skills from the blanket challenge:

- Learning how to share space
- Respecting space and ideas
- Listening to each other's feelings and ideas
- Discussing their feelings
- Working as a group to solve the challenge
- Brainstorming ideas

The blanket challenge was a successful way for the children to practise their group-building skills. However, many things can influence the social structure of the group, including the number of children, their ages, and their experiences.

If a new group of children is joining a program in which there is a group that has already been together for a while, remember that the new entrants may not yet have had the experience of being part of this kind of group, so they may not be sure what is happening or what is expected of them. The educator can ask the more experienced children to tell the new arrivals what happens during the blanket challenge (for example, how they brainstorm ideas of how to solve the problem and decide as a group what to do), or ask them to suggest different ways in which the new children can be involved in the blanket challenge. The educator can also get the new children to walk alongside the blanket during the challenge and get them to describe to the group what happened. Afterwards the educator should encourage them to join in the next game.

Children need to participate and practise group-building skills. If the group is new, the educator may play more of a role by modelling and demonstrating some of the skills. During a community meeting, for instance, the educator will facilitate open communication and demonstrate how to be the chair of the meeting. The educator can provide, demonstrate, and implement co-operative games (such as parachute games), team-building exercises (moving a log), and group challenges (redesigning the indoor environment) to promote group-building skills and learning experiences. A variety of materials and loose parts can be used in the environment for children to work and create together.

5. Group Dynamics

Group dynamics is the second step in developing an understanding of how groups work and the educator's role in the group. A group is made up of children with different personalities, learning styles, motivation needs, and special needs, and with a variety of experiences. All of this can affect the community, and depending on the educator's skill and experience can change the community in either a positive or a negative way.

Developing group-building skills and skills such as open communication, sharing ideas, and problem-solving techniques is the basis for children to understand how group dynamics work. Group dynamics help children to understand their role in the group, how they can influence it, and what group membership means. Children lean naturally toward being either leaders, observers, listeners, or collaborators, and many are a combination of all four. These different roles will depend partly on the amount of experience each child has had with working in a group, and whether they have had opportunities to practise and develop different strategies.

Maintaining community and building group-dynamic skills depend on fostering an inclusive atmosphere in which all children—regardless of personality, learning style, or special needs—are included in the group. An active child who has trouble sitting through a meeting may be given the job of taking photographs of the process. The attention-seeking child may be great at chairing the meeting. A child who has difficulty with verbal communication may be best suited to taking minutes or illustrating the meeting. A reflective child may feel more comfortable adding ideas later by using a suggestion box. It takes a creative educator to make sure all children have the opportunity to participate in their own unique way.

Another creative faculty is to find the children's hidden talents and skills so as to encourage their personalities in positive ways. Instead of allowing the typical group dynamic brought about by a directed-power approach, which is based on conformity and focuses on peer pressure, the educator should try to facilitate the unexpected. This is done by involving all the children in the discussion, always with the aim of throwing light on the questions of what community is, what it means to be part of a group, and how this particular group works.

The dynamics of a particular group will change over time as children gain more experience with how it works, although their mood will also be affected by factors such as the season or the weather. If it has been raining for a number of days and the children have not been able to get outside to play, the group's mood may have more of an edge. This is the time to relax the program by de-emphasizing unnecessary routines and transitions. How can you make a 20-minute snack time more relaxed? Can you arrange larger blocks of time for the children to play indoors, or access the gym as much as possible? If you don't have access to a gym, think about ways you can modify the indoor environment to promote more physical activity. It is important for the educator to be flexible and to be able to adapt to the mood of the group.

6. Co-operation

Co-operation is one of the guiding principles of building community. It naturally tends to include all children, and can be demonstrated when children are participating in group-building and group-dynamic experiences. Children of different ages and abilities learn to work together, to communicate and share ideas, and to develop trusting relationships and a willingness to help each other. Positive peer relationships and friendships are reinforced when children are practising and learning how to be co-operative, as the following scenario illustrates.

> The children spent time keeping the school play yard clean. Some would sweep the asphalt area during playtime; others would pick up paper garbage. During one icy winter, the children were concerned that the ice on the asphalt was becoming dangerous. They decided they wanted to get rid of the ice, and so developed a plan to chip away at it and create a "production line" to get rid of it. They started by using a variety of metal shovels, garden edgers, and ice picks to chop away at the ice, and soon found that the heels of their winter boots also worked well. All the school-age children worked on this project, and each had a specific job. They created an assembly line of children: chippers, collectors, haulers, and pilers. They wanted to see how large a pile of ice they could create in the middle of the yard. During the school day some of the school children also participated in the chipping activity. After two weeks, the asphalt area was cleared of ice. By working together, and by involving the broader community, the school-age children were able to create a safer environment for all children to play.

In the above observation, the children had a common goal of removing the ice from the asphalt to make the play yard safe. They discussed and brainstormed different ways to approach the task of moving the ice, and the different tools that could be used. Each child had an active role to play from chipping, moving, or building piles of ice. During the process there was a natural flow of conversations, sharing ideas, and solving problems, and a "hum" of activity occurred. Everyone was involved in the experience of chipping and piling the ice, and the project lasted for two weeks. Eventually the school children got involved in the project during school time, and the school-age children received praise and a certificate from the school for their community spirit.

7. Friendships and Peer Relationships

School-age children enjoy playing and spending time together. As they do so, they are developing friends and peer relationships. They have the opportunity to develop and practise their communication skills, learn how groups work, support each other, negotiate, solve problems, help each other during conflict, and have fun as they develop positive peer relationships. When we asked a group of school-age children what the word

TABLE 8.4	Different types of peer pressure	
Direct Peer Pressure	**Indirect Peer Pressure**	**Silent Peer Pressure**
• The child is given a challenge in order to become part of the group. For example, he is told, "If you steal Kevin's book, you can become part of the group."	• The child is told what is and isn't "cool" in the opinion of the group. For example, how to dress and behave (such as using slang words).	• The child fears to speak up if he does not agree with the group or the group's leader.
• Failure to take up the challenge means the child will be excluded from the group.	• Failure to fulfill the group's expectations means the child will be excluded from the group.	• The child fears becoming the next victim of a bully if he does not conform to the bully's wishes.

"friendship" meant to them, their responses illustrated the different qualities and expectation of friends:

"A friend is someone you like. They play around with you and have fun." (age six)

"Friends don't act snobby, and they don't argue or disagree with you." (age ten)

"If you're nice to them, they're nice to you." (age seven)

"A friend is a person who helps you do things like going to movies or skipping. When you need something, they get it, and you will do the same [for them]." (age nine)

"They understand you when you feel sad and feel happy. You can count on them being there." (age eleven)

"It's someone who you talk to and share your secrets with. They will do the same with you." (age twelve)

When children first enter a school-age program, their friendships are likely to be limited to one or two close friends, and are generally based on a common interest, such as riding bikes or playing hockey. As they mature and develop, they start to form wider networks of friends and peer groups, and in particular same-sex groupings. They expect more from their friends than from others considered to be outside this group, including loyalty, understanding, and support. They will start to spend time in small groups, having conversations about the latest fads, discussing issues, and playing similar games. Eventually they will group together in cliques where they adhere to peer-group norms such as having the same hairstyle or clothing. During this period, peer pressure may influence children in both negative and positive ways by the expectation to conform to the group's (or its leader's) preferences (see Table 8.4). It is important for children to develop ways—such as "I" statements and bully-prevention strategies—to counter this pressure (examples can be found in Chapter 9). With these skills, children will be able to challenge peer pressure and not fall into the trap of conforming for the sake of being part of the group or for fear of being excluded. The educator will help in this process by developing strong self-esteem and confidence in the children, by modelling appropriate behaviour, and by challenging the children when they exclude others from play. Clear boundaries for interactions with members of the opposite sex occur later in the development of school-age children.

TABLE 8.5	Peer relationship skills

- Show the children how to introduce themselves to a group. Educators should model specific techniques, such as moving into the group and having a discussion about what the children are doing or creating.
- Show the children some joining in group activities, such as asking to join the play, co-operative games, sharing information, and getting involved in discussions.
- Show the children the importance of sharing their toys, materials, and belongings. Make sure it is clear which materials are being shared, for how long, and when the toys should be given back.
- Encourage the children to offer help to others, and to ask for help themselves if they need it.
- Show the children how to negotiate play rules. Make sure all children clearly understand the rules of a game.
- Show the children the importance of learning how to laugh and have fun with their peers.

In a community-oriented environment children are encouraged to have friends and to understand what it means to be a friend. They support and help each other, and they respect each other. Friends can offer support and help when there is a conflict with another child, or can encourage others to try a new activity. By having friends, children will learn how to communicate, negotiate, and compromise, and to understand another point of view. As children develop different peer-relationship skills, the sense of community will become more complex, based on shared experiences, mutual respect, and willingness to help each other.

Peers are important for the following reasons:

- They provide a sense of belonging to a group.
- They develop a sense of security and trust.
- They develop a sense of inclusion and community.
- They build self-esteem and confidence.
- They help children to develop and grow, both emotionally and socially.

Table 8.5 lists some of the strategies that can be used to help children develop peer-relationship skills.

A community-oriented environment also means that not all children are forced to be friends. But all children are expected to be supportive and respectful of each other.

8. Leadership

Children in a community-based program will have the chance to develop strong leadership abilities by practicing communication, debating, and group-dynamic skills, such as collaborating, co-operating, problem-solving, and negotiating. As children develop and practice their leadership abilities, more sophisticated skills and abilities will emerge—for example, mentoring and coaching skills and envisioning their role in the group and in society. Educators should mentor the children by modelling (Bandura schema) these skills, guided by the values and philosophy of the program. It is important for children to have the opportunity to develop leadership skills, because our society needs leaders with strong communication abilities who are able to advocate for everyone. If we start to develop leadership qualities in children while they are young, they will be able to take these skills with them when they grow into the wider community as youths and adults.

The basis for developing leadership skills is being able to recognize how your behaviour can influence, help, and affect individuals and groups without needing to control them. Leadership is thus based on the guided and facilitated use of power, rather than directed power. Children who demonstrate these qualities can become, as adults, the kind of people who are mentors for others, and whom children instinctively look up to, following their example, attitude, and behaviour. As leaders they will be the sorts of people who take seriously responsibilities (such as being a problem-solver), and are able to use their influence in a positive way, perhaps by motivating children to raise money for the victims of a local fire. They will become people who enjoy communicating and debating about various social issues (for instance, how to deal with strangers, drugs, violence, and so on), will participate in discussions, and will advocate for different groups and causes.

Children gain leadership experience when they participate in community meetings. They have the opportunity to take turns at chairing meetings and gain skills and develop strategies enabling them to work with groups of people, to negotiate, and to follow a process (the agenda). During meetings they also have the opportunity to communicate opinions, ideas, and concerns, to give input into the values and rules of the program, and to participate in developing curriculum webs and charts. Children should have the opportunity to participate in and take ownership of meetings, which will help to develop an understanding about their role in the group and to experience how adults run meetings.

When children have opportunities to be involved in co-operative group activities, group-building exercises, consensus-building, and planning, they are developing and practising leadership qualities necessary to be part of society. In a supportive community environment, a leader acquires skills and insights, develops respect for and empathy with the other participants, and grows in self-esteem and self-evaluation skills by participating in activities and helping other children. The following experience illustrates leadership skills in action.

In one program the children decided they wanted to create an herb garden, and during one planning session one of the children assumed more of a leadership role. This occurred outdoors as the children were preparing the soil for spring. This leader made sure that all children had the opportunity to be involved in discussion by asking them all questions about what herbs they would like to plant. The leader decided to take the initiative by creating a list of herbs that the group wanted, while another child volunteered to research the soil conditions needed for each type of herb. During this process, the children negotiated and brainstormed about the herbs they wanted, and the leader took on the role of supporting all the children through the process. The leader demonstrated strong mentoring skills by communicating and listening to the needs of the group. The leader involved the children in the problem-solving process by guiding them through the planning and collaboration process and demonstrating the webbing planning process.

9. Activism
When building community, the educator should encourage children to speak up and take a stand, especially if someone is not feeling safe or if something needs to be

challenged. Children are encouraged to problem-solve about how to take action, and are encouraged to be decision makers when they are involved in activism skills. Co-operation is encouraged between everyone, and critical-thinking skills are fostered. It is important to teach children different strategies and techniques when developing activism skills, such as "I" statements (see Chapter 9). When successfully implemented, activism leads to a shift in the power structure from guided power to facilitated power, with the educator supporting the process. Children who speak up about, say, wanting to make changes to planned activities or types of snacks, or who are opposing bullying are demonstrating activism skills. They feel trusted and safe in the environment, and they know the educator will not judge them and the other children will not shoot down their ideas. All of the foundation skills and building blocks (such as communication, respectful language, inclusion, and problem-solving) are in place when activism occurs. Children feel empowered and strong enough to stand up for their rights and the rights of others, which is the basis of a true sense of community.

COMMUNITY MEETINGS

Why Have Meetings?

Community meetings are an important part of building community because they bring children and educators together, provide an opportunity for everyone to connect with each other, give everyone a forum to speak out and raise issues and ideas, and help develop a positive playroom culture. It is a structured time for children and the educators to gather as a group to brainstorm, share, discuss, plan, support, solve problems, and express their feelings about the program and each other. It is a time for the children to learn to be part of a group, understand their role in the group, and learn skills that will help them to support each other—all essential elements in building community.

During community meetings children are considered a valued part of the group because they are actively involved in developing a structure for the meetings. By being involved, they become part of the program's community by having input into the values of the group (for instance, what it means to be part of the group), curriculum development, developing rules, and developing leadership and community skills. Community meetings support children's critical thinking and give them the opportunity to voice their concerns, issues, and ideas and to problem-solve solutions—for example, brainstorming the types of herbs to plant in the garden.

What Happens During Community Meetings?

The following six things occur during community meetings:

1. Discussion
2. Sharing of feelings, ideas, opinions, and issues
3. Reflection
4. Planning
5. Documentation
6. Developing of rules, consequences, and solutions

The Six Elements

1. Discussion
Community meetings are a time for children and educators to share information about what happened at school, at home, or on the weekend. They should be kept natural, spontaneous, and geared to encouraging everyone to participate. It is important to have a time when children can practise their conversational skills, which will give them the opportunity to share personal history, issues, opinions, ideas, and concerns.

2. Sharing of Feelings, Ideas, Opinions, and Issues
Community meetings should be environments in which both children and educators feel safe to share their feelings. The educator should share her own feelings, ideas, opinions, and issues, which will help the children do the same. Encourage children to listen reflectively, to use caring and respectful language, and to focus on the ideas being shared.

3. Reflection
Community meetings can be a time when children have the opportunity to reflect about past experiences. Relaxation activities such as deep breathing can help children to connect to their past experiences and create a good base for visualization activities. Children can think back and visualize something they enjoyed, such as a field trip to a museum. This information can then be brought back to the group for a discussion about what they enjoyed during the field trip, which can be useful for identifying common interests among the children and for planning future field trips. Reflections can also be used to sum up what occurred during a meeting, what the group talked about, and what future activities are planned. These overviews can help ensure the meeting ends on a positive note.

4. Planning
Community meetings can be used for planning the program. Planning time can give the children the experience of using books to do research, of brainstorming webs, charts, and materials lists, and of bringing new ideas to the group. Planning also gives the educator the opportunity to follow up on any planned activities and the materials needed for an activity.

   Children have the opportunity at meetings to brainstorm as a group what they would like to do in the program, what to have for their snacks, where to go on field trips, what projects to implement, and so on. Community activities such as fundraising, developing job lists, and volunteering can be planned and implemented during the meeting.

5. Documentation
A community meeting is a time for children to be involved in developing and constructing documentation panels from experiences such as field trips (going bowling, perhaps) and projects (like sewing). Children should have the opportunity to use cameras, tape recorders, and camcorders to document the community process and when planning curriculum. In one program, a group of children who were friends decided to use photographs of the group playing skipping games together to create a panel about friends. They mounted the photographs on bristol board and added stories about what it means to be friends. This occurred during a "documentation meeting time," and

All children should be involved in the planning process by having the opportunity to brainstorm and share ideas.

when they finished their panel, they displayed it with pride on the parents' bulletin board.

The meeting process should be documented in the form of written minutes, which can be supplemented with photographs showing important events of the meeting, success stories, and a transcript of the discussion that took place. These forms of documentation will help to keep a visual record of what happened, and they show the success of the children and the group. Children, educators, and families can use this documentation to remember what happened in the past and prepare for what is going to happen next.

6. Developing of Rules, Consequences, and Solutions

Rules, consequences and solutions for the program can be brainstormed and developed during community meetings. Involving the children in the development of rules and proactive solutions helps to give them strategies to deal with issues before they become problems and empowers them to help each other and to be responsible for their own actions. Rules about what is expected of the children and the educators should also be developed with the children during community meetings. Table 8.6 provides examples of broad, respectful rules and strategies to resolve issues and conflict.

TABLE 8.6	Rules and strategies for dealing with conflict

Rules	Strategies
• Respect people and property	• Talk it out
• Respect people's bodies	• Listen to each other
• Respect people's feelings	• Use caring language and avoid "you" statements (See Chapter 9)
• Respect other children's material and toys (e.g., Lego structures, forts, games still in progress, lockers)	• Use "I" statements
	• Ask for help

All rules and consequences were developed for and by school-age children.

Nine Tips to Remember When Structuring a Community Meeting

1. Children's Experience

The author had the experience of facilitating a community meeting with a group of children who were already well-acquainted with the meeting process. They were planning what kinds of games they would like to play in the gym. There was a new child in the program whose previous child-care experience had been in an educator-directed program, with no input from the children. During her first meeting, she made it clear she thought the meeting process "was stupid" and that it was the educators' responsibility to plan the program. From her statement, it was clear she had no experience with giving input into the planning of the program. The educator and the other children explained why it was important for the children to be involved in the planning—the program belongs to the children, and their involvement demonstrated this. Over time the child slowly developed a sense of security and trust, and an understanding of how the program worked. Two months later she was a full member of the group, saying, "I can't believe we have choices here! I love being part of making the decisions."

If children have not had any experience of being part of community meetings, the structure of the meeting may seem strange. Children need to have the process explained to them and modelled for them. They need to understand why community meetings are important and all the different ways in which they can be involved. Be patient with the children and work through the process slowly. This way, children will develop the necessary skills to participate and to be effective members of the group.

2. Consistency

Be consistent with the location, time, length, and frequency of the meetings. When you first initiate a community meeting you may want to have it once a week so children and educators can both get into the habit of having meetings and understanding how they work. Once everyone is familiar with the process, meetings can be held less frequently if desired.

3. Location

Find a comfortable space in which a large group of children can feel safe participating in a meeting. The living room or dining room area in the indoor environment may be the best location to hold community meetings at first. When first implementing meetings, find a location with the fewest distractions—for example, try to avoid having a meeting in front of a window, which can be distracting for some children. Meetings can occur very naturally during snack time, lunchtime, in the dining room area, or during outdoor "waiting" transitions. When children are familiar with and have had experience with community meetings, expand them to a variety of other spaces: outdoors, or in the gym or lunchroom. The authors have been successful in having meetings in tents, in children's forts, and during play. As children become more experienced, ask them where they would like to have their meetings.

4. Time Management and Flexibility

As mentioned in point 2, meetings should be held at the same time of day to begin with. As children become familiar with the routine, you can become more flexible about the time. If you notice children are having difficulty listening and seem overly energized or overly tired, you should probably take it as an indication that it is not a good time for a meeting. The weather, time of the day, and school routines (such as report-card time, grade three testing in Ontario, or seasonal holidays) can affect children's behaviour and therefore may affect your meetings. Be sensitive to the moods of the children, and modify the meetings or move them to a different time or a different day.

5. Meeting Structure

It is important to have a structure for your meeting; without one, children will not know what is expected of them. The structure will also help keep each meeting consistent. The following are some of the elements that need to be in place for a meeting:

- *Beginning activity.* Start the meeting on a positive note. The following are options to start or end your meeting: relaxation exercises, a chant or cheer, a group-building game, or visualization activities.
- *Chairing.* Have a process for choosing a child or educator to chair the meeting.
- *Minutes.* Have a child and an educator take minutes of the meeting.
- *Documenting.* Have children document the meeting (for instance, with a camera, camcorder, or audiotape).
- *Following the agenda.* Follow the order of items on the agenda.
- *End activity.* End the meeting on a positive note, by reflecting on the positive results that have been reached, or use the chant or cheer from the beginning.

6. Democratic System of Voting

Children enjoy being involved in making changes and decisions in the program and can be confident decision makers. It is important for all children to be involved in having input into the program and to be involved in the voting process. Brainstorm with the children about how they would like to bring ideas and issues forward. Suggest different ways to make decisions (including voting, counting-out games, flipping a coin) and

TABLE 8.7	Sample agenda template

AGENDA FOR SCHOOL-AGE MEETINGS
DATE: June 20, 2007
TIME: 4:00
LOCATION: Drop-and-flop area

1. Beginning activity: group chant and cheer

2. Read agenda

3. Read expectations for a meeting

4. Share stories about how we have included others in our thoughts and our play

5. Group activity: Creating a peace pledge

6. Other business:

    i) Voting on baking or cooking: The educators would like to brainstorm and plan future baking experiences.

    ii) Storage space for Lego structures: Warsame would like to discuss the issue of why other children are taking pieces of Lego off his structures and to ask if he can have a different space to store them.

7. End Activity: What happened during the meeting, group chant and cheer, etc.

explain the difference between voting systems based on majority or on consensus. Explain to the children the way decision-making and voting work in our municipal, provincial, and federal government (that is, through elections) or how adults make decisions at team meetings.

7. Developing an Agenda
Develop an agenda format, as seen in Table 8.7, and post it the week before, so children and educators can add to it if necessary. Mount a pen or pencil beside the agenda for children to use, and remind them before the meeting starts what the agenda is used for. The person who puts the items on the agenda will be expected to facilitate that part of the discussion. The items discussed will dictate the structure and flow of the meetings. Everything on the agenda should be discussed, and a forward-action plan— deciding who will implement the meeting's decisions—needs to be developed after each discussion.

8. Taking Minutes
Encourage the children to take minutes, either in writing or using visual pictograms. Develop a sign-up sheet so children can have the opportunity to take minutes; all the children should be encouraged to take a turn at one time or another. When children are doing the minutes, have another educator take minutes also. When the meeting is finished, post the minutes (both the children's and the educator's) beside the agenda for next week. Provide clipboards, paper, pens, pencils, and dictionaries for children taking minutes. See Table 8.8 for an example.

TABLE 8.8	Example of minutes

Minutes for August 17, 2005

Agenda

Planning for kindergarten show
Movie for Friday
Bowling next week
School is starting

Minutes:

Planning for kindergarten show

Plan a date for the show (raps, comic acts, and air band).
Plan date: Wednesday, August 20th at 10:00
Leslie and Kevin are the masters of ceremonies for the show.
Continue to write rap for show.

Movie for Friday

Voted on movie for Friday. *Wizard of Oz.*

Bowling next week

We have a bowling field trip planned for next week.
Hodan volunteers to call the bowling alley and organize a time and date. Tuesday and Thursday are possible dates.

School is starting

School is starting soon. Would like to find out who will be our teachers this year and visit the classroom before school starts.

9. Chairing

When first starting the process of holding meetings, it is important for the educator to model how to chair a meeting. The role of the chair is to ensure the following:

- Everyone is safe and ready for the meeting.
- There is a beginning and end activity.
- The order of the agenda is followed.
- Everyone is aware of the group expectation of appropriate behaviour.
- The discussion is facilitated.
- Everyone has the opportunity to express their ideas and concerns.
- The flow of the meeting is kept going.

Meetings should not be thought of as occasions to lecture children or to control proceedings toward a predetermined end. The educator's role is, rather, to demonstrate what is expected so that everyone can follow an agreed procedure. Once the children have observed how to facilitate a meeting, the educator's aim should be for all the children to have the opportunity to be the chair at some point or other. Remember, you are still involved in the process by sitting close by to guide children through it and to step in if necessary (for instance, if some children are not listening or are being disruptive).

ROLE OF THE EDUCATOR IN DEVELOPING COMMUNITY

In the Chapter 2 overview section, the many roles of the educator are listed and described. When developing community, the educator at times will be a facilitator, director, model, and communicator. The educator's role in developing community is to set up an environment and curriculum where children can become part of a group, learn group membership skills, and develop positive attitudes, so that they eventually become productive, active members of society. The educator's knowledge of childhood development theories and understanding of the value of community will affect the type of community that the program develops. The educator's roles can be thought about in more detail as follows.

Role Model

Educators must be positive role models when they are building community by interacting and communicating with children, parents, and other educators. Bandura's theory talks about how children are keen observers and will model themselves on what they see and hear the educator doing and saying. Children will expect the educators to follow the same model they have for the children, and will be quick to pick up on any discrepancies. The educator therefore needs always to be aware of what influence his words and behaviour will have on the children. For example, the educator can remind children that if they are respectful when another child talks, the other child will respectfully listen when they are talking; the educator can then back this up by being seen to listen respectfully when a child is talking, rather than breaking off into a discussion with another educator. If two educators need to discuss

Group meetings give the educator and the children the experience of working together and being a valuable part of the group.

TABLE 8.9	Involving children in the program environment and activities

- Rearrange the physical layout of the room. For example, have the children redesign the room, move the living room areas to the construction areas.
- Encourage children to bring out new materials and to organize the shelves.
- Move materials and loose parts to different areas of the room (for example, plastic pipes and tubes from the construction areas to the living room areas to create a communication system).
- Children can be involved in making things for the room (e.g., pillows or curtains).
- Encourage children to bring artifacts from home to represent their families.
- Have a day each week where the children will help to clean the room.
- Encourage the children to take turns watering plants and taking care of pets.
- Encourage the children to pick up litter from the play yard and to help to shovel the snow off pathways.

something urgently between themselves during a meeting, they should move away from the group so they do not disturb the meeting.

Developing the Environment and Curriculum

The educator is responsible for creating a home-like environment that facilitates group experiences and allows the children to develop a sense of ownership and opportunities to connect with each other, and to be involved in building community. Table 8.9 provides ideas on how to involve children when creating the environment. In developing a sense of community the educator's role is to plan and implement a number of activities for children to learn about and experience community. Table 8.10 lists learning experiences that will help the children to develop various community strategies and techniques.

TABLE 8.10	Learning experiences to promote a sense of community

- Co-operative and team development games
- Group challenges (e.g., cleaning the room)
- Taking turns making snack
- Gardening experience such as brainstorming, planning, and creating a herb garden
- Dramatic play activities (e.g., mirroring, mime, skits, body machines)
- Community walks and field trips (e.g., going to the farmers' market to purchase fruits and vegetables for snack)
- Group storytelling activities
- Creating and implementing air bands, skits, and plays
- Fundraising activities
- Taking care of the outdoor environment, for example, sweeping the yard
- Sponsoring animal welfare groups or environmental groups
- Social action activities (e.g., recycling, taking care of the environment, protecting animals.

TABLE 8.11	Developing community over time

Step 1: Introducing community time to the children

- Provide a time to share ideas and interests with others.
- Explain what meetings are for (discussions, sharing, planning).
- Explain that each child is considered a valuable member of the group.
- Explain how meetings are structured and model communication and conflict-resolution techniques.
- At this stage, meetings may be brief.

Step 2: Beginning of community

- Ask the children to develop the rules and consequences for the group.
- Discuss the group needs, including everyone's need for respect, trust, independence, and responsibility.
- Develop the agenda, minutes, and procedure for chairing a meeting.
- Talk about specific questions, such as what the children want to have for their snack.
- Continue to **model** communication and conflict-resolution techniques.
- Meetings may remain brief.

Step 3: Working toward community

- Discuss with the children what they would like to play with in the program.
- Brainstorm ideas, ways to implement the program, necessary resources, and influencing factors (such as the available time).
- Record ideas and process using webbing. If children have never experienced this process, the educator will demonstrate. Explain the purpose of a web and what it looks like.
- The children start to develop learning experiences, projects, and clubs.
- Continue to **model and facilitate** effective communication and conflict-resolution techniques.
- Encourage the children to practice and demonstrate effective communication and conflict-resolution techniques.
- Encourage the children to develop the agenda, write the minutes, and take turns at being chair with the guidance of the educator.
- Meetings tend to be longer. Be flexible.
- Meetings may be held in different locations. Small group may have community meetings during play—perhaps in a tent or fort. Or designate a specific play area as a meeting space.

Step 4: Community

- Children tell the educator that they want a community meeting based on their needs.
- Children develop the agenda, taking turns at being the chair and the minute-taker. A system for keeping track of taking turns will be developed.
- Children will become more adept at conflict-resolution and will initiate the resolution of conflict and the solving of problems, demonstrating a strong sense of community.
- The educator will become **less of a facilitator** as the children begin spontaneously to take a more active role in developing community.
- The children are structuring how to schedule their time and the educator's time in the program. For example, who will facilitate clubs or who will bake.
- Children are developing projects, clubs, and resources.
- An inclusive community and attitude is emerging.
- The children are developing a shared history and ownership of the community.
- The educator is become a **resource person and advisor.**

Encouraging Group-Building

Children should have the opportunity to be a part of the group. For example, if the children are creating a mural for the room, the experience will give them the opportunity to work together to brainstorm, research, design, and paint the mural. The mural becomes a co-operative experience in which all children are encouraged to contribute in different ways. They can contribute their ideas and skills and have a sense of pride when the project is finished.

Children should have opportunities to contribute as active members of the group. Developing curriculum and values by participating in community meetings will give the children a forum to contribute. For example, if they are missing things from their lockers, they can bring this issue to a community meeting. Once missing belongings have been returned to their owners, the children can have the opportunity to contribute to the brainstorming and decision-making processes about how to avoid such incidents in the future.

DEVELOPING A COMMUNITY OVER TIME

Finally, it is important to remember that developing a sense of community and helping children feel comfortable with the process of community meetings takes time. Table 8.11 shows the various steps and the roles of the educator and the children in building community. The process described in the table came from a program that was implemented over a 12-month period. However, it is important to remember that during the year the program may revisit an earlier step to reflect on past experiences or to fine-tune skills.

Summary

This chapter illustrates why a sense of community is important and how it can be developed in a school-age program. This sense of community is the foundation for educators' guidance of children's behaviour when implementing an emergent curriculum. Building blocks such as safety, open communication, and respect are foundation skills crucial for children, parents, and educators to develop a sense of ownership of the program. The nine building blocks, including group dynamics, friendships, and problem-solving, help children and the educator to develop and practise strategies and skills in building community. It is essential for educators to understand their roles in facilitating community with children and how their application of the three types of power—directed, guided, and facilitated—can affect community. Community takes time to develop, and the chapter demonstrates how to develop and implement a program that nourishes this sense over a period of one year.

Student Learning Experiences

Community Activities

Part 1: Visualizing Community

Visit a school-age program and undertake the following exercise with the children: Ask them to close their eyes and think about what community is. Use these questions to guide the children during the visualization:

- What is community?
- What does community sound like?

- What does community feel like?
- What happens in a community?
- Is community the same in the classroom and the play yard?
- How would you develop community in the classroom and the play yard?

When the activity is over, encourage the children to discuss with each other what community means to them.

Part 2: Illustrating Community

Provide individual children with a variety of paper, markers, pencil crayons, or pastels. Ask the children to illustrate what the following statements mean to them:

- What does your community look like?
- What does your community feel like?
- What happens in your community?
- Who is in your community?
- What happens in your school community?
- What happens in your home community?

Part 3: Write a Story about Community

Ask the children to tell or write a story about their community based on the above visualization and illustrations. Provide them with paper, markers, or pencils. The story can be added to their illustrations. Using staplers or binders, children can be encouraged to create their own community books. Use the following questions to guide the children.

- What does your community look like?
- What does your community feel like?
- Who lives in your community?

Part 4: Create a Community Mural

Create a group mural with children in a school-age program. Involve all the children in the process of designing and creating the mural. What did the children learn during the process? What did you learn? List the different community strategies and techniques used to implement this activity (e.g., respect).

Resource File Create a file of community activities using the community building blocks sections for the resource file (Table 8.1). For example, for each section, provide activities for communication, group-building, friendships, co-operation, and problem-solving activities. Include at least 15 entries for each section.

Internet On the Internet, find at least five articles to support the philosophy of community. Compare and contrast the five articles. Give two examples from each article when comparing and contrasting. Back them up with your understanding of building community and child development concepts.

Review Questions

1. List and describe in your own words the three different types of power used by the educator in relation to a school-age program.

   Part A: Give an example of when you would use each type of power. Give an example of how you would change the type of power to another type. For example, how would you change directed power to guided power?

   Part B: What do you think would be the main challenge for you to make this change? How would you meet the challenge?

2. Describe why it is important to develop community *with* children. Which of the five building blocks would you implement first with school-age children, and why?

3. Describe why community meetings are important. How would you structure a community meeting? What do you think would be the main challenge for you in facilitating a community meeting? How would you meet this challenge?

4. From the nine building blocks for creating community, choose three and describe the educator's role in each. List four activities (include the educator's role) that you would implement with children for each of the three building blocks.

5. Review Table 8.10: Developing Community Time. List at least three activities that you would implement to help to support and develop each step.

CHAPTER 9

Guiding Behaviour

OVERVIEW

This chapter will focus on the educator's role in guiding children's behaviour by helping children to understand what conflict is, how to respond when conflict is happening, and how to prevent conflict in the program. The educator's role is to facilitate and guide the children through the process by including them in the planning and developing of a peaceful community and environment. The importance of developing an appropriate physical environment and a sense of community illustrates the need to develop a safe environment and facilitate community skills when guiding children's behaviour.

A variety of strategies will be discussed in this chapter to illustrate the five behaviour-guidance components that need to be considered. We will also address the causes of conflict, its different varieties, the educator's role in de-escalating it, and questions of resources, power, and values. Developing rules, consequences, and solutions during community meetings will also be discussed, and different steps of how to involve children in the process will be highlighted. We will also explore the importance of children having opportunities to develop and practice conflict-resolution skills, and develop their mediation skills.

Finally, the nature of bullying and the components of a bullying-prevention program will be discussed. In this section the different types and effects of bullying will be discussed to show how bullying can impact the development of the child in a school-age program. A number of different strategies and activities will demonstrate how bullying prevention can be implemented in a school-age program.

WHAT IS BEHAVIOUR GUIDANCE?

The term *behaviour guidance* rather than *behaviour management* emphasizes "guiding" children's behaviour rather than "managing" negative behaviours. It is an approach that focuses on changing the behaviour of the child rather than being judgmental of the child's personality. Guiding children's behaviour is a proactive approach. In this approach the educator facilitates the learning of the children by teaching a variety of techniques to help the children to problem-solve and determine the best way to deal with a specific conflict situation, such as name-calling. Children will have the opportunity to practise and demonstrate specific techniques during play or other activities.

DEVELOPING SELF-REGULATED PROBLEM-SOLVING STRATEGIES

The goal of guiding children's behaviour is for children to develop self-control and self-regulated problem-solving strategies (Bandura's and Erikson's schemas). With support, guidance, and modelling from the educator, children will be encouraged to practise and develop self-regulated problem-solving strategies. This happens when children have the opportunities to develop, practise, and implement conflict-resolution skills by brainstorming and developing rules, consequences, and solutions during community meetings, and opportunities to express their problem-solving strategies through creative and language arts, such as writing stories about what it means to be safe or using role-plays to practise different strategies ("I" statements). In an environment that is based on community, children will have the opportunity to see, experience, and practise their peacemaking and conflict-resolution skills. They will be better equipped to deal with challenging behaviours, peer pressure, violence, bullying, or harassment.

The following steps will help children to understand and learn how to develop their self-regulation and problem-solving strategies and skills. Encourage the children to think about each step when they are problem-solving how to deal with a conflict or trying to understand a "power on" situation.

- Defining the problem
- Identifying several possible solutions
- Predicting the outcome
- Practising the technique
- Evaluating the effectiveness of the technique
- Modifying the technique

WHY GUIDE CHILDREN'S BEHAVIOUR?

Behaviour guidance in the school-age program gives the child the opportunity to practise and demonstrate developmentally appropriate strategies and techniques in a safe and supportive environment. It is important to consider the child's developmental level, past experiences, strengths and challenges, (e.g., English as a second language), and family practices when guiding her behaviour. It is important to remember that the aim is to guide behaviour (facilitated power) rather than to direct or dictate it, although there will be occasions, such as when there is aggression toward others, when the educator will need to use a directive approach (directed power) to ensure that all the children are physically and emotionally safe.

Developmentally, school-age children have the ability and skills to demonstrate and implement behaviour-guidance practices and conflict-resolution/mediation skills. Table 9.1 illustrates why behaviour guidance is developmentally appropriate for school-age children. Their advanced communication skills and ability to consider another person's point of view mean they will be able to understand the importance of telling their stories by using "I" statements, not interrupting each other, and understanding how the other children felt during the conflict,

TABLE 9.1	**Skills and abilities school-age children possess that help them implement behaviour-guidance practices**
School-age children	
• Are logical in their thinking	
• Have advanced communication skills	
• Can considers another person's point of view	
• Desire increased independence	
• Are willing and able to accept increased responsibility	
• Need to feel power and ownership over their own behaviour	
• Know how to use a variety of non-defensive communication and conflict-resolution skills	

skills that are important to the mediation process. It is important to note that these skills will not emerge without help. Children still need the educator to teach mediation skills and encourage them to use these skills during play and when participating in group activities, such as planning and performing an air band.

Providing appropriate behaviour guidance will help the child develop self-control and self-regulated problem-solving strategies, develop self confidence, communicate effectively, develop independence, become more responsible, build decision-making skills, and interact with others in a positive, safe, and respectful manner. Children who participate in group-building and group dynamic learning experiences (e.g., group clapping games) will have the opportunity to practise and demonstrate these skills.

Behaviour-guidance strategies help children become integrated into their micro-community (Bronfenbrenner). Behaviour-guiding skills, such as developing leadership and mentoring skills, will also help the children to effectively participate in the larger society/macro-community (Bronfenbrenner).

CONFLICT

Before starting to discuss how to develop and implement strategies and techniques, it is important to understand what causes conflict, what it looks like, and what it sounds like.

When we think about conflict, what come to mind are anger, emotional rather than thoughtful reactions, not listening, and interrupting each other. We think of it as an exercise in power in which one party must win and the other lose. Everyone reacts to conflict in different ways—for example, by an immediate, explosive reaction, by shutting down, by trying to avoid the situation, or by continuing to revisit the source of the conflict again and again. Conflict is seen as being negative, not productive, and at times as something that has no resolution. Yet the following are all ways of thinking about conflict in a positive light:

- It stimulates solutions to problems by promoting discussion.
- It makes changes to the group dynamics through negotiating and solving problems.
- It helps build positive communication skills.
- It helps develop self-assessment skills.

Conflict is a natural process that children, educators, and parents go through. It can be healthy, but a lack of communication during conflict can make it destructive. Children need to be taught how to communicate effectively and how to express their emotions during a conflict through coached by the educator and through having the opportunity to practise self-regulated problem-solving strategies that the educators demonstrate. They need a safe and supportive environment in which they are treated equally and in which they are able to practise and demonstrate skills. The educators also need to model positive communication when interacting with children and with colleagues. Conflict should be seen as a win–win situation in which everyone agrees to work it out with a willingness to listen, generate ideas, discuss solutions, and compromise.

When children learn the appropriate strategies, they can help each other by modelling the techniques, suggesting different ways to resolve an issue, or mediating a conflict. They can be part of the mediation/mentoring process, which helps them to develop empathy, positive expression of emotions, appropriate communication skills, problem-solving strategies, and a sense of ownership and community. The more experienced children can help the children with less experience, and can be seen in a leadership/mentoring role in the program.

What Causes Conflict

Conflict can occur at any time of the day. It can occur during snack time, during indoor or outdoor play, during routines and transitions, or during community time. Causes of conflict between children can be triggered by physical needs (for example, lack of sleep, low blood sugar, hunger, physical disabilities) and by their physical appearance as school-age children enter puberty. Emotional and social needs can also cause conflict—for example, worrying about being bullied, wanting to be liked by peers, or stress from a situation at school. The child may have had a disagreement with his parents or teacher, and so lash out at other children as a way of releasing anger or frustration. Cognitive and language abilities can cause conflict, such as having a different learning style and different academic abilities, or speaking with an unfamiliar accent. There are situations in which having different physical abilities—such as different eye–hand–foot co-ordination, upper body strength, or fine motor abilities—can trigger conflict.

When working with children from the ages of six to twelve, it is important for the educator to ensure that the program meets all their developmental and individual needs. By doing this, the educator can help reduce conflict among the children and between children and staff.

Three Types of Conflict

Educators observe that children's conflict generally falls into one of three broad types, according to the source of the conflict. Once this is understood, the educator will be able to make a proactive response, helping to develop strategies that will enable the children to deal with the conflict.

The three types of conflict involve:

- Resources, materials, and loose parts
- Power over the group
- Values, culture, and family practices

Resources, Materials, and Loose Parts Conflict over resources is the most visible and easiest type of conflict to deal with. It occurs when children are sharing play materials or toys. This might happen because there are not enough materials to go around. For example, if you have only one or two basketballs for a group of 30 children, conflict is likely to arise. The educator must thus make sure that there are enough materials, toys, and developmentally appropriate pieces of equipment for all children to use. By observing how the children play, and with what, the educator can work out if more materials of a certain kind are needed. Also, children can tell the educator what materials or toys are needed during community meetings.

Wanting other children's materials and toys can also create conflict even when there is no overall shortage. This can happen when a specific item—perhaps a Gameboy or a marble of a certain colour—is particularly desirable. Many programs have policies to limit, or even eliminate, situations in which toys and materials are brought to the program from home, in order to avoid these situations. Make sure the program's policies are developmentally appropriate for school-age children and are based on their development. For example, children of this age enjoy collecting. If collectible toys brought from home, such as sets of cards, are not allowed, then collecting may be stifled. All policies should be communicated verbally and in writing to the parents and children. During community meetings, encourage the children to express their views in creating the policies about toys from home to ensure they will have an interest in following the policies.

The following is an example of a statement developed with children from a school-age program about toys from home.

Children in the school-age program have established the following rules for toys from home. They must meet the following criteria:

- *The toy does not promote competition.*
- *The toy does not promote violence.*
- *The toy does not promote racism, sexism, homophobia, or any other form of discrimination.* [For instance, this might affect some games played on Gameboy units.]
- *Wheeled toys require the proper safety equipment, i.e., helmets and wrist, knee, and elbow pads; these toys will be used only once a week.*

In some programs, children are allowed to bring in toys such as bikes, scooters, or skateboards on special days.

Power Over the Group Power imbalance, which over time can lead to bullying, is the biggest factor in conflict among children, and between children and educators. At times it is easy to identify a misuse of power—for example, when children are having a discussion that deteriorates into physical conflict. At other times, it can be very difficult to see the power struggle going on when the conflict is a psychological one. Such conflicts can be the most damaging, however, since they have the potential to dig deep emotionally, becoming detrimental to a child's self-esteem and confidence. Such a conflict can be seen when a child is excluded from a group. The children initiating the exclusion have the power in the group, and are therefore able to persuade other members to exclude a specific child. Exclusion can be based on personality traits, physical appearance, disabilities, or cultural family practices. The exclusion can take such subtle forms as giving the child a hard look, whispering about her, or turning their backs on the child.

Influences from society and from children's culture (such as TV, advertisements, and music) can also create an imbalance of power. For example, wearing a fashionable clothing label can give you a certain status with the group, so if you do not have such clothes you may be seen as not having power.

Having access to money, housing, and food can also be seen to confer status and power in a school-age program, particularly when that gives children access to expensive toys. If they are flaunting an expensive toy, a computer, or a watch, then the children without will feel powerless, setting up the conditions for conflict.

Conflicts over power are thus very subtle, and the educator needs to continually observe and be visible during learning experiences and play time so as to monitor situations in which such conflicts might arise. The educator needs to be aware of what is happening to the group dynamics and to individuals by asking specific questions and by challenging the group when power is being misused. The educator can then help the group to develop curriculum addressing the issues that have been raised. It is important for the educator to bring back to the children, during community meetings, examples of behaviour in which power has been misused and to ask the children for input on how to deal with the issues.

Values, Culture, and Family Practices Conflict over values is a clash of beliefs based on cultural and religious practices, societal issues, or family dynamics. This type of conflict arises because of discrimination and prejudices that stem from a lack of awareness and knowledge. It can be the most difficult type of conflict to address because you are dealing with potential clashes between societal norms and family expectations. It can be very emotional for children when they face any type of discrimination. The following are some examples of conflict over values.

- Family practices; for example, being walked to school. The child may be teased or excluded from the group by others who are not walked to school.
- Family structure; for example, same-sex families or single-parent families. Children who do not fit the societal norm; for example, a child whose parental figures are both women, may face name-calling or exclusion, and may be physically hurt.
- Cultural and family practices; for example, how you dress, what you eat, and what holidays you celebrate. Girls who wear a sari or a headscarf or Sikh boys who wear a top-knot may be teased or excluded for having a different appearance.

By creating a sense of community in a diverse multicultural setting, the educator will help to develop and promote appreciation of and respect for each child's own culture and family life and that of others. Educators need to implement learning activities within the curriculum that will challenge assumptions the children might have about different cultural and religious practices and that are accepting of the individual experiences of each child. Teaching children activism skills and explaining diversity to them will help them to understand each other better. It is also important to teach children strategies for dealing with racism, sexism, and homophobia in a safe and trusting environment.

THE EDUCATOR'S ROLE

Educators influence and guide children's behaviour in four different ways. First, by the physical environment they provide for children to interact in. Second, by their own verbal interactions with the children. Third, by teaching a variety of strategies, techniques, and problem-solving skills to resolve conflict, and fourth, by modelling appropriate behaviours and actions when interacting with children.

The educator guides the children's behaviour during play by implementing a variety of techniques. Some of these are as follows:

1. *Positive comments and encouragement.* It is important to use a variety of positive comments when guiding children's behaviour during play. For example, a comment such as "I've noticed that everyone is solving problems and working together to put the puzzle together. How does it make you feel?" tells a child what behaviour is expected, describes the behaviour, and focuses on feelings. The comment ends with a question for children to respond to, prompting reflection on what is happening.

2. *Redirection.* Some behaviour can be directed during play experiences. The materials provided in the environment, and their location, can direct play. For example, by providing skipping ropes, basketballs, building materials, art materials, loose parts, and digging equipment such as shovels throughout the outdoor environment, educators can direct children to different areas and different play materials. Educators can also direct a child to a different area if they feel a potential conflict may occur.

3. *Setting appropriate limits.* The educator needs to set appropriate limits and must follow through on enforcing them. Limits should be appropriate for the age of the child and should help to promote independence and responsibility. Limits help to guide children and are there to make sure children are safe. For example, if children want to climb a 3-metre fence with a drop of 15 metres on the other side, the educator may set limits on how high the children can climb up the fence, or he may decide the fence is off limits. The educators can negotiate limits with children as they become more accomplished at different skills (such as balancing, running, and jumping).

4. *Establishing physical proximity.* The educator needs to observe children in the environment and move around between groups of children. Children will know that the educator is observing and is there to help them. If the educator knows that particular children tend to get involved in conflict when they play board games, she should be close by to help the children. For example, if the conflict tends to be interpretation of the rules or their observance, the educator can be part of the game by helping to read the rules and explaining how the game is played. Sometimes just being close by will help the children to focus on what is expected.

5. *Teaching strategies, techniques, and self-regulated problem-solving strategies.* Teaching a variety of strategies, techniques, and problem-solving strategies to individual children and to groups of children is one of the main roles the educator will undertake when guiding children's behaviour. The educator will help children to understand the different types of conflict and how it occurs, practise different strategies, such as "I" statements, to gain self-control by participating in role-playing activities, and identify which strategy will help to de-escalate a conflict. At the end of this chapter, in the bullying prevention section, a variety of hands-on activities will be listed to help children understand conflict and develop self-regulated problem-solving strategies.

6. *Modelling appropriate behaviour.* The educator plays an important role in children's learning and understanding behaviour-guidance strategies by modelling appropriate behaviours and strategies when interacting with children, other educators, and parents. Bandura's social cognitive theory states that children learn by watching others (observer), and will imitate another person's (model) behaviour. Children are always observing the interactions and communication skills of the educator, and by observing they gather information and insights about what is appropriate. Modelling is a powerful tool that the educator can use daily when guiding behaviour.

Tables 9.2 and 9.3 show what can cause conflict to escalate and de-escalate. It is the educator's role to develop play experiences, learning experiences, activities, strategies, and techniques to help guide a child's behaviour in such a way that conflict does not escalate.

By implementing a variety of techniques (such as observation skills and physical proximity) and the foundation skills and building blocks of building community (see Chapter 8), the educator will be able to help children deal with conflict.

FIVE COMPONENTS TO CONSIDER

There are five components to consider when guiding children's behaviour:

1. Planning the environment
2. Developing a peaceful community and environment

3. Implementing and developing effective rule-making and community meetings

4. Demonstrating and practising creative conflict-resolution techniques

5. Implementing a bullying prevention program

Planning the Environment

Planning of Space The layout of the indoor and outdoor environments can either encourage or discourage desired behaviour. Areas should be designed to complement each other. Are you setting up the children by having an active construction site beside a quiet reading area? If play areas are small and crowded, the likelihood of conflict occurring between the children will be increased. If the area for construction with large blocks, boards, and crates is confined to a small corner of the room, children will not have enough space to work and are more likely to trip and have accidents. If the construction area is large and adaptable in size—defined by

TABLE 9.2	Conflict will ESCALATE

Conflict will ESCALATE if:

- Educators do not supervise and observe children playing
- Rules and natural consequences have not been developed
- Children and parents have not been involved in the development of the rules and consequences
- A positive expression of emotions does not take place
- Children are not taught, and educators do not model, communication skills and self-regulated problem-solving strategies (self-control)
- All children are not supported, and children are encouraged to take sides
- Positive team-building and co-operative learning activities are not implemented, and there is an overemphasis on competitive learning activities
- There is a lack of self-regulated and self-control skills

TABLE 9.3	Conflict will DE-ESCALATE

Conflict will DE-ESCALATE if:

- Educators supervise and observe children playing
- Educators react and deal with conflict by modelling appropriate techniques
- Rules and consequences are enforced consistently by the educators
- Rules and consequences are developed in conjunction with the children
- Various strategies and tools for creative conflict resolution and self-regulated problem-solving strategies are taught and modelled by the educators
- Children are encouraged to express their emotions in a positive manner
- Attention is focused on the problem and not on the personality of the child
- Educators implement team-building and co-operative learning experiences

movable shelving units, for example—children will have space to work in an environment less likely to cause conflict. Space should be planned in such a way that children can move about, in, and out of the area and have access to materials.

The traffic flow between play areas both indoors and outdoors can also cause conflict when children are moving around the room or moving materials between areas. If there is only one entrance/exit to a play area, this may cause congestion, increasing the likelihood that children will bump into each other or intrude into each other's personal space. To avoid this situation make sure there are a number of entrances and exits into play areas. As observed in Chapter 5, straight, wide paths that could lead to running should be avoided, since they increase the chances of children colliding with each other, an obvious source of conflict.

Space needs to be carefully planned based on the children's developmental level and needs. For example, school-age children should have more adult-sized equipment than that used by younger children, and the environment should be home-like. Space that is well organized and aesthetically pleasing, perhaps including a variety of artifacts such as woven baskets, will contribute to a positive sense of well-being, diminishing the chances for conflict to arise. Children need spaces appropriate for private time as well as group experiences, so having smaller areas in which children can get away from the group will help to de-escalate tension and conflict.

Children need to have both outdoor and indoor experiences, and opportunities to "blow off steam" after school; if they spend all their time indoors participating in quiet activities, conflict will occur. School-age children need to have opportunities to run and play and to release their physical energy—whether positive or aggressive.

Finally, conflict can be reduced when children have the opportunity to be designers of the program. They should have the opportunity to redesign space and to have a variety of materials, loose parts, and equipment at their disposal.

Large Blocks of Playtime Children should have large blocks of playtime to interact with their friends and with the materials, to develop independence, and to gain self-control and respect for each other and the environment. Children should have a balance between active and quiet play, indoors and outdoors.

Schedules, Routines, and Transitions A schedule serves as a general framework of how the routines and transitions work in the program; it tells children what will happen during the day. Children come from school, have a snack, play indoors or outdoors, and go home. The framework can help children to gain trust, security, and order in their lives, all of which contribute to positive behaviour guidance. By providing snacks at the same time and location each day, children will know what to expect.

Schedules, routines, and transitions should be flexible and based on the developmental level and needs of the children in the program. They should be adaptable to the weather and to circumstances in their school lives. For example, if children are going through a week of provincial testing at school, it is probably not the time for a schedule of quiet activities after school or teacher-directed art activities. Instead, children will need to have the opportunity to socialize with their friends or to expend some energy outdoors. If children have been inside during school because of extreme cold or heavy rain, it is important to change your schedule to meet their needs by, for instance, letting them run around in the gym or have free play in the room.

Too many routines and transitions can cause the children to be dependent on the routine. If children spend all their time in routines without a long period of free play, it may lead to negative behaviour (such as not sharing, a lack of trust, or physical aggression). Children will not have the time to interact or to participate in learning activities. For example, programs that ask all the children to go to the toilet at the same time need to ask whether it is developmentally appropriate, or causing negative behaviour.

Routines and transitions that are not flexible, and are based solely on what the educator feels is important, can cause negative behaviour. For example, if children are given only ten minutes to eat a snack because the educator thinks it is important to get into the room to practise a play, the educator misses the point that school-age children need to have time to eat their snack and to socialize. Routines and transitions should be based on the needs of the children and should be flexible in nature, based on what is happening in the lives of the children.

Materials, Loose Parts, and Equipment Materials, loose parts, and equipment should be developmentally appropriate for the group of children or individuals. A variety of items, including materials that are structured (hammer and saw) as well as unstructured (wood and clay) need to be readily available for all children to use. To avoid conflict, the environment should have plentiful amounts of materials and loose parts for children to use. The following examples illustrate this point:

> Six pieces of plumbing tube are not sufficient for children to be creative with, and will cause conflict over the ownership of the pieces. A variety of sizes and length of plumbing tube should be provided. One program we observed had 250 pieces of varied plumbing tubes, which were donated to the program.

> Twenty-five kilograms of clay would only be enough for a group of about six children to sculpt. Not having enough clay will cause conflict over the lack of resources. In a program we observed, they used 200 kilograms of clay during the summer months.

> A 350-piece Lego kit is not sufficient for groups of children without conflict arising over the sharing of individual pieces, and over the ownership of Lego structures. The educator needs to provide the children with many more pieces—perhaps 2500—for all the children to have the opportunity to share and to build with it. If the program were to purchase one or two Lego kits a year, it will soon have enough Lego for all the children to build with.

Developing a Peaceful Community and Environment

Developing a philosophy for a peaceful environment is an essential component when facilitating and guiding behaviour in school-age programs. A peaceful community and environment will help all children to feel safe, respected, and valued. Children will have the opportunity to experience a peaceful community by being involved in developing and participating in peacemaking activities.

Laying the groundwork for a peaceful community and environment may take a number of months to implement. The involvement of the children, educator, and parents in developing of a peaceful environment is a key element in developing strategies based on peace. Everyone will play a part in working together by developing a sense of ownership that emphasizes the strengths of individuals in the group. The following six components are needed and should be put in place when developing a peaceful community and environment: developing clear and concise policies and procedures; creating a safe environment; building a sense of community; participating in community meetings; developing self-control and practising self-regulated problem-solving strategies; and engaging in interactive activities. The following activities will help to promote and develop a peaceful community and environment.

- **Peace art.** Create peace art, such as origami peace cranes, peace pins, and flags.
- **Discussions.** Have discussions about peace and how to deal with conflict.
- **Music.** Create raps, chants, and air bands about what peace means to the children.
- **Peace table.** Create a space in the environment for children to spend time discussing peace issues. Include books, a peace manual, drawings about peace, artwork, stories, posters with images of diversity, etc.
- **Peace gardens.** Brainstorm, plan, and create a peace garden or plant a tree for peace. The peace garden can be a place where children can go to talk about or reflect on peace or about strategies they can use to make sure the environment is peaceful.
- **Creative arts.** Create paintings, drawings, and group murals about peace and community.
- **Creative writing.** Have the children create a peace newsletter and write stories or poems about peace and community.
- **Civic engagement.** Encourage the children to volunteer in their community. For example, link up with a seniors' program and have the children perform plays and songs or serve tea to the seniors.

Implementing and Developing Effective Rule-Making and Community Meetings

Rules should be developmentally appropriate and should have a strong theoretical base in psychology. In Bandura's and Erikson's schemas, developing self-regulated problem-solving strategies is an important skill because it helps children to learn how to deal with conflict identify problems, and discuss solutions, evaluation, and modifying techniques. For example, developing rules, consequences, and solutions with children will help them to develop their own self-control, problem-solving, and self-governance skills. Children will be able to solve problems with the group about why rules are important and which rules are important for the group, and identify several possible solutions and outcomes for not following rules. Rules should be clear and concrete, and implemented in a fair, firm, and consistent manner. Expectations of behaviour should be the same for both boys and girls. All children should be involved in developing rules and thus have a stake in creating a safe, peaceful community in which they are able to demonstrate skills and strategies learned previously and have the opportunity to learn and practise new skills and strategies. Rules should be based on the philosophy of the program, theories of development and learning, the history of the program, past experiences of the children, and cultures of the children and families of the group. Effective rule-making develops a sense of community, mutual respect, independence, group relationships, responsibility, and self-regulated problem-solving strategies. Table 9.4 illustrates how rules help to define how the group works, the expectations of behaviour, and the expectations of the community (Bronfenbrenner).

TABLE 9.4	What do rules define?	
How the Group Works	**The Expected Behaviours for the Group and for Individuals**	**What the Community and Society Expects**
Decisions must be made together.	Help each other when needed.	All children from age six to twelve go to school.
Treat each other with respect.	Use a respectful tone of voice.	If someone needs help, we help them.
Play together and do not exclude.	Be both a listener and a speaker.	
	Keep our bodies and feelings safe.	
	Say no to violence and bullying.	

Consequences and Developing Solutions Consequences (the results of not following rules) should focus on the child's behaviour, not personality. All consequences should be natural and logical by nature. For example, if one child takes apart another's fort without asking, he should be responsible for helping to rebuild it. As long as everyone can see that the consequence flows logically from the original action, they will support it. The educator needs to be firm, fair, and consistent when implementing consequences. Consequences are effective only when they are enforced respectfully and consistently.

Natural consequences help children to understand the chain of causation—that behaviour has inevitable, unavoidable outcomes, whether for good or bad. When developing consequences, children should be involved in the brainstorming process, which will offer them choices about what might help them most. It is important to focus not on the past but on the future. Group meetings and brainstorming should therefore always be about the consequences of a theoretical action, not the actual behaviour of a particular child, otherwise the child will feel persecuted. Focus on the positive behaviour you want to see, and avoid adding something to the consequence that isn't necessary or does not relate to the behaviour.

Some behaviours for which you will need to develop consequences will be inadvertent actions (or forgetting to take an action) that rebound on the child herself (or her environment) rather than on other children. For example, the following questions illustrate how children can think about the outcome of their behaviour and develop solutions for it.

Issue-based question: What would happen if you forgot to water your plants?
Solution-based question: How can you make sure all plants are watered?

Issue-based question: What would happen if you left your lunch out in the play yard?
Solution-based question: How can you make sure you have food for lunch?

Issue-based question: What would happen if you didn't wear a winter coat or winter boots when it is minus 20 degrees outside?
Solution-based question: How can you make sure you are warm outside when it is minus 20 degrees?

Developing Rules During Community Meetings The following is an example of what can occur during a community meeting to develop a policy on group expectations.

> In a school-age program, community meetings have been one of the methods used to foster mutual respect, group membership skills, and expectations of behaviour. Social bullying in the form of gossiping and excluding children was starting to become evident during play, and a number of children were beginning to complain about it. The educator decided to put the issue on the agenda. At the next meeting, he described what he had been seeing and hearing in the yard (though without identifying individual children), reinforced the expectation that everyone should feel safe, and then asked the children to help resolve the issue. After a few minutes of describing the behaviour and sharing anecdotes, many of the children felt they wanted to create a brainstorm web on the theme of what a group is, and what it means to be part of a group. The children took turns writing and recording their main ideas (see Table 9.5).
>
> Once the children finished adding their ideas to the web, they discussed each idea and talked about how it would affect them. Each child signed the brainstorming web and agreed to all the ideas. The educators also signed the brainstorming web and agreed to bring in different co-operative games and group challenge games, and to provide opportunities for the children to role-play different ways of resolving conflict.

Many things need to be in place before you are able to facilitate a successful community meeting such as the one described above.

1. Get your group accustomed to having meetings. Children need to learn how to take turns, listen respectfully, and not laugh at other people's contributions, so everyone will feel safe participating in the discussion.

2. The educators should act as role models with their own behaviour, interaction, and communication, for example, by demonstrating "I" statements and problem-solving strategies.

TABLE 9.5	What is a group?		
Respect		**Work as a Team**	**Group Games**
• Respect each other's bodies, feelings, ideals, and equipment.		• Remember that we are all winners.	• Share ideas and thoughts.
• Take responsibility for behaviour.		• Communicate.	• Play fair.
• Play fair.		• Co-operate and share ideas.	• Include everyone in games.
• Be peaceful and resolve conflict by using "I" statements.		• Negotiate and solve problems, and get help if you can't come up with a solution.	
• Play with everyone.		• Think twice before you say something.	
• Listen to opinions.		• Be a teacher and helper.	
• Be a part of the group by participating in meetings, planning projects, and clubs.		• Be a part of the group in making decisions.	
		• Follow expectations of the group.	
		• Participate in community meetings.	

3. All who want to participate should get a fair chance to share their own feelings, ideas, issues, and opinions. Encourage the same expectations for boys and girls during community meetings.

4. Community meetings can be used as an opportunity to talk about conflict-resolution by getting the children to ask questions about the behaviour causing the conflict, such as:

   - Why do I do this?
   - What can I do about it?
   - How important is it for me to feel safe?
   - How can I resolve or de-escalate conflicts?
   - What techniques can I use to feel safe and de-escalate conflict?
   - How can I help other children when they are having a conflict? What is my role?

5. Use the meeting time as an opportunity to develop rules and consequences. Ask the following questions:

   - What does it mean to be a community member?
   - What is respectful behaviour? What does it mean to be respectful?
   - What does it mean to be safe?
   - How can I make sure my body, feelings, and materials are safe?
   - Which rules are important to make sure my body, feelings, and materials are safe?
   - What are the consequences for not following the rules?
   - How can I take responsibility for my actions and behaviour?

6. Brainstorm for creative solutions. One idea will generate others. Don't reject any idea out of hand, no matter how crazy it might sound.

7. Use the meeting to discuss activism, strategies for dealing with bullying, and planning and participating in anti-bullying projects.

Making Decisions During Community Meetings

The following are the steps that a group of school-age children went through in developing rules and consequences during a series of community meetings that took place over the course of a month.

Step 1: Brainstorming Rules
Decide as a group which 10 to 15 rules seem the most important. Encourage the children to develop a web or a list of rules. Once this is done, help the children to reclassify them into broad rules and specific rules, as seen in the examples given in Table 9.6.

Change negative wording to positive wording. For example, instead of saying "No name-calling," phrase the rule as "Call people what they want to be called."

The following rules were developed by a group of school-age children:

- Keep everyone's body safe.
- Keep everyone's feelings safe.
- Keep everyone's thoughts, ideas, and words safe.
- Keep everyone's work safe.

TABLE 9.6	Developing broad and specific rules
Broad Rule	**Specific Rule**
• Respect each other (Define respect with the children).	• Treat other children as you would like to be treated. • Use a voice tone that is respectful when you are talking with another child. • Call people what they want to be called. • Listen to the other people's points of view without interrupting.

Step 2: Understanding Rules

Encourage the group to explain the reason for each rule and illustrate it with examples. At this point, ask the group what each rule means to them. Children can be encouraged to write a story or draw a picture to illustrate how they feel about each rule and what it means to them during this process.

Step 3: Developing Consequences and Solutions

Once the children have had the opportunity to understand the rules, brainstorm with the group one consequence or solution for each rule. Consequences should relate to the rule and focus on the behaviour involved. Children often want severe consequences for not following the rules. In one program, all the children at a brainstorming session wanted to expel children from the program for physical aggression such as kicking. Educators must help children to moderate their punitive instincts by asking them how they would feel if they were expelled from the program. Would they accept this consequence for themselves? It is important to expand children's thinking by having them address issues before they happen and develop solutions. For example, if children's bodies are expected to be safe in the program, ask the children how to make sure other children's bodies are safe. The solution might be to keep our hands to ourselves or the idea that hands are used to help each other, such as building a fort or making a friendship bracelet together. Help the children to develop conflict-resolution strategies that will key them safe by enabling them to defuse potentially aggressive situations, to evaluate the effectiveness of the techniques, and to modify the techniques for specific conflict situations.

Step 4: Committing to Rules, Consequences, and Solutions

When the group agrees to the final list, post a large master list of rules and consequences in a prominent place in the environment. All the children and educators should sign the list.

Step 5: Reflections

Post photographs of children demonstrating positive play behaviour around the written rules and consequences. If the group needs to develop collaboration skills, put up photographs of children demonstrating these skills, such as planning and painting a mural together. Children's drawings, paintings, or stories about how they feel during positive play experiences can also be mounted around the list of rules. Reflective activities, such as painting and drawing a peaceful environment, will help children to predict outcomes of behaviours and evaluate the effectiveness of rules and consequences.

Step 6: Review
Review the list often, perhaps once a month, until everyone, including all the educators, is aware of what each rule and consequence means in practice. Give the children positive feedback about desirable behaviour that educators have observed.

Creative Conflict-Resolution Techniques

Conflict resolution allows children to realize that they are capable of resolving conflicts and preventing future conflicts by implementing a variety of techniques and strategies. Conflict-resolution techniques help children recognize that they have the skills necessary to deal with conflict, and are responsible for being kind and respectful to each other.

Creative conflict resolution encourages children to consider different options when communicating with each other and to interact with one another in a positive manner. It helps to de-escalate conflicts, and can be successful at nipping problems in the bud before they become worse. It helps to decrease negative emotion and perceived threats by expressing feelings in a positive manner and by using caring language. It helps children to focus on the problem, to negotiate, and to come to a resolution with each other.

Once they begin to take part in this process, children gain a sense of responsibility and are empowered to resolve conflict in creative ways. The process helps to promote mutual respect and interdependence, and allows children to develop skills for living and participating in a democratic community. Creative conflict resolution helps to promote a sense of trust and safety in a community. Children have the opportunity to practise and demonstrate a variety of strategies and techniques. For example:

- Positive non-defensive communication
- Demonstrating respectful language
- Using caring language, such as "I" statements (see below)
- Using reflective listening as a tool to gather information
- Reading non-verbal cues (body language)
- Participating in the mediation process

Steps in Resolving Conflict

The following are seven steps in resolving conflict: cool down; focus on the problem; be a mediator; use caring language and "I" statements; resolution; brainstorm for ideas and solutions; and follow through.

Step 1: Cool Down
Establish a cool-off area or space for the aggressor and victim to go to (these do not need to be dedicated spaces). A cool-off area should not be used as a form of punishment, but to calm down, regain self-control, and have the opportunity to reflect. It should be located where both the aggressor (bully) and the victim (bullied) can be safe, so ask both of them to find areas to cool down away from each other. Let them know that it's all right to say, "I am angry and I need time to cool down. We'll talk later."

Help the children to develop ways to cool off, relax, and centre themselves, which will help to develop self-control. For example, taking slow, deep breaths, visualizing a solution, or drinking a cool glass of water can all help. Make sure children have had enough time to calm down, think about what the problem is, why they feel like this, and how they can resolve the conflict.

Tip #1: For repeated aggressors, you may have a designated area for them to regain self-control and reflect.

Step 2: Focus on the Problem

After children have calmed down, it is important to have them focus on the problem and not the person. It is important to discuss with each child what the issue is, the source of the conflict, and what needs to happen to resolve the conflict. Using reflective listening or "I" statements can help to focus on the problem. You want to make sure that children avoid using disrespectful language when speaking to or about the other child, since it tends to escalate the conflict. Name-calling, threats, put-downs, blaming, bringing up the past, making excuses, not listening, sarcasm, and not taking responsibility for their actions are all examples of behaviour that will not help resolve the conflict. Focus on changing language from "You ought to ..." to "What can we do?"

Step 3: Be a Mediator

The goal of mediation is for the educator to help children solve problems by guiding and facilitating, not directing. Being a mediator helps give the power back to the children by

TABLE 9.7	The role of the child and the educator in the mediation process
Role of the Child	**Role of the Educator**
• To listen without interrupting once the other child has calmed down.	• To make sure the children all calm down before starting the process.
• To use respectful language and focus on "I" statements.	• To explain to the children the process involved, making sure they understand
• To be willing to tell his story. Encourage the children to use "I" statements. Each child should have the opportunity to tell her story without interruption from the other child.	that they will take turns talking and listening.
	• To use reflective/active listening. Active listening is a way of paraphrasing by reflecting back to the speaker what he said. Example: "It sounds like you're saying that..."
• To be willing to tell how he feels. Focus on the needs of each child. Each child should have the opportunity to say how she feels without interruption from the other child.	• Not to take sides or make judgments about either child.
• To think of several solutions to the problem. If they are having trouble coming up with solutions, give them a couple of examples to help to move the process along.	• To focus on feelings and ask, "How did that make you feel?"
	• To give suggestions for resolutions.
	• To check that both children agree to the resolution, and to give positive feedback when they demonstrate positive play and behaviour.
• To pick the solutions they can live with. Make sure both parties agree to the chosen solution, and evaluate the situation to make sure one child is not manipulating the other into accepting it.	
• To be responsible for carrying out the agreed-upon solution.	

getting them to solve the problem together and come to a resolution. It takes a while to develop the mediation process, and there is a time and place for it. For example, if there is a physical conflict between two children during a basketball game, the mediation process should not hold up the game for the other children. The two children who are having the conflict should be asked to move away from the game and find separate locations to cool off. Once they have cooled off, bring the children together and start the mediation process.

   Tip #2: Post the mediation process chart for all to see so children can review it when they want to. Involve the children by creating the chart and by adding stories and poems about how they resolve conflict. Note that the chart must focus on the principles of mediation, not on any particular incident or child.

   Tip #3: Around the chart, post photographs of the children participating in the mediation process or in positive play experiences.

Step 4: Use Caring Language and "I" Statements

Caring language begins with a non-blaming, respectful attitude that helps children listen to and to understand each other. Caring language helps identify problems by taking the emotion out of the conflict and focusing the children on thinking about their own needs and feelings.

   An "I" statement is not primarily a conflict-resolution technique, but is a generalized format for stating your feelings clearly. "I" statements are often used to encourage assertiveness. There are many possible variations, but all "I" statements are important because they allow the individual to express her ideas, needs, concerns, and feelings.

   "I" statements can be difficult to implement because children need the educator and other children to model them, need to believe in the technique, and need time to practise them. As children first grapple with making "I" statements or are not yet convinced that they work, they can come across as having a patronizing tone, rather than being a natural part of the child's vocabulary. Sometimes this also occurs because children have memorized a format they are repeating without thought, or they want to please the teacher with their skills. Children need to get past the stage of worrying about the phrasing of an "I" statement and see it as an opportunity to express their feelings and needs in a way that can lead a conflict situation toward a resolution. Table 9.8 shows the "I" statement format.

Step 5: Resolution

Identifying a resolution is the last step in the "I" statement format, as illustrated in Table 9.9. After each child has expressed how he or she feels, the next step involves thinking about solutions. Focus on the needs of each child and what they want to happen. This is an important exercise in developing negotiating skills and the ability to compromise. If the problem still persists, help them develop some possible solutions by asking the following questions: What do you want to happen? What are your needs? What are the ways you can solve the conflict?

   Tip #4: During community meetings, children can have the opportunity to practise the "I" statement format. Provide the children with a number of conflict situations and have them take turns with a partner in role-playing the situation. Encourage the children to focus on their own feelings and needs, and to listen to what the other is saying. After each role-play, discuss with the group what happened.

   Tip #5: During the role-play, freeze the conflict situation and ask the group what they would say and do next. Then un-freeze the role-play and continue. Afterwards, discuss

TABLE 9.8	"I" statement format
I feel......... (**using specific feelings**)	
when ... (*specific behavior*)	
because ... (tangible effect)	
Example:	
I feel **angry** when *people hit me* because it hurts.	

TABLE 9.9	**Example of an "I" statement with resolution**
Use the person's name ... Faven	
Tell how you feel. ... I feel angry when	
Identify the problem. ... You look in my journal	
Tell what you want done ... Respect my privacy	

with the group what happened. Focus on the positive results and ask them to think how the situation would make them feel.

Tip #6: Videotape the role-play and let the children review the recording. Focus on the techniques being used.

Tip #7: Post examples of the "I" statement format (such as in Table 9.8) so children can review it whenever they want.

Tip #8: Create a rap using "I" statements. Encourage the children to share their raps during community meetings or during playtime.

Step 6: Brainstorm for Ideas and Solutions

Encourage both children in a conflict situation to pick a solution and carry out the resolution. The educator's role at this point is to make sure both children agree to the resolution. Sometimes the more powerful or articulate child might attempt to manipulate the resolution into a win–lose outcome in his own favour. The educator, however, must make sure that the needs and opinions of both children are voiced and heard, and if she feels that one child is manipulating the other, she must identify the problem and prevent it from occurring. If children are having issues over a resource need, for example, the use of a toboggan, and after the resolution one of the children still has no access to the toboggan, the process has not worked properly and the educator must step in and help the children reach a resolution that is fair. Also, the educator can use "I" statements to reflect, and reflective listening to paraphrase, what each speaker is saying, thus modelling the process for the children.

If the problem persists, children should be encouraged to get help from the educator or from a peer.

Step 7: Follow Through

The children involved decide together what the solution should be, and they carry it out. The educator should continue to observe them during play, and praise and encourage them when they are following through. If the conflict continues, however, the educator should bring the children back together and give them a gentle reminder of the solution they agreed to.

Tip #9: Role-play the situation with the children. Have the children involved reverse roles with each other. Ask the children how they were feeling during the role-play. How did they feel when they reversed roles? What techniques did they use? What was successful? What would they do next time?

Tip #10: Children can make drawings or paintings to illustrate how they resolve conflict, and what it means to be safe both indoors and outdoors.

Step 8: Follow-Up Questions to Ask Yourself

The following questions can be used for children to reflect on how they resolve conflict, and can also be used as a self-checker. Did we solve the problem? How did we solve the problem? Did we use "I" statements? What did I say? Did I use caring language? How do I feel about the way I handled myself? What did I learn that would help me in future conflict situations?

Implementing a Bullying Prevention Program

What is Bullying Prevention? A bullying prevention approach is a proactive process where the educator creates a safe and peaceful environment for children by facilitating and teaching strategies and techniques to prepare and prevent bullying before it happens. This is accomplished by changing the power dynamics of the group and by developing positive peer relationships to help to support the process. Intervention is a process of responding to bullying as it is happening. When bullying behaviours de-escalate, a prevention program should be implemented. Developing and building a sense of community is the foundation of a bullying prevention program. The educator accomplishes this by planning and implementing a variety of interactive activities to promote group-building and group dynamics, co-operation, peer relationships, communication skills, and problem-solving skills.

Goals and Objectives There are four long-term goals and eight short-term objectives to consider when developing and implementing a bullying prevention program. The four long-term goals are as follows:

- **Creating safe and peaceful environments**
  Create a safe and peaceful environment by developing policies and procedures for educators and parents; creating and implementing clear and concise rules, consequences, and expectations for all children; and developing prevention strategies.
- **Protecting the victim**
  The educator supports the victim by making a clear statement to the group that all children are safe (physically and emotionally) in the program and that bullying is not acceptable. It is important to support victims by teaching them different ways to stay safe (prevention) and different techniques and problem-solving strategies to deal with bullying. The goal is to change the imbalance of power between the victim and the bully.
- **Working with the observer**
  The educator works with and teaches the observer (bystander) different types of strategies and techniques to help the victim or to seek help from peers or adults.
- **Changing bullying behaviour**
  The educator teaches and works with children who are demonstrating bullying behaviour by identifying the behaviour as bullying and by making it clear it is not acceptable.

It is important to work with the child who is exhibiting bullying behaviour by changing the power imbalance and her behaviour, and to teach different ways to interact appropriately with peers and the group.

The short-term objectives of a bullying prevention program are for children to learn the following:

- Recognize bullying and name it.
- Say no to bullying.
- Know when to report bullying.
- Implement conflict-resolution skills.
- Chose a variety of different strategies to deal with bullying.
- Problem-solve and evaluate which strategy is the right one to use.
- Learn how to modify the strategy for different types of conflict.
- Know which strategy is the most effective before bullying becomes a problem.

Developing a Bullying Prevention Program with the School Children who attend school and school-age programs need to feel and know they are in a safe environment free from social and physical bullying. It is important for the schoolteachers and school-age educators to meet and work together to reduce bullying behaviour by developing appropriate strategies, consistent rules, and consequences. Consistency between both settings will help children to understand that rules and consequences are the same in both environments and that teachers and educators will deal with bullying behaviours in the same way. Children will also understand what is expected of their behaviour and that they will be safe in both environments.

What Is Bullying? Bullying occurs when one or more children are exposing another child to negative physical, verbal, and social behaviour such as teasing, hitting, and isolation from the group. This behaviour happens continually over time. Bullying is about intimidation and the misuse and imbalance of power. The bully has the power—which is generally based on fear and intimidation—over the child who is being bullied. It is not bullying when two children of approximately the same age, strength, or developmental level fight or quarrel. Nor is bullying a physical attack in the heat of the moment caused by sudden anger. Rather, it is planned and deliberate: the bully has intent to harm her victim, and the victim is targeted by the bully over a sustained period.

Bullying happens at school, in after-school programs, in the play yard and indoors, on the way to school, at the park, at home, and on the weekend. Bullying can be either direct (physical) or indirect (psychological). **Direct bullying**, for example, tripping or hitting another child, is easier to see and hear compared to **indirect bullying**, such as gossiping or excluding children from the group. Bullying behaviour can undermine and destroy the sense of community and the emergent curriculum process because it takes power away from all the children and leaves it with only a few. It is important for both educators and children to have an awareness of bullying and to know how to deal with it.

The main reason that children turn to bullying is to gain a sense of power. The bully uses whatever tools are available to gain power and control over someone weaker in order to elevate his own feeling of self-esteem and to achieve status with his peer group. The

TABLE 9.10	Types of bullying

Physical (direct bullying)	Social (indirect bullying)
• Pushing, shoving, hitting, spitting at, tripping, or beating up another child • Stealing or damaging another child's property • Physical acts which are demeaning and humiliating	• Gossiping and spreading rumours about others • Excluding others from the group, based on appearance or type of clothing • Threatening with total isolation by peer group
Verbal	**Sexist/sexual**
• Name-calling and mocking, such as based on sexual orientation • Teasing about appearance, clothing, and language • Verbal threats against property	• Starting rumours about sexual activities • Passing unwanted notes or pictures of sex • Inciting others to behave in sexist ways • Refusing to work with, play, or co-operate with others
Cyber bullying—through e-mail or text messaging	**Racist**
• Gossiping and spreading rumours • Excluding from the group • Sexual innuendo	• Making fun of music, accent, dress or dietary habits of anyone from a different culture or religious observance • Singling someone out because of her skin colour, cultural practices, religious background, or ethnic origin • Insulting or degrading comments • Refusing to work with, play, or co-operate with others • Inciting others to behave in a racist way

imbalance of power means that the children being victimized have trouble defending themselves—they are easy targets. Table 9.10 illustrates the different types of bullying.

Effects of Bullying It is hard to overstate the potential negative effects of unchecked bullying. It affects the victim's emotional well-being, self-esteem, and mental health if it is allowed to continue. Children who have been bullied can have low self-esteem, develop a number of unexplained illnesses (for instance, complaining of a sore stomach and not wanting to go to school), become anxious, withdrawn, and insecure, suffer from depression and anxiety, and sometimes have thoughts of suicide. Bullying should never be ignored or avoided by parents, educators, or other children. For example, brushing it aside with remarks such as "Oh, they are just children playing," or "I was bullied, it's just part of life" is not acceptable when children do not feel safe and are being physically and mentally hurt. By not accepting the importance of the situation or dealing with it, we are giving the bully power and creating an unsafe environment for children.

The Bungee school-age program (not the real name) was having some challenges with bullying. A number of boys were complaining about not feeling safe because one or two children were bullying them, using physical threats to get what they wanted. A small group of boys and girls were complaining about not being allowed to play in the fort that they had helped to build. Also, a group of five girls would not play with one other because she was not wearing the "right" style of clothes. They had started to spread rumours about the girl to other groups. Also, a number of parents had raised their own concerns about bullying in the program.

Stopping Bullying Behaviour by Using Directed Power The bullying situation occurring in the above program was of concern to the program director and the educators. The sense of community had eroded over time and children did not feel safe in the program. During a staff meeting, the educators shared their observations and understanding of what was happening in their program. They were aware children did not feel safe and bullying needed to stop.

The educators decided to implement a bullying prevention program, but before they could do this they needed to stop the bullying behaviour and give a clear message that all children are safe and bullying behaviour is not accepted. The educator initially implemented a "directed power" approach to stop the bullying behaviour by taking control of the environment and telling children what is the expected behaviour and that bullying behaviour is not allowed in the program. Directed power helps children feel physically and emotionally safe, because the educator is giving a very clear message about being safe, and taking control over what is and isn't acceptable behaviour; for example, excluding children from play isn't acceptable. At this point in the prevention, children have limited input in the program.

Creating a Safe and Peaceful Environment

Group Meetings: Developing Rules, Consequences, and Solutions In the above example, the educators decided to have a discussion with the children about bullying during the next community meeting. Initially the educators spent the first two weeks (guided power approach) discussing with the group about feeling safe and not feeling safe in the program. The bottom line was that any form of bullying behaviour (direct or indirect) was not allowed in the program and children who were bullying would be asked to cool off and have time away from the group to think about how they could change their behaviour.

If appropriate, the victim would talk to the bully about how they felt about being bullied and what type of behaviour they are expecting from the bully. This is a great opportunity for the educator to facilitate new learning for the victims by helping them to understand their feelings and to model what to say to the bully. Over the next few weeks, the bullying behaviour started to de-escalate and children were being bullied less. The educators decided it was the opportunity to start a new program (facilitated power approach) called "**SAY NO TO BULLYING AND YES TO PEACE!**"

The educators realized they needed to start reviewing and redeveloping a sense of community in the program. The educators decided to revisit the various building blocks when developing a sense of community, such as respect, inclusion, communication, and conflict-resolution skills. They felt by promoting discussions during community meetings children would have the opportunity to discuss what bullying is and what it means to be safe in the program. Together, the children and educators brainstormed different ways of dealing with the bullying behaviour and how they could control and stop bullying. The educator implemented a number of activities to promote communication strategies, group-building skills, inclusion, peer relationships, and mentoring skills. Table 9.11 describes a number of activities the educators facilitated during community meetings.

TABLE 9.11	Bullying prevention/peacemaking activities

Activity #1: Thank You for Peace!

One technique the educators used was to start to focus on the positive behaviour of the children instead of the negative behaviour. During community meetings the children had the opportunity to thank other children for random act of kindness, such as helping to clean the yard, fixing a Lego structure, or helping with a conflict. A suggestion box was created for children to write who should be thanked and why they were being thanked. During community meetings the suggestion box was opened and the educator or children took turns reading the messages.

Activity #2: Feel Safe Illustrations

Provide the children with a variety of paper and drawing tools to create illustrations based on the following questions. Chose one or two questions or combine questions, depending on the age and abilities of the children.

- What does it mean to feel safe?
- What is it like when you do not feel safe?
- What does it mean to be safe?
- What does bullying look like?
- What does bullying sound like?
- What does bullying feel like?
- What is harassment? (Grade 4 and up)

Activity #3: Posters and Banners

Provide the children with a variety of paper, poster board or foam core, and drawing or painting tools. Think back to the discussions about bullying and being safe when creating your poster. The poster will tell other children why we are saying "NO" to bullying or why we are saying "YES" to peace. Create a picture, slogan, saying, or rap-poem and add it to your poster. Display the posters in the school-age program and outside. Foam core and acrylic paint work well for outdoor displays.

Adaptation:

- Work in small groups and pre-plan the design or text of your poster.
- Create banners from cloth or other materials with the same information.
- Create a poster contest between groups.
- Display the posters in the community or in the play yard.

Activity #4: Create a Rap or Chant

Create a classroom rap or chant using the "SAY NO TO BULLYING AND YES TO PEACE" information from the above activities. Children should be encouraged to create their own lyrics or rhythms. Present to other classes and during assemblies at the school.

Adaptation:

- Small groups can develop their own raps. Present to the whole group or to other classes in the school.
- Develop a two-, three-, or four-voice rap.
- Add acoustic drumming to the rap by using plastic garbage cans and small pieces of dowelling to drum.
- Have a "Rap Off" session with other school-age programs or with other classes in the school. Present the "Rap Off" in the gym or outdoors.

> **Activity #5: Dramatizations and Skits**
>
> Encourage the children to write a play or short skits about being safe, peace, or why we are saying "SAY NO TO BULLYING AND YES TO PEACE." Small groups can develop their own play or skit with the support and guidance of the educator. This process may take a number of weeks or even a number of months to complete. Do not rush the process. When they are ready to perform their play or skits, they can present them to the whole group, to other classes in the school, or to other school-age programs.
>
> - Videotape their final production.
> - Create props, flags, and banners for the production.
> - Invite parents to an open house and perform the play. This is a great opportunity to celebrate the success of the prevention program.

Proactive Prevention Strategies The following six prevention strategies were developed and implemented. This process occurred at the same time as the group started to implement the new "SAY NO TO BULLYING AND YES TO PEACE" program.

1. **Stay Safe—Avoid Places where Bullies Are**
   Encourage children not to be alone in potentially dangerous or unsafe places, but to play in areas where they feel safe. Help the children to identify areas where they do not feel safe, both outdoors and indoors. For example, if they feel physically or socially unsafe behind the bushes or the garbage dumpsters in the corner of the play yard, suggest to the children not to go there.

2. **Stay with a Friend—Avoid Bullies**
   Encourage children to hang out with friends and build connections with new friends. Staying with a friend is one of the best prevention measures against bullying. Encourage children to play with a friend or a group of friends who like the same things they do. If someone is bullying one child, the child's friend or friends can go for help or they may tell the bully to leave their friend alone.
   Make it clear to children that bullying behaviour is not to be tolerated.
   Make sure children understand what bullying behaviour is and what it looks like—it is important for all children to have the same definition and knowledge. Children also need to feel confident and have positive communication skills when dealing with bullying.

3. **Activism—Say "No" to Bullying**
   Children observing bullying (bystanders) play an important part in reducing bullying behaviours. Once the group understands what bullying is and why it isn't accepted in the program, teach them about the importance of speaking up and how to make a stand against bullying. If they see another child being bullied, they can seek help from the educator, or in some instances can support the victim by telling the bully to leave him alone. Children with more experience with conflict resolution and the mediation process can become a "champion" or "mentor" to less experienced children. They can help to monitor the behaviour in the program to make sure everyone feels safe. Make sure the "champions" have the appropriate communication and leadership skills for this new role. Children need to be clear about their role and the role of the "champion".

You don't want to create another bully by giving the "champion" or mentor inappropriate power and control within the program.

4. **Reporting—Tell, Tell, and Tell**
   Teach the children the difference between tattling (ratting) and reporting. Reporting is when children seek out help from the educators or a peer because they feel their body and feelings are not safe. This information is based on a shared understanding of bullying. Tattling (ratting) is when children are telling on someone because they want the other child to get into trouble; it is not based on bullying or feeling unsafe. Many children don't tell anyone they are being bullied because they are afraid the bullying will get worse if they are seen as "tattle-taling." It is important for the educator to create a system for children to be able to report a bully in a safe, trusting, and private way—for example, discussing the behaviour away from the bully or sitting at the craft table.

5. **Helping the Victim and Bystander**
   The following tips and strategies were developed to help the victim and bystanders to develop a variety of techniques to deal with bullying and to change the power structure between the victim, bully, and bystanders.

   - Teach children to stay within sight of the educators and groups of children.
   - Demonstrate different conflict-resolution strategies, such as "I" statements and mediation skills, to help de-escalate conflict and bullying. Children should be encouraged to practise these skills each day. Brainstorm with the children what they could do or say if anyone bullies them again.
   - Encourage children to role-play "I" statements and teach them how to walk away and get help—for example, by saying, "I don't like how you are speaking to me!" then leaving. The more opportunities and practice they have with using "I" statements, the more the techniques will start to become a part of their natural communication style.
   - Teach children to check out their body language and not to give the impression they are afraid of the bully—for example, by slouching, looking at the ground, or at their feet. The bully will pick up on body language when looking for the next target. Teach children to look confident by standing tall, looking forward, etc.
   - Use visualization or guided imagery (self-regulated strategy) to help the child to visualize the experience, to rehearse what it feels like to use conflict-resolution strategies, and to gain control of the situation. Encourage the children to think of the visualization process as similar to creating "visualization movie" which they are re-playing in their own mind. During the process ask the children to use a technique called self-talk (talking to yourself), which will help them to hear what they sound like when they are dealing with bullying behaviour. Ask the children to observe their own body language and identify whether it is confident. When the children put the visualization exercise into practice they will be able to play back the positive experience. The more times the children practise their "visualization movies" and self-talk experiences, the more control they will gain over the experience, and they will develop assertive and non-defensive language.

Reduce Bullying Behaviour The following techniques may help to change the bullying behaviour and the bully's need for power and control. If the bullying behaviour has been ongoing and has been pervasive in the program, a doctor or counsellor may be needed to work with the bully. Talk to the bully's parents and with the school about what you have been observing to see what kind of resources are available to help the bully. It is important to remember school-age programs need written consent from the parent to be able to discuss behaviours of the bully with the school. The following strategies may help to reduce bullying behaviour.

- Make a clear statement about how bullying behaviour isn't acceptable. Describe what bullying is, why a behaviour is bullying, and the consequences for bullying.
- Direct the child who is displaying bullying behaviour to a place in the play space, away from other children, to think about how she can change her behaviour. Your attention at this point should be on supporting the victim. If too much attention is given to the bullying behaviour, then the it may continue to escalate. The bully will be gaining attention through her negative behaviour.
- Encourage the child to practise and implement conflict-resolution skills and explain why it is important to use these strategies when dealing with conflict.
- Use role-play, creative writing activities such as creating a journal, or drawing/painting to help children express their feeling, about bullying or to reflect about how they can change their behaviour.
- Read a book about bullying, such as "The Bully Ant," to younger children; this will encourage to facilitate a discussion about why we don't bully.
- Participate in co-operative activities as a way to experience and understand the meaning of being part of a group, how a group works, and the opportunity to practice new communication skills. Gardening and baking are great co-operative activities where the bully will gain appropriate group dynamic skills, such as working together and listening skills.
- Taking care of the pets or watering plants in the environment will help the bully to develop empathy skills.

Educator's Role

Observing Observe the children indoors, outdoors, and on field trips. Observe how children play, who they are playing with, and the formation of groups. Observe the body language of each child and take your cue from any overt changes to body language, such as a shrug of the shoulders, which may be telling you the child is afraid of a certain situation. A child storming off from a group may be telling the educator he is a victim of a bully or he isn't getting his own way—two different reactions and responses by the educator. Physical aggression such as kicking, tripping, or pushing is easy to see; it is important for the educator to react and to resolve the conflict. When the educator is observing, it is important to listen very carefully to children's conversations and discussions and act when you hear anything that may lead to direct or indirect bullying. For example, if a group of girls are having a discussion about excluding another girls from their play because she has a language delay, the educator needs to react by having a discussion with the group about excluding children who are perceived as different.

Supervising When supervising the play environment, you are visible in the program. It is important to move around the play spaces and support the children when needed. When you are visible in the program, the children will know that you are there to support and guide them, making sure they are safe from bullying. The educator will gain an understanding of how the group is working whether children are practising conflict-resolution skills, the impact of community, and whether all children are safe. If you notice that a group of children are starting to demonstrate bullying behaviour such as name calling/teasing, you may want to hover around the group and listen very carefully to the interactions. It is your role to offer suggestions by asking different questions, challenging inappropriate behaviours, and sharing with the group the philosophy of the program—for example, we are all safe.

Helping Help children to develop friendships and peer relationship skills. Encourage the children to meet and interact with new peers by creating icebreaker games, co-operative activities, and play ritual games such as skipping and clapping. Involve children in community meetings; they may develop new friendships, for example while planning the next field trip.

Summary

Guiding behaviour is a process in which the children learn what behaviour is appropriate and what is expected of them. They also learn and have the opportunity to practice a variety of strategies, such as self-regulated problem-solving strategies to deal with conflict (e.g., communication).

The educator guides behaviour during play experiences, in the environment, and during community meetings to help the children build a peaceful community. One of the educator's key aims in guiding behaviour is to make sure that all children are safe from aggression and bullying behaviour. The educator needs to have an understanding of what causes conflict; this will help them implement the appropriate strategies in response. Teaching children how to use creative conflict-resolution and peacemaking skills are two strategies that will help to guide their behaviour. The educator should give children the opportunity, through role-playing, dramatizations, creative writing, and creative arts to practise and demonstrate these skills. The role of the educator is to model, observe, support, and teach children a variety of social skills and ways to implement techniques and strategies.

The importance of having clear and concise policies and procedures will help educators to implement programs and strategies and to be consistent.

Student Learning Experiences

1. What Would You Do?
Fatima is in the block/construction area. Evan is sitting on the couch, which is beside the block area, reading a Harry Potter novel. He has been relaxing on the couch for 45 minutes. The following conversation occurs.

> **Fatima:** "I like making really tall towers and then knocking them down. I like the crashing sound. *Crash! Crash! Crash!* Then I can build the tower again and knock it down again!"
> **Evan:** "I'm trying to read. I'm at the best part of the book, and I'd like some peace and quiet."

Answer the following questions:

- What are the needs of each person in the conflict?
- How can you turn this into a win–win situation? Give examples.

- What would you say to the children? Describe the process.
- What do you think is the resolution for the conflict?

2. **Construct an "I" Statement to Open a Conversation.**
   i) You and your friend were planning to do homework together after school. Your friend gets a chance to go to the mall with someone else. You do your homework alone.

   I feel_____

   when_____

   because_____

   ii) When you go to your locker you find your new neon-green highlighter pen is missing. Looking around, you see it in your friend's locker.

   I feel_____

   when_____

   because_____

   iii) The friend you are talking to keeps interrupting you.

   I feel_____

   when_____

   because_____

3. **Internet Activity**
Search the Internet for bullying-prevention programs in England, Scotland, Australia, and Canada. Copy the information to create a research file for each country. What are the common elements in each program and the strategies being used?

4. **Visiting a School-Age Program**
Visit a school-age program, and during a community meeting develop rules based on the four broad sample rules given earlier (keeping everyone's body safe; keeping feelings safe; keeping thoughts, ideas, and words safe; and keeping work safe). Describe the process. What did the children learn, and what did you learn?

Review Questions

1. List and describe the three different types of conflict. What is the role of the educator in dealing with each one? What would you say and do during the conflict?

2. What are the five components to consider when guiding children's behaviour? Choose two components and in your own words describe the role of the children and the educator. List and describe four strategies for the two components.

3. Describe why developing rules and consequences with children is important. How would you involve the children in the process? What are the barriers to developing rules and consequences, and how would you get over those barriers?

4. List and describe each of the steps in resolving conflict. What is the educator's role during each step? List one activity that would support the skills for each step.

5. In your own words, describe what bullying looks and feels like. List and describe the five bullying-prevention strategies.

PART 4

Planning
and Implementing Curriculum

CHAPTER 10

Traditional Curriculum

OVERVIEW

Traditional programming may mean different things to different people, but there are some programming elements that appear to be common in more traditional out-of-school programs. This chapter will describe various aspects of traditional programming and identify ways that educators in programs can ensure they address the various needs of the children.

WHAT IS TRADITIONAL CURRICULUM?

Traditionally, educators in out-of-school programs have observed children, and used this knowledge, along with their knowledge of child development, to plan centres and activities that school-age children will find interesting. When planning the curriculum, educators use a theme-based approach to plan activities for the various learning centres. Because educators recognize the impact of school on the children, one of the areas in the room is usually identified as an area where children can "drop and flop"—a place where they can relax and chat with their friends about what is happening in school and in other areas of their lives.

In the traditional curriculum, the educators will plan the program for a week or more in advance. Although known interests of the children may be included in the planning, the majority of the planning is based on the educators' knowledge of what school-age children tend to be interested in. As well, most traditional programs make it clear that the goal is to complement the school day, and this means that the focus tends to be on recreational activities (games, art, building blocks of many types, reading for pleasure, gross motor activities, and so on) and social activities (such as co-operative games, drama, and the drop-and-flop area). As well, some programs offer homework clubs or an area that children can use to do their homework.

Many programs indicate that they want to offer children the same activities they could do if they were at home, though there is some controversy around this aim. There are two schools of thought regarding access to computer or video games that are solitary or somewhat violent in nature. Some educators think that children should have opportunities to play these types of games in the program (as long as the rating of the game is all right) while others feel that the program should focus more on group activities, the arts, and informal outdoor activities, since children are less likely to have these types of opportunities available to them once they get home. Educators are less divided over the issue of violence. All agree that violent games should not be allowed, though people differ on their definition of violence.

Because educators plan the environment and activities in advance, children are not actively involved in curriculum development in traditional programs. This does not mean that children have no opportunities to make choices for themselves. Within the planned environment the children will decide what to do, and good educators have the flexibility to take advantage of serendipitous events and capitalize on the children's interests by using these events to support learning. For example, when a child comes back from March break with a collection of shells, a good educator will provide time and space for the children to explore the shells and obtain resource materials to help them with their exploration. This will be done regardless of the current theme for the week.

Table 10.1 illustrates some of the essential components of the traditional curriculum.

TABLE 10.1	Traditional curriculum

Educator-developed:

- pre-planned experiences are based on goals for the group
- goals are based on observations and knowledge of development
- planning is usually done for a week or a month in advance
- spontaneous learning experiences arise from ongoing play and serendipitous events

Theme-based:

- usually, although not always, themes are used to help structure the curriculum
- themes often last one or two weeks
- environments are often arranged around specific activity centres:
- although activities within centres will vary throughout the year, the areas themselves tend to remain constant
- centres are designated for specific learning experiences (e.g., construction play) and materials (e.g., art)
- centres include private, small group, and large group spaces
- learning activities are identified as appropriate for one activity centre or another
- planning tends to occur around the activity centres

PLANNING A TRADITIONAL CURRICULUM

The Roles of Development and Theories

Educators developing the curriculum for a school-age program may be tempted to rely on their memories, thinking about what they liked to do after school when they were that age. Although an educator may come up with many excellent ideas this way, curriculum planning is much more than this. The educators' knowledge of development, theory, and the individual needs and interests of the children in the program all influence the curriculum that they develop.

As the chapter on development indicated, school-age children have mastered, or are developing, skills that preschoolers seldom have, and these skills will influence the activities that educators develop. For example, knowing that the children in the program tend to be logical thinkers and have some reading skills means that the educator can provide board games and the children will be able to play them as long as the directions use words the children can read. Knowing that the children are already successful with basic gross motor skills such as running, throwing, climbing, and bouncing a ball means that the educator should provide more complex activities for them (such as soccer drills, hopscotch, or cycling).

Educators use their child-development knowledge to ensure that all developmental domains are addressed in the program. If educators based their curriculum only on what they themselves liked to do as a child, many developmental areas might be ignored. The educator who hated sports might not plan for many outdoor activities, while the educator who did not enjoy reading might not provide a very extensive library, and might ignore research books altogether. If educators ignore the children's developmental needs, the program could be influenced in other ways as well. For example, the educator who cannot stand untidiness would not think about the fact that school-age children still need hands-on, concrete experiences, and the educator might prevent messy play from occurring.

Along with a general knowledge of child development, educators will use their knowledge of theory to help create a curriculum that children will be interested in and learn from. Educators who understand Vygotsky's theory know that children need to be in the Zone of Proximal Development for learning to occur. This understanding will result in educators who find out what kind of knowledge children already have on a topic before developing a theme. If the educators are planning a theme based on the Olympics, for instance, they will want to find out what information children have on the Olympics before planning various activities. If children in a program already have a clear understanding of the history of the Olympics and the sports people compete in, the educators may want to spend more time during theme week on some of the unusual things that have happened in the Olympics (e.g., Britain's ski jumper, Eddie the Eagle, at the 1988 Calgary Winter Olympics) or have an activity where the children develop their own unusual Olympic games. On the other hand, if the children in the program know very little about the Olympic Games, the educators will want to plan accordingly and include more basic information and activities in their theme. In addition, there will have to be a variety of learning experiences around any theme in order to accommodate individual differences with respect to knowledge and skills.

Both development and theory should guide traditional programming, and result in theme-based programming that is not static but changes from year to year and from child to child. Educators working in traditional programs may use themes to help plan the year, but they cannot complete their planning until they know the children in the program. They need to know what stage each child is at developmentally, since this will influence the types of activities they offer, and they need to know how knowledgeable the children are with respect to the themes being planned, since this will influence the content of the activities. Although educators in a traditional program may have ideas regarding the topics they would like to introduce throughout the year, a good program will not plan all of their curriculum weeks or months in advance because it is unlikely that they will project their knowledge of what the children need that far in advance. Educators in traditional programs may have kits for various themes, but a good program will not just pull out the kit each year and implement its activities. A kit in a traditional program should contain materials and ideas for activities that could be used with a theme, and educators will use those materials that are appropriate for the current group of children, while adding to the kit the new ideas that come from working with this particular group of children. If an educator is simply using the same activities every year, he need to ask if he is providing curriculum that meets the needs of the children, or if he is simply meeting his own needs (because it is easier to keep doing the same thing).

The Role of Observations

At the Mapleridge school-age program, an educator is observing a group of children in the drop-and-flop area. On the pad she carries to record observations, she makes a quick note that two of the three groups of children in this area are discussing hockey and the Stanley Cup playoffs. As she moves into the construction area, she observes a group of children building forts and records that some of the older children in the area have solved the problem of keeping the roof on their fort. While outside with the children, she is able to observe a large group of children playing hockey. As she watches them, she notes that some of the older children are getting frustrated with the younger ones, who are having difficulty controlling the puck. She also makes note of the children who remain on the sideline throughout the game without being asked to participate. At the end of the day, she puts her written observations in a file with other observations that have been taken throughout the week.

Observation plays an important role in the development of curriculum in any school-age program. Educators learn a lot about the children's abilities, interests, and knowledge as they observe the children in play activities. As an educator watches how a child handles losing at a board game, how competently a child throws a ball, or how a child participates in conversations, he better understands what stage the child is at developmentally, and what kinds of topics or activities motivate the child.

Observations of the child may be formal or informal in nature. The educator may use anecdotal observations to identify some of the children's interests and skills, while she may use checklists to help keep track of overall skill development. Direct conversations with both children and parents also provide invaluable information on children that can help the educator with programming. Depending upon the wishes of the parents and the school a child is attending, information from the school can also help the educator know a child better, and thus program more effectively. If a child in the program has a disability, other professionals may be able to share information with the educator. Information specifically geared to the child's disability can help the educator understand or use techniques to help the child learn.

The Role of Goals in Planning

Through observations, discussions with parents, and input from other professionals (when necessary), general and specific goals emerge. Educators record these goals and keep them on file (in the children's individual files as well as the program files). Educators keep these goals in mind and use them to help plan experiences that will support learning and help the children attain various goals.

For example, a child in the program might have a hearing impairment, resulting in limited oral communication skills. The educators observe that she spends most of her time alone in solitary play, but frequently watches the other children playing. They also observe her in group situations and notice that she stays close to other children but seldom tries to communicate either orally or through sign language. Finally, observations indicate that the other children do not display negative behaviours toward her, but simply ignore her. Both the educators and the child's parents have identified friendship as an important goal for the child. With this goal in mind, the educator will make sure to include learning experiences that require children to work together (such as co-operative challenges) or help all the children communicate more effectively with one another (such as teaching sign language). The educator might also institute a buddy system for the child to help make it easier for her to enter play situations and to get to know the other children in the program.

The challenge for an educator is to keep in mind the various goals for the children, and to find ways to incorporate these goals into the play activities. Fortunately, many children will have similar goals, and many activities can address more than one goal type or level. For instance, fort-building can support social skills (like negotiating), science skills (physical properties of materials, gravity) and physical skills (co-ordination, strength). Fort-building can also support the development of these skills at several different levels. The child who has difficulty negotiating may succeed if the educator is there to provide some guidance, or if the educator is able to encourage the child to build with children who already have the skills. To help develop the science skills at different levels, the educator would ask different questions, or offer different materials, to help the children solve the problem. To help with motor skills, the educator might encourage different children to use different materials when building forts (for instance, small v. large pieces; flimsy v. stiff materials).

Goals for children should always be in the back of the educator's mind, and this will influence what is planned, the objectives for the learning experience, the materials provided, and the educator's role during the experience. In summary, observations combine with child development and learning theory to produce goals for children, which in turn provide a basis for much of the curriculum planning.

The Role of Themes

In a traditional curriculum, themes are used to provide some structure to the curriculum delivery. Educators identify themes they know school-age children tend to be interested in and want more information on. Educators know that children coming to the program after a day in school need some active play. They also know that school-age children tend to be interested in games with rules. Combining this knowledge with what they have observed the children doing may result in a theme around sports. By identifying this theme, they have a topic to use when trying to decide on activities that would help the children move toward their learning goals. By letting parents and children know what the theme is, the children can anticipate what will happen in the program during the week, and perhaps find materials to bring in that relate to the theme.

Educators use themes to provide a structure or framework for the curriculum, but themes should never dictate everything that occurs in the program. Educators planning a theme around music will incorporate music-based activities throughout the program, but will not restrict the program to musical activities only. For example, although the educators will make sure there are books related to music available, they will continue to make a variety of other books available. In the construction area, although the educators will post illustrations of instruments (perhaps of instruments being made, as well as played) and will provide a variety of materials that could be used to make instruments, the educators will also allow children to engage in other types of constructions in this area. In addition, if, during the music theme week, a child brings in some seeds and wants to plant them, a good educator will take this moment as it comes, and incorporate it into that day's curriculum.

The Role of Centres

In traditional programming the curriculum planning occurs around centres. The room has areas for different types of activities that educators know tend to support different types of learning. For example, every program will have an art centre, and educators know that this area will support the development of eye–hand co-ordination, spatial awareness, problem-solving, and creativity. With this knowledge in place, the educators will then plan weekly activities that support the goals they have for children in these areas. If one of the goals for the children is to refine their eye–hand co-ordination, the educator may provide pencil crayons and fine-tipped paint brushes; they may put up art posters that illustrate detailed pen and ink work; and they will take time to talk to the children about what they see in the art posters and help them develop their pencil and paintbrush skills. Often the activities provided in the area will be developed around the theme. In the above situation, if the theme is music, the educator may have materials laid out for the children to make musical instruments. A model of the instrument may also be placed in the centre of the table for the children to copy, or the educator may change the activity to reflect the theme while still encouraging the development of skills (for example, the activity could be making minia-ture instruments).

The centres found in a school-age program will vary, but most programs will have the following:

- large construction (blocks, boxes, etc.)
- small construction (Lego, etc.)
- art (drawing, painting, crafts, etc.)
- drop-and-flop (chapter and picture books, magazines, pillows, etc.)
- table-top toys (board games, cards, puzzles, etc.)
- dramatic play (dress-up, props, etc.)
- computer and technology
- writing area (clipboards, markers, pencils, blank books, etc.)
- science (experiments, natural materials, loose parts, etc.)
- snacks (often doubles with art or table-top areas)

Outdoors, the areas may differ widely since many centres share outdoor space with schools or other organizations. Most programs try to identify space outdoors for

- active physical play (organized sports, small group games, running games)
- quiet play
- climbing (usually limited to a climber)
- sand play (sand pits, or under the climber)
- dramatic play (space for putting on air bands, plays, etc.)
- traditional outdoor games that do not require running (skipping, hopscotch, four square, etc.)
- sitting space (picnic tables, etc.)

For instance, if the school yard is also being used by the school or a recreational group, the program may have access to only part of the yard. This may mean that the children have limited space for running games, or that they have limited access to the paved area where four squares and skipping usually occur.

Educators in a traditional program may or may not extend the theme into planning for outdoor activities; however, they will keep their goals for the children in mind when developing the program. They will always plan for activities that require movement, especially running and other rapid movements, since children often get insufficient opportunities for these types of gross motor activities during the school day. When planning for the outdoors, educators will always want to include several types of gross motor activities to ensure that different individual abilities and skill levels are being addressed. The curriculum might include opportunities for older children to get involved in a game of soccer so they can practise the coordination of a variety of skills, while younger children might have the opportunity to dribble balls through an obstacle course. There would also be opportunities for basketball or skipping, which provide opportunities for coordination and rapid movement but in a format that some children find more appealing. If there are children in the program with mobility impairments, educators must also find ways to provide various gross motor activities for them to participate in, working on their coordination skills and movements. For example, if a child in the program is interested in basketball but has trouble with balance and coordination, educators have to be creative and find a way the child can actively participate in the play.

The Role of Children

In traditional programming, the children do not play an active role in curriculum development because the curriculum is seen as the responsibility of the educators. This does not mean that the children do not influence what direction the curriculum takes. Through observations and conversations with the children, educators discover their interests and use this to help determine the themes that will be used and the activities that will be planned. Unfortunately, in traditional programs in which planning occurs months or even an entire year in advance, this indirect influence is missing, and the program is less likely to meet the needs of the children as a result.

Many programs also offer some more concrete ways for children to get involved. Some will have meetings with the children to discuss what they would like to do on special days (such as Professional Development Days), or to discuss an issue that has arisen (such as problems with children not following the rules). The educator will run these meetings, but the children will have opportunities to share their ideas and help solve the problem being discussed.

In other programs, educators may provide a suggestion box where children can place ideas for themes or indicate solutions to problems. Some educators favour this technique because, like observation, it provides them with recorded information that can be used to help plan curriculum.

The Role of the Educator

The educators in traditional programs are responsible for planning the curriculum. As indicated earlier, they have to be able to combine their knowledge of development and theory with the information they have obtained on the children in their program, and incorporate this into the planned curriculum. In order to do this successfully they have to determine what types of themes children will be interested in, and how the goals for the children can be effectively addressed in the various theme-based activities.

Educators in the traditional program may ask children and families for information regarding interests and topics for curriculum, but, ultimately, it is the educators who make the decisions regarding themes and activities.

Turning Knowledge into a Weekly Plan

The easiest way to understand the planning process is to follow an example of it as it occurs:

> The staff of Mapleridge school-age centre are in the midst of a program-planning meeting. The goal of the meeting is to develop the curriculum for the next couple of weeks. The program's two educators are basing their discussion on their observations of the children as well as the curriculum goals for the program.

Step 1 They began by discussing some of the observations they have made on things that the children were interested in. One topic that kept coming up was making forts, while another was hockey (the Stanley Cup playoffs were on). The educators decided to go with hockey as a theme.

Step 2 Next, they began to discuss how the theme of hockey would work into various areas of the program. Planning outdoors seemed relatively easy since they knew that pick-up games of street hockey would occur, but they also decided to add some skill development by setting up some targets for children to try to shoot pucks at. Knowing that Alice, one of the most avid hockey fans in the group, would have trouble getting involved in a pick-up game, the educators decided to organize a simple hockey game. This game would have to have some adaptations made in order to accommodate the fact that Alice needs to use a wheelchair as a result of spina bifida. Even though the theme was hockey, the educators also planned some different activities for the sandbox and other areas. For example, along with the usual toys for sand building, they included some ropes and pulleys to encourage the children to work at a solution to finding new ways of moving buckets of sand from one area to another when building.

Step 3 The indoor environment seemed as though it might be a bigger challenge with a theme of hockey than the outdoors. The educators posted various hockey pictures in the art area and made sure that the pictures were varied, not only in content, but also in the art style used to make the picture. The children were given access to pencil crayons, tempera paint, and brushes of various sizes and shapes. The educators did not make markers available, because they had observed that children often headed straight for them because markers were a familiar medium and children were not sure their pictures would look good if they tried to use pencil crayons or pastels. The educators also included black paper and white chalk in the art area and encouraged the children to use these materials to create a winter hockey scene.

In the science centre, the educators provided examples of hockey equipment that was old and could be thoroughly examined by the children. They also provided resource books that described various aspects of hockey equipment, and a variety of loose parts so children could try to make equipment themselves.

In the drama centre, the educators had hockey equipment that the children could wear and examples of music that is often associated with hockey. There was also a puppet theatre and an area where children could work on making puppets. Sports magazines that had pictures of hockey players were provided as well, and the children were encouraged to cut them up in order to use them to make stick puppets.

In the construction centre, there were posters of hockey arenas. Some of the pictures showed modern arenas (such as Ottawa's Corel Centre) while others were pictures of old community arenas and outdoor rinks. The educators also provided a toy Zamboni along with the other cars and trucks.

In the table-top centre, the educators made sure that there were board games, a hockey foosball game, and puzzles that related to hockey (remembering that there had to be a number of puzzles of varying difficulty levels).

In the drop-and-flop centre, the educators added hockey books to the general library. These included resource books, books on hockey greats, and story books about hockey. By providing a variety of books, the educators addressed not only the different interests of the children, but also their different reading levels. In addition, the educators brought in blankets with hockey logos and hockey banners to decorate this area.

Step 4 After making the decisions regarding activities for each area, the educators double-checked to make sure that they identified any special considerations that needed to be made in each area (for example, the hockey game had to be playable by someone in a wheelchair).

Step 5 Once the ideas had been identified, the educators recorded their curriculum on the weekly planning sheet. As well as simply recording the name of the activity, the educators took the time to identify the various objectives for the activities, any adaptations that would have to be made, and the materials they would need to collect to put the plan into action. Once this was completed, they then looked to see what materials were available in the "hockey theme kit."

Step 6 At the end of the planning meeting, the educators divided up the tasks that needed to be completed before beginning the theme. One of the educators took on the responsibility for ensuring that the equipment and materials were available for the science, art, reading, and drama centres, while the other took on the task of collecting the materials for the rest of the centres.

Strategies for Planning Traditional Curriculum

The above example describes one way that educators can develop the theme-based curriculum, but not all programs involve the educators meeting and working together on all aspects of curriculum development. The above method requires programs to provide staff with sufficient time to meet and come up with curriculum ideas. Although this is a potential drawback, the advantage of this method is that it ensures that all goals are being addressed, that each centre is providing a unique activity, and that all educators are committed to the curriculum.

A different strategy for curriculum planning is for educators to meet and determine the theme, and then assign each educator some centres to plan on his or her own. This approach requires less meeting time, and educators who prefer to plan on their own may appreciate this. If this technique is used, educators need to make sure that all the goals are being addressed. This might be accomplished by assigning goals to various centres, or by providing a follow-up meeting to discuss which activities are addressing which goals, and make changes if some goals are not being addressed in any of the activities. Although this method does reduce the meeting time, it has the potential to result in a duplication of activities (or at least the creation of very similar activities) and a failure to address all of the goals.

Another approach to planning the curriculum is to have one educator responsible for planning the curriculum for the week. This method requires very little meeting time and, since one person is responsible for everything, and thus has an overview of the whole process, no goals should be missed. One drawback to this method is that without the brainstorming component, the curriculum may not be as effective at meeting the diverse needs of the children. Another drawback is that with only one person making the decisions, the others may not be as fully committed to the curriculum that results, perhaps because they think certain activities are inappropriate.

Formats for Weekly Planning

There is no set format for recording a weekly plan. It may take the form of a chart, a web, or a timetable. The educators developing the plan will use a format that best complements their planning style. Regardless of the format being used, a weekly planning sheet should provide readers with information regarding the experiences being provided and their links to learning and development.

The information included in the planning should be clear enough that a supply educator would be able to come in and implement the curriculum. Some centres will try to provide all the information on one form, while others might provide an overview with additional information recorded on a separate sheet of paper. This additional information could be a detailed planning sheet for each activity, or simply a materials list. What a centre chooses to use will once again depend upon the needs of the educators and those working with them.

Figure 10.1 and Table 10.2 show how the planning done by the Mapleridge educators would look using different formats.

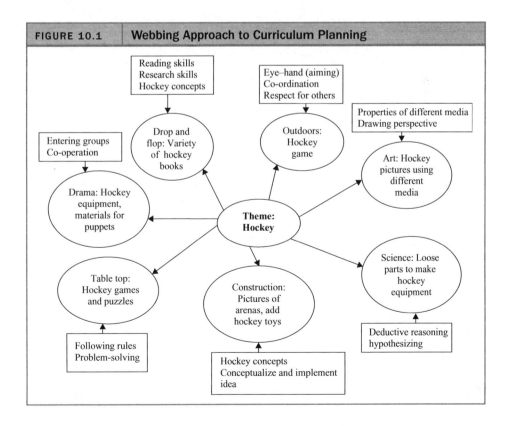

FIGURE 10.1   Webbing Approach to Curriculum Planning

TABLE 10.2 Chart approach to curriculum planning

Week of: April 16 — Theme: Hockey

Main Observations (Compiled from Ongoing Observations on File)	Development (Highlight Development for This Week)	Weekly Plan	Special Notes	Evaluation of Activites (Were the Objectives Met? How Should I Change or Expand Activity?)
Interest in hockey and forts	Beginners to advanced readers	*Flop and drop*: Incorporate a variety of hockey books and magazines in drop-and-flop area.	Find hockey novels and magazines to encourage non-reader hockey fans to get involved.	
Younger children having trouble controlling the puck	Practise eye–hand co-ordination for aim	*Art*: Post hockey pictures in the art area and include similar media as that used to create the pictures.	Discuss perspective techniques with children who need this knowledge.	
Some children excluded from games	Control how hard one hits an object	*Science*: Provide loose parts and resource books so children can try to build hockey equipment.	Need a large space.	
Lots of discussions occurring around how to build forts, communication systems, and science experiments	Problem-solving skills in a number of areas Social skills needed to enter groups Develop respect and empathy for peers	*Construction*: Have posters of arena, etc. and include toy zambonis, etc.		
Children asking educator to draw pictures	Develop perspective in drawing skills	*Drama*: Provide hockey equipment to wear and magazines to create hockey puppets.		
		Table top: Have games and puzzles related to hockey.	Find some 15-piece puzzles that don't seem too childish	
		Outdoors: Provide hockey equipment, set up pylons for puck control practice, organize a hockey game, provide pulleys and ropes in the sand area.	Organize a hockey game that Alice can participate in.	

Interest Clubs and the Weekly Plan

A club has a specific focus (for instance, baking) and usually meets once a week, with a limited number of children participating. Many programs incorporate clubs into their weekly planning. Clubs provide children with an opportunity to explore a theme in more depth. Unlike weekly themes, clubs will run for many weeks or months. During this time the children know that they will be able to go back each week and learn more about, say, photography, how to put on a play, or a particular sport. Clubs are one way that traditional programs engage children in long-term projects. A club provides children with a recurring theme that they have chosen to become involved in, and because it is long term, the children have time to think about what they have learned, ask questions, and come back to experiment with new ideas on the same topic.

Some programs will encourage children to sign up for one or two clubs. Each club usually has identified goals that the children are aware of when joining it. For instance, children sign up for a photography club knowing that they will learn how to take digital photographs, download them onto the computer, and manipulate the pictures before printing them. Other children sign up for the drama club knowing that they will eventually put on a show.

Clubs are often led by an educator or volunteer who has an interest in and some knowledge of the topic. The club leader will help the children learn the skills outlined in the club goals, and will also help children find answers to their questions on the subject.

The following six steps in setting up a club will help guide the educator in developing them.

Steps in Setting Up a Club

1. Brainstorming
The educators will brainstorm together to decide which clubs they feel the children would enjoy based on their observations of the group or from past experiences—for example, a homework, games, or art club.

2. Scheduling
The educators decide what day of the week and time the club should meet. Clubs usually meet in a program once or twice a week and will continue for a number of months. Some centres will have set times for clubs throughout the week. If all the clubs meet on Tuesday and Thursday afternoons, a child may be able to join only one club. If some clubs meet on Thursday and others on Tuesday a child has a chance to join more than one.

The one complaint that some children have about clubs concerns scheduling. If the club meets only once or twice a week, children who become very interested in the topic may find this too infrequent. In one program, the children in the science club wanted to meet every day because they were creating experiments and wanted to check them and add additional ingredients, but unfortunately the club met only twice a week, and the materials were not available in between meeting times.

3. Planning
The educators will plan what the club will focus on: activities the children would participate in, any field trips connected to the club, and guest speakers. In some programs, the children are given the opportunity to make some of these decisions. In this type of club the educators facilitate the meetings, but the children themselves decide what direction the

club will take. They brainstorm what they want to know about the topic and determine how they will get this information. Besides facilitating the meeting, the educator will take a more vocal role if the ideas, or the ways the children want to obtain the information, are inappropriate. For example, if the children in the drama club decide that they want to create a dance using music with violent lyrics, the educator will have to step in and let the children know why that music cannot be used.

4. Signing Up and Organizing

Children sign up to participate in a club they are interested in. Whether or not a child can sign up for more than one club will depend on how the clubs are scheduled into the program.

5. Implementing

Initially, the educators will implement the club, with some input from the children. During the process, the educator may decide with the children if new materials or activities are needed or if they should bring in a guest speaker. For example, in an art club, if the children are busy working with clay, the educators may feel it is important to bring in an artist to teach some different techniques.

6. Concluding

The club is finished when the educator feels the children have met the goals of the club or have finished all the activities. The final conclusion of a drama club would be putting on a play for the other children and the program's parents.

Long-Term Projects in Traditional Programs

Even though traditional programs base their curricula around themes that usually last a week or two, they will at times incorporate long-term projects into the curriculum. Examples might include putting on a play for the parents or performing a concert for the families.

The idea for long-term projects may come from interests the educator has observed in the children, or it may be an idea that could not be accomplished within the ordinary curriculum time constraint of a week or two. It may also be a project that is done on a yearly basis (such as a school concert). Once the educator has identified a project, she will discuss it with all the children in the centre. This will be done to help them understand exactly what is going to happen, what their roles will be, the time-frame for the project, and so on. In a traditional program, a long-term project will involve all of the children, and each one will be assigned various tasks. The assigning of tasks will often be done in consultation with the children, since it is important to the success of the project that the children want to participate in the task. For example, once the educator has discussed putting on a play about one of the Harry Potter books, she will help each child decide if he or she wants to be an actor, design the backdrop, be a director, do lighting, or decide on costumes. The educator knows that some children will want to be on stage while others would dread that role, and she helps them understand the responsibilities of each of the roles, so the children, with the help of the educator, can choose wisely.

In long-term projects, the educator takes a leading role in the development and delivery of the project. The educator does not simply tell the children to go off and develop the play. Instead, she sets up meeting times and comes to the discussion with ideas on how to put on the play successfully. As the children work on costumes or practise their roles, the educator is there to help them. Because all of the children are involved in the project and the educator needs to be actively involved as well, there is usually a time set aside during the day that is devoted to project work. The amount of time may vary from day to day, but it has been planned in order to ensure that the project is completed by the due date (that is, the date of the performance).

When the decision has been made to incorporate a long-term project into the curriculum of a traditional program, the educator must carefully determine if this project is something that can engage all of the children. The educator must look at them and plan components of the project that will appeal to their diverse interests and abilities. When planning a play, the educator will encourage children who love construction activities and machines to help build the sets (children would love to try and build something that looked like Hogwarts School!). Children who enjoy art can help paint backdrops, while those who like crafts might be involved in other areas of set and costume design. By knowing the children, the educator can create aspects of a project that will appeal to everyone, and in doing so will actively engage all of the children in the project.

Documentation of a long-term project is determined by the educators and is typically posted after the project has been completed. The purpose of the documentation is to show others the type of involvement the children had in it, as well as to highlight the final outcomes. Although the children may help the educator create the documentation display, it is the role of the educator to determine the purpose of the documentation, and how it will be developed.

Evaluating the Learning

As educators plan the various activities for the week, they will also determine how each activity will be evaluated. Since each activity should have learning objectives, the educators know in advance what skills and abilities the activity should be encouraging and therefore what they want to look for and evaluate. For instance, if the objective of the art activity is for children to develop perspective in their pictures, the educators would then look at the drawings to determine if perspective was demonstrated. To keep track of their findings the educators might use a chart, or even simple jotted notes that could be added to children's files later on.

If the observations indicate that the objectives are not being met, the educators will have to decide why the activity did not work and try to create a more appropriate one. For example, they might discover that they were trying to get the children to look at too many aspects of perspective at one time, thus confusing them. If this happened, the educators would then make sure that they focused the new activity on only one perspective technique.

If the activity objectives were met, the educators would have to decide if they needed to continue with similar activities to give children time to practise their skills, or if the children had mastered the objectives and needed a more complex activity.

Planning for the Unexpected

All educators know that some of the best learning is very serendipitous in nature. When these unexpected situations arise, educators should be prepared to take advantage of them.

One way they can do this is by allowing flexibility in the structure of the day. The educators may have planned to go inside at 4:30, but if a child finds a large earthworm just before then and several other children want to look at it, the educators will realize that they all need to stay outside for a bit longer.

Educators also provide for the unexpected by having a variety of resources available. Books are one of these resources. When children want to look at an earthworm, the educator may or may not have the knowledge needed to share information about the worm's body parts. If an educator does not have this knowledge, there may be a book in the centre's library that could help. Another useful resource would be a clear plastic container that the worm could be placed in along with earth, so that the children could see how it works its way through the earth before letting it out back into the soil outside.

Finally, questioning skills are important if educators are going to be able to take advantage of the unexpected. The educator needs to be willing to ask children questions to get them to think and solve problems. The educator may know the answer to the questions being asked, or she may want to learn about the subject as well. In the example of the worm, the educator might ask the children how the worm feels to the touch, and follow this up by asking if snakes feel the same way. The educator could ask the children how they think the worm moves without any legs or what it eats in the earth. The educator's own curiosity can lead to a variety of questions, and can get children to ask their own questions and to try to find the answers.

Unexpected learning situations can also help the educator determine future planned curriculum. If the children are motivated to learn because of the discovery of a worm, the educator might build this interest into the next theme. This interest might result in a theme such as "worms and snakes" or "things that live in the ground."

Influence of Routines and Transitions on the Curriculum

Routines and transitions are often used as a framework around which a curriculum is planned. There are daily routines around which educators have no control (such as buses picking up children to go to school, or the start of the school day). There are other routines that are more flexible in nature (such as deciding when to have a snack). Along with the routines, educators have to look at the transitions during the day (such as moving from free play to leaving for home, or moving from snack time into outdoor play).

When setting up the daily schedule, educators keep these routines and transitions in mind. They know at what time some will have to occur and how long it usually takes children to go through the routine or transition. This in turn will help them plan activities for the children.

Routines and transitions can also influence a program's curriculum. For instance, if a program has children coming from four neighbouring schools, the first group might arrive at the centre at 2:45 and the last group not until 3:30. Most will arrive wanting something to eat and drink. Keeping this in mind, the educators decide that there will be an open snack time from 2:45 until 3:45 to accommodate the children's different arrival times and needs. Free play is scheduled during this period, and at 3:45 some children begin the transition to outdoor play.

The activities available during free play include activities that can be completed quickly, since children arriving later may not want to get involved in complex activities, though these should also be available for the children who have more time (because they arrived earlier) or who do not mind stopping their play to go outside. Aside from providing a snack, the educators avoid any directed activities during this time because the children need a change from the very teacher-directed activities found in the school day. If there are, say, two educators in the program, one might begin the transition to outdoor play with those children who are ready and wanting to be outside, while the other handles a later transition for those still eating their snack, or who want to complete an activity before going outdoors.

If the weather is good, the children are likely to stay outside longer than the schedule indicates, and educators might do some activities outdoors that were scheduled when the children went back inside. For example, on a really nice spring afternoon the educators might hold a group meeting outdoors to discuss an upcoming field trip, or they might set up an outdoor homework area for children whose parents expect them to have completed their homework at the centre.

Although the educators may adjust the schedule slightly to take advantage of the great weather, the usual timetable has the children come back inside around 4:30. This is because the centre closes at 5:30 and the children will need time to finish activities they began before going outside, do homework if required, participate in a long-term project, or attend clubs (depending on the day) or group meetings.

Because the educators know how long the various routines take (for example, 20 minutes for group meetings, 15 minutes for children to get ready to go outside) they are able to determine how much time is left for free play activities, and therefore the types of activities that will occur. This does not mean that educators plan only for activities that can be completed in that time slot, but it does mean that they need to know how long the children will need to complete each part of the activity, so that it can be broken down into discrete steps that can each be accomplished on separate days. It also means they have to ensure that there is storage space for the materials used in partially completed activities. If the educator has planned making papier mâché animals, the first day may consist only of putting paper strips on the balloons, while the next day's activity is putting the details on the shapes, and the last day is spent painting the animals.

Routines and transitions occur regularly throughout the week, and because they are known quantities educators can slot other curriculum activities into the time left between them. Educators need to be careful, though, that routines and transitions do not become the most important aspect of curriculum planning. If children are very involved in fort construction or in a science experiment, the educators can extend the indoor time accordingly, and go outside at the end of the day rather than at the usual time. If the children come to the program with lots of energy and want to be very active, the educators do not need to make them wait until 3:45 to go outside. Instead, the educators could take the snack outside and find a quiet area where it could be served (do not forget hand-washing just because you are going outside!).

Role of Routines and Transitions in the Curriculum and in Learning

Most school-age children like being able to anticipate what will happen during the program, though they also like to have some say regarding routines and how they will be run. At this age they want more independence and responsibility, and routines provide them with opportunities to develop these abilities. In planning meetings, educators can identify the routines that are essential and inflexible as well as those that can be implemented in a more flexible manner (for instance, under what conditions could educators extend the outdoor play period?). Once educators have identified routines in which children have greater participation, they can provide children with increased opportunities for decision-making. For example, given some parameters (such as the Canadian Food Guide), children can help determine the snacks that will be served and the routine for having them. By allowing the children some input into some routines, the educators are helping them learn to see things from others' points of view, negotiate, listen, and work co-operatively.

Unlike for younger children, most school-age children are capable of following the routines without constant reminders. Educators will probably not need to take the children to the washroom to wash their hands before eating, for instance; the children will generally be able to do so on their own, with the occasional reminder. When educators acknowledge this, they show the children that they consider them capable and competent individuals. This in turn helps the children develop self-confidence and self-esteem.

Field Trips and Summer Activities

In a traditional program, the educators are responsible for determining field trips and summer activities. The same process used to plan the regular curriculum is used to plan these activities, though due to scheduling issues (such as organizing buses), educators often plan these activities well in advance of implementation. In many traditional programs, field trips and summer activities are planned many months in advance based on the types of trips and activities from the year before.

In some programs the educators will find out what the children would like to do, while in others the educators base the planning of field trips and summer activities on the theme for the week or on activities that their experience tells them school-age children enjoy (such as pajama day). Summer programming tends to provide children with more recreational types of activities, and more outdoor activities. Because summer programs are full-day programs, activities that require extended time to complete are more frequently included than during the school year.

TRADITIONAL CURRICULUM AND THEORIES

Regardless of what curriculum approach is used by educators, it should be supported by a firm theoretical understanding of learning and development, and a traditional curriculum is no exception. As previously mentioned, however, educators may implement such a curriculum in more than one way, which in turn will affect how well the theories support what is happening. In order to address this issue, this section will first look at best practices for traditional curricula with respect to their theoretical base, and then look at the impact that variations of traditional programming methods will have on the theoretical base.

The educator-directed aspect of traditional curriculum could be supported to some extent by social-cognitive theory. This theory recognizes that educators need to observe children and create situations where they will be rewarded for completing appropriate tasks. Such a curriculum can also support Bandura's vicarious learning theory, as educators model skills they want the children to use, though it may also result in children learning inappropriate behaviour if educators make all or almost all of the decisions for the program, since children will learn that those who are bigger and older have power and make decisions. This can be translated by older children into the idea that they can control the younger children and don't need to listen to their ideas.

As long as the traditional curriculum provides opportunities for more knowledgeable children to act as mentors to their peers (that is, providing scaffolding), and as long as the educators use information obtained from observations and child development concepts to help determine the themes and activities offered (thus relating to the idea of the zone of proximal development), Vygotsky's theory would support a traditional-curriculum model. This theory is not supported, however, when educators plan the program well in advance, implement the same theme kits year after year, and do not allow ongoing observations of the children to influence themes and activities.

When educators provide loose parts so that children can engage in hands-on exploration, and when they use knowledge obtained from observations to create activities that provide children with challenges suitable to their developmental stage (preoperational, concrete operational, or formal operational) and previous experiences, Piaget's theory is being supported. This theory is not supported, however, under the same conditions that would also compromise a Vygotskyan approach, as outlined above.

If the planned activities are meaningful to the children and help them develop skills that are valued in society, the program is addressing the conflict identified in Erikson's "industry v. inferiority" stage of development (the stage most school-age children will be dealing with). Unfortunately, if the program fails to provide the supports necessary for children to feel competent when working on their skills, it will be creating a situation where the resolution of the conflict is negative rather than positive. This means that it is important for educators to provide a variety of activities to support different types of skills, activities that can accommodate different skill levels, guidance as to how to develop the skills, and recognition of the children's efforts in order that they develop a sense of competence as they work on mastering various meaningful skills (such as reading, drawing, or woodworking).

A weakness of the traditional approach with respect to Erikson's theory is that social skills are some of the most important real-life skills children are developing at this age. When educators alone determine what will occur in the program, they limit the children's ability to develop effective social skills. Our society wants individuals who can think for themselves, take others' perspectives into account, and find solutions to problems in a variety of situations. Having children participate in curriculum planning requires them to use all of those skills in a very meaningful way, but this does not occur in a traditional-curriculum model.

Educators in traditional curriculum models are less likely to use IPM to help them determine the curriculum. When using an information processing model, educators base much of the curriculum on previous experiences and knowledge. Educators using this model would take the children's current interests and use them to help them learn; a themed approach would therefore not be appropriate, since children's interests are varied and are not limited to a week or two of study. IPM also encourages children to revisit experiences and concepts, since the more they do so, the better the learning. Unfortunately, a themed approach often discourages children from revisiting experiences, since the theme changes regularly.

The one aspect of IPM that a traditionally programmed, theme-based model can address is the impact that a multi-sensory approach can have on learning. IPM indicates that learning is more likely to occur if more than one type of sensory input occurs. By having a theme that encompasses all areas of the program, multi-sensory input should occur.

Because educators are responsible for curriculum development, some of the multiple intelligences identified by Gardner will not be supported as much as others. Planning is especially good for engaging what is known in Gardner's model as *practical intelligence*. Children will have to work out how to access resources both within the classroom and within the community, and this is something they often have little opportunity to practise in other areas of their lives.

Although a traditional model may address some of Gardner's intelligences very well, other areas may be missed. The interpersonal and intrapersonal intelligences are directly related to a number of social skills and, as identified in the section on Erikson, some of the best ways to support these skills are not addressed very well in a program where the curriculum is pre-planned by educators.

The final theory we will discuss here is Bronfenbrenner's ecological theory. According to Bronfenbrenner, there are various social systems that are unique to each individual and affect development and learning. If educators make observations of the children while obtaining knowledge of other parts of their lives (such as what is happening in school, the family, and the larger community) and this information is used to determine themes and appropriate learning experiences, then components of the ecological theory are being addressed. If educators plan the themes and activities well in advance, and ongoing observations of and communication with the children are not the foundation for curriculum development, then this theory does not support the educators' approach.

In conclusion, when the traditional theme-based, educator-directed model of curriculum planning bases the development of the themes and activities on the observed skills, abilities, and interests of the children attending the program, this approach can be at least partially supported by several theories of learning and development. If observations of the children are not used as the basis for determining themes and planning, then few theories will support this approach.

Even though educators may be able to use certain aspects of the various theories to support their theme-based, educator-directed curriculum, there are aspects of many developmental and learning theories that tend to conflict with this thematic approach to curriculum development. For instance, using a theme to drive the activities designed for the various areas of the program does not recognize the individuality of children. Not all children will be interested in a particular theme (motivation to learn, multiple intelligences) or will be able to coordinate their interest with the educators' timetable (themes usually last a week or two) that will determine how long they study a concept (cognitive stage, ease of learning). When individuality (expressed in needs and interests) is not a major component of the planning process, the process cannot be supported by many of the theories (including Gardner, Piaget, Vygotsky, IPM, and Bronfenbrenner).

Educators may also have difficulty using theories to support curriculum in programs where they make all the curriculum decisions (that is, where all activities are planned by the educators with little or no active input from the children). When educators do all the programming, the children lack important opportunities to develop or use abilities and skills that theories such as Piaget's and Erikson's identify as important for them. In fact,

Bandura's concept of vicarious learning even indicates that children might learn inappropriate skills in this type of environment.

Summary

Traditional programming is a theme-based, educator-directed approach to curriculum development. This approach uses themes as a framework to guide the development of pre-planned learning experiences. In this approach the environment consists of various learning centres that remain fairly constant throughout the year (such as dramatic play, drop-and-flop, and construction centre).

Educators following best practice in a traditional program will use ongoing observations to determine themes and plan learning experiences. Educators will not plan themes and activities weeks or months in advance, but will use their observations from the past few weeks to determine the theme for the upcoming week and what types of learning experiences will best support the children's learning both within the context of the theme and outside it.

Educators following best practice will use themes as one of their tools for creating learning experiences. Along with the theme-based activities, they will make sure other activities are available as well, since they recognize that some children may want to engage in other types of play. Educators will also take advantage of serendipitous experiences to engage children in learning.

Educators working in traditional programs must avoid falling into the trap of planning so far in advance that there is no way the curriculum can truly meet the needs and interests of the children. They must also avoid the temptation to simply recycle themes and activities. Any theme developed for the program should arise from ongoing observations of the children. Although themes may reoccur over the years, educators should never base a decision for a theme on the fact that they have used it before, and so have a ready-made "kit."

Finally, the very basis of the traditional approach (theme-based, educator-directed) poses some problems for educators wanting to use theories of learning and development to support their practices. Although good traditional programs can be partially backed up using theories, the use of broad-based themes and a very directive approach by the educator poses some problems.

Student Learning Experiences

1. Scenario
Using a case scenario, complete a curriculum plan utilizing each of the formats discussed: chart, webbing, and timetable. After completion, have a discussion around each tool and its effectiveness for planning.

2. Designing Curriculum
In groups, design your own curriculum planning form/s that would address: development, objectives for learning experiences, special considerations that may need to be noted, and restrictions of the daily schedule.

3. Debate
Debate the appropriateness of traditional planning for school-age children. Use your theoretical understanding to back up what you say.

Review Questions

1. Describe how and why observations are used in traditional theme-based programming. What is the relationship between observations and developing goals?

2. What is the difference between a theme, a club, and a project in a traditional curriculum?

3. Identify the theories that would not support determining themes and activities weeks in advance of implementation. Explain why these theories cannot support this practice.

4. List and describe in your own words the steps in the planning process.

5. What are the roles of children, parents, and educators in a traditional curriculum?

Employee Name	Employee ID	Saturday
Allen, Stephanie	101279	02:00 PM-08:30
Baron, Andrew	101289	11:00 AM-08:30
Bonner, Dallas	101402	09:00 AM-05:00
Campbell, Jordan	101333	07:00 AM-05:00
Church, Cherlyn	101334	07:30 AM-06:00
Coombs, Lisa	101403	02:00 PM-08:30
Deavitt, Wendy	101332	07:00 AM-05:00
Greer, Susan	101287	
Hashem, Ocean	101291	08:00 AM-05:00
Maurdev, Peter	101387	
McGale, Patricia	101319	07:30 AM-06:00
McGourty, James	101398	
Moore, Ryan	101298	
Moran, Kenzie	101400	
Nagy, Szilvia	101335	
Patterson, Sarah	101385	02:30 PM-08:30
Raymond, Samantha	101278	09:00 AM-07:00
Rendon, Mona Lisa	101386	11:00 AM-08:30
Russell, Kathryn	101389	11:00 AM-08:30
Sage, Jean	101354	10:00 AM-08:30
Sharp, Michelle	101397	10:00 AM-07:00
Thompson, Kella	101401	07:00 AM-05:00
Thornton Raymond, Lesley	101323	09:00 AM-06:00
Wilson, Michael Anthony	101399	07:00 AM-05:00
Zoney, Roxanne	101286	07:00 AM-05:00

CHAPTER 11

The Emergent Child-Directed Curriculum

OVERVIEW

This chapter will focus on the child-directed curriculum, a form of emergent curriculum, and will discuss the philosophy, definitions, and the emerging processes that underlie it. Developing and building a sense of community in a home-like environment is the basis of an emergent child-directed curriculum approach, and for the emergent process to be successful the components of building community from Chapter 8 need to be implemented and developed in the social environment. For example, without having the necessary experiences and skills such as communication and leadership skills, children will have more difficulties in participating in community meeting and in developing, planning, and implementing curriculum. The role of the educator will be discussed and different strategies and techniques about how to involve children in the curriculum process will be illustrated throughout the chapter. Case studies, play experiences, examples of webs, and short-term and long-term project examples will illustrate the collaborative approach between the children, educators, and parents. Tips about how to involve children in the planning process will be discussed and will feature stories and examples from a school-age program whose philosophy is based on an emergent child-directed approach. The importance of play experiences, observations, loose parts, research, and community meetings will be featured in discussing how to develop full-day curriculum. Finally, the development of curriculum over the year will demonstrate the role of the educator in the emerging process.

WHAT IS EMERGENT CURRICULUM?

The term "emergent" has been used for many years in the school system for a specific area of the curriculum, namely literacy (hence the common term in education theory, *emergent literacy*). The process of the emergent curriculum is similar in concept and processes to emergent literacy. Emergent curriculum occurs in both the social and the physical environments and it emerges over time. Cultural practices and values of the children and families in the program are incorporated in an emergent-curriculum approach. It is an ongoing process in which the children, educators, and parents interact, share ideas, and collaborate. The educators and children use a variety of tools (perhaps a camera or a camcorder) to document what children are learning, what they are interested in, how they are using materials, and how they are playing.

Children are an important part of the process and should be involved in all areas of developing curriculum. Emergent curriculum should ensure that children are part of a collaborative process and have an active role in community meetings, developing documentation, and having input into the curriculum.

Elizabeth Jones, a professor at Pacific Oaks College in California, coined the term "emergent" in relation to curriculum development in the 1970 NAEYC publication *Curriculum Is What Happens* (see bibliography: Braun). Others experts including Lillian Katz, George Foreman, Rebecca News, and Marjorie Schiller have discussed the value and process of emergent curriculum.

TABLE 11.1	What is emergent curriculum?

Child-driven:

- Educators meet regularly with children to plan the program.
- Goals are developed through observations and children and family input, as well as the educators' knowledge of development.
- Meetings occur regularly to plan for both short- and long-term experiences.
- A variety of documentation is used to convey interest, learning, and play experiences.
- Spontaneous learning experiences arise from ongoing play and serendipitous events.

Project-based:

- Program is not theme-based, although there will be a number of short- and long-term projects occurring that may look at times like a theme.

Environment:

- Environments are often arranged around a variety of loose parts and resources that might change throughout the year as interests and skills vary.
- Children can move materials from one area to another.
- The play areas are flexible in nature and include areas for private, small group, and large group spaces.

Learning:

- Learning experiences can arise in one play area and move into other areas.

Planning:

- Planning tends to occur around the children's interests and play.
- Planning is a collaborative process between the educator and the children.

Table 11.1 illustrates some of the essential components of an emergent curriculum.

How Emergent Curricula Lead into Projects

The following story illustrates how the emergent process can lead into a project.

The children started collecting rocks from the many visits to a local beach. During these visits, they would collect rocks, stones, and pebbles based on a variety of characteristics, such as shape, texture, and sparkle. They would carry the rocks back to the centre and spend time showing each other what they had found and how they wanted to use it. A shelf and a countertop were turned into a "rock garden" for children to visit, add to the collection, or take and use in other parts of the room. Based on the interest—rocks and collecting—the educator decided to bring into the program at least 60 large rocks ranging in diameter from 7 centimetres to 15 centimetres. He placed several of the rocks on a table. The children, for the first few days, did not bother to approach the table, so a few days later he placed a large piece of shiny black satin on top of the rocks, and on another table close by he placed acrylic paint, brushes, glue, and natural materials. Eventually, the children gravitated to the table, removed the piece of satin, and starting handling the rocks. After a few days, they discovered the acrylic paint and starting painting the rocks. Many of the rocks contained messages (some in code) or poems. Over a number of weeks they started connecting the rocks up to create a maze-like sculpture by linking their messages, poems, and codes. During the process the children and the educator took pictures and decided to create a bulletin board about the rock experience. Some children wrote stories and poems about the experience and added them to the bulletin board.

During a community meeting the educator decided to bring in resource books about secret codes, mazes, labyrinths, and rock gardens. The children created a brainstorming-planning web of what they wanted to do with the rocks.

Eventually, the maze-like sculpture became a part of the outdoor garden and was also used in the playroom during different play experiences. After two years, many of the rocks, and the maze sculpture, could still be found in the environment.

Why Is This Curriculum Emergent?

The children had a specific interest based on community and play experiences—collecting rocks—which the educator observed. He facilitated this interest by providing materials in an innovative way, including cloth on the table as a way of displaying the rocks. Space was provided in the environment for the children to handle and experiment with the rocks in both the indoor and the outdoor environments. The children were not rushed through the experience, and had time to observe, manipulate, and experiment with the rocks. The educator did not remove the rocks early on when it seemed the children were not immediately interested; instead he asked questions and waited until the children were ready to use the materials. The experience lasted a number of months without the children being rushed off to begin a different activity. Children had the opportunity to connect with people in the community by interacting at the beach. Children worked collaboratively by connecting the rocks together and developing secret codes and messages. The educator again picked up on this new direction to their interest by bringing in a variety of resources about codes and mazes, helping to expand the children's experience. During community meetings the children were actively involved in curriculum development as they helped plan (using webbing) what they wanted to do with the rocks. Finally, the children and the educator were able to document the experience and the ever-changing process of the project through photos and stories. Eventually, the whole rock experience became a natural part of the program's physical environment. Each new facet of the process was allowed to emerge naturally from what had come before, and each new emergence was encouraged and further developed.

COMPONENTS OF EMERGENT CURRICULUM

1. Observe

Observations are the starting point for emergent curriculum. Using a variety of observational tools (such as anecdotes, jotted notes, photographs, illustrations, dictation, stories, videotapes, and audiotapes) the educators observe children's learning, skill development, interests, backgrounds, and values. They observe children interacting with each other, having discussions and conversations, in the context of both small and large groups. They observe children manipulating and experimenting with materials and loose parts, and observe them making links between activities, concepts, and new subject areas.

Once the observations have been documented (say, written in a log book) the educators, as a team, should review their observations at least twice a month and ask the following questions:

- What are the children telling you about how they are playing?
- What do you think children are learning?
- What are the children telling you about how they are using the loose parts and materials?
- How can you facilitate their play and learning?

As educators reflect on these questions, they should begin to get a clearer picture of where the children are going with their interactions, ideas, and interests. Once the educators have formulated their thoughts about what the children are interested in, or what new ideas they have connected to from the original project idea, they should discuss how they could support the children's learning, what resources are needed, and how to involve the children in the process.

2. Communicate: Sharing of Feelings, Ideas, Opinions, and Issues

Children and educators are encouraged to share and communicate ideas and opinions, and to question each other. This will occur during playtime, routines, and transitions, and during community meetings.

During community meetings children will have the opportunity to share with the group the following: what's happening at school, at home, or on the weekend. Children will have time to develop their conversational skills by sharing their family history, interests, opinions, ideas, and concerns. Everyone should be encouraged to participate. It should be kept natural and spontaneous. The educator should encourage discussions and conversations by asking questions and sharing their own interests, ideas, and opinions.

In order for children to become active participants in the development of the curriculum, they need to feel that what they are thinking and saying will be accepted and respected by the educator and by the other children. During community meetings, interactions, and play experiences, the environment should be safe, secure, and trusting. Children should feel comfortable sharing their feelings, opinions, and issues with the group. Educators must encourage children to listen reflectively and to focus on their feelings and the feelings of others. Educators should help the children learn how to use caring and respectful language.

As the children and educators plan the curriculum, the educators should also feel comfortable sharing their own ideas and feelings. It is important for the educator to model appropriate language, attitudes, and questions.

3. Based on Interest

The educator will develop curriculum from observing and interacting with the children. She will note the interests coming from play experiences, conversations, discussions, and brainstorming sessions and, with the help of the children, will decide how these interests will influence the curriculum development.

The educators will also bring their own interests to the program. For example, if an educator has an interest in reading to children, she may set aside a time in the day to read a chapter from a story to them. Or if he enjoys growing things, an educator might bring his passion, skill, and knowledge of gardening into the program.

Educators are a vital part of the community and the program, and should feel comfortable bringing their own passions into these areas. They should not impose their ideas or enthusiasms on the children, but should present them during group planning sessions or through discussion and conversations.

The interests of parents can also be integrated into the curriculum. During parent orientation at the beginning of a school year, and throughout the year, parents can be surveyed about their interests and talents, and asked how they would like to be involved in the program. Also, parents can be a good resource for materials and loose parts for the program. In one program, one parent loved to make pies, and her work schedule enabled her to come in once a week to make pies with small groups of children. Another parent had access to large amounts of wood. The children were involved in a woodworking project, and the wood this parent donated kept the project going.

4. Active Input by Children Planning the Curriculum

In an emergent philosophy, children should have input in the planning of curriculum. School-age children are verbally capable of communicating their ideas, needs, and problems. Children's interests, ideas, and opinions are essential to curriculum development. By creating a process where the children can take part in curriculum planning, you are developing their self-esteem, critical-thinking skills, group-building skills, leadership skills, and language skills. You are also showing the children that their ideas, suggestions, and opinions are valued and worth sharing.

The children's input is also important for ensuring that the curriculum is actually meeting their needs. Even the closest observation by the educator cannot take the place of a child's direct comment, because observations help the educators only to make informed guesses, and these may be wrong. For example, in one program we observed an educator watching a group of children building an indoor fort with cloth. They were using a variety of tapes to attach the cloth to the wall and storage unit. This process went on for a few days. The educator finally said, "It's interesting watching the group constructing the fort. It looks like you are working together to develop a fort with plenty of space inside." But the children responded, "No, we are interested in connecting the cloth with different kinds of tape."

In this observation, if the educator had not asked the children about their fort, he would never have known that his assumption about their interest was wrong. As a result, the educator knows that to support the children's learning, he can bring in different types of tape for them to experiment with. A new area of interest had emerged.

5. Materials and Loose Parts

In an emergent approach, educators and children will develop together the material webs and the lists of loose parts and materials that the children need for their play experiences, interests, and emerging projects.

Using information obtained from observations and conversations with children, the educator will provide sufficient and appropriate materials, loose parts, and research books to expand play, learning, and projects. For example, if children are constructing a hammock between trees, the educator can continue this type of play by providing a variety of different kinds of cloth and plastic sheeting. To expand the play, an assortment of fasteners can be used, including rope, twine, and duct tape.

6. Connect and Collaborate

Developing a collaborative approach in which power is equally shared between the educator and child is a component of an emergent curriculum for school-age children.

The educator plays a vital role in the collaborative approach by:

- Facilitating and modelling the steps in planning, for example, developing the agenda and taking minutes for meetings, brainstorming sessions, organizing information, making decisions, creating documentation, and developing material resource lists
- Demonstrating how group meetings work
- Providing time and space to develop the collaborative approach
- Observing and documenting the process
- Facilitating discussions
- Sharing ideas
- Offering advice
- Encouraging problem-solving

In emergent programs, educators provide children with opportunities to play with and connect with other people and ideas. As children make numerous connections in their play and interactions, they are developing a variety of concepts and skills.

In the hammock experiments mentioned above, if the educator brings in a pre-made hammock and encourages the children to study it by manipulating, exploring, experimenting, and even taking it apart, she is providing an opportunity for the children to make the connections with their hammocks. Hopefully, they will transfer this knowledge to their own hammock-making play. By having this experience, they may learn some of the techniques of making a hammock, and acquire some of the skills necessary to create their own hammocks successfully.

During community meetings and the planning process, as children and teachers share ideas, the children are connecting new ideas with ideas from the past and, as a result, are developing new hypotheses, questions, ideas, and thoughts.

Children should have the opportunity to connect to the community at large by visiting libraries, hardware stores, markets, recreational centres, and seniors' residences. This will help children create links between their community, their play experiences, and their projects.

Besides getting the children to go out into the community, educators should also bring the community into the children's space (the program). Both types of connections are valuable, and provide different experiences for the children. For example, if children are interested in snakes they could visit a pet store that sold snakes, but they could also invite a reptile expert to come in to talk to them and show them reptiles. Each of these experiences will connect the children to the community, but will also be a very different experience for the children.

7. Plan During Community Meetings

During community meetings, children will have the opportunity to discuss and, share their feelings, ideas, and opinions, and to reflect plan, and document. It is a time to involve the children in the community meetings by becoming a part of the playroom community. Children should be encouraged to share ideas, concerns, and issues. It is a time for children to develop assertive, positive, and respectful communication skills.

Meetings are a structured time for the children and educator to develop and implement the curriculum through brainstorming planning sessions. All participants bring both new and old ideas to a planning session. Planning webs or lists can be used to give the ideas some coherence. Although educators should always be open to new suggestions from the children, they should also not be afraid to repeat something popular. In one program, when children were brainstorming ideas for the summer, they made sure corn roasts were included on the planning web. The program had held corn roasts every year for the past six years, but the children were clearly not bored with them. Corn roasts had become part of the program's tradition and sense of identity.

Children and the educators will have the opportunity during community meetings to develop material lists (with budget) and weekly or monthly charts of activities. A list of research material, or a request for a speaker, can be developed during this time. So can planning snack menus and play experiences, vacation events, clubs, and special projects.

Community meetings are also a time for children and educators to follow up on decisions made at earlier meetings, and to evaluate how the program is doing.

8. Implement the Curriculum
Once the emergent curriculum process has begun, the educators provide ongoing support for the process by supplying materials, loose parts, and equipment for the children. The educator will support and extend the learning by using open-ended questions to encourage children to think about what is happening. They will also use their observational skills and conversations with the children to gather information about the play experience and the learning. During the implementation process, children and educators will continue to use research to support the play experience, concepts, and projects. Children will continue to develop brainstorming webs and lists of materials and ideas.

9. Connect Emergent Curriculum and Projects
The connection between the emergent curriculum and projects will vary depending on the children's and the educators' experience with the process. It will also depend upon the type of play experiences and level of previous knowledge the children and educators have. In an emergent curriculum, not all play experiences need to contain all the components that exist in the emergent curriculum process (such as documentation or research). At any one time, several play experiences are occurring, and each will be emerging slightly differently. It is important for the educator to go with the flow and be flexible, observe carefully, and involve the children, colleagues, and parents in the process. The children will determine which play experiences will eventually emerge into projects, and which will remain simple play experiences that they are enjoying in the moment but have no real interest in pursuing.

The warning "not to fall down a rabbit hole" is one to remember when developing curriculum. For example, if a child approaches the educator and says how much she enjoys playing in the wind, the educator might do one of three things. First, she may think the child is interested in flying kites, and so decides to provide materials for building them and books about how to build them. Second, she might wait to see if other children feel the same way. Third, the educator might ask the child questions about the wind, and from these questions find out what exactly interests the child about it. It may be constructing kites and flying them, or it may just turn out to be the experience of feeling the wind on the face, or a sense of the power of the wind.

The first response is the one that can be characterized as "falling down a rabbit hole": grasping onto the first interpretation that presents itself by assuming the child's interest is in flying kites. In an emergent philosophy, the child could be making a personal statement about her "joy" when feeling the wind, and will feel comfortable telling the educator this. The lesson is that if the educator is not sure quite how to interpret a child's interest, she needs to ask more questions. Children will tell you what their needs and interests are. Projects are simply one possible outcome of emergent curriculum.

10. Research

Educators using an emergent-curriculum approach support the development of research skills as they encourage the children to use a variety of books and magazines, the Internet, telephone research, community guest visitors, and community field trips; and as they identify what materials are needed for the children's play experiences. As the children participate in the emergent curriculum process, research skills such as questioning, hypothesizing, locating information, organizing research findings, and drawing conclusions will naturally be developed.

In one school-age program, a group of children were building 3-D boxes from pieces of Plexiglas. One child asked what Plexiglas was made from and if they could they make it at the centre (question). He thought that, if they could make their own Plexiglas, it would save the centre money and they would have access to as much Plexiglas as they needed (hypothesis). The educators felt it was an interesting question and asked the children how they thought they could find the answer. The children decided to use the yellow pages of the phone book to make a call to a store that sold Plexiglas, and to the company that made it. They organized their questions and made the call (locating information). After making the call and discussing the information they had learned, they decided it was "not safe" to make Plexiglas at the centre (drawing a conclusion). In the course of their research, they found out that they could receive a discount the next time they purchased Plexiglas (unexpected conclusion).

In the above story, the children used a telephone book to do research. Books, the Internet, magazines, community visitors, and community fieldwork can also be used for research.

11. Document

Documentation is an important aspect of an emergent curriculum, because it records what has happened (process, learning, and so on) and communicates this information to one or more audiences (parents, the wider community).

Documentation takes on a variety of forms. It can be a story about play, or a book with photographs. For example, if children are creating new co-operative games, the documentation can demonstrate the beginning of the process (planning and brainstorming), the middle (creating the various games), and the end (playing the games and producing a games book).

The children and educators should have access to a variety of documentation tools: camera, audiotape, camcorder, clipboards, writing pads, drawing and painting tools, computers, overhead projectors, and light tables can all be part of the process.

When creating documentation, children are encouraged to make 3-D models of their thinking, for example, from clay, wood, wire, dioramas, cloth, and loose parts. Children are also encouraged to create 2-D representation of their thinking, such as illustrations, blueprint plans, maps, mazes, and panel and brainstorming webs, as well as writing stories, poems, lists, and charts.

Community meetings can be used for children to develop and construct their documentation, such as by discussing how they want to use the photographs from a garden project. They might decide to use the photographs to create a timeline showing the development of

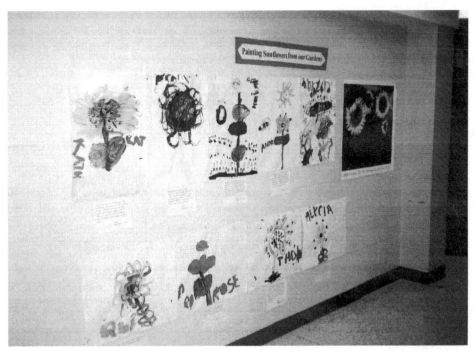

Documentation can be displayed in various locations of the program.

the garden from April to October. They can use pieces of bristol board for each phase of the garden (sprouting plants, preparing the garden, planting, watering, and harvesting), then add the appropriate photo and dictation. The bristol board panels will be hung in the hallway for parents to see what happened in the garden project.

Other ways in which projects can be documented include photographs, illustrations, painting, mapping, creating 3-D models of projects and play experiences, audiotaping of stories and of the process, videos, and writing stories, songs, and raps.

As part of the documentation process, the educator should develop a system of communicating with parents, such as newsletters, open houses, and workshops. Developing a parent information board, with photographs and other types of documentation, will help to demonstrate the emergent-curriculum process and how it supports the children's learning.

AN EMERGING CURRICULUM IN ACTION

Because emergent curriculum development is a dynamic process, the best way to understand it is to observe it in action. The following example demonstrates how emergent curriculum unfolds, the respective roles of the children and the educator, and the learning that can occur.

Purchasing Games with a Budget of $300

During a community meeting children made the following request: they wanted to purchase new board games. The older children wanted more challenging logic games while the younger children wanted fantasy-type games. The educator felt it would be the perfect opportunity for the children to learn about budgets and to be responsible for purchasing and taking care of the games. The educator gave the children a budget of $300 to purchase the games. The process took place over four weeks. Here is how the curriculum emerged.

Brainstorming Ideas

The children brainstormed what types of games they wanted. One child developed a web for the group and put all their ideas on the web. The main question from the group at this point was: how many games could you buy for $300?

Researching

Catalogues from different wholesale companies were brought out for the group to price and select games. They worked in small groups and spent time discussing the cost of games, the types of games, and reading the description of each game. The older children helped the younger ones to read the catalogue and showed them how it was organized.

Developing Individual Webs and Lists

Each group developed a web or a list of the games they wanted to purchase and the cost of each game. The page numbers and names of the catalogues were added to the web or list. The older children helped the younger ones to write down the names of the games and the price for each ones and helped them to add up the final cost.

Developing a Group Web

The group decided to take all of the information from the individual webs and lists and put the ideas on a large group web. They felt it would be easier to have all the information on one web when the time came to make the final decision. Children took turns at developing the group web as they recorded the names of the games, the prices, and the catalogue each game came from. They classified each game by its type (logic, fantasy, and so on).

Voting (for a Shortlist)

The group decided to vote on the games they wanted. The 12 games with the most votes would be the ones that the group would use to make the final selection.

Group Discussion (Purchasing Within Budget)

The children added up the cost of the games to see if they were within their budget. They realized that if they purchased all 12 games they would be over budget. They predicted that by taking out three games they would be within their budget. The group decided to vote to find out which games would be eliminated. After voting out three games, they were under budget by $10.

Purchasing Games

The children nominated two children to fill out the order form with the educator and be responsible for mailing the order.

Finding a Space for New Games

In five weeks, the games arrived. The boxes of games were brought to the community meeting and the group opened the boxes and checked off the games against the order form.

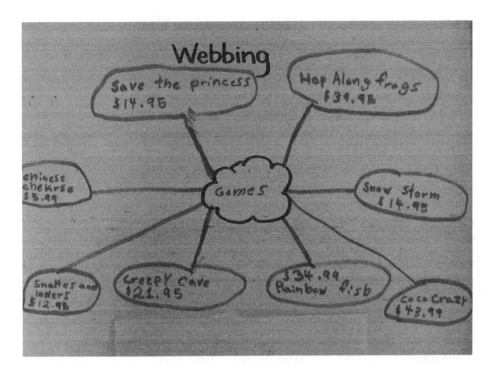

The children were very excited and wanted to play the games immediately, so they spent that afternoon doing so. Two children took the initiative to clean off a couple of shelves so there was room to store the new games.

Surveying Which Games Were Their Favourites

Two weeks after the delivery of the games, a number of children developed a survey. They wanted to find out what each person's favourite game was, and why.

Documenting

During the process of brainstorming, researching, developing webs, and playing with the games, the educators took photographs. They created a documentation board with the children's webs, lists, and photographs, and added their own story about what the children were learning during this process. The following are examples that illustrate what the children learned during the process of purchasing the games:

- Problem-solving: brainstorming, planning, voting, and playing the games
- Negotiating skills: discussing and determining the process to use and what types of games to purchase
- Decision skills: selecting the games and voting
- Research skills: using research materials for predicting, questioning, locating information, analyzing options, and drawing conclusions
- Reading skills: using research materials and reviewing webs
- Writing skills: creating webs and lists

- Math skill: fractions, adding, subtraction, and data management
- Organizational skills: working within a budget, organizing the process, finding space for games
- Social skills: working as a group toward a common goal, purchasing games, developing group webs, and playing the games
- Peer teaching: older children have the opportunity to help younger ones with reading and writing
- Building self-esteem by being a part of the group and being able to purchase games within a budget
- Physical skill: developing eye–hand co-ordination when playing the games

TOOLS IN AN EMERGENT CURRICULUM

Informal Conversations as Tools in an Emergent Curriculum

Informally, children can be involved in planning the program. During play experiences and routines and transitions (such as snack time), children will have discussions and conversations about what they are interested in and whom they want to play with. This is a good opportunity for the educator to have conversations with children and ask questions. It is a natural and spontaneous way to develop curriculum. The educator can also have an audio-tape recorder on during this time to tape the discussions. Some educators carry a small note pad and a pen to jot down notes on the children's conversations and ideas.

Suggestion Box

By adding a suggestion box in the program, children and parents will have the opportunity to offer suggestions for different play experiences. When using a suggestion box, educators should locate it in areas that all children have easy access to. Placing pens and pads of paper close by gives children a clear message to use the suggestion box. One program used this method to gather snack ideas and suggestions for field trips.

Documentation Area

In the program, create documentation areas by providing blank webs in the play space. Include pads of paper, pens, rulers, pencils, and clipboards. One idea is to attach a file folder full of blank webs to the wall or on the back of a storage unit where children have easy access to them.

Webbing

Although there are a variety of methods used to record planning ideas, webbing is frequently used in emergent-curriculum situations. It accommodates a variety of information, facilitates the brainstorming process, and is easy for the children and educators to use. The children are able to grasp the concept of webbing very fast after observing the educator model creating a web. In one program, a child commented, "Wow! I can see my thinking."

Children can create their own planning webs by having access to blank webs in the environment.

Webbing can be used for:

- Brainstorming and gathering information (general or research-based), ideas, and interests from children, educators, and parents
- A record of ideas and interests for the children and the educator
- Demonstrating divergent thinking. One can actually see the thinking process when a web is read. It is a visual way of organizing ideas
- Demonstrating ways of organizing play experiences, observations over time, materials or loose parts, ideas, thoughts, and concerns
- Developing a sense of community and group membership

Types of Webs

Play-Based Webs It was observed in a program where children were familiar with webbing that they used the blank webs naturally during play. For example, a group of children who were playing in a fort were discussing creating a band and writing songs. One child raced over to the web bank, grabbed a web and some markers and went back to the fort. She announced, "Let's have a meeting and plan what we need for our band." They presented their final web to the educator and this web was used as a basis for developing a band and writing songs.

Planning Webs When webs are used for different purposes, their names will change to reflect the content. If educators are going to post the webs for others to read, having titles will increase the reader's understanding of the content. The following three webs (brainstorming web, materials and time frame web, and project web, Figures 11.1–11.3) illustrate what various webs look like and different ways to use webbing with school-age children. The following webs emerged from the interest a group of school-age children had in Plasticine. They spent a number of weeks during indoor and outdoor play manipulating and experimenting with Plasticine. Eventually, they expanded their interest to sculpting Digemon characters, as part of creating a mini environment about a fantasy world. While making their characters, they expressed an interest in making a Digemon movie.

Initial Brainstorming Web The focus of the initial web is creating a Plasticine world. The children and educators organize ideas, thoughts, and opinions around the focus. In the web shown in Figure 11.1, the brainstorming ideas are organized around research, materials, community, and documentation.

Material and Time Frame Web The central focus of the web shown in Figure 11.2 is the materials and loose parts. In this type of web, all materials are placed in the centre. Additional materials can be added at a later point in another colour pen to demonstrate the emerging process. Around the materials, information (in the form of jotted notes) about how children are using the materials can be placed. To keep track of this information, place a date beside it. Also, the educator or children can add to the web the documentation tools that they would like to use during their Plasticine play.

The process of webbing gives children the experience of working together by brainstorming and recording their ideas.

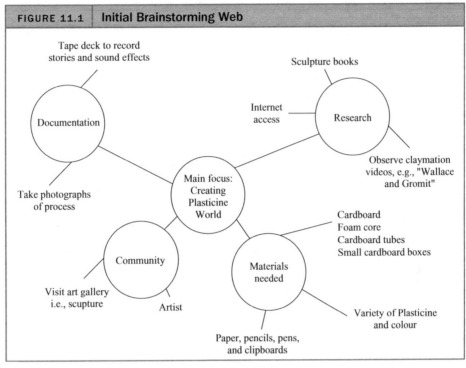

FIGURE 11.1 | **Initial Brainstorming Web**

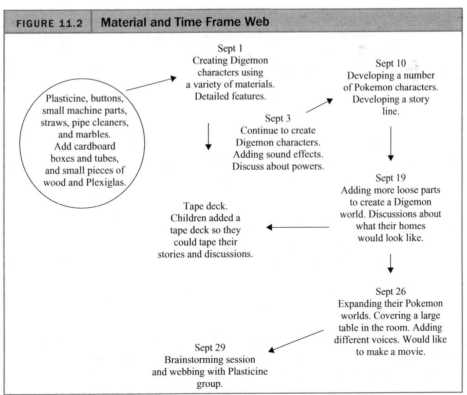

FIGURE 11.2 | **Material and Time Frame Web**

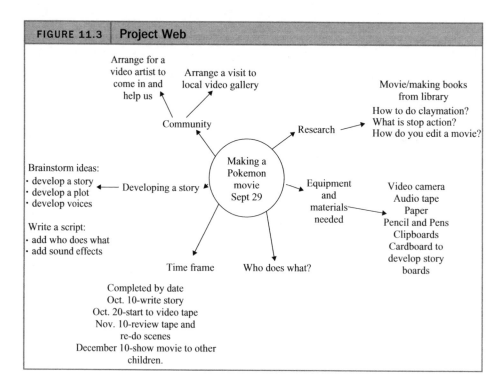

FIGURE 11.3 | Project Web

Project Web During the Plasticine Pokemon play experience, the educator sat down with the group and webbed with them on September 29 (shown in Figure 11.3). The children wanted to make a movie of their Pokemon fantasy world. By creating Pokemon characters and fantasy worlds, the children's play has emerged as a special project. The central focus is making the movie.

EMERGENT CURRICULUM AND SPONTANEOUS PLAY

Emergent curriculum does not always lead to projects; often it simply ends in a variety of spontaneous play. Spontaneous play evolves as the children are given the freedom to simply enjoy using the materials. They are not worried about engaging in research or documenting what is occurring. This type of play still provides a wide range of learning opportunities, and can be just as rewarding as projects. For this reason, educators should not always push the children to turn their play into a project. The following vignette shows how having fun creating forts can lead to a variety of spontaneous play with numerous learning outcomes.

The children in a school-age program were building forts in the outdoor environment during the summer. They used a variety of loose parts, equipment, and props in constructing their forts. The children were able to leave their forts up overnight and on the weekend because of the location of the yard and the fact that it had a locked gate. Several of the children lived across the street from the yard, and they and their families took care of the forts during the weekend. Each morning the forts were inspected for any hazardous materials or wildlife. Building and maintaining the forts became a communal experience where all the children were involved, and the forts became very complex. They consisted of separate rooms connected by corridors or tunnels so that the children could visit each other. A communication system made out of small plastic hoses and funnels was used between the separate rooms. A pulley system made from nylon rope was suspended from tree to tree, which enabled the children to move materials and messages from area to area. Inside the forts, the children were starting to design furniture for each room, and were decorating the walls.

The observations in Table 11.2 were made after the summer, when the fort play was extending into the fall. The observations demonstrate how play experiences emerge over time. The role of the educator in the process of expanding play experiences is to observe, ask questions, provide materials, research materials, and document the play experience. The observations start on August 22 and end on September 12.

TABLE 11.2	Constructing and designing forts
August 22	**August 27** →
Materials: Tape rope foam core, pillows, cloth, and telephone.	**Materials:** Foam core, fabric, table, boards, tape, long tubes, streamers, pipes, tape, rope.
Observation: Building forts under the climber and connecting to fence. Designing rooms with floors, walls, and ceiling.	**Observation:** Constructing forts behind bench and under table. Creating various size rooms (3 in total) and decorating each room. Developing a communication system with small plastic tubes between rooms. Attaching flags to their forts.
Documentation tools: Camera and camcorder.	**Documentation tools:** Camera and camcorder.
	Research: Photos of forts from different countries, Internet search on the construction of forts and tents.
September 6	**September 12** →
Materials: Cloth, tape, foam core, rocks, plastic tubes, broom, boards, cardboard, cards, crates, pots, and pans.	**Materials:** Cloth, fun fur, tape, string, boards, tubes, paper, streamers, crates, tape.
Observation: Creating new rooms (bedroom and swimming pool area) and walls. Constructing canopies. One new room has a window, which becomes the "Dairy Queen." Inside the Dairy Queen area, they are creating a workstation to make ice cream. Designing an indoor garden with the rocks.	**Observation:** Creating private spaces and separate rooms. For example, bedrooms, homework, meeting, babies and cats, and clapping game spaces. Making costumes in the bedroom area. Creating a 3D pinball machine from boards and tubes.
Documentation tools: Camera, blueprint plans, clipboards, paper, and pens (create room plans).	**Documentation tools:** Camera, camcorder, and tape deck.
Research: Architecture books, photos, and postcards.	

In this example, the play began with creating forts, then emerged into a process of designing rooms with specific functions. Role-play and play re-enactment became a part of the fort construction as the children created a Dairy Queen serving window and added elements of storytelling. Some children made a pinball machine and set up flags to watch the wind. They created blueprints and illustrations to help design their forts. Eventually, the children decided to create a tree fort by brainstorming ideas about the materials needed, the location, and eventually the construction.

Throughout the process, the educator provided a variety of materials based on observing which materials the children were using, and how. There was no requirement on the part of the educator to keep the children focused on one aspect of fort-building, or to encourage them to go into a more in-depth study of forts. The focus was on allowing the play to evolve spontaneously, and by doing so the educators were able to watch it transform into a variety of different activities. Not surprisingly, since the children were familiar with research and documentation, many of them took it upon themselves to use these tools in their play, but there was no sense that this was because they felt obliged to do so.

EMERGENT CURRICULUM SHORT-TERM PROJECTS

The observations seen in Table 11.3 demonstrate how the emergent process developed over time and showed how the play experience of mixing different food dyes and paint became a focus for the children. Role-play and play re-enactment became a major part of the activity,

TABLE 11.3	Transforming play: emerging curriculum	
November 29	**December 5**	**December 15**
Children mixed different colours of food dyes, paint, water, and oil in bottles. They imagined the mixtures would transform into potions called "Monster Blood Infections" and "Biohazards."	Children started to assemble plumbing pipes and attached them to a table to create a winding potion machine. They were pouring the water into the top of pipe so it would travel down through the pipes and into a bucket. The children discussed how the water transformed into a secret potion when the water went through the pipes and ended up in the bucket.	The children mixed paint with water in small and large containers with lids and shook the liquids to create a potion called "Monster Breath." The children imagined the water changed from water into Monster Breath potion. The children used a tape deck to describe the process.
January 9	**January 11**	**January 12**
The children used a variety of materials and loose parts to create costumes and a lab from *The Island of Dr. Moreau*. They created potions from water, food dye, paint, oil, and sparkles, which transformed the children into animals.	The children used cloth and tape to create walls for a laboratory and costumes to become "Mad Scientists." They created science experiments with different materials such as flour, water, oil, and paint, documenting them with a camera.	The children and educators developed a list of materials needs and gathered materials to make Obblik (a commonly-used modelling clay).

and transformed the experience from cause-and-effect experiments to more sophisticated play (for example, acting out *The Island of Dr. Moreau* and other stories of a "mad scientist" genre). The educators used observations, jotted notes, and anecdotes to document the play experience.

Developing Short-Term Projects

At this point in their playing, the children and the educator were looking at photographs of potions transforming. The children expressed an interest in developing a science club. They wanted to experiment with different materials and liquids to create chemical reactions and transform liquids.

Potion transforming had now emerged into a project. The educator and children brainstormed questions and ideas on how they wanted to set up the science club. They developed a list of materials and research books they wanted to use. The three observations seen in Table 11.4 demonstrate how research books and research skills were used to develop a short-term project.

EMERGENT CURRICULUM LONG-TERM PROJECTS

Long-term projects are in-depth studies of concepts, ideas, and interests. Projects may vary in length from a few weeks to months or even years. They are in-depth investigations by the children that involve play, planning, researching, implementation, reflections, and documentation. Projects can be specific to an individual child, a small group of children, or a larger group. They can be broad in nature, such as planning and creating a garden, or specific in focus, such as making plant- and vegetable-based food dyes from the above garden

TABLE 11.4	Science club: developing short-term projects	
January 27	**February 10**	**February 17**
Research Book: *Art of Science*	Research Book: *Baking Soda Book*	The children continued to use the *Baking Soda Book* and *Art of Science*.
The children spent time looking for experiments in the *Art of Science* book. They created materials lists and collected the materials for the environment. Some children demonstrated the experiments in bottles and started to predict what would happen next and what would happen if the experiments were left out overnight. Children illustrated the process.	The children spent time looking for chemical experiments from the *Baking Soda Book* and developed a web of materials they needed. The children, with the help of the educator, gathered materials and set up the environment. Some of the children demonstrated the experiments. During the process, the children predicted what would happen next and asked different questions. Children took pictures during the experiments.	The children started to create their own experiments by combining experiments and predicting what would happen when you mix . . . together? The experiments changed from using bottles to create their experiments into using a variety of flat shallow pans. Many of the children were keeping track of their experiment by using clipboards and pens and illustrating the chemical reactions.

project. They can also branch off into smaller projects or connect to other ongoing ones. For example, the plant and vegetable dye project may become part of another project, such as tie-dyeing. The newly created dyes may be used during the process as children continue to experiment with different types of synthetic and natural dyes when tie-dyeing. During the process of implementing long-term projects children should have the opportunity to document the projects by representing their ideas, planning, and findings through both 2-D items (drawings and painting) and 3-D ones (sculpture, woodworking), as well as in writing. In a gardening project, for example, children might draw a design of their garden, create a 3-D model from clay or boxes and tubes, or take pictures of the garden. This process will also illustrate the project over time. The following four steps will illustrate the components needed in developing a long-term project.

Four Steps in the Process of Developing and Implementing Projects

Step 1: Beginning of the Project:

Observations, interest, and generating new ideas

- The educator observes children during play experiences and uses a variety of tools to document their play, interactions, and conversations.
- There is an initial community meeting to discuss observations and children's interests and to generate ideas for projects with the children.

Step 2: The Planning Process: Initial Community Meeting

Community meetings are held to generate ideas or to plan the project. The following points will guide the process during the meetings.

- Create documentation to support the planning process: planning webs, minutes of meetings, photographs of the process, audiotapes, and dictations.
- Use research books to find out more about the project and to answer any questions about it.
- Develop material, loose parts, and equipment lists to support the project.
- Locate areas to implement the project and times and date to start it.
- Brainstorm whether you need any support for the project from experts in the community or whether you need to visit the community before the project starts to gather more information.
- Collect materials, loose parts, or equipment needed for project.

Step 3: Implementation and Documentation:

Connecting to the micro and macro environment

- Start implementing the project in the indoor or outdoor environment.
- Invite guest speakers, such as experts from the community, to come to the program.
- Link the project to the community by going on a field trip into the community.
- Use a variety of documentation tools (illustrations or photographs) to document and record the project over time.

- Continue to hold community meetings to talk about the project, successes, and new materials needed or linking to other projects.
- Continue to observe and document the project.

Step 4: End of Project: Reflections and Documentation

- During community meetings, children and educator discuss what they enjoyed about the project or what they would change next time.
- Children and the educator create a record or the history (timeline) of the project by creating bulletin boards from any of the documentation, such as photographs, stories, illustrations, and dictation.
- Invite parents to a potluck to connect with each other, observe the documentation, and celebrate the end of the project. This will also give the children the opportunity to talk to their parents about the project.

Long-Term Clubs

School-age children enjoy being involved in clubs. Clubs are, in essence, specifically focused projects, and many of them will last up to a year. Clubs give children a sense of belonging to a group and promote peer friendships and mentoring. They give children the opportunity to plan, develop, and implement projects based on their interests. The following description of a music club illustrates the different components of a child-driven approach, such as planning sessions, researching, developing activity and material webs, implementing activities, connecting to community guest speakers, documenting the process, and finally celebrating the success of the club.

Development of a Music Club (October to June)

During a community meeting, a group of children used a web to brainstorm about different clubs they wanted to participate in. There were suggestions for at least 20 clubs, and the group then decided to vote on which clubs they wanted. After voting a number of times, the group decided on three clubs and scheduled the time and dates to implement them. A music club was one of the three clubs that were implemented.

The Club in Action

The educator sat down with the group and asked what they wanted to do in the music club. The children said they wanted to learn more about jazz, in particular Louis Armstrong. During this session, the children created group webs of what they wanted to do during the club.

The following was the process used to develop the club.

October

- Resource books about jazz were brought into the program.
- The educators purchased jazz CDs from different eras. Several of the parents also brought in CDs.

November

- Different types of instruments were brought in for the children to use. The camera was used to take pictures of the process.

FIGURE 11.4	Jazz Music Webbing

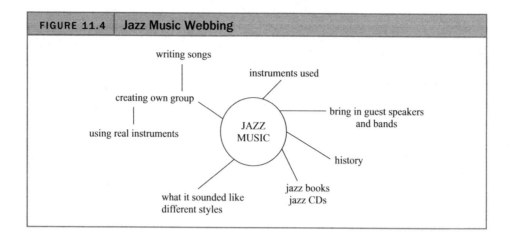

- Old trumpets were brought in for the children to play and experiment with.
- Children developed a number of designs and illustrations of the instruments they wanted to make. They created their own instruments from a variety of loose parts and materials. A variety of books and web searches on the Internet were used for resources. The camera was used to take pictures of the process.
- Children listened to the new jazz CDs. They decided to create a music club bulletin board with their documentation.

January

- Guest speakers and musicians participated in the program. One parent who plays in a jazz band brought the band in to play for the children. The local high-school jazz band participated in the club at different times. Children had the opportunity to play their instruments. The children asked the high-school jazz band questions about how to write a song. Cameras and the camcorder were used to document the process.
- Children continued to make their own instruments by creating new designs and illustrations. They researched a number of books about jazz (including types of instruments). An area was created in the environment to display their instruments.

February

- Children started to write songs and lyrics and decided to create their own jazz band. The children listened to the jazz CDs to get some new ideas about the "jazz sound."
- Cameras and the camcorder were used to document the process. Children continued to add to the documentation board.

March

- The group decided to make a demo tape of their music. A guest speaker from the local radio station was invited to talk about promotion and making demo tapes. The children continue to add to the documentation board.

- The children made a demo tape and decided to name their group The Cooool Katz. They continued listening to jazz CDs to get new ideas about the jazz sound.

June

- The Cooool Katz planned to give a performance. They created posters to announce the time and date of the performance.
- They performed for the other children and parents and sold copies of their demo tape. Cameras and the camcorder were used to document the process. They continued to add photos and dictation to the documentation board.
- A wrap-up party was held with lots of food and discussion after the performance.

During the wrap-up party, the parents had the opportunity to view the documentation board and documentation panels created by the children, which consisted of the photographs from October to June (including guest speakers, taking the trumpet apart, planning, creating instruments, and so on). The initial webbing material list, designs, and illustrations of the instruments were included. The educators also included a number of stories that illustrated the process, the importance of clubs, and what the children were learning from the music club. The children and educator also created a display of all of the instruments created, and had a video of the performance for parents and community members to view.

This project lasted over several months. Not all long-term projects will last this long (although some will last longer), but all of the projects will help the children gain an in-depth understanding of a topic or concept.

Documentation panels created by the children can be displayed in the environment to celebrate the end of a project.

EMERGENT CURRICULUM AND PLANNING FOR FULL DAYS

In an emergent-curriculum program it is important to include the children in the planning and implementation of the full-day curriculum that occurs during the various holiday times (especially spring break and the school summer holiday) and on school's Professional Development days. During full-day programs, children could potentially be in the school-age program from 7:00 a.m. to 6:00 p.m. With more time to participate in the program, the children and educators will have the opportunity to plan and implement more activities, field trips, clubs, and in-depth long-term projects. There will be more time for the educators to plan and hold community meetings with children and they will have the opportunity to be completely involved in the planning process. With larger blocks of time, community experts can be invited to come to the program (musicians, reptile experts, etc.) to share their knowledge and expertise with the children. Community visits can be expanded and the visits may link to ongoing long-term projects. For example, if the children from the "Crazy Science Club" are interested in reptiles, they may invite a reptile expert to the program or visit a pet store that sells reptiles. After visiting the pet store the children may have many new questions about reptiles or other pets. Children can be encouraged to explore research books and the Internet to find answers to the questions generated by the reptile expert or the field trip. In a full-day program or over the summer, children have the time and opportunity to explore projects over many days and weeks. The learning opportunities are less fragmented because both the children and educator have the time, space, materials, and opportunity to engage in project work.

Eight Steps in the Planning Process

The following eight steps and key components in the planning process for March break are the same steps used when developing curriculum for Professional Development days and the summer program. Many of the steps are similar to community meeting sessions and the process of developing long-term projects. The steps illustrate the importance of connecting and collaborating among the children, educators, and families.

Step 1: Preplanning

Community Meetings

- Facilitate a community meeting before the actual planning meeting and remind children that March break is coming up. Encourage the children to think about what they enjoyed about last year's March break experience. Have the children think back to the different examples of field trips, snack food, guest speakers, and long-term projects.

Tip #1: Use photographs or photo albums from last year's March break to promote discussions.

Environment

- Suggestion Boxes. Set up suggestion boxes in the environment and provide Post-it notes and markers for children to spontaneously write their ideas and put them in the suggestion box.

Tip #2: A Kleenex box works well for a suggestion box. Cover the Kleenex box with construction paper and have the children decorate it and write a catchy slogan on the box, such as "We need your ideas!"

- Webs. Provide blank webs and markers in the environment for children to create their own individual planning web during play.

Tip #3: A letter- or legal-size file folder with the ends stapled works well to hold blank webs. Decorate the folder and add a catchy slogan to it. The folder can be taped to the back or side of a storage unit or tacked onto a bulletin board.

- Photographs. Post photos of last year's activities, field trips, and projects in the environment.

Step 2: Community Meetings and Brainstorming as a Group

- Facilitate a community meeting to start the brainstorming and planning process. Bring the suggestion box with ideas and any of the individual webs completed by the children during play.
- Create a preliminary group web to classify ideas (for example, field trips). The web can be a general web with the central idea being what to do for March break, or a specific web with sections to classify ideas (field trips, special foods, or projects).
- Include ideas from the suggestion box or any ideas from the individual web on the preliminary group web.
- Ongoing play experience, emerging projects, and projects already underway are included on the large group web. Highlight these ongoing activities with different coloured markers so children can see the difference between ongoing activities and new ideas.

Tip #4: Educators and the children should take a few minutes and document the process by taking photos of creating a group web.

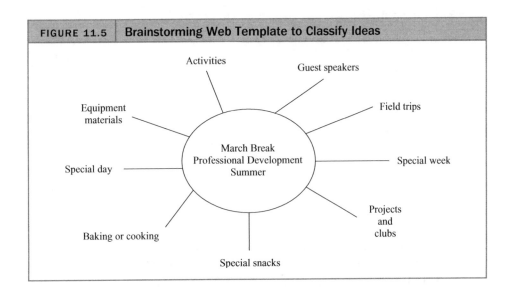

| FIGURE 11.5 | **Brainstorming Web Template to Classify Ideas** |

Activities

Guest speakers

Equipment materials

Field trips

March Break
Professional Development
Summer

Special day

Special week

Projects and clubs

Baking or cooking

Special snacks

Step 3: Making Decisions

- Combine preliminary webs and suggested ideas in a central web and review the information with the children.
- Vote on the suggestions from the group web in a democratic way (either by a show of hands or by using a ballot box).
- The voting may take one or two days to process or it can be done over one or two weeks. Not all the activities can be implemented during March break, but they may be integrated into the program of activities afterwards.

Tip #5: Review the section of Chapter 8 about the democratic system of voting.

Step 4: Planning and Charting

- Develop a weekly chart (Monday to Friday) with sections similar to your large group web, such as field trips, guest speakers, projects, and clubs. Include a section for materials or loose parts needed.
- Write ideas that were voted on on Post-it Notes, which will help to move ideas around on the weekly chart.
- Analyze for balance between indoor and outdoor activities.
- Use a voting system for group decisions such as whether the group wants one field trip or two field trips in a day.

Tip #6: Be flexible, adaptable, and creative when planning and moving Post-It Notes around the chart. If children agree not to have any outdoor play for a week, it is the role of the educator to use guided power and directed power to ensure the children have outdoor play experiences.
Tip #7: Make sure the program is not over-planned and children have enough time, space, and opportunity to play.

Step 5: Final Decision

- Develop the final chart with activities for parents and children to take home. Children can help to develop the final chart by helping to create a computer-generated or free-hand chart.
- Decide who is responsible for what—e.g, shopping for materials and loose parts, inviting guests, finding recipes for baking activities, making telephone calls to potential guest speakers, or arranging field trips.
- Develop materials lists and decide who will be gathering materials, such as food needed for baking or loose parts needed for a project.
- Follow up to check that, for example, the person who was asked to find out bowling times and dates has actually done so.

Step 6: Implementation

- Continue to expand learning opportunities by using open-ended questions and enrich the environment with loose parts, research books, and other materials.
- Encourage the children to participate in activities and play experiences.

FIGURE 11.6	**Webbing for March Break**

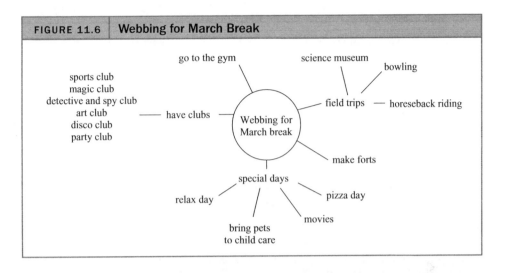

Weekly planning chart developed by the children.

- Prepare the children and parents for upcoming field trips and play experiences by reminding them about these at the end of the day. Create a newsletter or memo for parents with a schedule that includes all trips and play experiences.
- Review the planning chart daily with the children and parents.

Tip #8: Discuss any safety issues and rules as they apply to being out in the community.

Step 7: Documentation

- Children and educators should document the process of activities and play experience by using a variety of tools such as cameras, camcorders, audiotape decks, markers, etc.
- Post completed documentation, such as illustrations, panels created by the educator or children (pieces of bristol board with photographs and dictation), or stories created by the children in the indoor and outdoor environment.

Step 8: Reflections

- Once the activity is over, look at the documentation that has been created.
- Review the plan and discuss what was successful and what should be changed next time.

Tip #9: Post documentation on the parent bulletin board to tell parents what is happening in the program. Documentation should tell the parents what the children are learning both in the program and in the project or activity.

CHILDREN'S AND EDUCATORS' CONTRIBUTIONS IN AN EMERGENT CURRICULUM

Table 11.5 illustrates children's and educators' contributions when developing, planning, implementing, and documenting a process using an emergent approach. The table reflects a collaborative approach in which children and educators alike contribute to developing skills, projects, and documentation during an emergent process. For example, in the planning section the children generate ideas through the webbing process, while the educator contributes by helping the children develop webbing skills and group-dynamic skills. This can be done by modelling the process and by having actual examples of webs posted in the environment.

THE EMERGING EDUCATOR

Emergent curriculum takes time to develop and to implement. It is important to remember that it is a process, and when implementing it the educator will guide and facilitate the skills the children need to plan the curriculum. Children and educators alike are planners and researchers for the program, and those who have not experienced this way of working before may need to take small steps to begin with. Throughout all aspects of the process, educators should continue to observe the children, ask open-ended questions, evaluate the process, and modify it when necessary.

Children new to the emergent process will need to be reassured, supported, and empowered when developing the curriculum. New children joining the group, as well as school and family stress, may affect how successfully the program is working, and at times the educator will need to modify the approach to give children extra support.

Table 11.6 outlines the process of developing an emerging curriculum over a year, over which time educators will also be working out their own educational philosophy and attitudes to the process.

TABLE 11.5	Children's and educators' roles when developing and implementing curriculum	

Curriculum Elements	Children's Contribution	Educators' Contribution
Play	• Express ideas and interests to peers and educators during play.	• Observe children's interests, needs, and strengths during play.
	• Add new materials and loose parts to environment and play experiences.	• Facilitate and implement activities by providing loose parts and materials based on observed interests, needs, and strengths.
	• Commit to working together and respecting others during play.	• Develop group activities for social/peer interactions and co-operation during play.
	• Share ideas, opinions and questions during play.	• Ask open-ended questions in order to expand play.
Planning short-term and long-term projects and clubs	• Brainstorm and develop ideas by using webs during community meetings.	• Work with the children to develop webbing skills and group dynamic skills.
	• Develop material lists for projects, during meetings and play.	• Facilitate children's planning of projects and activities during play and community meetings.
	• Work in groups to develop projects and clubs.	• Model the use of documentation tools to record the planning process.
	• Use documentation tools to record the planning process.	
Implementation	• Implement plans for projects and clubs.	• Model various planning, implementing, questioning, and evaluation skills.
	• Choose loose parts, materials, and resources to be included in the environment for projects.	• Add loose parts, materials, and resources to the environment.
	• Make decisions during community meetings about what is needed for projects.	• Use books and the Internet as resources to expand projects.
	• Use books and the Internet to research projects.	• Use documentation tools to record projects.
	• Use documentation tools to record projects.	
Documentation	• Create 2D and 3D documentation of projects.	• Provide space to display project work.
	• Display projects and documentation in the environment.	• Use documentation tools to document projects.
	• Use documentation tools to document projects.	
Additional planning and links to the community	• Use additional resources and activities to create new experiences.	• Plan new experiences and materials to expand projects.
	• Plan field trips and community involvement during meetings.	• Plan field trips and community involvement during meetings.

TABLE 11.6	The emerging educator over a year

Stage 1: Beginning of Emergent Process

a) Observe and interact with the children to discover the following:
   - How they handle conflict.
   - Types of interactions with others.
   - Interests of the children.
   - What stage of development each child has reached.
   - How experienced they are with self-directed activities.
   - How experienced they are in participating in curriculum development.
b) Introduce community meeting to the children.
   - Provide a time to share with others (ideas, interest, etc.).
   - Model effective communication and conflict-resolution techniques.
c) Plan activities based on the children's ideas and interests.
d) Provide loose parts in the program.

Stage 2: Starting to Emerge Curriculum

This step is taken when you see the children are comfortable with the community meetings, making things with loose parts, and have begun to develop a sense of community.

Continue to work on all aspects of Stage 1, and in addition:

a) Introduce conflict-resolution techniques in appropriate situations. The educator should model conflict-resolution techniques when dealing with the children.
b) Discuss the needs of the group with the children.
   - Need of everyone for respect and trust.
   - Need for everyone to feel safe.
   - Need of everyone for independence and responsibility.
c) Ask the children to develop class rules.

Stage 3: Emergent Curriculum

This step is taken when you see that the children are developing some skill in conflict resolution and there is an increased sense of community.

Continue to do aspects of Stages 1 and 2. In addition:

a) During community meetings, discuss with the children what to do in the program:
   - Brainstorm ideas and resources needed.
   - Record ideas and process using the webbing format.
   - Plan and implement clubs and projects.
   - Document meetings and play activities.
b) Follow through on request from children.
   - Support the children's endeavours.
   - Encourage the children to take the next steps in their planning and implementation.
   - Follow up on the commitments you have to the children (such as providing materials).
c) Review and adapt classroom rules.

Stage 4: Emerging Projects

This stage is reached when the educators see the children becoming adept at conflict resolution and demonstrating a strong sense of community. The educator will gradually become less directive and the children will begin to spontaneously take a more active role in planning and implementing curriculum.

Continue to do aspects of Stages 1–3. In addition:

a) The children will tell the educator what they would like to work on and then take the initiative to do some brainstorming and carrying it through to completion. At this point, they may often require the educator only as a resource and advisor.
b) Children will be developing projects and are responsible for the planning and gathering of resources.
c) Children will create their own documentation.

OBSERVATION TOOLS AND TRACKING SHEETS

The following tables are examples to show how educators can track an emergent curriculum, short-term projects, and long-term projects. The goal of the observation tools and tracking sheets is for the educator to take note of which elements are emerging, which are completed, and what materials are needed to expand the experience. Tracking sheets can also be posted to keep families, children, and other educators informed of what is happening in the program.

Log Book

Table 11.7 shows an anecdote about snow-fort–building recorded in the play log of a school-age program. Educators would use such a log to document the daily indoor and outdoor play that the children were involved in, conversations with the children, and notes on how the children were using materials in the environment. Once a month, the educators would analyze all the anecdotal observations from the play experiences and emerging projects.

Tracking of Emergent, In-Progress, and Completed Projects

The first column of Table 11.8 illustrates emerging play experiences (such as developing secret codes) based on observations from indoor and outdoor play. Over time, the play experiences will either turn into a long-term project, or they will remain spontaneous play experiences. The educators will continue to observe the children and ask questions during play time and community times to gauge if the emerging play experiences are becoming a project. The second column shows the many projects currently being pursued by children in the program (such as gardening), whether singly or in small groups. The third column illustrates projects that are now finished, whether because they have reached

TABLE 11.7	Play log book
January 31	**February 1**
There had recently been a large snowfall. Some children were using the large snow shovels to push snow around the yard. The children made ridges of snow with the shovels. Some children added doorways by digging out sections in the walls. Other children got involved with the building by collecting snow chunks and piling them to create more walls. The children also added a slide and one window.	There was another snowfall. The children used the new snow to add to the snow fort. They piled the snow to make the walls higher and wider. One of the windows had broken, so repairs were made.

In the afternoon, some children brought out the water and began to pour it onto the slide. They said that when it freezes, it will become a slippery slide. They also made some slush with water and snow. They made slush balls and piled them beside one of the windows to use later. They also used the slush to add to the walls and chairs. One of the children added a paper roll to the fort. This became a telescope. |

TABLE 11.8	Emergent experiences, tracking projects, and completion of projects	
Emerging Play Experiences	**Projects Children Have Been Involved in Over the Past Two Months**	**Completed Projects from the Past Three Months**
Secret codes: Developing and writing secret codes during out door play.	**Gardening:** Harvesting the garden and preparing for winter.	**Natural Dyes:** Final stage of creating natural dyes project has been completed.
Sewing: Children are interested in sewing. They have been asking to make puppets and they will be discussing this at the next community meeting.	**Newsletter:** Developing the monthly newsletter. **Air Band:** Developing air band. Making costumes.	**Air Band:** Stage has been completed for air band. **Aqueduct:** The children have dismantled the aqueduct.
Seeds: A number of children are collecting seeds and are interested in saving them for next year.	**Architecture:** Conceptualizing, developing, and planning arches for the indoor play space.	
Raps and games: A small group of children are creating raps and singing games outdoors and in the gym.	**Developing Clubs** • Crazy Science • Breakdancing • Art Club	
Planned Experiences		
Community Visits	Visiting local architect to discuss the arch project and to help design blueprints.	

the goals that were originally set out, or the children's interest has faded. This table will help the educator to see the flow of ideas move from the emerging play experience toward the initiation of projects, and finally their completion.

Summary

Emergent curriculum is a collaborative approach to curriculum development in which both educators and children have active roles in the planning. It is based on the interests and needs of the children, which educators gage through observations and direct conversations with the children and their families. It is not a pre-planned approach, but is constantly changing as the educators use their skills to help the children develop the abilities necessary to actively participate in the planning and implementation of learning experiences. Although an emergent curriculum can result in spontaneous learning experiences, it often leads the children and educators toward more in-depth projects on various topics and concepts. These short- and long-term projects are not limited to a week or a month, but continue as long as the children maintain their interest in pursuing an in-depth study of the topic.

Educators in an emergent curriculum have many roles. They facilitate the learning by creating a sense of community in which the children feel safe, by encouraging children to use and develop the new skills they need for the exploration they want to do, and by providing the necessary materials and resources. At times, educators will model techniques and at other times they will need to be more directive (such as not allowing cooking because of health regulations).

Children also play an active role in developing an emergent curriculum. Most ideas for the curriculum will come from the children, and they actively participate in the planning process through group meetings, arranging for guest speakers, engaging in the research activities, working on documentation, and so on. Only as the educators and children work together to develop a respectful community that allows active participation of all its members is an effective school-age curriculum achieved.

Student Learning Experiences

1. Interview Children

Interview six school-age children in a school-age licensed program. Brainstorm with the children, using the webbing format, asking them the following questions.

- What are they interested in doing in the program?
- What would they like to have for their snack?
- What kinds of field trips would they like to have?
- What kinds of activities do they want to have more of?

What did you learn from this experience? What new information did you learn from the children?

2. Internet

On the Internet, find at least three articles to support the emergent approach. Compare and contrast the three articles. Give two examples from each article when comparing and contrasting. Back the examples up with your understanding of child development concepts.

3. Resource File

Create a file of community resources with the following sections: people (e.g., musicians, artists, carpenters); business and education (museum, video studio); recreation (pools); and materials and loose parts. Feel free to add others. Include the contact name, name of business if appropriate, address, phone number, services offered, how to get there, fees or other costs involved, and any special features. Include at least 30 entries for each section.

4. Observations

Observe children in a licensed school-age program for 30 minutes during outdoor playtime. Keep track of the observations by using jotted notes or anecdotes. Evaluate your information to work out what types of play the children are interested in. Use the webbing format to record your ideas of how the play experiences you observed could be expanded, under such headings as materials, loose parts, research books, and community visitors. Describe what you would say when introducing your findings during a community meeting.

Review Questions

1. List and describe the stages in developing a curriculum over a year. What are the roles of children and educators during each stage?

2. Describe in your own words what an emergent curriculum is. What are the main differences between emergent and traditional curricula?

3. Identify the planning process when developing a curriculum for a full-day program. What do you need to consider when developing curriculum for a full-day program as it relates to children and parents?

4. Describe the difference between play, short-term projects, and long-term projects. Use one concrete example to describe each type of project.

5. List the six components of an emergent curriculum and discuss the importance of each when involving children in developing curriculum and when implementing projects and clubs.

CHAPTER 12

Supporting Skill Development through the Curriculum

OVERVIEW

According to Erikson's psychosocial theory of development, school-age children are interested in developing abilities that are valued in their society. In Canada, this means that there are numerous skills children will want to master. Some of these skills are necessary for academic success, some for arts and crafts, and still others are necessary for participating in sports and other recreational activities.

According to Piaget's theory of cognitive development, the majority of children in school-age programs will be in the concrete operational thinking stage, which means that they will have the logical thinking abilities necessary to master these skills.

Vygotsky's cultural social theory of learning indicates that children learn when they receive appropriate support from educators and more knowledgeable peers, while IPM and social-cognitive theories of learning indicate that motivation and past experiences play important roles in influencing the learning that occurs.

This chapter will identify some of the skills that children are developing during the elementary school years, and indicate ways that educators can facilitate this learning by making it meaningful for the children and by providing appropriate supports. This chapter will look at how skill development can be incorporated into various activities that children are interested in. Some of the techniques that educators can use to help the children master the skills will also be identified.

WHY INCLUDE SKILL DEVELOPMENT IN A SCHOOL-AGE PROGRAM?

Children have been in school all day by the time they arrive at a school-age program, so many adults do not look to the program as a place for learning. However, children do not stop learning once school is out; nor do schools teach children *all* the skills necessary for societal success. As well, some children find learning academic subjects in the traditional school environment difficult and need additional opportunities to practise the skills in real-life situations so that they can master these subjects.

Many children are also interested in developing skills that may not be emphasized in the school, such as athletics, art, or music. In school-age programs, educators have the opportunity to provide learning experiences that promote skill development in these areas.

It is unrealistic to expect educators to be very knowledgeable in all the skill areas the children are interested in. But it is realistic to expect educators to be able to find resources for various skills (such as art books or the rules of games) and to learn or improve their own skills while facilitating the children's learning. Educators can also incorporate opportunities for more knowledgeable peers or adults to help children in the program. For example, if none of the educators has woodworking skills, they could find a volunteer with those skills who would donate some time to help the children in this area.

In order to master skills such as woodworking, acting, drawing, or sports, most children will need some guidance from others to facilitate their learning. During the school week, and during holidays, children in out-of-school care spend many waking hours in the program. Therefore it is important that the program support the development of skills that children want and need. Educators are in the unique position of being able to support the children's school-based academic learning while providing additional learning in the non-academic, but just as essential, recreational and social skills.

INDIVIDUALITY AND SKILL DEVELOPMENT

In any given school-age program, at any given time, children will be working on a variety of skills. Even if two children are developing skills in the same area (such as drawing), the actual skills they are developing may vary greatly. For example, a child in grade one who is very interested in art and who has attended drawing classes will know to make the trees in the background smaller than those in the foreground. At the same time, a child in grade three whose drawing opportunities up until now have been limited to the weekly art time during the school year may still draw all the trees the same size.

The *range of skills* in a school-age program can vary widely, not simply because of past experiences and age, but also because some children in the program may have physical or developmental disabilities, while other children may be gifted, and still other children fill the entire range of abilities in between. Ongoing communication with parents and children is important if educators wish to understand fully where individual children are at in terms of skill development.

The skills developed in the program will also be *influenced by the diverse interests* that children bring with them. Some of the children may be very interested in developing effective soccer skills, while others are more interested in skipping, crafts, socializing, or nature. A high-quality school-age program will ensure that there are opportunities for children to develop their interests.

The skills that children want to develop will be *influenced by their families*. A child from a family that is very interested in music may want opportunities to engage in musical activities or to practise playing a musical instrument. Some children will come from families that emphasize sports, and others from families that encourage the development of social skills or art skills. Some children in the program may have recently immigrated to Canada, and this can also influence the skills they value and want to develop in the program. Educators need to speak to parents as well as children to identify the types of skill development they want the program to support.

The following sections identify some of the skills that may be supported in a school-age program, and indicate strategies for doing so. The skills that will be discussed are:

- Academic skills
- Research and science skills
- Social skills
- Athletic skills
- Artistic skills

SUPPORTING ACADEMIC SKILLS

Many out-of-school programs support the development of academic skills by offering an area where children can complete homework if they or their parents prefer to have it done in the after-school program. Educators offering this type of activity may further facilitate the learning by offering help if a child needs it.

Academic support does not have to be limited to homework clubs or a homework area in the centre. Through discussions with parents, educators can find out what academic skills parents want their children to practise. When asked, most parents indicate that practice in reading, spelling, and math is important, even if their child is doing well in school. Once educators know what the goals are for the children, they can incorporate these goals into the learning experiences they offer. For example, if a group of children have been showing an interest in air bands, the educator might find out if they want to put on an air band presentation. If they like the idea, it becomes a great opportunity to incorporate academic skills. Meetings will have to be held to determine how they are going to put together the performance, so the meeting will need to be minuted. The children will create posters to advertise the event. If several groups are going to perform, they will need to work out the running order. All these activities give children opportunities to practise their reading, writing, and spelling skills, and the educator who knows the children will be able to ensure that the child who has trouble spelling takes the minutes. The same educator will also make sure to review the minutes with the child so that he has a chance to correct any spelling mistakes and isn't embarrassed when the minutes are posted. When children develop any project, documentation of the process should occur, and school-age children should be involved in creating the documentation. As they develop the documentation to post for parents and others to see and read, they continue to work on advancing their academic skills.

Another example of incorporating academics into ongoing learning experiences would be math skills in activities such as sewing, woodworking, or cooking. If children want to sew costumes, educators should help them to take the necessary measurements, and to use the measurements when sewing. If material needs to be bought, the children can help decide what they can purchase with the money available. Even simple sewing projects such as making pillows (see Table 12.1) will require children to take measurements and determine what size pillows can be made with the fabric that they have. Table 12.1 shows the relationship between the learning experience (sewing), academic skills (reading, writing, and math) and the role of the educator (facilitator and provider of resources).

Cooking is a great opportunity to use math skills in a real-life situation. It provides opportunities for children to practise and understand fractions, weights, addition, multiplication, and so on. As children measure out the amount of an ingredient, or as they have to double a recipe in order to make enough for everyone, they are finding meaningful ways of using math skills. The role of the educator working with these children is to know which skills the children have, and which ones they need to develop. For example, if the children were going to double a recipe, the educator might ask the child in grade three how much flour was now needed, but wouldn't ask the child in grade one the same question. The child in grade one, however, might be asked to fill a dozen muffin tins and then asked what the number is that means the same thing as one dozen. Through specific questions and requests, educators facilitate the learning of meaningful academic skills.

TABLE 12.1	Academic skills supported through sewing and fabric crafts

Learning Experiences	Academic Skills Supported	Role of Educator
Sewing and fabric crafts	Reading, writing, various math skills (e.g., measurement, counting, fractions, multiplication, money)	• Encourage children to read books on the crafts they want to make. • Involve children in determining the amount of fabric, etc., that they need and in buying the fabric and supplies. • Provide tape and other measuring tools to help children when sewing, etc. • Encourage children to use measuring instruments when cutting yarn, designing patterns, etc. • Have children keep a list of supplies that they need. • Get children involved in documenting their activities.

Practically any activity available to the children can reinforce one type of academic skill or another, and educators can encourage children to expand the activity so as to further increase learning. An example of this would be board games. Most board games encourage reading skills, either through reading directions or reading cards that are part of the game. If the children enjoy playing games, educators can further enhance learning in a couple of different ways. One way is described in Chapter 11, where the children are involved in the process of purchasing new games for the program. By involving the children in this activity, the educator is able to create additional opportunities for the children to practise reading, writing, and math skills. Another way to enhance the learning is to encourage the children to develop their own board games. As children plan, design, and create their board games they will practise reading, writing, spelling, drawing, math (designing the board), and organizational skills. Many school-age children find that creating a board game is fun and exciting. Checking one's spelling, or writing neatly in complete sentences, is not a chore or boring in this context, because they realize how important it will be for someone else playing the game. Table 12.2 shows the relationship among the learning experience (board games), academic skills (reading, writing, and math), and the role of the educator (facilitator and provider of resources).

Many educators may not think about it, but sports and other physical activities can be used to help support academic skills. For example, while some children who excel at a sport, such as basketball, may not be interested in traditional academic activities, educators can use a child's interest in basketball to help with academics. Table 12.3 shows the relationship among the learning experience (sports), academic skills (reading, planning, writing, and math), and the role of the educator (facilitator and provider of resources).

DEVELOPING RESEARCH AND SCIENCE SKILLS

Any project or learning experience that a child is very interested in lends itself to the development of research skills, and one of the important roles of educators in the school-age program is to make research materials available for children to use and to provide opportunities for children to engage in research activities.

TABLE 12.2	Academic skills supported through board games	
Learning Experiences	**Academic Skills Supported**	**Role of Educator**
Board Games	Reading, writing, math (e.g., counting, money, measurements), numerous concepts	• Encourage children to read the rules for games. • Rewrite rules for games so that younger children can successfully read them. • Make sure that games that include cards use language that children can read. • Buy games that support learning of different concepts (e.g., *Snakes and Ladders*: counting; *Life*: reading skills, counting skills, money skills) • Get children involved in buying games. • If children are interested in board games, encourage them to create their own.

TABLE 12.3	Academic skills supported through sports	
Learning Experiences	**Academic Skills Supported**	**Role of Educator**
Sports	Reading, planning skills, writing, math skills (e.g., measurement, division, counting)	• Have children read books to find out exact rules for the game and then have them record and post the rules they are going to use. • Take pictures of the children playing and have them create documentation to go with the pictures. • For older children who are into stats, have them find out how stats are determined and use the information to create stats on themselves. • If children decide to create a sports club, have them keep minutes of the meetings. • Involve the children in the process of buying some of the equipment. Have them calculate the costs and determine what can be bought. • Challenge the children to find out if the fields they're using are official field sizes. • Encourage children to develop their own games.

School-age children are big collectors, and are often very interested in information on the materials they collect. A child who is very interested in collecting rocks will need resources available to look up information on rocks and, perhaps, to perform experiments on the rocks. This means that the educator will need to provide books about rocks in the centre. These resource books might be specifically about the classification of rocks, or they might have more general information on topics such as volcanoes. Other resources might include a scale for weighing the rocks, a hammer (and eye goggles) for trying to chip small pieces of rock off a larger piece, a magnifying glass to look at structures, and duct tape to hold the rocks together while trying to build something.

As well as providing resources, educators also encourage the development of research skills through the questions they ask the children and the suggestions they make. When speaking with the child who is interested in rocks, the educator could ask how the child was organizing the rocks he had collected, and how many differences the child saw between them. The educator could also suggest that the child might want to record some of the information, to make it easy to find later on. If the educator wants to encourage the child to use books to find information, she could ask the child what the proper names are for the rocks in the collection. If the child does not know, the educator could then ask him how he could find out the names, and perhaps show him some books that might help. If the educator takes this approach, she should make sure that she returns later to see if the child has found an answer to the question and to thank him if he has. She might even encourage him to make labels for the rocks so that other children can learn the names.

If the child is interested in experimenting with the rocks (such as finding out which ones break easily and which ones are hard), the educator can encourage research skills simply by asking the child to predict which ones are harder than others, and helping him set up a chart to record his actual discoveries. Educators should also ask children what they want to know about the topic they are interested in, and then encourage them to follow through on finding this information. This follow-through may take the form of first-hand experimentation (such as the child who wants to put as many different food colours into the oil as possible to see if she can make black) or acquiring information indirectly through the Internet (such as using it to find out what colours are used to make black).

Besides providing resource books or magazines related to various topics of interest, educators should help children learn how to access these books, as well as other types of resources, for themselves. If children want to find out information on an aspect of gardening or photography, for instance, the educator can use it as an opportunity to take them to the library and have them locate the material on their own. As well, the educator could help the children access some information on these topics using the Internet, or even using a phone book to find out who in the community might have the information they are looking for (such as a garden centre or a photography studio). Table 12.4 shows the relationship between the learning experience (gardening), research and science skills (using the Internet, mapping, and recording), and the role of the educator (facilitator and provider of resources).

As children learn research skills, they are also developing the skills that support an understanding of science and the scientific method. Science is all about learning how the world around you works, and it is through research and experimentation that this happens. As children experiment with rocks or research gardening they are engaging in the study of the natural sciences. As they build ramps and try to get their model cars to jump a gap of a metre they are learning about how gravity and velocity work. As children cook snacks or experiment with liquids (such as water and oil) they have the opportunity to learn about chemical reactions and how different materials interact. As children hypothesize about the outcomes of their experiments or record what occurs, they are actively using scientific methods. As children research a topic of interest, and in the process absorb a lot of information on other topics as well, they are learning a wide variety of science concepts,

TABLE 12.4	Research and science skills supported through gardening

Learning Experiences	Research and Science Skills Supported	Role of Educator
Gardening	Using library and Internet, using tables of contents and indexes, predicting, hypothesizing, mapping, recording data, classifying	• Have children research the plants they want in the garden to determine where and how to grow them. • Provide the centre with seed catalogues and books on gardening and plants. • Take the children to the library or have them use the Internet to locate information. • Have children draw designs for their garden. • Have children decide how to organize the garden plantings (e.g., plants that require sun located in same area). • Have children periodically record what is happening (e.g., watering schedule, when different plants are ready).

and educators can support this learning by asking them questions and providing them with challenges that encourage science skills.

DEVELOPING SOCIAL SKILLS

It is important for school-age children to be accepted by their peers, and a child with poor social skills is less likely to find acceptance. Educators find many ways to provide opportunities for social interaction in the program, and they need to take advantage of these social situations to help children develop effective social skills.

Some children do not know how to enter *group situations*. They may simply barge into the group and assume that they will be accepted; they may hang around the periphery of the group but never let the other children know that they want to be a part of it; or they may use aggressive tactics such as grabbing the ball a group is playing with as a way of trying to indicate a desire to join in the group activity. Regardless of the cause of a child's difficulty (perhaps a developmental disability, or personality, or past experiences), when children consistently exhibit these behaviours, educators should recognize that they will have to facilitate the development of their social skills. The educator may do this in a number of ways, and the approach taken will be influenced by the underlying cause of the inappropriate behaviour. Suggesting alternative methods for entering a group, modelling ways to enter groups, or having a discussion during a group meeting about when and how children want others to join them in their play are just a few of the approaches an educator could use.

The school-age program is an excellent place for children to develop leadership and co-operative skills and to become aware of group dynamics. Although educators will probably use some group time to facilitate discussion of these topics, most of the skill development will occur during practical experiences.

Group meeting time is one arena for *developing leadership skills* and increasing one's awareness of group dynamics. As discussed in Chapter 8, educators will have to help children learn the various roles that individuals play in successful meetings, but as children work to make their meetings successful, they will develop leadership and co-operative skills.

As children are given *responsibilities for daily routines* (such as preparing snacks and caring for pets and plants) educators have an opportunity to develop the children's social skills. If groups of children are responsible for working together to prepare the snack, there are numerous opportunities for them to practise listening, negotiating, compromise, and delegating skills. As the children gain more advanced skills the educator can allow them more independence, but the educator should always be observant to ensure that children are not being excluded or always relegated to the follower role. Children who may have language challenges, either because of a disability or because English or French is their second language, may often find themselves at a disadvantage in these types of situations and may require additional support from the educator as they participate in activities that require a lot of language use in order to foster social skills.

Another way educators help children develop these skills is through conflict resolution. Children who learn and implement the techniques necessary for conflict resolution are also learning co-operative and leadership skills. Strategies educators use to help children learn these skills have been previously discussed in Chapter 9.

Co-operative games are another excellent way for educators to facilitate the development of social skills. Because co-operative games and activities require children to work together to complete a task, they are encouraged to work on all the skills necessary for successful group dynamics. A co-operative game could be a non-competitive scavenger hunt or challenge put forward by the educator (for instance, a challenge to build a ramp that will make a model car go right across the room). Although co-operative games and activities will, by their very nature, encourage the development of social skills, the educators can also support this learning through comments and questions. If a group is trying to solve a scavenger hunt riddle and one child in the group is being ignored, the educator can indicate to the group that they haven't heard from this child yet. If the educator sees that the group trying to build the ramp is having difficulty and the cars always fall short, she might ask what is happening and follow this up by asking what they have already tried and what they think might make a difference, and so on. Table 12.5 shows the relationship between the learning experience (co-operative games), social skills (co-operation, leadership, team-building, problem-solving), and the role of the educator (facilitator and provider of resources).

DEVELOPING ATHLETIC SKILLS

Many school-age children are interested in sports and want to develop the skills necessary to play well. Children who are well motivated will happily practise these skills (such as shooting hoops) on their own, but many will benefit from having educators give them pointers and provide them with opportunities to practise some of the skills (such as setting up a soccer drill with pylons).

Developing athletic skills does not need to consist only of planned activities. Providing plenty of opportunities for children to run and use numerous gross motor muscles is also

TABLE 12.5	Social skills supported through co-operative games

Learning Experiences	Social Skills Supported	Role of Educator
Co-operative games	Co-operation, leadership skills, team-building, follower skills, organization, establishing roles for each group member, problem-solving within a group, negotiating, compromise	• Provide co-operative board games in the centre. • Provide challenges to the children that require them to work together. • Through questions and comments, support co-operation and negotiating. (e.g.,if the children have identified something that needs to be done, the educator can ask how they're going to decide who does it). • Make sure that the children who decided to participate in the activity are actively participating. Find out what the problem is if a child isn't involved.

important for the development of athletic skills. Given room and opportunity, children will spontaneously organize a variety of traditional games, such as tag. These games help children develop the endurance, strength, and agility necessary for many sports.

But when educators think of helping develop athletic skills, they need to think in broader terms. Providing children with mats and facilitating the development of tumbling skills develops athletic skills for different types of sports. Taking children on regular trips to the local pool is another way the development of athletic skills is supported. In winter, educators can create ice rinks or use local rinks so some children can practise skating skills while educators can help other children learn to skate.

Many educators in school-age programs are hesitant to actively support athletic skill development because they think they do not have the necessary expertise. Although a school-age program can benefit from having an educator with a recreational diploma, those without may choose to take additional training in a sport area that children are really interested in, or they may simply speak to others who are knowledgeable in order to find out how to help children develop the skills. There are many resource books that can provide educators with the rules of various sports and with information on activities that can help the children with their skill development. Educators do not have to be good at a sport to help encourage its development, but they do have to show a willingness to learn more about the sport (often from the children themselves) and to provide opportunities for children to practise their skills.

Educators who are concerned about the competitive side of sports can encourage the children to work on skill development rather than focusing on actual games. When the children do play the game (and they will want to) the educator can help de-emphasize the winning aspect by commenting on specific things children did well, whether or not they were on the winning team. The educator should recognize that, for some children, developing specific skills is just as important as playing the game, so skills should be recognized and developed in their own right. Just as educators will make comments to a child about how well she reads, they should also be willing to comment on how well a child controls a soccer ball. These comments are especially important for the children who may do well in sports but struggle in academic subjects. Table 12.6 shows the relationship among the learning experience (sports activity), athletic and physical skills (general co-ordination, eye–hand co-ordination), and the role of the educator (facilitator and provider of resources).

During play, children will have the opportunity to practise and demonstrate a variety of athletic skills.

TABLE 12.6	Athletic and physical skills supported through sports	
Learning Experiences	**Athletic and Physical Skills Supported**	**Role of Educator**
Sports activities	Co-ordination, ball control, dribbling, kicking, problem-solving, planning, running with control, eye-hand co-ordination, flexibility, balance, ability to jump with control, throwing, catching, and hitting skills	• Provide books on rules and history of games, skill development, athletes, etc. • Provide lots of opportunities for children to engage in active play both indoors and out. • Make sure active play is not limited to the use of a few skills but provides opportunities for children to perform a wide variety of skills (e.g., tumbling, running, jumping). • Encourage children to engage in more complex skills (e.g., running while dribbling a ball, using tumbling movements to create gymnastic routines). • Provide a variety of materials and equipment that encourage the development of athletic skills (e.g., various balls, tumbling mats, loose parts to create obstacles courses, balance beams, ropes, rackets, nets). • Provide opportunities for children to use roller blades and bikes. • When children express an interest in becoming better at a skill (e.g., dribbling a soccer ball) discuss with them how they might practice this and then set up the activity. • Participate in activities with the children.

DEVELOPING ARTISTIC SKILLS

Preschool children love experimenting with a variety of art materials, but school-age children want to create as well as experiment, and they want the skills to do this.

Children interested in drawing generally want to know how to make their pictures look life-like—with realistic perspective and shading, and with figures that give the impression of movement. Some children will develop these skills without support from others, but most children will need some form of scaffolding to help them learn these skills.

Children are also interested in learning how to draw using a variety of materials. Although markers and crayons are always popular, children also enjoy the challenges provided by pastels, charcoal, and watercolour pencils. In order to use these materials successfully, children need to learn skills such as holding a pastel so you do not smudge what you have already drawn, using your finger to smear charcoal to create shading, and learning how to use the watercolour pencils so colours do not bleed together. Table 12.7 shows the relationship among the learning experience (drawing), artistic skills (perspective, shading, self-expression), and the role of the educator (facilitator and provider of resources).

By the time children reach the school-age program, many of them have done a lot of experimenting with tempera paints and are ready to create artworks that require both drawing and painting skills. They are also interested in finding out how to use other types of paints and paint brushes. Acrylic paints and watercolours can be introduced to children at

TABLE 12.7	Artistic skills supported through drawing	
Learning Experience	Artistic Skills Supported	Role of Educator
Drawing	Perspective, shading, proportion, creating texture, elements of design, awareness of detail, colour, self-expression, observation, and interpretation of the physical and social environments	• Provide books on art and drawing. • When children ask how something is drawn, take the time to show them the technique or help them locate the information. • Locate community experts who would be willing to come to the program to demonstrate techniques. • When having conversations with children about things they see around them, take the opportunity to point out shadowing, perspective, etc. • Have pictures and posters that clearly illustrate aspects of design, texture, shading, etc. • Provide books and pictures that show how objects, landscapes, and people can be drawn in a variety of ways.

this age, but only if educators are willing to teach the techniques necessary to use the materials successfully and avoid frustration. Children should have access to a range of brushes and know what kind of results each brush can produce.

Although some children may be familiar with clay, many children will have had little opportunity to work with this medium. In order that children not become frustrated with the results of their work (such as finding that the arms fall off sculptures they make) educators will have to help children learn a number of techniques. Children will need to learn how to cut clay, how to get air bubbles out, how thick to make objects for successful drying, how to make slip, how to attach pieces so they do not fall off, and how to use tools to create detail. Children will also need to learn some basic rules, such as not dumping clay-laden water down an ordinary drain. Children with experience in clay work may want to learn about firing clay and using glazes. Although a school-age program is unlikely to have a kiln, educators may access community resources to help children learn more about these topics.

By having access to painting materials, children can demonstrate and practise painting techniques.

Mosaic is an art form that is not used with younger children, but can be successfully done with school-age children. As with many art forms, children will need to learn techniques for creating designs and for using the materials. Mosaics may be done using paper and glue, but children often prefer more three-dimensional materials, such as tile pieces. Even though educators could provide children with tiles that have already been cut, it is often more interesting for children to be involved in breaking up the tiles that will be used. Because tile pieces may have sharp edges, educators will need to teach safety techniques along with design techniques. Fortunately for educators who may not be familiar with these materials, there are many art books that provide this information in an easy-to-read format (such as *Ceramics for Kids* by Mary Ellis).

Children can also learn to use a variety of other materials to create sculptures and constructions. Each of these materials will require different skills. Wire, wood, Plasticine,

Children will have the opportunity to practise a number of sculpting techniques by experimenting with clay.

papier-mâché, and a variety of loose parts (such as machine parts, plumbing pipes, and bamboo) are all used to create three-dimensional sculptures and constructions, but will require different techniques.

Music is another art form children are interested in. While many children are content to simply listen to their favourite music, some are very eager to learn how to play a variety of instruments. Some educators who have proficiency in music have encouraged the formation of clubs where the educator has helped the children learn to play a simple instrument like the recorder. Educators who do not have this ability can facilitate learning by finding a more knowledgeable person to guide the club. They can also provide an area where children who are taking music lessons outside of the program can practise, or they can provide an instrument, such as a keyboard, that children can try to learn with a minimum level of support (if educators choose to include a keyboard in the program they should pick one that allows the children to use headphones, so others do not have to listen as they practise). Table 12.8 shows the relationship among the learning experience (musical instrument), artistic skills (rhythm, interpretation, understanding notes), and the role of the educator (facilitator and provider of resources).

Music skills are not limited to those associated with instruments. They also include song and dance. Like preschool children, those of school age continue to enjoy singing and dancing to music, though the types of song and dance are becoming more complex and varied. School-age children are generally aware of the popular songs of the day and want to perform them. As well as actually singing the songs, many children will want to do "real

TABLE 12.8	Artistic skills supported through musical instruments

Learning Experiences	Artistic Skills Supported	Role of Educator
Musical instruments	Rhythm, ability to follow a beat, reading music, understanding of notes, ability to use instruments correctly, understanding of how instruments create musical notes, ability to interpret music and rhythms, ability to express one's own emotions and ideas	• Provide real musical instruments in the program. • Provide a variety of resource books on music (e.g., song books, how-to books, history books, magazines about music). • Help children when they try to read music or find a more knowledgeable peer or adult to help them. • Incorporate music into the program (e.g., allow children to help select music to play). • Support children's efforts to put together air bands, dance routines. • Have pictures and posters that look at a variety of music and musical instruments (make sure that these are not only limited to traditional Canadian music and instruments). • Invite experts in to share their skills with the children (e.g., high school students, community musicians).

dancing" to the music, and this may take the form of imitating the movements they have seen on the music videos. Children may want to know and discuss the various types of popular music (such as rap or country) and many will be beginning to try to create their own songs. Educators need to be willing to discuss musical and dance styles with the children and help them identify some of the strategies for creating their own songs or dances. Table 12.9 shows the relationship between the learning experience (dancing), artistic skills (rhythm, self-expression, limb co-ordination), and the role of the educator (facilitator and provider of resources).

During the preschool years, drama is usually associated with the dress-up area and the imaginary play that children engage in. During the school-age years, drama slowly transforms into the more adult-like theatrical productions. Although the spontaneous, imaginative play will continue, children will begin to try to act out specific stories, television shows, and so on, often planning the performance in advance by deciding on the script, the backdrops, the costumes and the role of each child in the production. As children begin to move into this more organized type of dramatic production, they will need the educator to help facilitate some of the discussions where decisions are being made, or to monitor their progress to ensure they have considered all aspects of the production. The educator may also need to be there to help them follow through on the commitment they have made. Often children initially decide to aim for a certain outcome, but when the process actually includes some hard work they want to give up. Educators can provide the support the children need to get through the more difficult aspects of a project. Table 12.10 shows the relationship among the learning experience (drama), artistic skills (body language, interpretation, vocal delivery), and the role of the educator (facilitator and provider of resources).

TABLE 12.9	Artistic skills supported through dancing	
Learning Experiences	Artistic Skills Supported	Role of Educator
Dancing	Rhythm, ability to follow a beat, ability to interpret music and rhythms, ability to convey a message, ability to express one's own emotions and ideas	• Provide a variety of resource books on music and dance (e.g., song books, how-to books, history books, magazines about music). • Provide recording equipment so children can create and sing their own songs or songs they are familiar with. • Discuss dance with children when they express an interest in it. • Encourage children to share the types of dances they've learned from their family and/or cultural community. • Incorporate music and dance into the program (e.g., allow children to help select music to play and provide an area where they can feel free to dance). • Support children's efforts to put together air bands, dance routines. • Have pictures and posters that look at a variety of dance styles (make sure that these include traditional Canadian dances and dances from other cultural backgrounds). • Invite experts in to share their skills with the children (e.g., high school students, dancers from various community groups).

TABLE 12.10	Artistic skills supported through drama	
Learning Experiences	Artistic Skills Supported	Role of Educator
Drama	Ability to convey a message using both words and body language, ability to express one's own emotions and ideas, ability to interpret what others have written, ability to develop and implement creative ideas	• Provide resource books that show various types of drama activities as well as types of costumes, set designs, etc. Include resources on movie making, animation, *etc.* Provide materials that will help children create various dramatic productions (e.g., fabrics and other loose parts, CD player, movie maker software, camcorders, digital camera). • Provide an area where children can engage in dramatic play. • When children express an interest in a dramatic performance they've seen or hear about (e.g., a movie, musical, or concert), get them to discuss the acting, production, etc. • When children express an interest in air bands, or putting on a play, facilitate this interest by asking questions (e.g., How do you think you could make it happen?), helping them problem-solve, and providing encouragement when they decide it's too much work.

Folk art usually refers to those activities that are craft-like in nature but that contain creative elements as well. For instance, knitting can be a very utilitarian craft when a child is simply given yarn and expected to knit a scarf using the basic knitting stitch. When one allows children a say in selecting the knitting materials used and the pattern to be created, however, the experience moves from a simple craft into the realm of folk art.

School-age children can easily learn the skills necessary for knitting, crocheting, weaving, and braiding, as long as another child or educator can help them. Some children may be able to learn the skill by simply reading the description in a book, but many will learn best by watching someone slowly demonstrate the technique, and then being guided through the steps. Educators can help children learn not only by demonstrating the techniques but also by providing them with large needles (though not so fat that they are hard to use) and heavy yarns that are not shaggy. Children who have learned some of the techniques need to be provided with a variety of needles and yarn, so that they can make choices about what they want to do. Educators also need to make sure that there is sufficient yarn for children to finish a project that they have started.

School-age children can master a variety of types of sewing. Many educators hesitate to let children use a sewing machine, but in the authors' experiences with children, none has ever been injured using the sewing machine, although many have been pricked while sewing by hand. The key to success is that the children are taught how to use the machine before they are allowed to use it without the direct assistance of an adult. (Educators should, however, exercise caution in judging when a child is ready to use a sewing machine—or any other potentially dangerous machine—on their own, bearing in mind that they are legally responsible for the child's safety during the time the child is in their care.) Children want to sew in order to make costumes for themselves, accessories such as bags to hold precious objects, puppets, cushions to sit on, and other decorations such as wall hangings. If children are not provided with the materials to sew fabric they will find substitutes such as staplers or tape; however, in many situations, they would prefer to use a needle and thread to hold the fabric together. When children are learning to sew by hand, educators will want to provide needles with large eyes, since otherwise the educators will constantly be threading the needles for the children or the children will become frustrated at not being able to do so themselves. Educators also need to provide a variety of materials for the children to use while, at the same time, making sure the materials will not be too difficult to manipulate. For instance, children with experience using a sewing machine may be able to sew slippery materials successfully, while those with less experience will not be able to do so. Similarly, children may have difficulty sewing material like vinyl that is thick, or that tears easily.

Helping children learn to sew not only lets them create a variety of folk-art objects but also allows them to sew on a loose button on a shirt or jacket, thus averting both lost buttons and upset parents!

Other craft activities using fabric also lend themselves to folk art. Tie-dyeing and batik are two crafts that children can easily learn and that provide numerous opportunities to be creative. Once educators have helped them learn the basic techniques, children can experiment with the process to create diverse results.

TABLE 12.11	Folk art skills supported through woodworking	
Learning Experiences	Folk Art Skills Supported	Role of Educator
Woodworking	Reading and following directions, planning, designing, and implementing projects, learning how to safely and skilfully use a variety of tools	• Provide a variety of woods, wood fasteners, and loose parts to use with wood. Provide books, etc., on woodworking and encourage children to use them to help them with ideas and solutions to problems. • Provide a sufficient variety and quantity of woodworking tools and equipment. Get children involved in determining what they need in order to complete projects. Provide graph paper and blueprint paper for children to create designs. • Ask children questions such as: "How can you make it more stable?" and "What would happen if . . . .?"

Other forms of folk art use wood. As mentioned previously, educators will need to help children learn a variety of skills and safety practices in order to complete woodworking projects successfully. Once children have learned the necessary skills, they can create a variety of objects with minimal supervision.

Table 12.11 shows the relationship among the learning experience (woodworking), folk-art skills (reading and following directions), and the role of the educator (facilitator, model, and provider of resources).

WHAT SKILLS AND ATTITUDES DO EDUCATORS NEED TO SUPPORT THE CHILDREN'S SKILL DEVELOPMENT?

Parents cannot expect every educator working in a school-age program to have extensive knowledge of all the topics the children are interested in, but centres can help increase the chances that diverse interests are met by trying to ensure that the skills of various staff members complement each other. For example, if a centre needed to hire a second educator and the existing staff member had strong artistic skills but little interest in sports, the centre would be wise to hire an individual with sports skills.

Two important characteristics of educators in these programs are curiosity and a sense of adventure. Educators need to be willing to try new things and learn with the children. An educator may come to a program with little knowledge of origami, but when children express an interest in it, the educator should be willing to help them find information on the topic, decipher the directions, and participate in the activity with them if the children want that.

Educators who are able to support the children's learning successfully will have compiled resources and located experts who can also support skill development. The skills children want to learn are many and varied. They range from drawing techniques to ball handling when playing soccer. Table 12.12 provides a few examples of skills children will learn, and indicates some of the knowledge that educators require when helping the children to be successful in developing their reading, artistic, athletic, and folk-art skills.

TABLE 12.12	Knowledge educators need to help children develop their skills

Sample of Reading Knowledge Educators Need

Phonics:

- If there is only one consonant between a vowel and the "ing" ending, the vowel in the word will have a long vowel sound (e.g., hoping) but if there are two consonants the vowel in the word will have a short vowel sound (e.g., hopping).
- If two different vowels are together in a word, they will usually say the name of the first vowel (e.g.,boat, heat).

Sample of Research Knowledge Educators Need

Recording Data:

- Identify what you want to find out (hypothesis).
- Identify what type of information you want to record.
- Determine what will be the best way of recording the information (e.g., chart, point form, pictures).
- Decide how frequently you'll need to record information.
- Set up the equipment and materials you'll need (e.g., get a camera, make a chart).
- Locate the materials in the area where your observations are being done.

Sample of Artistic Knowledge Educators Need

Perspective in pictures:

- Create a horizon line in the drawing (this is where the land meets the sky) and when drawing an object such as a road that goes from the foreground to the horizon, have the space between lines narrow as the lines approach the horizon line.
- Draw objects closer to the horizon line smaller than objects closer to the bottom of the page.
- When drawing buildings, make sure the side of the building angles back toward the horizon. Like other lines heading toward the horizon, the line at the base of the building and the top of the building will get closer together the nearer they get to the horizon line.

Creating mosaic pieces:

- Determine if you want all of your pieces to be the same size and shape or if random shapes will work for your design.
- Tiles can be broken with a hammer by placing the tiles in a bag and hitting the bag with the hammer. Care must be taken that the pieces aren't hit so often that they become too small.
- Tiles can be broken with a tile cutter (follow directions included with the cutter). Tiles cut this way will be more uniform in shape and size than when using a hammer.
- Paper can be ripped or cut into small pieces.

Dance (feeling the dance):

- Use familiar concepts when trying to create a dance.
- Visualize what you want to express.
- Think about and feel the emotions involved.
- See how different music will influence your movements.
- Talk about how the dancing made you feel.

Sample of Athletic Knowledge Educators Need

Trapping (soccer):

- Keep your eye on the ball as it comes toward you.
- Move into position so that you're directly facing the oncoming ball.

(Continued)

TABLE 12.12	Knowledge educators need, continued

- Raise your leg from the hip, keeping your knee slightly bent.
- As your leg makes contact with the ball, apply pressure to the top of the ball.

Dribbling (basketball):

- Keep your head up and eyes on the target as you dribble.
- Relax the wrist, spread the fingers, and cup the hand that dribbles the ball.
- Push the ball toward the floor rather than slapping the ball downward (slapping will result in a loss of control).
- As the ball rebounds, the fingers, wrist, and arm ride back with the ball.
- As you move, lean forward with the knees slightly bent.

Tumbling Skills (dive forward roll):*

- Begin in a partial squat position (knees bent in L shape, body bent forward).
- Extend arms in front of you.
- Spring forward (slightly arch back and push off with both feet).
- As your feet leave the ground, your hands should be pushed toward the mat.
- As hands touch the mat, tuck in your chin and bend arms at the elbows.
- Continue forward movement, so you land on the base of the neck and the top of the shoulders.
- Push off with the hands and continue the forward motion. The force of the forward motion should allow you to stand up at the end of the role.

*This should be done on a mat

Sample of Folk Art Knowledge Educators Need

Batik:

- Synthetic fabrics are harder to dye than natural fabrics.
- Synthetics fabrics may not take the wax.
- Dye fabrics starting with the light colours and moving on to darker colours.
- Wax needs to be kept at the correct temperature for the wax to be able to adhere to the fabric.
- Designs need to be pre-planned.
- Wax needs to be applied in a water bath.
- Iron the finished product between two pieces of paper.

Summary

The school-age program should support children's learning by more than just providing materials and allowing children to experiment with them. School-age children are interested in learning techniques to become more successful at a variety of tasks ranging from academics to sports.

Educators in out-of-school programs need to support this skill development by providing information on and demonstrations of the skills. This can be done in a variety of ways. Educators can provide resource books that they can use with the children, or that can be used to develop their own skills in order to provide demonstrations. Educators may also obtain the necessary skills by taking courses themselves (such as knitting classes offered through the school board's continuing education program) or by getting a knowledgeable person to demonstrate to them, and possibly the children, how to perform the skill. Another option is to find experts in the community to come in and give a workshop in a skill area or to devote time to engage in ongoing work with the children.

Student Learning Experiences

1. Pick a learning experience commonly found in a school-age program and identify five things you could do that would support a grade two child's reading and math skills (find out what skills the grade two curriculum is teaching before completing this assignment).

2. Review an art book designed for use by children. Analyze for the following:
   - What age is the book best suited for?
   - Does the design of the book appeal to children?
   - Does it use language that the children can understand?
   - Are directions easy to follow?
   - Does the book help children learn techniques that can be applied to a variety of art activities?
   - Do the illustrations help clarify the written words?
   - Does it encourage the children to think of a variety of ways to use the information in the book?

3. Interview school-age children to discover what skills they want to know, and then find resources to help the children develop those skills.

4. A child in the school-age program may have a physical disability. When supporting artistic skills, explain how a physical disability might influence the use of materials, space, time, and/or people.

Review Questions

1. List and describe the various skills (academic, research and science, social, athletic, artistic, and folk art) that educators should be developing in a school-age program. Choose two skill areas and describe one activity to support each skill.

2. Describe in your own words why it is important for the educator to include skill development in a school-age program. What is the educator's role in developing skills?

3. Why is it important for the educator to understand how his own attitude and skills can affect how he implements skill development for the children?

4. Explain how team-building can be used to support both academic skills and social skills.

Glossary

Accommodation: An adjustment or adaptation to suit a special or different purpose.

Anecdote: A written observation that briefly describes what is happening in a particular situation.

Assimilation: Taking in new information and incorporating it into existing concepts.

Behaviour guidance: The techniques used by adults to help children learn appropriate behaviour and interaction with others. This includes setting up environmental conditions and adult–child interactions that support appropriate behaviour. This term is often viewed as referring to techniques that encourage prevention and active child participation, as opposed to more adult-dominated interventions (commonly called behaviour management).

Checklist: A written observation that consists of a list of skills and abilities that the observer then checks off to indicate that the child is able to perform the skill.

Child abuse: Physical, emotional, or sexual injury intentionally inflicted upon a child. It also includes the failure of adults who are responsible for the child to provide adequate physical and emotional care.

Child-care worker: An individual working in programs for children up to twelve years of age outside the educational system. This individual may or may not have specialized training.

Child-directed curriculum: Curriculum development that is based on the interests and abilities of the children in the program, and that actively includes children in the planning process.

Cognitive development theory: Jean Piaget's theory of how individuals construct knowledge and how the nature of thinking changes from birth to adolescence. It consists of four stages of cognitive development.

Community: A place (both physical and conceptual) where children feel safe, cared about, and encouraged to care about others. There is a sense of belonging, being valued, and respect. In a community-oriented approach, children and educators work together to be inclusive when developing classroom values and group expectations. Community is the base when developing emergent curriculum and guiding behaviour.

Conflict resolution: A win–win approach used to help children to acquire skills, strategies, and understanding to resolve conflict independently. Communication skills, caring language, co-operation skills, and respect for diversity are some of the strategies used in conflict resolution.

Convergent questions: Closed questions that solicit a particular answer.

Curriculum: The content and processes that children and educators engage in to achieve learning and developmental goals within a program. It includes set-up of the environment, learning experiences, the subjects addressed, and educator–child interactions that promote learning.

Developmental domain: The areas of children's psychological development. The following four domains are commonly used to study changes that occur during childhood: cognitive, language, social/emotional, and physical.

Disability: Condition that impedes typical development in any or all of the following areas: physical abilities, learning abilities, social adjustment, and sensory abilities.

Divergent questions: Open-ended questions that encourage and accept more than one answer.

Diversity: The variety of differences found among school-age children and their families with respect to factors such as religion, culture, socio-economic background, special needs, individual interests and personalities, and family structure.

Documentation: Written, pictorial, visual, or auditory records of what children have learned as they engaged in various aspects of the curriculum.

Ecological theory: Uri Bronfenbrenner's theory that explains how the various levels of society and social structures (from personal interactions to cultural expectations) influence a child's development.

Educator: An individual with specialized training who develops programs for children up to the ages of twelve outside the educational system, and who facilitates learning in these programs.

Emergent curriculum: Curriculum that evolves as educators and children work together to develop learning experiences based on the interests and needs of the children.

Event sampling: A written observational tool that focuses on a particular event and what is happening when that event occurs.

Extended family: A family in which two or more generations live together or close to each other.

Flexible materials: Materials including loose parts as well as furnishings and equipment that can be used in a variety of ways.

Hierarchy of needs theory: Abraham Maslow's theory that explains how a variety of needs, from physiological to self-actualization, influence an individual.

Home child care: Out-of-school care for children up to age twelve in a private residence supervised by an adult who may or may not have training.

Informal observations: Jotted notes that educators take to quickly record interests, behaviours, and development of children.

Information processing model: Theories that focus on how sensory input, perception, cognitive strategies, and previous experiences all influence what an individual learns from a particular experience.

Kindergarten-age child: Preschool child who attends pre-grade-one school board educational programs.

Latchkey kids: Children who are responsible for their own care between arriving home after school and their parents' return from work.

Learning/play activities: Pre-planned or spontaneous activities designed to support learning and play.

Learning disabilities: A variety of conditions that impede a child's learning or require a child to use alternative strategies when approaching learning situations.

Learning experiences: Spontaneous or pre-planned activities designed to support learning. This term is often used when the activities are open-ended in nature.

Licensed out-of-school care or licensed school-age care: Regulated centre-based care outside school hours for school-age children up to twelve years.

Loose parts: Open-ended materials that do not predetermine how children will use them. Children will see a variety of applications for these materials, even though adults might find them more restrictive.

Multiple intelligences: Concept proposed by Howard Gardner that intelligence is not a single entity but consists of various facets that may or may not interact but that will determine how an individual responds to a situation.

Occupational standards: A set of criteria for a profession that individuals use to guide their behaviour when developing and implementing programs, interacting with children and families, working with other professionals, and so on.

Philosophy: A statement of beliefs that guides the behaviour and practices of individuals in a program.

Psychosocial theory: Erik Erikson's theory of how individuals adapt to the social demands of family and society. It is a developmental stage theory and indicates that the demands placed on an individual change as they enter different stages of their lives. It has eight stages that span infancy to old age.

Punishment:　A method used to reduce occurrences of an unwanted behaviour by giving the individual something he does not want or taking away something he does if he performs the behaviour. Corporal punishment (which educators are not allowed by law to practice on children in their care) involves physically disciplining the child by smacking.

Recreational program:　A program where the primary purpose is to provide some form of leisure activity; it may include activities such as organized sports.

Routines:　Scheduled activities to meet children's physical needs (e.g., bathroom, snack, lunch, dressing).

Running record:　A detailed written narrative observation of an individual or situation.

Scaffolding:　Support given to children to help them learn a concept or task. This support can come from an adult, a more knowledgeable peer, or the planned environment.

School-age children:　Children of elementary school age. This usually means children between the ages of six and twelve.

Self-care:　The practice of allowing children to care for themselves without adult supervision after school or for other periods of time. Educators should be aware of the law in their province or territory regarding the youngest age at which a child can legally be left at home alone.

Self-efficacy:　The individual's assumption regarding the likelihood of success or failure on a particular task.

Self-esteem:　One's opinion of one's own value or worth.

Self-regulation:　The ability to refrain from using inappropriate behaviours and replacing them with socially acceptable ones.

Sibling care:　The practice of allowing an older sibling to care for a younger child after school or for other periods of time. Educators should be aware of the law in their province or territory regarding the youngest age at which a child can legally be left at home alone.

Social-cognitive theory:　Albert Bandura's theory that proposes how individuals learn through observation and imitation.

Sociocultural theory:　Lev Vygotsky's theory that looks at how language, culture, social interactions, and the individual's current skills and knowledge all influence what an individual will learn from a situation, or if any learning will even occur.

Special needs:　Exceptionalities that alter typical development in any or all of the following areas: physical abilities, learning abilities, social adjustment, and sensory abilities.

Teacher:　An individual with specialized training who implements curriculum for children under the mandate of the Ministry of Education (public and private school board educational systems).

Theme-based curriculum:　Curriculum planning that is done by choosing a theme for a set period of time and planning learning experiences based on that theme.

Time sampling:　A written observational tool that focuses on whether a behaviour occurs or the number of times a behaviour occurs during a set period.

Traditional curriculum:　Teacher-directed program plan in which the majority of learning experiences are pre-planned by the teacher, with or without input from the children.

Transitions:　Scheduled activities to help children move from one routine or activity to another.

Vicarious learning:　Learning that occurs by watching someone else be rewarded or punished for a behaviour.

Webbing:　A curriculum-planning method that allows individuals to record brainstorming ideas and to link these ideas with aspects of the program and potential learning.

Zone of proximal development:　The zone where learning occurs. In this zone, the task is not so difficult that an individual cannot learn regardless of how much support is offered, or so easy that the individual already knows everything the task involves.

Bibliography

Books and Articles

Abbeduto, L. (2002). *Taking sides: Clashing views on controversial issues in educational psychology.* Guilford, CT: McGraw-Hill.

Allard, A., and Wilson, J. (1995). *Gender dimensions: Developing interpersonal skills in the classroom.* Armadale, Australia: Eleanor Curtain.

Allen, K.E. and Marotz, L. (2003). *Developmental profiles: Pre-birth through twelve.* Clifton Park, NY: Thomson.

Baden, R. and Seligson, M. (1993). *School-age child care: An action manual.* (2nd ed.). Boston: Auburn House.

Baird, H. (1997). *Mosaics.* London: Lorenz.

Bender, J., Elder, B. and Flatter, C. (2000). *Half a childhood: Time for school-age child care.* (2nd ed.). Nashville, TN: School Age Notes.

Bigner, J.J., and Jacobsen, R.B. (1989). Parenting behaviors of homosexual and heterosexual fathers. *Journal of Homosexuality, 18 (1/2)*, 173–86.

Braun, S.J. *et al.* (1970). *Curriculum is what happens: Planning is the key.* Washington, D.C.: National Association for the Education of Young Children.

Canada Mortgage and Housing Corporation. (1979). *Play opportunities for school-age children, 6–14 years of age.* Ottawa: CMHC.

Canadian Child Care Federation. (1999). *Partners in quality: Vol.1. Issues.* Ottawa: Canadian Child Care Federation.

Chard, S. (1998). *The project approach: Developing curriculum with children.* New York: Scholastic.

Chen, J. (1998). *Project spectrum: Early learning activities.* New York: Teachers' College Press.

Childcare Resource and Research Unit. (2000). *Early childhood care and education in Canada: Provinces and territories, 1998.* Toronto: CRRU.

Childcare Resource and Research Unit. (2004). *Early childhood care and education in Canada: Provinces and territories, 2001.* Toronto: CRRU.

Copple, C. and Bredekamp, S. (1997). *Developmentally appropriate practice in early childhood programs.* Washington, D.C.: National Association for the Education of Young Children.

Crary, E. (1994). *Love and limits: Guidance tools for creative parenting.* Seattle, WA: Parenting Press.

Doherty, G. (2003). *Occupational standards for child care practitioners.* Ottawa: Canadian Child Care Federation.

Doherty-Derkowski, G. (1995). *Quality matters: Excellence in early childhood programs.* Don Mills, ON: Addison-Wesley.

Elkind, D. (1994). *A sympathetic understanding of the child: Birth to sixteen.* (3rd ed.) Boston: Allyn and Bacon.

Esbensen, S.B. (1987). *An outdoor classroom: The early childhood playground.* Ypsilanti, MI: High/Scope Press.

Flaks, D.K., Ficher I., Masterpasqua, F., and Joseph, G. (1995). Lesbians choosing motherhood: A comparative study of lesbian and heterosexual parents and their children. *Developmental Psychology, 31*, 105–14.

Gardner, H. and Hatch, T. (1989). Multiple intelligences go to school. *Education Researcher, 18 (8)*, 4–10.

Gardner, H. (1991). *The unschooled mind: How children think and how schools should teach.* New York: Basic Books.

Gauvain, M. and Cole, M. (eds). (2005). *Readings on the development of children.* (4th ed.). New York: Worth.

Gay and Lesbian Parents Coalition International. (1992). What science knows about homosexual parents and their kids. *GLPCI Network, Summer*, 1–2.

Gestwicki, C. and Bertrand, J. (2002). *The essentials of early education.* (2nd ed.). Toronto: ITP Nelson.

Glenn, S., Lott, L., Nelsen, J. (2000). *Positive discipline in the classroom.* (3rd ed.). Rocklin, CA: Prima.

Green, S. (2005). Aiming for higher standard of care. *School-Age Connections, 13/2,* 1–2.

Harms, T., Jacobs, E. and White, D. (1996). *School-age care environmental rating scale.* New York: Teachers' College Press.

Harris, B. (2002). *Winning together: Successfully resolving conflicts with your kids.* Toronto: CGS Communications.

Harter, S. and Pike, R. (1984). The pictorial skill of perceived competency for young children. *Child Development 55 (6),* 1969–1982.

Hendrick, J. (2003). *Total learning: Developmental curriculum for the young child.* (6th ed.). Toronto: Prentice-Hall, and Upper Saddle River, NJ: Merrill.

Hergenhahn, B. and Olson, M. (2005). *An introduction to theories of learning.* (7th ed.). Upper Saddle River, NJ: Pearson/Prentice-Hall.

Hughes, F.P. (1999). *Children, play, and development.* (3rd ed.). Boston: Allyn and Bacon.

Hunt, M. (1993). *The story of psychology.* New York: Doubleday.

Jacobs, E., Mill, D., Gage, H., Maheux, I. and Beaumont, J. (1998). *Directions for further research in Canadian school-age child care.* Ottawa: Child Care Visions, Human Resources Canada.

Jones, E. and Nimmo, J. (1994). *Emergent curriculum.* Washington, D.C.: National Association for the Education of Young Children.

Judson, S. (1977). *A manual on nonviolence and children.* Philadelphia: Friends Peace Committee. Reprinted, Philadelphia: New Society, 1984.

Kazura, K. (2000). Fathers' qualitative and quantitative involvement: An investigation of attachment, play and social interactions. *Journal of Men's Studies, 9/1,* 41–57.

Kirchner, G. (1992). *Physical education for elementary school children: Lesson plans.* Dubuque, IA: Wm. C. Brown.

Kohn, A. (1996). *Beyond discipline: From compliance to community.* Alexandria, VA: Association for Supervision and Curriculum Development. Reprinted, Upper Saddle River, NJ: Merrill/Prentice-Hall, 2001.

Lajoie, G., McLellan, A., and Seddon, C. (1997). *Take action against bullying.* Coquitlam, BC: Bully B'Ware Productions.

Lefrançois, G. (1995). *Psychological theories and human learning.* (3rd ed.). Pacific Grove, CA and Toronto: Brooks/Cole.

Linderman, M. (1997). *Art in the elementary school: Drawing, painting and creating for the classroom.* (5th ed.). Dubuque, IA: Wm. C. Brown.

Luxbacher, I. (2003). *The jumbo book of art.* Toronto: Kids Can Press.

Martin, S. (2004). *Take a look: Observation and portfolio assessment in early childhood.* (3rd ed.). Toronto: Pearson/Addison-Wesley.

Maslow, A. (1987). *Motivation and personality.* (3rd ed.) New York: Harper and Row.

McCullagh, J. (1994). *Milestones in child development.* Ottawa, ON: Algonquin College.

McLoyd, V.C. (1990). The impact of economic hardship on black families and children: Psychological distress, parenting, socio-economics and development. *Child Development, 61,* 311–46.

Musson, S. (1999). *School-age care: Theory and practice.* (2nd ed.). Don Mills, ON: Addison-Wesley Longman.

Nash, C. (1989). *The learning environment: A practical approach to the education of the three-, four- and five-year-old.* (2nd ed.). Don Mills, ON: Collier Macmillan Canada.

National Institute on Out-of-School Time. (2000). *Understanding basic standards for a quality out-of-school time program.* Wellesley, MA: Center for Research on Women.

National School-Age Care Alliance. (1998). *NSACA standards for quality school-age care.* Dorchester, MA: National School-Age Care Alliance.

Neugebauer, B. (ed.) (1989). *The wonder of it: Exploring how the world works.* Redmond, WA: Exchange Press.

O'Connor, S. (1991). *ASQ: Assessing school-age child care quality.* Wellesley, MA: Center for Research on Women.

Ontario Coalition for Better Child Care. (1994). *School's out! Who cares?* Toronto: Ontario Coalition for Better Child Care.

Ontario Coalition for Better Child Care. (2000). *School-age care: A question of quality.* Toronto: Ontario Coalition for Better Child Care.

Ontario, Government of. (1997). *Day nurseries act: Regulations.* Toronto: Queen's Printer for Ontario.

Ontario, Government of. (1998). *Ontario child care licensing: Day nurseries manual.* Toronto: Queen's Printer for Ontario.

Ontario Ministry of Education and Training. (1997). *The Ontario curriculum: Grades 1–8: Language.* Toronto: Government of Ontario.

Ontario Ministry of Education and Training. (1997). *The Ontario curriculum: Grades 1–8: Mathematics.* Toronto: Government of Ontario.

Ontario Ministry of Education and Training. (1997). *The Ontario curriculum: Grades 1–8: Science and technology.* Toronto: Government of Ontario.

Park, N. (1992). *A comparative study of school-aged child care programs.* Toronto: Ontario Ministry of Education.

Pellegrini, A. and Perlmutter, J. (1988). Rough-and-tumble play on the elementary school playground. *Young Children, January,* 14–17.

Piaget, J. (1997). *The origin of intelligence in the child.* London and New York: Routledge. (Original work published as *Origins of intelligence in children,* 1952.)

Piaget, J. (1962). *Comments on Vygotsky's critical remarks concerning "The language and thought of the child" and "Judgement and reasoning in the child."* Cambridge, MA: MIT Press.

Richmond Child Care Resource and Referral Service. (2000). School-agers. *Child Care Today, Summer.*

Rivkin, M.S. (1995). *The great outdoors: Restoring children's right to play outside.* Washington D.C.: National Association for the Education of Young Children.

Santrock, J. (2004). *Educational psychology.* (2nd ed.). Boston: McGraw-Hill.

Sapon-Shevin, M. (1999). *Because we can change the world: A practical guide to building cooperative, inclusive classroom communities.* Boston: Allyn and Bacon.

Steinberg, L. (2005). *Adolescence.* (7th ed.). Boston: McGraw-Hill.

Van Hoorn, J., Nourot, P., Scales, B., and Alward, K. (1993). *Play at the center of the curriculum.* (3rd ed.). Upper Saddle River, NJ: Merrill/ Prentice Hall.

Vygotsky, L. (1986). *Thought and language,* translated by Alex Kozulin. Cambridge, MA: MIT Press.

Wadsworth, B. (1978). *Piaget for the class-room teacher.* New York: Longman.

Wiener, J. and Lidstone, J. (1969). *Creative movement for children: A dance program for the classroom.* New York: Van Nostrand.

Williams, J.E. and Best, D.L. (1990). *Measuring sex stereotypes: A multination study.* Newbury Park, CA: Sage.

Winsler, A and Berk, L. (1995). *Scaffolding children's learning: Vygotsky and early childhood education.* Washington, D.C.: National Association for the Education of Young Children.

Woolfolk, A., Winne, P., and Perry, N. (2004). *Educational psychology.* (2nd ed.). Toronto: Pearson Education Canada.

Young, N. (1994). *Caring for play: The school and child care connection.* Toronto: Exploring Environments.

World Wide Web Resources

Afterschool.gov (United States)

www.afterschool.gov/cgi-binh/home.pl

Canadian Association for Young Children

www.cayc.ca

Canadian Child Care Federation

www.cccf-fcsge.ca

National AfterSchool Association (formerly the National School-Age Care Alliance) (United States)

www.naaweb.org

National Association for the Education of Young Children (United States)

www.naeyc.org

National Network for Child Care (United States)

www.nncc.org

School Age Child Care Association of B.C. (SACCA)

www.wstcoast.org/affiliates/sacca

Index